Gardening with Perennials
Month by Month

Joseph Hudak

Gardening

with Perennials

Month by Month

Second Edition, Revised and Expanded

TIMBER PRESS
Portland, Oregon

Flower drawing ornamentation from *Landscaping with Perennials* by Emily Brown (Portland, Oregon: Timber Press, 1986).

Reprinted 1994, 1996, 1998, 2000

ISBN 0-88192-264-1
Printed in Hong Kong

TIMBER PRESS, INC.
The Haseltine Building
133 S. W. Second Ave., Suite 450
Portland, Oregon 97204-3527, U.S.A.

Library of Congress Cataloging-in-Publication Data

Hudak, Joseph.
    Gardening with perennials month by month / by Joseph Hudak. -- 2nd
ed., rev. and expanded.
        p.   cm.
    Includes bibliographical references (p.   ) and index.
    ISBN 0-88192-264-1
    1. Perennials--Handbooks, manuals, etc.   I. Title.
SB434.H8 1993
    635.9'32--dc20   92-18902
                                                                          CIP

Contents

To the memory of my maternal grandmother,
who introduced me as a child
to the joys of horticulture

Preface

When this book originally appeared in 1976, it was considered unusual. First, it came from the hands of a landscape architect who actually used the majority of the perennials described, either for himself or for his clients. Next, it pointed to wider gardening horizons in the United States and southern Canada by detailing the growing information about hundreds of herbaceous perennials attractive in all sizes and shapes. Some of these plants were then scarce in the marketplace, but all had some worthwhile appeal and just needed more publicity. In a short time growers did notice, happily enough, and today you can easily purchase a truly expanded perennial selection. Also, the book's focus included hardy bulbs of every description and reliable ferns as well. Such information had often been isolated in many separate books on these topics.

The format of the book was unique. It presented the blooming time of every plant in a monthly calendar organized according to the color of the flowers. Such handy information recorded in one book was novel at the time. It still is.

This format benefited both the professional and the amateur with substantial guidance. The book, originally published by Quadrangle/New York Times Book Company, found an interested audience, was reprinted by Timber Press in 1985, and earned a welcome niche in many home libraries.

Gardening with Perennials Month by Month, Second Edition, is completely revised and updated. The original approach is the same, but the book has been enlarged, expanded, and fully illustrated with my own color photography. The current scientific and common names have been updated according to new taxonomic information, and popular ornamental grasses have been added. These adjustments should make the revised book an even more beautiful, useful, and valuable perennial reference for many years to come.

Joseph Hudak
Westwood, Massachusetts

Introduction

This book represents a comprehensive effort at cataloging the majority of the noticeably attractive and reliable plants for garden use called "hardy herbaceous perennials" and "winter-tolerant bulbs," recognized for satisfactory performance throughout most of the United States, southern Canada, and other north-temperate growing areas of the world. Many dependable ferns and ornamental grasses have also been included here for additional interest. A high percentage of the plants discussed in the book originated in either Europe or Asia and have been garden-cultivated there for centuries.

In the world of horticulture there are the *annuals,* which complete their full life cycles in one year's time; the *biennials,* which need the first year to produce roots, stems, and leaves but the second to flower, set seed, and then die; plus the *perennials,* which persist at least three years just to earn their name. Local conditions may alter a known perennial into a shorter-lived biennial or even an annual, but 1000 days of endurance is the criterion used here for the hardy perennials discussed.

Trees and shrubs are also perennial plants, but they differ importantly in their far greater size and persistent woody stems and branches. In the simplest terms, the soft stems and leaves of herbaceous perennials and winter-hardy bulbs wither to the ground by the end of their growing season. Unlike annuals, they maintain living roots throughout the enforced dormancy of winter to start growth again the following spring. Although technically classed as shrubs, a few dwarfed plants with evergreen stems and foliage are included here since they regularly appear in gardens as specimens, useful edgings, or ground covers. They are also frequently included now in major catalogs with the herbaceous perennials.

FORMAT

A calendar (March through September) of blooming times and available colors begins each monthly chapter. The schedule of blossoming is based upon the flowering span for gardens in the Boston, Massachusetts, area (Zone 6)—the one where I have lived and grown plants for almost 40 years—and needs adjustment, of course, for those of you in different locales. Because there can be three to four days difference in the listed start of flowering for each degree of latitude

9

change, those north of Boston should expect a later start for the blooming schedules, while those to the south of Boston should anticipate earlier starting dates. For example, Boston is approximately at 41 degrees latitude, while Montreal is 46 degrees. This means that identical plants will likely be in bloom two to three weeks later in Montreal. In Dallas, Texas, at 33 degrees latitude, the same plants normally would flower nearly a month earlier than in Boston. For the sake of brevity, those carryovers still in bloom from a previous month are not listed again in any current month's flowering schedule.

Cool spring weather and consistently overcast days can delay the projected start of bloom for any early perennial, while drought or prolonged heat can shorten the blooming spans of summer-flowering plants. Early and repeated autumnal frost slows down or resolutely stops all growth in our colder growing areas, yet mild sections enjoying little or no frost action often experience blooming periods longer than those listed. All plants eventually pause for some period of rest, however, or else they would exhaust themselves. It is at this dormant or resting stage that herbaceous perennials are often best transplanted or perhaps divided for propagation.

The monthly calendar is further categorized by alphabetized lists of the plants displaying the separate color values occurring in each month. Every color division includes the shades, tints, and tones of the dominant color value. It is a genuine time-saver. As with all descriptions, however, the true color of any flower may exist only in the eye of the beholder. While my text entries attempt to be precise, each coloring given is still a gamble of nomenclature offered in good faith. At least one factor about color is consistent: it changes everywhere with the light intensity at the time of day. Those of you who are also color photographers already well understand this situation.

With both of these speedy chapter references you can readily determine *before* you plant the expected blooming time as well as the potential color spectrum available within that month. Such handy information should prove invaluable for all garden designers and flower arrangers.

Following each monthly calendar is an alphabetical listing of the plants blooming within that period. Each entry begins with a standardized block of pertinent information starting with the current scientific and common names (as defined by *Hortus Third,* supplemented by additional sources endorsed by the Royal Horticultural Society of Great Britain) and includes any alternate or former names still in common use. The listing progresses to ultimate height, preferred amount of sunlight, zones of expected hardiness, flowering time span, natural color potentialities for the parent plant, and distribution or, for horticultural hybrids, origin. A detailed but concise description of the plant follows, including recommended cultural needs, propagation techniques, insect and disease nuisances, and the available varieties or cultivars found today in nurseries or plant catalogs. Major, complex categories, such as *Hemerocallis, Lilium,* and *Narcissus,* are given expanded essays usually where each first appears in the text.

Because ferns are botanically nonflowering plants, they are not compartmentalized under any month in the calendar but have a fully developed section of their own. They appear in the chapter following the September entries. The various ornamental grasses, however, are included alphabetically in the month where the showiness of their seedheads is first apparent, usually by late summer.

At the end of the book are useful lists for many specialized growing conditions: shade, dryness, wetness, long-term bloom, and the like. Naturally, the same plant might appear in several categories by its special adaptability, a bonus set of points well worth noting. Again, such lists will aid you in easier decision-making since the tabulations are also in calendar form and carry, as well, either recommended light intensities or moisture requirements.

The main thrust of this book is to provide all pertinent information about perennials in one convenient place, concisely stated, and illustrated generously with informative photos. It is the kind of knowledge I enjoy having available for myself that I now share willingly with other horticulturists.

LIGHT INTENSITY

While the majority of perennials favor locations with at last six hours of full sun, others prefer reduced light. The ones listed as needing *semishade* expect only half that sunshine period or just three hours of strong sunlight. Perennials tolerant of full shade need the sun's brilliance blocked or filtered all day long, yet most will accept open light reflected from the sky in any amount. Bear in mind that shade is often accompanied by soil dryness when sizeable, water-seeking tree or shrub roots are also nearby and in quantity. Extra irrigation, coupled with a moisture-saving organic mulch, then becomes an additional cultural need for shade-grown perennials. Select your planting areas with the future growing conditions always in mind. It can save you time, effort, and money.

HARDINESS

The listed zones of hardiness (tolerance to cold) refer to the 1990 United States Department of Agriculture map (see p. 17). The range of zones provided for each perennial is hardly exact, but it does represent what major plant growers, botanic experts, and professional gardeners in this country believe reasonable to support. More wide-ranging data will surely change some of this information in the future.

For mountainous growing areas within any zone, adjust the hardiness range to account for the year-round coolness there. High elevations can be at least a whole zone colder than surrounding valleys. Large bodies of water, fresh or salt, also create zonal differences by warming the local temperature more than identical growing zones without such moderating geographic features. Such variations are often called *microclimates* and can exist on a smaller scale wherever a garden wall, fence, or dense planting diverts wind and traps additional heat.

While a thick, long-enduring blanket of snow in cooler areas insulates perennials well during dormancy, its annual appearance is undependable. Without it, frequent freeze-and-thaw periods lift shallow-rooted perennials from the ground to suffer wind damage. For more reliable winter protection use a temporary covering of needle evergreen branches, salt marsh hay, corn stalks, or non-matting fallen leaves, all applied after a deep freeze. Remove this protection in early spring as new growth starts but when frost is no longer a concern.

Although the hardiness of any plant is primarily based on its known adaptation to the rigors of consistent cold, other factors in the course of a year also influence hardiness. Sustained drought, long-enduring summer heat both day and night, excessive wind, soil which drains either too quickly or too slowly, together with sudden changes of light intensity, just as certainly affect a plant's performance. Weed infestations claim space, water, and nutrients a perennial can otherwise use to its advantage, so maintain a regular weed-removal program and forestall new weed crops by using several inches of organic mulch at all times in all perennial beds.

SOIL

Because soils everywhere are often variable in their textures and nutrient contents, they often need to be improved before new planting occurs. Adequate water drainage is vital to healthy root development, especially in winter, when roots do not absorb water at the summer rate.

Mixing coarse sand with heavier clay soil helps aerate the stickiness of clay to improve subsurface drainage. Some chemical modifiers also have this same ability by coagulating the tiny clay particles into larger units, thus creating more separation between soil parts. Sandy soil can be upgraded to hold more moisture by thoroughly spading, forking, or rototilling large quantities of well-rotted manure, compost, leaf mold, or moistened peat moss deeply into the garden bed. Avoid working any soil when it is muddy or frozen since such activity can negatively change the original soil texture. Wait until soil has either dried out or thawed.

Soils are either *acidic* or *alkaline* by chemical composition, and each type has a separate influence on root growth and plant survival. Most of the world's soils are acidic. To alter acid conditions, apply agricultural ground limestone either dug into or at least scratched into the top layer. To modify alkaline soils, incorporate either sulphur or iron sulphate. Because permanent change from acid to alkaline—and the reverse—may require surprisingly large quantities of such additions over a period of time, you will find it more rewarding to start a perennial garden with only those plants already suitably adapted for growing well in your area's soil. To verify modest adjustments to acid or alkaline soils, check with your local county agent or soil testing laboratory for dosages.

The natural nutrients for all plant growth are normally found only in soil. When a major nutrient such as nitrogen, phosphorus, and potassium is deficient, any plant may soon show signs of discolored foliage, stunted growth, or paltry flowering. Trace elements such as iron, boron, zinc, copper, and magnesium, while not needed in large amounts, are also essential to best growth. An in-depth soil analysis can determine what is missing as well as suggest what chemicals to use to correct the imbalance.

Nitrogen is essential for stem and leaf development. Phosphorus is for root enlargement and expansion. Potassium is for flower and fruit production. Since nitrogen is easily dissolved both by repeated rainfall and by mechanical irrigation, it needs to be replaced more frequently than phosphorus or potassium. Manufactured products are available in either a quick-acting chemical form or a slow-acting organic formulation. *Always* follow the manufacturer's instructions for application exactly. Distribute the fertilizer evenly—never in clumps. Scratch it lightly into the top surface, and follow with a thorough watering to start the fertilizer into a useful solution. Excess amounts of water-absorbing, dry fertilizer left to nature's erratic rainfall schedules can damage delicate feeder roots at the surface of the soil.

Fertilizing established perennials is usually recommended at the start of spring growth, yet many spring bulbs benefit from feeding right after blooming ends in order to stimulate stronger budding for the next season's leaves and flowers. Newly divided perennials, having reduced root systems, are best left unfertilized until they show definitive new growth.

PROPAGATION

The creation and distribution of new perennial offspring in nature is mainly achieved from generous seed production (or by spores from ferns) during summer and autumn in the North Temperate Zone. Seed planting by gardeners is economical of time and expense but slower for results than other propagation methods and has the drawback of not always producing parental duplicates. Seed, either collected from a garden or the wild or bought from a reputable seed company, must be fresh and sown either into prepared ground outdoors or into shallow containers indoors. Store unused seed in a cool, dry place.

Natural seeding of some perennials occurs in every garden over the course of time. Learn to identify seedlings desirable for your needs as well as those likely to dominate a garden space quickly. The prompt removal of spent flowers (called "deadheading") forestalls production of unwanted seeds, a technique which also conserves a plant's energies for the formation of additional roots and leaves.

Another popular propagation method is reproduction by stem cuttings, which assures you the new plant will be a parental duplicate. Spring and early summer are the usual collection times. This schedule involves the removal of three to four inches of new top or side growth by scissors or sharp knife before the plant blooms. Drop the cuttings into a pail of water to keep them cool and moist, and when all of one type are taken, strip off the lower sets of leaves, dip the moistened ends into a root-inducing hormone powder, and set the cuttings into closely spaced rows in shallow wood or plastic flats. The rooting medium in the flat should be either coarse sand, peat moss, vermiculite, perlite—all moistened and compacted beforehand—or a mix of these as experience and cultural practices dictate.

Water the installed cuttings, label and date the collection, and place the container in a wind-protected, outdoor location away from bright sunlight. Maintain even moisture in the flat at all times and inspect for new root development after a few weeks. When roots begin, take the flat into more sunlight. As soon as both stem and leaf enlargements are evident, place the individual cuttings into pots or permanent garden locations. Millions of hardy chrysanthemums are propagated yearly by growers in just this way.

A variation is to make root cuttings, which are usually thick pieces of root removed by sharp knife or clippers from a parent plant in early autumn as stem growth halts. Dig up the entire plant, wash off the soil, cleanly slice thick root pieces two to three inches long, and then replant the parent. Store the cut root parts until the following spring in a cool but frost-free location either in boxes or plastic bags containing moistened sand, peat moss, or sawdust. Inspect the material intermittently through the winter for mold, rot, or the need for another light watering. Discard any decaying pieces promptly.

When your garden soil is workable in spring, set out the stored cuttings into well-prepared but unfertilized soil in rows in a semishaded location with about six inches of space between each piece. Of course, they can also be planted above ground in shallow containers of a preferred soil mix with at least an inch of covering. Keep these cuttings consistently moist, and when substantial stem and leaf growth emerges—which may take several months—lift and install at permanent locations.

By far the quickest method to obtain quantities of new plants is simple division of an established plant. Schedule this either for early spring as growth begins or else in late summer as growth slows down. The technique involves lifting the entire plant with a spading fork, shaking off the soil, and then carefully separating the combined stems and roots into plantable sections. Some fibrous-rooted perennials can be simply pulled apart, but deep-rooted types require slicing with a newly honed straight-edged spade or a sharp knife. Relocate these divisions into well-dug planting holes, water well, and forego fertilizing until the following season. Protect the emerging foliage of spring divisions from undue abuse, but by autumn you can be less cautious in handling plants since only additional root growth is anticipated then. Plan this work for cool, overcast days, especially in the spring.

Crowded bulb colonies are handled for division in a similar way by lifting the clumps after bloom is finished and foliage starts withering. Spring bulbs can be immediately replanted or else lifted and stored for autumn installation in a cool, dry, inside location. Because they are never really dormant, all lilies should be replanted immmediately after division. Retain all bulb foliage since it is essential for creating the next year's flowering.

SPACING

Recommended spacing for perennials is *not* provided here because too many variables exist: the purchase size, annual growth rate in your locale, immediate effect wanted, your site exposure and rainfall amounts, plus the time available for weeding and cultivation. What spacing works happily in Zone 4 is not likely to prove useful in Zone 8 due to the very different lengths of the growing season between them. Spacing becomes a trial-and-error experience for all of us at some point.

Nevertheless, you can develop some practical knowledge about spacing from a careful reading of the text regarding mature plant size, normal leaf size, and expected vigor, while also observing actual growth habits locally. For example, if a plant has 8-inch-long foliage, it then will normally spread at least 16 inches edge to edge in a season. A similar-sized plant nearby is best set at twice this leaf spread (or 32 inches) to allow for several years of normal expansion of new stems and leaves from both plants without undue crowding in a short time. Because most bulbs expand slower and produce far fewer stems and foliage than many other perennnials, they can be spaced closer from the beginning. In any event, only you can decide how a spacing program works best.

NOMENCLATURE

Official labels for plants are organized into a system of scientific names—never intentionally duplicated—as formulated by the International Union of Biological Sciences and published through their International Code for

Cultivated Plants. There is no formal code for common names, however, and these are frequently duplicated at whim in different places, creating identity confusion for entirely separate plants. Knowing only common names for perennials can soon prove less than beneficial, but learning the proper scientific names will assure precise identification no matter where you are.

Each plant is provided first with a *genus* name (plural: *genera*), which is always capitalized. Next follows the *species* name (plural: *species*), set in lowercase type, and if it exists in nature, a *variety,* also lowercase, identifying a definitive, single alteration from a species, such as prostrate (lying flat on the ground) habit (for example, *Geranium sanguineum* var. *prostratum*). A true variety reproduces accurately from seed.

Recently the coined world *cultivar*—from "cultivated variety" of garden use—has emerged. It is often identified by the abbreviation *cv.* (*cvs.* for plural) followed by a set of single quotation marks enclosing the identifying, capitalized name taken from any modern-day language. Some authors and publishers, however, omit the cv. designation as redundant, remarking that the single-quote system is identification enough. I am one who has eliminated the cv. mark here, particularly since it is not used in conversation. Be that as it may, cultivars are propagated asexually to ensure the uniformity of their progeny because their seed delivers erratic results.

The scientific name of hybrid plants, those hoped-for improvements created by the deliberate intervention of people in fertilizing flowers from members of the same family, are preceded by the multiplication sign—×—which is not pronounced in discussion. If the × comes *before* the genus (a rare happening horticulturally), the hybrid resulted from the cross-pollination of two separate genera within that family. If the × *follows* the genus name, then the fertilizing took place between two—often more—species from that family. In talking about such hybrids, the × translates either into "hybrid genus" or "hybrid species."

SUMMARY

Generally economical to buy and to grow, the hardy perennials represent a generous range of garden effects from flower to foliage—at times both—to provide attractive, seasonal interest for most of the horticultural year. If they have any particular drawback, it is their usual need to be lifted, divided, and reset after a few years because of crowding from their own exuberance. The bonus for you is an increase in perennial wealth.

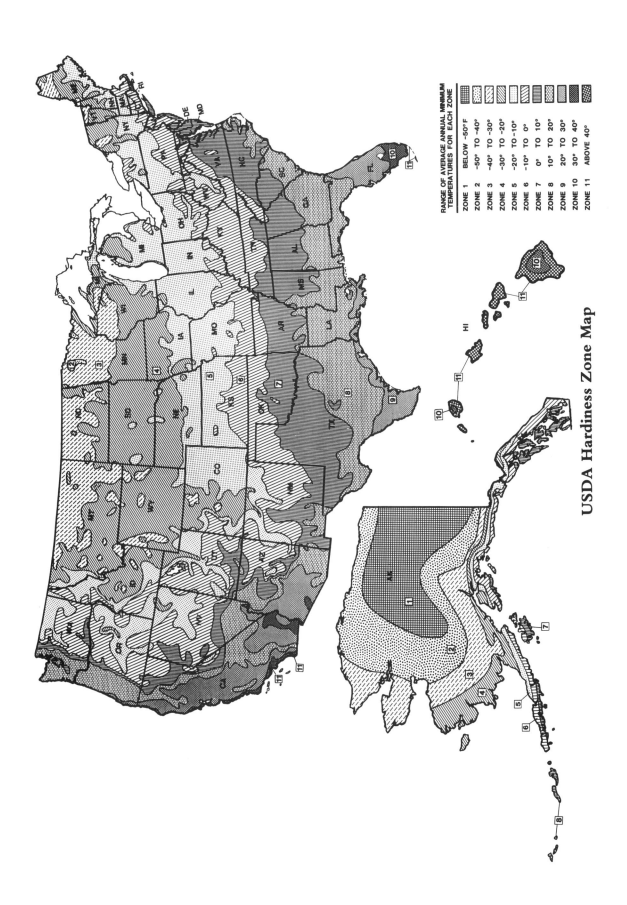

USDA Hardiness Zone Map

RANGE OF AVERAGE ANNUAL MINIMUM
TEMPERATURES FOR EACH ZONE

ZONE 1   BELOW −50° F
ZONE 2   −50° TO −40°
ZONE 3   −40° TO −30°
ZONE 4   −30° TO −20°
ZONE 5   −20° TO −10°
ZONE 6   −10° TO 0°
ZONE 7   0° TO 10°
ZONE 8   10° TO 20°
ZONE 9   20° TO 30°
ZONE 10   30° TO 40°
ZONE 11   ABOVE 40°

The Monthly Calendar

March

(Photos for March are between pages 24 and 25.)

T H E   P L A N T S

Chionodoxa luciliae (glory-of-the-snow) 3–6 in Sun Zones 4–8

FLOWERING SPAN: Late March to mid-April

NATURAL COLOR: Violet blue with a white center

DISTRIBUTION: Asia Minor

Six-pointed, 1-in, upward-facing flowers with conspicuous white centers, generally 8–10 to a stalk, emerge from deep green, 3-in, straplike foliage. Easily naturalized by self-seeding and bulb offsets, this autumn-planted perennial enjoys cool, moist, well-drained locations in either full sun or light shade. Ants are attracted to the sugar coating on the seeds and often move them to their nests some distance away, thereby starting new plant colonies inadvertently. Foliage disappears by early summer, and disease or insect problems are nonexistent. The cultivars include: 'Alba', white and scarce to find; 'Gigantea', large-flowered; 'Pink Giant', blush pink and floriferous; 'Tmolusi', clear blue but dwarfed and later-flowering; and 'Rosea', violet-pink but skimpy for blossoming. (See photo.)

Chionodoxa sardensis   4–6 in   Sun   Zones 4–8
   FLOWERING SPAN: Late March to mid-April
   NATURAL COLOR: Porcelain blue
   DISTRIBUTION: Asia Minor
   Deeper blue and more open-flowered than *C. luciliae,* the ¾-in blossom here has 6–8 florets with small white centers on purplish brown stems. Culture is the same for both.

Crocus chrysanthus   2–3 in   Sun   Zones 3–9
   FLOWERING SPAN: Mid-March to mid-April
   NATURAL COLOR: Yellow, blue, white, often interblended
   DISTRIBUTION: Bulgaria to Asia Minor
   Many chalice-shaped, stemless flowers emerge from each tiny bulb before the 4–6 white-lined, grassy leaves develop fully. Colonizing readily into dense masses in rockeries, borders, and lawn displays where winters are consistently cold, these mountain crocuses prefer full sun or light shading in enriched, well-drained locations. (In warmer climates the flowers tend to "blast," or look ragged.) Foliage elongates after flowering and should remain in place until dried. Natural self-seeding or autumn planting and division of crowded colonies propagate it easily. While insects present no difficulty, a sooty fungus on the corms can spread rapidly. Chipmunks like to eat them, too.
   Named cultivars are many: 'Advance', yellow-bronze outside, straw yellow inside; 'Blue Bird', light blue outside, buttercup yellow inside; 'Blue Pearl', silvery blue outside, yellow inside with an orange stigma; 'Blue Peter', purple outside, blue with a gold throat inside; 'Cream Beauty', creamy yellow throughout with an orange stigma; 'E. A. Bowles', sulphur yellow with a bronze base; 'Ladykiller', deep mauve outside, lilac-white inside; 'Princess Beatrix', clear light blue throughout with a gold base; 'Snow Bunting', white throughout with a bronze-yellow center, very early; 'Warley', cream and deep blue outside, white and yellow inside; 'Yellow Hammer', golden brown outside, yellow inside; and 'Zwanenburg Bronze', garnet-brown outside, saffron yellow inside. (See photo.)

Crocus tomasinianus   2–3 in   Sun   Zones 3–9
   FLOWERING SPAN: Early March to April
   NATURAL COLOR: Purple to mauve

DISTRIBUTION: Central Yugoslavia

Very hardy, free-flowering, and probably the easiest crocus to grow, its prominent orange stigma is its identifying characteristic. Impervious to dryness or being inadvertently disturbed by digging when dormant, it self-seeds readily. New plantings and division are autumn operations for sunny, average-fertility locations. No special pests or diseases bother it. The cultivars include: 'Barr's Purple', mauve-white outside, purple-lilac inside; 'Ruby Giant', purple outside, silver-mauve inside; 'Taplow Ruby', reddish purple throughout; and 'Whitewell Purple', purple-mauve outside, mauve-white inside. (See photo.)

Crocus vernus (Dutch crocus) 4–6 in Sun Zones 3–9
  FLOWERING SPAN: Mid-March to mid-April
  NATURAL COLOR: White, yellow, purple
  DISTRIBUTION: Central and southern Europe

The largest flowering of all, these crocuses have showier blossoms and wider, thicker foliage, and they self-seed readily. Install in autumn in a sunny, average-fertility location for best results. Cultivars are many: 'Blizzard', white; 'Cinderella', white with pale and deep lilac stripes; 'Enchantress', silvery blue; 'Flower Record', rich violet-blue; 'Grand Maitre', deep blue-purple; 'Haarlem Gem', pale lilac-mauve; 'Jeanne d'Arc', pure white; 'Kathleen Parlow', white with prominent orange stigma; 'King of the Striped', white-striped lilac; 'Little Dorrit', lilac; 'Peter Pan', ivory white; 'Pickwick', purple-striped lilac; 'Purpureus Grandiflorus', silvery deep purple; 'Queen of the Blues', blue-lavender; 'Remembrance', silvery violet; 'Sky Blue', lilac-blue; 'Snowstorm', white; 'Striped Beauty', white-striped lavender; 'The Bishop', deep reddish purple; 'Vanguard', pale silvery lilac; 'Victor Hugo', light purple; and 'Yellow Mammoth', rich yellow. (See photo.)

Eranthis cilicica (Cilician aconite) 3–4 in Sun Zones 4–8
  FLOWERING SPAN: Mid-March to early April
  NATURAL COLOR: Deep yellow
  DISTRIBUTION: Greece, Asia Minor

A sizeable, frilly collar of leafy bracts supports solitary, fragrant, 1-in flowers above 2-in bright green leaves. Favored locations in spring sun need to be followed by summer shading once the foliage disappears. Moist, alkaline soil is best, but it is not fussy about dryness. Plant new tubers immediately upon receipt in the autumn since they dry out quickly. Once established, the plant seeds freely. Diseases and insects are not bothersome.

Eranthis hyemalis (winter aconite) 3–6 in Sun Zones 4–7
  FLOWERING SPAN: Early March to April
  NATURAL COLOR: Lemon yellow

DISTRIBUTION: Western Europe, Asia Minor, North America

Similar to *E. cilicica* but slightly taller, this perennial carries thinner foliage and blooms earlier. Its solitary, buttercup-shaped, 1-in flowers sit atop a jagged rosette of green bracts. Culture is the same.

Erica carnea (spring heath) 8–12 in Sun Zones 5–8
    FLOWERING SPAN: Mid-March to May
    NATURAL COLOR: Reddish purple
    DISTRIBUTION: Europe

This plant is often regarded solely as a dwarf shrub because of its woody stems and evergreen foliage, but it is included here for its common use in rock gardens and seashore gardens in many parts of the country. Widely but slowly creeping and trailing thin stems with needlelike whorls of ½-in evergreen leaves produce long-lasting terminal spikes of ¼-in bell-shaped flowers. Best in full sun, it prefers a well-drained, sandy soil enriched with peat or acid humus; however, this is the only heath species in the United States to grow well in limed soil. Summer tip cuttings or layered stems are the reliable propagation methods since older plants do not divide or transplant satisfactorily. No problems are apparent with insects or diseases. The cultivars are all superior to the parent: 'Atrorubra', deep pink, late-flowering: 'Eileen Porter', carmine red; 'King George', deep pink, dwarfed; 'Ruby Glow', ruby red, compact; 'Sherwood Early Red', rosy red, early; 'Snow Queen', white, dwarfed; 'Springwood Pink', bright pink; 'Springwood White', white, showy flowered; 'Vivelli', light red, dwarfed; and 'Winter Beauty', rosy pink. (See photos.)

Galanthus elwesii (giant snowdrop) 6–9 in Semishade Zones 3–9
    FLOWERING SPAN: Late March to mid-April
    NATURAL COLOR: White
    DISTRIBUTION: Asia Minor

Two grayish, 1-in-wide leaves lengthen to 4 in and surround the 6–9-in flower stalk with 1½-in blossoms. The flowers have 3 outer petals which flare out to reveal a narrow, notched tube colored green at both ends. It naturalizes slower than other species and prefers a rich, moist, well-drained soil that is cool in all seasons. Division and replanting of crowded colonies right after flowering, when the foliage disappears, is best, but new plantings should be made in the autumn. Pests and diseases are not problematic.

Galanthus nivalis (common snowdrop) 4–6 in Semishade Zones 2–9
    FLOWERING SPAN: Early March to April
    NATURAL COLOR: White
    DISTRIBUTION: Central Europe

Chionodoxa luciliae

Crocus chrysanthus
'Cream Beauty'

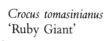

Crocus tomasinianus
'Ruby Giant'

Crocus vernus
'Yellow Mammoth'

Erica carnea

Erica carnea
'Springwood White'

Galanthus nivalis

Galanthus nivalis

Helleborus niger

Helleborus orientalis

Puschkinia scilloides

Scilla bifolia
'Rosea'

Scilla siberica

Its two, gray-green, ¼-in-wide leaves emerge pressed together at the base. The drooping 1-in flowers have outer petals much longer than the green-rimmed inner cylinder. Naturalizing freely from self-seeding, new plantings should be made in autumn into woodsy, moist, well-drained, enriched soil. Spring foliage disappears completely by early summer. No pests or diseases of consequence are known. Several cultivars exist: 'Arnott's Seedling', fragrant, robust, 6–10 in tall; 'Flore Pleno', somewhat double; and 'Simplex', larger-flowered. (See photos.)

Galanthus plicatus (Crimean snowdrop) 6–9 in Semishade Zones 2–9
FLOWERING SPAN: Early March to April
NATURAL COLOR: White
DISTRIBUTION: Crimea

Two very grayish 1-in-wide leaves emerge face-to-face but with the edges rolled back to form a pleat. Blooming slightly earlier than the other *Galanthus* species here, it has a broad, dark green collar on the 1-in flower tube. Culture is the same as for *G. nivalis*.

Helleborus niger (Christmas rose) 9–12 in Semishade Zones 3–8
FLOWERING SPAN: January through March
NATURAL COLOR: Greenish white
DISTRIBUTION: Southern Europe

Although very poisonous, this plant maintains the constant interest of gardeners. Five-petaled, 3-in flowers centrally ringed with a band of noticeable yellow stamens emerge from a clump of long-stalked, evergreen, leathery, deeply indented leaves with just a few serrations on the margins. The flowers fade to a blush pink coloring, and if cut will last longer if you slit the stem. Established plants have long, deep roots and resent transplanting. Disliking heat and intense sunlight, they enjoy a rich, acid, constantly moist but well-drained soil mulched each spring with a layer of leaf mold. Nursery-grown plants or seed (which is very slow to germinate) are the preferred methods of increase. Slugs occasionally feed on the foliage or flowers, and a fungus disease can discolor the leaves in humid summer weather. The cultivars include: 'Angustifolius' and 'Praecox', both smaller-blossoming; and 'Major', larger-flowering. (See photo.)

Helleborus orientalis (caucasicus) (Lenten rose) 15–18 in Semishade Zones 3–8
FLOWERING SPAN: Early March to mid-May
NATURAL COLOR: Purple-pink to cream
DISTRIBUTION: Greece, Asia Minor

Also poisonous and similar in foliage to *H. niger* except that the 12-in glosssy leaves are lighter colored and have many small, marginal teeth. Its 2-in flowers appear on leafless, branched stems with 2–6 blossoms. Culture is the same for both. The cultivar 'Atrorubens' is purplish, shorter, and carries only 2–4 flowers. (See photo.)

Iris danfordiae (Danford iris) 3–4 in Sun Zones 4–8
  FLOWERING SPAN: Mid-March to early April
  NATURAL COLOR: Canary yellow
  DISTRIBUTION: Eastern Turkey
      Often neglected because of its habit of quickly subdividing into many tiny bulblets which diminish flowering, this plant has squat blossoms 2-in wide before its 2-ft-long leaves appear. Light, annual fertilizing may help produce regular flowering. Initial plantings are made in the autumn and are best set in protected, well-drained sites of average fertility. Insects are no problem, but a fungus called "ink disease" can quickly destroy the bulbs.

Iris reticulata (netted iris) 5–6 in Sun Zones 4–8
  FLOWERING SPAN: Mid-March to mid-April
  NATURAL COLOR: Deep purple
  DISTRIBUTION: Asia Minor
      Violet-scented, this showy flower appears between narrow, upright, 8–10-in leaves which stretch almost to 18 in and then disappear by early summer. Attractive when used in drifts for rock gardens or borders, the bulb likes any well-drained, average soil in full sun. Pests are unknown, but the "ink disease" fungus can prove troublesome. Cultivars offer some interesting variations: 'Album', white; 'Cantab', light blue; 'Clarette', violet-blue with white markings; 'Harmony', deep sky blue with gold markings; 'Royal Blue', deep blue; and 'Violet Beauty', dark purple with orange markings, free-flowering.

Puschkinia scilloides (libanotica) (striped squill) 4–6 in Sun Zones 3–8
  FLOWERING SPAN: Late March to mid-April
  NATURAL COLOR: Blue-white
  DISTRIBUTION: Asia Minor and Caucasus
      Related to both *Chionodoxa* and *Scilla,* this bulb has stalks of 5–20 florets growing from a pair of fleshy, ½-in-wide leaves at ground level. Its ½-in white blossoms carry a central blue stripe on each petal. Preferring cool, moist locations in sun to light shading, it does not survive long in sun-baked areas. Overcrowded colonies can be separated and replanted when the foliage disappears by early summer, but new plantings should be made in the autumn. Pests and diseases are no problem. The cultivar 'Alba' is pure white but hard to find. (See photo.)

Scilla bifolia (twinleaf squill) 3–6 in Sun Zones 3–8
  FLOWERING SPAN: Mid-March to mid-April
  NATURAL COLOR: Bright blue
  DISTRIBUTION: Southern Europe, southwestern Asia

  Appearing just before *S. siberica,* the starlike, ¾-in flowers have noticeable anthers jutting beyond the petals. The flowers appear on slender, reddish stalks in clusters of 3–8 above twin, bronze-green leaves. Not so vigorously spreading as other species, it likes a cool, moist, humusy soil, well-drained in full sun to light shade. Self-seeding normally takes care of propagation, but plant new colonies in the autumn. Pests and diseases are not worrisome, but they need winter mulching where the climate is severe. Several cultivars are available: 'Alba', white; 'Praecox', bright blue, earlier, larger; 'Rosea', pale purple-pink and warm-tolerant to Zone 9; and 'Splendens', cobalt blue. (See photo.)

Scilla siberica (Siberian squill) 3–6 in Sun Zones 2–9
  FLOWERING SPAN: Late March to late April
  NATURAL COLOR: Bright blue
  DISTRIBUTION: Southern Russia, Siberia

  Readily colonizing by self-seed into huge displays almost anywhere, these vibrant, 1-in flowers appear 3–4 to a stalk with several stems rising from each bulb. The 2–5 straplike, 6-in leaves disappear by early summer. Best grown in cool, moist, well-drained locations of average fertility in sun to light shading, it should be initially planted in autumn. Nothing appears to bother it. The white cultivar 'Alba' is rare, but the cultivar 'Atrocoerulea' (which is usually marketed as 'Spring Beauty') carries larger and earlier flowers on taller stalks. (See photo.)

Scilla tubergeniana 3–5 in Sun Zones 2–9
  FLOWERING SPAN: Late March to late April
  NATURAL COLOR: Pale blue-white
  DISTRIBUTION: Northwestern Iran

  Very hardy and blooming with *S. siberica,* these 1-in, upright flowers come 2–4 to a stem with, again, several stalks from each bulb. Individual petals have a dark blue dividing line at the top, giving a close resemblance to *Puschkinia,* but the stamens here are bright yellow. The 3–5 bright green leaves completely fade away by early summer, when overcrowded colonies can be divided. New plantings are best made in early autumn into moist, cool locations with sun or light shade. They dislike hot and dry exposures. Slugs are occasionally a pest, but there are no problematic diseases.

April

_____ WHITE _____

Actaea pachypoda
Actaea rubra
Anemone blanda cvs.
Anemone caroliniana
Anemone nemorosa
Anemone pulsatilla cvs.
Anemone quinquefolia
Arabis alpina
Arabis caucasica
Arabis procurrens
Caltha palustris cvs.
Claytonia caroliniana
Dicentra canadensis
Dicentra cucullaria
Dicentra eximia cvs.
Erythronium albidum

Erythronium dens-canis cvs.
Fritillaria meleagris cvs.
Hepatica acutiloba
Hepatica americana
Hyacinthus orientalis cvs.
Iris pumila cvs.
Leucojum aestivum
Leucojum vernum
Mertensia virginica cvs.
Muscari botryoides cvs.
Narcissus cvs.
Ornithogalum nutans
Pachysandra procumbens
Pachysandra terminalis
Phlox subulata cvs.
Primula denticulata cvs.

Primula × polyantha
Primula sieboldii cvs.
Sanguinaria canadensis
Trillium grandiflorum
Trillium nivale
Trillium undulatum
Tulipa cvs.
Tulipa clusiana
Tulipa fosteriana cvs.
Tulipa kaufmanniana cvs.
Tulipa turkestanica
Vinca minor cvs.
Viola blanda
Viola cornuta cvs.
Viola odorata cvs.
Viola sororia cvs.

_____ YELLOW _____

Adonis amurensis
Adonis vernalis
Alchemilla alpina
Allium moly
Anemone ranunculoides
Aurinia saxatilis
Caltha palustris
Caulophyllum thalictroides
Draba sibirica

Erythronium americanum
Euphorbia epithymoides
Euphorbia myrsinites
Fritillaria imperialis cvs.
Hyacinthus orientalis cvs.
Iris pumila cvs.
Narcissus cvs.
Primula auricula
Primula veris

Primula vulgaris
Tulipa cvs.
Tulipa fosteriana cvs.
Tulipa greigii cvs.
Tulipa kaufmanniana
Tulipa kolpakowskiana
Tulipa tarda
Viola cornuta cvs.
Viola pubescens

_____ ORANGE _____

Fritillaria imperialis
Narcissus cvs.

Tulipa cvs.
Tulipa whittallii

Viola cornuta cvs.

_____ RED _____

Anemone blanda cvs.
Anemone pulsatilla cvs.
Fritillaria imperialis cvs.
Hyacinthus orientalis cvs.
Iris pumila cvs.
Phlox subulata cvs.
Primula auricula cvs.
Primula × polyantha
Primula vulgaris cvs.
Pulmonaria montana

Tulipa cvs.
Tulipa eichleri
Tulipa fosteriana
Tulipa greigii
Tulipa kaufmanniana cvs.
Tulipa linifolia
Tulipa pulchella
Tulipa praestans
Viola cornuta cvs.

_____ PINK _____

Anemone blanda cvs.
Anemone caroliniana
Anemone pulsatilla cvs.
Anemone quinquefolia var.
    oregana
Arabis alpina cvs.
Arabis × arendsii
Aubrieta deltoidea
Bergenia cordifolia
Bergenia crassifolia

Claytonia caroliniana
Claytonia virginica
Dicentra eximia
Erythronium dens-canis cvs.
Fritillaria meleagris cvs.
Hepatica americana
Hyacinthus orientalis cvs.
Mertensia virginica
Narcissus cvs.
Phlox × procumbens

Phlox subulata
Primula × polyantha
Primula sieboldii
Pulmonaria saccharata cvs.
Tulipa cvs.
Tulipa aucheriana
Tulipa fosteriana cvs.
Tulipa greigii cvs.
Tulipa kaufmanniana cvs.
Viola odorata cvs.

_____ PURPLE / LAVENDER _____

Anemone caroliniana
Anemone nemorosa cvs.
Anemone patens
Anemone pulsatilla
Aubrieta deltoidea
Dicentra eximia cvs.
Erythronium dens-canis
Fritillaria meleagris

Hyacinthus orientalis cvs.
Iris pumila cvs.
Muscari armeniacum
Primula denticulata
Primula × polyantha
Primula sieboldii
Primula vulgaris
Pulmonaria saccharata

Trillium sessile
Tulipa cvs.
Vinca minor cvs.
Viola cornuta
Viola odorata
Viola palmata
Viola sororia
Viola tricolor

_____ BLUE _____

Anemone apennina
Anemone blanda
Anemone quinquefolia var.
    oregana
Brunnera macrophylla
Hepatica acutiloba
Hepatica americana
Hyacinthus orientalis cvs.

Iris pumila
Iris verna
Muscari armeniacum cvs.
Muscari botryoides
Muscari comosum
Muscari latifolium
Muscari tubergenianum
Omphalodes verna

Phlox subulata cvs.
Polemonium reptans
Primula vulgaris cvs.
Pulmonaria angustifolia
Pulmonaria officinalis
Pulmonaria saccharata cvs.
Vinca minor

_____ BICOLOR _____

Aquilegia canadensis
Fritillaria meleagris
Iris pumila cvs.
Mertensia virginica
Narcissus cvs.

Primula auricula cvs.
Primula × polyantha cvs.
Tulipa cvs.
Tulipa clusiana
Tulipa fosteriana cvs.

Tulipa greigii cvs.
Tulipa kaufmanniana cvs.
Tulipa tarda
Viola cornuta cvs.
Viola tricolor

(Photos for April are between pages 32 and 33.)

_____ T H E   P L A N T S _____

Actaea pachypoda (alba) (white baneberry) 12–18 in Shade Zones 2–8
FLOWERING SPAN: Late April to June
NATURAL COLOR: White
DISTRIBUTION: Nova Scotia to Georgia, west to Minnesota and Missouri
　　　Compact spikes of small flowers appear atop large, smooth, compound leaves on stout stems and are followed by conspicuous clusters of ⅜-in, football-shaped, pure white fruit (occcasionally reddish) by late summer. These berries are poisonous—as are most other white-fruited plants, including poison ivy—and are attached by conspicuous, stiff, reddish pink stalks. Each berry has a forward, darker dot that provides the common name of "doll's eye" in some areas. Growth is best in moist, rich, cool woodlots with acid to neutral soil in shade to semishade. Divide only in early spring or sow seed in autumn for additional plants. There are no special pests or diseases. (See photo.)

Actaea rubra (spicata var. *rubra)* (red baneberry, snakeberry) 18–24 in Shade
Zones 3–8
FLOWERING SPAN: Late April to June
NATURAL COLOR: White
DISTRIBUTION: Nova Scotia to New Jersey and Pennsylvania, west to South Dakota and Nebraska
　　　Actaea rubra is similar to *A. pachypoda* except that its stems are slender, the ½-in fruit is red (but sometimes ivory—and still poisonous) on green stalks, and the leaves are usually downy with soft hairs. Culture is identical. The West Coast variety *arguta* has smaller leaves and almost-round fruit. (See photo.)

Adonis amurensis (Amur adonis) 4–15 in Sun Zones 4–8
FLOWERING SPAN: Early April to May
NATURAL COLOR: Golden yellow, occasionally white or rose
DISTRIBUTION: Northeastern Asia
　　　Multiple, 2-in flowers are terminal with 20–50 petals for a showy effect. They rise from an attractive ball of fernlike, bronzed, 3–6-in foliage. Enjoying a moist, rich, sandy soil, this is a good rock garden accent in full sun to semishade. The plant goes completely dormant by midsummer, however. Careful division of the fibrous roots in spring is best for propagation, but spring or autumn seeding also works well. No insect or disease is a problem. The double-flowered cultivar 'Pleniflora' has greenish yellow blossoms 6 in tall. The Japanese have hybridized white, orange, pink, and copper-toned cultivars, but they have not yet been widely distributed here.

Adonis vernalis (spring adonis) 12–15 in Sun Zones 3–8
> FLOWERING SPAN: Mid-April to mid-May
> NATURAL COLOR: Bright yellow
> DISTRIBUTION: Central and southern Europe
>   Usually taller and later-flowering than *A. amurensis,* this hardier species has 3-in, solitary blossoms with only 10–15 petals. Culture is the same for both. White and double-flowered forms are known to exist but are not easily available.

Alchemilla alpina (alpine lady's mantle) 6–8 in Sun Zones 3–8
> FLOWERING SPAN: Late April to mid-May
> NATURAL COLOR: Greenish yellow
> DISTRIBUTION: Mountains of Europe
>   Tiny, ⅛-in flowers appear in large, loose clusters above a vigorous set of 1–2-in-wide, silvery green leaves divided into 5–7 almost-separate sections with silver-haired undersides. A moist, average-fertility soil is suitable in sun to semishade. Seeding works better than division for propagation. There are no insect or disease problems.

Allium moly (lily leek) 6–18 in Sun Zones 4–9
> FLOWERING SPAN: Late April to June
> NATURAL COLOR: Bright yellow
> DISTRIBUTION: Southern Europe
>   Erect flower heads, 2–3 in across, of noticeable, ½-in star-shaped florets dominate the paired, gray-green, 1-in-wide leaves. Provide full sun to light shade in any well-drained, average soil with reasonable moisture to create colonies readily from self-seeding and bulbous offsets. Divide and replant overcrowded bulb clumps after the foliage fades, and install new bulbs in the autumn. Pests and diseases are rare. The cultivar 'Jeannine' is larger-flowered and may occasionally have two flower stalks per bulb.

Anemone apennina (Apennine anemone) 4–9 in Semishade Zones 5–9
> FLOWERING SPAN: Early April to May
> NATURAL COLOR: Sky blue
> DISTRIBUTION: Southern Europe
>   *Anemone apennina* is similar to *A. blanda* in general appearance and culture, except that its rootstock is an elongated rhizome rather than a fat tuber and that it accepts more shading to bloom. Its 1½-in daisylike flower has yellow stamens and up to 20 petals. The flower is carried above light green, coarsely cut foliage with hairy undersides that disappears soon after blossoming. Its resemblance to *A. blanda* keeps it commercially scarce. There are no problematic pests or diseases. Divide established colonies by late summer or plant new ones in early autumn. Cultivars include: 'Alba', white; 'Plena', blue, double; and 'Purpurea', mauve.

Actaea pachypoda

Actaea rubra (fruit)

Allium moly

Anemone blanda
'Pink Star'

Anemone pulsatilla

Anemone quinquefolia

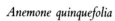

Aquilegia canadensis

Arabis caucasica

Arabis procurrens

Aubrieta deltoidea

Aurinia saxatilis

Bergenia cordifolia

Caltha palustris

Dicentra cucullaria

Draba sibirica

Erythronium americanum

Euphorbia epithymoides

Euphorbia myrsinites

Fritillaria imperialis
'Lutea'

Fritillaria meleagris

Hyacinthus orientalis
'City of Haarlem'

Iris pumila
cultivar

Leucojum vernum

Muscari armeniacum

Muscari armeniacum
'Blue Spike'

Muscari botryoides
'Album'

Muscari comosum
'Monstrosum'

Narcissus Division 1 (Trumpet)
'Spellbinder'

Narcissus Division 2 (Large-cupped)
'Carlton'

Narcissus Division 3 (Small-cupped)
'Pomona'

Narcissus Division 4 (Double)
'Mary Copeland'

Narcissus Division 5 (Triandrus)
'Thalia'

Narcissus Division 6 (Cyclamineus)
'Peeping Tom'

Narcissus Division 7 (Jonquilla)
'Suzy'

Narcissus Division 8 (Tazetta)
'Cragford'

Narcissus Division 9 (Poeticus)
'Actaea' (on right)

Narcissus Division 10 (Species)
N. triandrus

Narcissus Division 11 (Split-cup)
'Evolution'

APRIL

Pachysandra terminalis

Pachysandra terminalis
'Variegata'

Phlox subulata
cultivars

Polemonium reptans

Primula auricula
cultivar

Primula denticulata

Primula × *polyantha*

Pulmonaria angustifolia
'Rubra'

Pulmonaria saccharata
'Pink Dawn'

Sanguinaria canadensis

Sanguinaria canadensis
'Multiplex'

Trillium grandiflorum

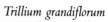

Tulipa (Single Early)
'Keizerskroon'

Tulipa (Double Early)
'All Gold'

Tulipa (Triumph)
'Apricot Beauty'

Tulipa (Triumph)
'Denbola'

Tulipa (Darwin Hybrid)
'President Kennedy'

Tulipa clusiana

Tulipa clusiana var. *chrysantha*

Tulipa eichleri

Tulipa fosteriana
'Orange Emperor'

Tulipa greigii
'Plaisir'

Tulipa kaufmanniana
'Gaiety'

Tulipa kolpakowskiana

Tulipa linifolia

Tulipa praestans
'Fusilier'

Tulipa pulchella
'Violacea'

Tulipa tarda

Tulipa turkestanica

April bulb display

Vinca minor

Vinca minor
'Alba'

Viola cornuta
'Jersey Gem'

Viola sororia

Viola sororia
'Alba'

Viola tricolor

Anemone blanda (Greek anemone) 2–8 in Semishade Zones 5–9
FLOWERING SPAN: Early April to mid-May
NATURAL COLOR: Intense sky blue
DISTRIBUTION: Eastern Europe and Asia Minor
    Daisy-petaled, 1½-in vivid flowers are carried above delicately divided, hairless, 3-in-wide leaves here. Effective in drifts which can remain undisturbed, it likes a moist, well-drained, humusy soil in dappled semishade. Divide the fat tubers when dormant in late summer or install new groupings by early autumn. Soak the wrinkled tubers overnight after buying new stock to ensure quicker response. No insect or disease is bothersome. Cultivars extend the colorings: 'Blue Star', blue; 'Pink Star', pink; 'Radar', raspberry-mauve; 'Bridesmaid', white; and 'White Splendour', white. (See photo.)

Anemone caroliniana (Carolina anemone) 5–16 in Sun Zones 5–9
FLOWERING SPAN: Mid-April to mid-May
NATURAL COLOR: White, pink, violet
DISTRIBUTION: Indiana to Florida, west to Texas and South Dakota
    Solitary, ½-to-1-in blossoms with up to 20 petals rise on slender stems above a basal clump of narrowly incised leaves. Attractive when naturalized in large rock gardens or open woodlots with rich, moist, alkaline soil. Tolerant of dryness when dormant, it produces densely woolly seedheads useful for indoor decoration. Insects and diseases are not a concern. This perennial is often grown and sold erroneously as *A. decapetala,* which is very similar but native only to South America.

Anemone nemorosa (European wood anemone) 6–10 in Semishade Zones 5–9
FLOWERING SPAN: Mid-April to mid-May
NATURAL COLOR: White, purplish white, or pinkish white
DISTRIBUTION: Europe, Asia
    Individual, 1½-in, drooping flowers with 5–8 large petals extend above low foliage with long leafstalks and deeply divided leaves. Good as woodlot carpeting where the soil is acid, constantly moist, humusy, and semishaded, this rampant species is intolerant of either dryness or high summertime heat. Division of the thick rootstock in spring or early autumn gives more productive results for propagation than seeding. It appears to have no important pests or diseases. The cultivars include: 'Alba Plena', double white; 'Allenii', silvery lavender, large-flowered; 'Blue Bonnet', soft blue; 'Major', white, large-flowered; 'Robinsoniana', clear lavender-blue; 'Rosea', reddish purple; 'Royal Blue', bright blue; and 'Vestal', double white with a pompon center.

Anemone patens (Pulsatilla patens) (spreading pasque flower) 4–8 in Sun
Zones 4–8
FLOWERING SPAN: Mid-April to mid-May

NATURAL COLOR: Lilac

DISTRIBUTION: Northern Europe

Cup-shaped, 2–3-in terminal flowers bloom before the basal clump of ferny leaves appears. These leaves are covered with silky white hairs. Later, the flowers develop into distinctive, long-lasting plumes of seedheads. Tolerant of extreme dryness when summer-dormant, *A. patens* likes a sandy, alkaline, well-drained soil in sun to light shade. Root cuttings and seed work better for propagation than division. Insects or diseases are rare.

Anemone pulsatilla (Pulsatilla amoena, P. vulgaris) (pasque flower) 6–12 in Sun Zones 5–8

FLOWERING SPAN: Mid-April to mid-May

NATURAL COLOR: Rich violet-purple

DISTRIBUTION: Europe

Showy, 2½-in cup-shaped flowers with a heavy ring of gold stamens appear before the fernlike 4–6-in leaves fully develop. Fluffy, durable, glistening seedheads follow. Well-drained, gravelly, neutral soil is best in full sun to light shade. Although spring division or root cuttings are feasible, seed works best for propagation. A root-decay fungus requires quick removal and discard of affected plants. Do not replant in the same place. Insects are not so troublesome. Cultivars are known but hard to find: 'Alba', pure white; 'Albacyanea', bluish white; 'Mallenderi', deep purple; 'Mrs. van der Elst', soft pink; and 'Rubra', maroon to brick red. (See photo.)

Anemone quinquefolia (American wood anemone) 4–8 in Semishade Zones 4–8

FLOWERING SPAN: Mid-April to mid-May

NATURAL COLOR: White, pinkish white

DISTRIBUTION: Southeastern Canada to North Carolina, west to Kentucky

Delicate, 1-in, solitary, up-facing blossoms are usually surrounded by a single, much-divided leaf lighter in color than that of *A. nemorosa.* Consistently moist, acid, humusy soil in open woodlots suits it best. Division of the wiry root system in either spring or autumn is the easiest propagation method. Serious pests or diseases are unknown. The West Coast variety *oregana* has ½-in blue or pink flowers. (See photo.)

Anemone ranunculoides (yellow wood anemone) 4–8 in Semishade Zones 4–8

FLOWERING SPAN: Mid-April to May

NATURAL COLOR: Golden yellow

DISTRIBUTION: Europe, Caucasus Mountains, Siberia

Except for its smaller, 1-in flower and its color, this species is very similar in habit, appearance, and culture to *A. nemorosa.* It thrives easily without becoming aggressive. The cultivar 'Flore Pleno' is partly double, while 'Superba' has deeper yellow flowers and bronzed foliage.

Aquilegia canadensis (wild columbine) 15–24 in Semishade Zones 3–9
    FLOWERING SPAN: Late April to June
    NATURAL COLOR: Red and yellow bicolor
    DISTRIBUTION: Southeastern Canada to Alabama, west to Texas
       Novel in configuration, the nodding flowers carry 1–2-in red spurs around an inner rosette of yellow sepals. These appear on branched, thin stems rising conspicuously above the rounded, blue-green, compound leaves. Best grown in light shade in wild gardens or rockeries, it wants a moist, sandy soil, well-drained, in sheltered locations. Seed is superior to root division. Leaf miner and root borer are destructive pests, while crown rot and mildew are serious diseases. The cultivar 'Nana' is only a foot tall. (See photo.)

Arabis alpina (mountain rock cress) 4–6 in Sun Zones 4–9
    FLOWERING SPAN: Late April to June
    NATURAL COLOR: Pure white
    DISTRIBUTION: Mountains of Europe
       Blooming conspicuously in dense, ¾-in-wide clusters of many-petaled flowers above low tufts of hairy green leaves, this compact ground cover is useful for sunny rock gardens and plant walls. Shear off the faded blossoms after flowering for continued compactness and potential repeat flowering. It wants well-drained, gravelly soil, marginally fertile, and can be propagated equally well from spring divisions, summer stem cuttings, or seeds. Very similar to but less vigorous than *A. caucasica* (which, some authorities believe, growers frequently offer instead of *A. alpina*), this species has no bothersome pests or diseases. The cultivars are: 'Compacta', dwarfed; 'Rosea', soft pink; 'Rosabella', rose pink; and 'Variegata', leaves striped in white or pale yellow.

Arabis × *arendsii* 6–9 in Sun Zones 4–9
    FLOWERING SPAN: Late April to June
    NATURAL COLOR: Pink
    ORIGIN: Horticultural hybrid of *A. aubrietioides* × *A. caucasica*
       Similar in general appearance and growth habit to *A. caucasica,* this hybrid has both creeping and erect stems, plus shorter flower stalks. Its culture is the same as for *A. caucasica,* and it has no particular pests or diseases. The cultivar 'Rosabella' develops light green foliage and rose red flowers, while 'Spring Charm' becomes bushier with large, carmine blooms.

Arabis caucasica (albida) (wall rock cress) 4–10 in Sun Zones 4–9
    FLOWERING SPAN: Late April to June
    NATURAL COLOR: Pure white
    DISTRIBUTION: Southeastern Europe to Iran

Slightly fragrant, ½-in florets (longer than those of *A. alpina*) crowd the many tall stalks rising above the vigorous, broad-growing mat of 1–3-in gray-green, soft-haired leaves, coarsely toothed at the tips. This popular perennial dislikes poor drainage, excessive fertilizer, and damp springtimes, preferring gravelly, sun-baked locations throughout the year. Severely cut back faded flowers and some foliage after bloom to encourage future compactness. Propagate the same as *A. alpina*. There are no special pests or diseases. Cultivars include: 'Flore Pleno', showy, double-flowered, long-lasting; 'Snow Peak', 4-in tall, very compact; and 'Variegata', leaves striped attractively in yellowish white. (See photo.)

Arabis procurrens (mollis) (downy rock cress) 6–10 in   Sun   Zones 3–9
FLOWERING SPAN: Late April to June
NATURAL COLOR: Pure white
DISTRIBUTION: Mountains of southeastern Europe
Oblong, 1-in, glossy, bright green leaves, which are slightly hairy beneath, form flat rosettes of evergreen foliage, slowly produced by thin, surface-creeping stems. The domed, ¾-in clusters of very tiny florets appear in an airy pattern on erect, wiry stems where sunshine is generous all day. It likes a sandy, well-drained soil of average or even low fertility to thrive. Spring division, summer stem cuttings, or seed all reproduce it readily, and it is untroubled by pests or diseases. (See photo.)

Aubrieta deltoidea (common aubrieta) 6–9 in   Sun   Zones 4–9
FLOWERING SPAN: Late April to June
NATURAL COLOR: Mauve to deep purple
DISTRIBUTION: Mediterranean Europe, Asia Minor
Resembling and related to *Arabis,* a well-grown specimen can become covered with hundreds of ¾-in flowers. Moundlike and wide-spreading in sun or light shade, it prefers a sandy, well-drained, neutral soil of average fertility. It dislikes waterlogged, clay soils and high heat in summer. Shear off the faded flowers after bloom (using the identical technique wildlife follows in browsing these mountain plants) to improve compactness of the ground-hugging, deep gray-green foliage. Division, layering of long shoots, autumn stem cuttings, or seed work equally well for propagation. Pests and diseases are not problematic. Many cultivars are available but are so confusingly identified that no correct listing of exact colorings or heights is possible here. (See photo.)

Aurinia saxatilis (Alyssum saxatile) (goldentuft alyssum, basket-of-gold, gold dust)
    6–12 in   Sun   Zones 4–9
FLOWERING SPAN: Mid-April to late May
NATURAL COLOR: Bright yellow
DISTRIBUTION: Mediterranean Europe, Turkey

Great masses of ¼-in, mildly scented flowers in compact clusters envelop the heavy, lancelike, 2–5-in, grayish, persistent leaves of this rambling perennial. Vivid in full sun for plant walls, rock gardens, and border edgings, it thrives on neutral sandy or gravelly soil with quick drainage. Soil too rich encourages straggly, soft growth less durable in winter. Trim off old flower heads for better plant shape. Division of the thick, long roots is difficult; spring or autumn seeding propagates it more satisfactorily, if slower. Self-seeding can be counted upon if the growing conditions are to its liking. Summer stem cuttings root satisfactorily, too. A club-root disease destroys feeding root hairs and requires removal and destruction of afflicted plants. Flea beetles bother the foliage occasionally. Attractive cultivars are available: 'Citrinum', pale yellow; 'Compactum', bright yellow, dwarfed; 'Compactum Flore Pleno', bright yellow, double-flowered, long-lasting; and 'Silver Queen', pale, creamy yellow. (See photo.)

Bergenia cordifolia (Saxifraga cordifolia) (heartleaf bergenia) 12–15 in Semishade
Zones 3–9
FLOWERING SPAN: Late April to June
NATURAL COLOR: Rose red
DISTRIBUTION: Siberia

The 6–10-in-wide, leathery, wavy-margined, evergreen leaves of this very hardy plant (cultivated since the 17th century) are as interesting as the stout flower stalk with its long-lasting head of waxy, bell-like, ¼–½-in blossoms. Turning somewhat limp and bronze-green in winter, the foliage is glossy green and upright when new. These leaves are probably better-looking for winter interest in Zones 6–9, yet they are still valuable in colder areas. The plant prefers moist, semishaded locations with average fertility but will accept more sun and moderate dryness satisfactorily, too. Division of the thick rootstock in early spring or early autumn is the usual propagation method, although seeding, while slow, is also workable. A fungus disfigures emerging foliage occasionally, and summer chewing insects may create some modest disfigurement. Recent cultivars are: 'Bressingham Salmon', warm pink-red, with erect leaves; 'Bressingham White', pure white, early, with downturned foliage; and 'Perfecta', warm red, taller. (See photo.)

Bergenia crassifolia (Saxifraga crassifolia) (Siberian tea) 12–18 in Semishade
Zones 4–9
FLOWERING SPAN: Late April to June
NATURAL COLOR: Rosy lilac
DISTRIBUTION: Mongolia, Siberia

Similar in general appearance and habit to *B. cordifolia,* this species carries oval to spoonlike, flat leaves up to 8 in wide and a flower stalk potentially 18 in tall. Its culture is identical.

Brunnera macrophylla (Anchusa myosotidiflora)   (Siberian brunnera)   8–15 in
Semishade   Zones 3–9
FLOWERING SPAN: Late April to mid-June
NATURAL COLOR: Clear blue
DISTRIBUTION: Western Siberia, Caucasus Mountains

Delicate sprays of ¼-in forget-me-not-like florets appear in great abundance here above a mound of rough-textured but neat, 6-in, dark green leaves. This very hardy plant enjoys moist but well-drained, humusy, semishaded sites. Where summers are consistently cool, it will accept full sun but must be kept constantly moist. Division in early spring or seeding are the usual propagation methods. Slugs are an occasional difficulty along with crown rot in poorly drained locations. The cultivar 'Hadspen Cream' carries cream-bordered leaves, while 'Variegata' shows wider margins of creamy white. Both are considered tender and need locations out of excess wind and bright sun to stay attractive.

Caltha palustris   (marsh marigold, kingcup)   12–18 in   Semishade   Zones 3–9
FLOWERING SPAN: Mid-April to June
NATURAL COLOR: Bright yellow
DISTRIBUTION: Newfoundland to Alaska, south to Tennessee and North Carolina, Eurasia

Durable, 1–2-in flowers profusely cluster atop the branched stems rising above this hardy perennial's deep green, heart-shaped leaves up to 7 in wide. The foliage is sometimes collected and cooked like spinach. At home on wet, acid soil in semi- to full shade, it thrives readily along stream banks, swamps, and bogs. If kept from drying out at any time, it will adapt to garden use in rich, moist locations. It can be divided when summer-dormant or else seeded where wanted. Pests and diseases are of no concern. The cultivar 'Alba' has white blossoms while 'Monstruosa' produces double, very showy, 2½-in yellow flowers over a long period. (See photo.)

Caulophyllum thalictroides   (blue cohosh)   24–36 in   Shade   Zones 4–8
FLOWERING SPAN: Late April to June
NATURAL COLOR: Yellowish green
DISTRIBUTION: Southeastern Canada to South Carolina, west to Missouri

Unshowy tufts of ½-in, star-shaped flowers in loose clusters rise above a neat foliage mass that is actually a single, much-divided leaf. The admired value here is the clustering of deep blue, ¼-in, berrylike fruit in late summer as the foliage withers. American Indians used the seed to treat uterine disorders. Plant in rich, woodsy soil with shade to semishade. Propagate by root cuttings or by seed. There are no special diseases or pests.

Claytonia caroliniana (Carolina spring beauty) 8–12 in Semishade Zones 4–8
FLOWERING SPAN: Early April to late May
NATURAL COLOR: White or pale pink with red stripes
DISTRIBUTION: Eastern North America
A solitary stem carries up to 15 widely separated, ¾-in, cupped flowers with long stalks above broad, lancelike leaves which disappear after blossoming. Its corm generates new foliage in late autumn that endures the winter. Best displayed in large drifts, it does well on consistently damp, acid woodlots with semishade, self-seeds easily, and transplants readily. Insects and diseases are uncommon.

Claytonia virginica (Virginia spring beauty) 8–12 in Semishade Zones 4–8
FLOWERING SPAN: Mid-April to June
NATURAL COLOR: Whitish pink with red stripes
DISTRIBUTION: Eastern North America
Blooming slightly later than *C. caroliniana,* this species has a pair of grasslike, fleshy leaves up to 5 in long, a sprawling habit, and ½-in flowers. Culture is the same for both.

Dicentra canadensis (squirrel corn) 6–12 in Semishade Zones 4–8
FLOWERING SPAN: Early April to mid-May
NATURAL COLOR: Greenish white with purplish tint
DISTRIBUTION: Southeastern Canada to North Carolina, west to Minnesota and Missouri
Erect flower stalks with heart-shaped, tiny, fragrant blossoms rise above a basal foliage cluster of feathery, gray-green leaves in the woodsy, moist, sandy soil it prefers. Division of the bright yellow tubers, which resemble kernels of corn, is best right after flowering and before the foliage disappears (so you can locate them). Seed, while slower, also works well. Dry rot may prove a serious nuisance after transplanting at times, but insects are no threat.

Dicentra cucullaria (Dutchman's-breeches) 6–10 in Semishade Zones 4–8
FLOWERING SPAN: Early April to June
NATURAL COLOR: White with creamy yellow tips
DISTRIBUTION: Nova Scotia to North Carolina, west to Kansas
Similar in habit, form, and culture to *D. canadensis,* here the flowers are more showy and end in wide-spreading spurs. (See photo.)

Dicentra eximia (fringed bleeding-heart, wild bleeding-heart) 12–18 in Semishade Zones 3–9
FLOWERING SPAN: Late April to September

NATURAL COLOR: Pinkish purple

DISTRIBUTION: Mountains of New York to Georgia

Durable, long-flowering, and very hardy, this wildflower has grayish green, heavily dissected foliage persisting until heavy frost. Long, nodding stalks of ¾-in, rounded flowers with short spurs appear generously in spring and intermittently through the heat of summer. Sandy soil enriched with peat moss or humus, reasonable moisture, and a shaded site meet its basic needs, yet it will accept full sun if kept consistently moist. Division of the fleshy rootstock can be made even when it is in bloom, and it self-seeds generously to the point of overcrowding. For the best flowering, divide and reset every three years. Dry rot and aphids are the chief nuisances. Cultivars are known but difficult to locate: 'Alba', white with a pink flush, sparse-flowering, and 'Gracilis', deep purple with narrow flowers and foliage. This species is often confused with the later-blooming *D. formosa* of May.

Draba sibirica (repens) (Siberian draba, Whitlow grass)   1–3 in   Sun   Zones 3–8

FLOWERING SPAN: Early April to May

NATURAL COLOR: Bright yellow

DISTRIBUTION: Siberia, Caucasus, eastern Greenland

A ground-hugging mat of creeping, wiry stems with ⅛-in, soft green leaves spreads readily in sun or light shade to produce an overwhelming coverage of bright flowers lasting for a month or more. The blossoms resemble alyssum. Repeat flowering is possible in early autumn, but it will be sparse. Light, gritty, average soil with peat moss or leaf mold enrichment is preferred. Because of its very shallow rooting, it may need a light mulch in severe climates if the snow cover is erratic. Division right after flowering is the simplest method of propagation and promotes thriftier plants. There are no special insect or disease difficulties. (See photo.)

Erythronium albidum (white dogtooth violet)   6–12 in   Semishade   Zones 4–9

FLOWERING SPAN: Late April to June

NATURAL COLOR: Bluish to pinkish white

DISTRIBUTION: Southeastern Canada to Minnesota, south to Kentucky, Arkansas, and Texas

Showy when colonized to any extent, this bulbous perennial has a narrow set of 1½-in leaves up to 6 in long, either all green or mottled in brown. The reflexed petals of the 1½-in, solitary, lilylike flower reveal a soft yellow center. Plant in cool, moist soil enriched with peat moss or humus in a definitely semishaded location. It will not tolerate excessive sun. Producing abundant offset bulbs when established, the mother plant dislikes being moved, but removing and transplanting the bulblets immediately after flowering may provide some success. Plant new corms in autumn when available since they dry out easily. Insect and disease problems are unknown. In colder locations apply a light mulch for winter. All species enjoy annual topdressing with bonemeal or wood ashes in spring.

Erythronium americanum (yellow adder's-tongue, trout lily) 6–12 in Semishade Zones 4–9
FLOWERING SPAN: Late April to June
NATURAL COLOR: Yellow
DISTRIBUTION: Southeastern Canada to Minnesota, south to Alabama and northern Florida

Another prolific offset-producer, this species enjoys the proximity of deep-rooted, deciduous trees, which may help remove any excess water that could keep the corm sulking. Its leaves are up to 6 in long and entirely mottled in brown and white. The blossom is flushed with brownish red outside. Culture is the same as for *E. albidum.* (See photo.)

Erythronium dens-canis (dogtooth violet) 6–12 in Semishade Zones 4–8
FLOWERING SPAN: Early April to May
NATURAL COLOR: Rose to purple
DISTRIBUTION: Central Europe, Asia

Twin elliptical leaves between 4–6 in long of mottled red-brown and white spread close to the ground and produce a solitary, 1-in, drooping flower with orange-red markings at the base and a slight fragrance. Culture is identical to that of *E. albidum.* Many cultivars are now available: 'Album', white; 'Congo', rosy purple; 'Frans Hals', light red-violet; 'Pink Perfection', bright pink; 'Rose Beauty', deep pink; 'Rose Queen', clear pink; and 'Snowflake', white. There also is a true variety *japonicum* with deep violet, 3-in flowers.

Euphorbia epithymoides (polychroma) (cushion spurge) 12–18 in Sun Zones 4–10
FLOWERING SPAN: Late April to June
NATURAL COLOR: Chartreuse yellow
DISTRIBUTION: Eastern Europe

From a hemispherical mound of many thin stems with ½-in, deep green leaves develop heads of 1-in, sulphur yellow bracts surrounding the true, green-toned flowers. Enlarging widely but neatly, the plant turns deep red in autumn. Preferring a marginally fertile, sandy soil with good drainage, it grows best in full sun but will acccept light shading. Seed, which is self-sown indiscriminately and generously, readily propagates the plant, while division or stem cuttings also work well. There are no special pests or diseases. (See photo.)

Euphorbia myrsinites (myrtle euphorbia) 6–9 in Sun Zones 6–8
FLOWERING SPAN: Late April to June
NATURAL COLOR: Greenish yellow
DISTRIBUTION: Mediterranean Europe

Prostrate and sprawling, this tender evergreen has cupped, gray-green, ¾-in, fleshy leaves arranged spirally around heavy stems. The terminal flowering is noticeable with 3-in heads of showy, yellowish bracts which surround the true, green-toned flowers. Needing wind and temperature protection in winter where the climate is harsh, this plant thrives in hot sun on a well-drained, gravelly, or sandy soil that is often dry. Division is unworkable, and seed propagation is the better system. Blight or stem rot can be serious diseases at times, but insects do not bother it. (See photo.)

Fritillaria imperialis (crown imperial) 30–48 in   Sun   Zones 5–8
   FLOWERING SPAN: Late April to June
   NATURAL COLOR: Reddish orange
   DISTRIBUTION: Northern India, Afghanistan, Iran
   Imposing when in flower, the sizeable bulb (at least tennis ball-sized) produces glossy, straplike leaves up to 6 in long on a lengthy flower stalk capped with a novel, dense crown of green, leafy bracts. The 2½-in flowers clustering beneath the cap are bell-like, strongly scented with musk to be disagreeable, and form a noticeable circle of elevated color. It thrives in full sun or very light shade on well-drained clay soil enriched with humus. The foliage disappears by midsummer, and then transplanting can take place. New installations should be made in either late summer or early autumn. Set the bulb on a 2-in sand cushion in the planting hole and place it less than upright to prevent rot. Be careful to avoid bruising the bulb since you will be overwhelmed by its skunklike odor, which obviously prevents wildlife from eating it. Pests and diseases are not problematic. The cultivars are more vividly colored than the species: 'Aurea', orange-red; 'Aurora', deep orange-red; 'Lutea', bright yellow; 'Lutea Maxima', deep lemon yellow; 'Orange Brilliant', rich orange; 'Rubra', rusty red, very large flowers; and 'Sulphurea', sulphur yellow. (See photo.)

Fritillaria meleagris (checkered lily, guinea-hen tulip)   6–12 in   Sun   Zones 3–8
   FLOWERING SPAN: Late April to June
   NATURAL COLOR: Brown-purple checkered with white
   DISTRIBUTION: Middle Europe, British Isles, Caucasus
   These uniquely mottled flowers always excite interest. Egg-shaped, drooping, solitary, and 1½ in long and wide, they appear above slender, gray-green leaves between 3–6 in long. The bulb naturalizes well in consistently damp, cool, acid, sandy soil enriched with humus in full sun to light shade. Divide and replant overcrowded colonies after the foliage withers, but plant new colonies in the autumn. There are no apparent problems with insects or diseases. Dutch growers have developed many interesting cultivars: 'Alba', pure white; 'Aphrodite', white, vigorous; 'Charon', deep purple; 'Pomona', white with violet markings; 'Poseidon', purple-pink, 3-in blossoms; and 'Saturnus', bright red-violet. (See photo.)

Hepatica acutiloba (sharplobe hepatica) 4–6 in Shade Zones 2–8
FLOWERING SPAN: Mid-April to June
NATURAL COLOR: Pale blue, white
DISTRIBUTION: Southeastern and south central Canada to Georgia and Alabama

Anemonelike, 1-in flowers with prominent stamens appear with three-lobed, pointed leaves on hairy stems. This foliage, often browned, persists through the winter, so it cannot truthfully be called ever*green*. Wanting no direct sun, the plant likes a rich, neutral, moist soil that is well drained. Spring division or seed propagates it readily. Smut fungus is sometimes troublesome, but insects present no problem.

Hepatica americana (triloba) (roundlobe hepatica) 4–6 in Shade Zones 2–9
FLOWERING SPAN: Mid-April to June
NATURAL COLOR: Pale blue, white, pale pink
DISTRIBUTION: Southeastern and south central Canada to northern Florida and Missouri

Just as super-hardy as *H. acutiloba* and with a broader southern range, this species is almost identical except for foliage with rounded ends and a slight increase in flower color potential. Culture for both is identical.

Hyacinthus orientalis (common hyacinth, Dutch hyacinth) 8–12 in Sun Zones 4–8
FLOWERING SPAN: Mid-April to mid-May
NATURAL COLOR: White, blue, red, pink
DISTRIBUTION: North Africa, Greece to Asia Minor and Syria

Intensely and enticingly fragrant, this ever-popular bulb has retained a featured place in gardens since the 17th century. A sturdy spike of slightly nodding, heavy-textured, bell-shaped florets rises centrally from a ring of light green, erect, fleshy, 4–6-in leaves which later elongate to as much as a foot before fading. Best grown in full sun on a light, neutral, sandy soil with reasonable moisture, it displays better in large drifts or bedding than in soldier lines outlining borders. The bulbs have a natural habit of subdividing into smaller, skimpy-flowered offsets within a few years, and replanting with new stock every 3 years is almost routine. Bulbs smaller than top size withstand wind and pelting rain better and are less expensive. Propagation is highly complex and its wisely left to the growers. Problems with insects and diseases are not serious. A light fertilizing after blooming encourages a stronger bud for flowering the next season.

While the latest hybridization efforts lean toward double-flowered forms, the main appeal continues for these dependable single cultivars: 'Amethyst', violet; 'Amsterdam', rose red; 'Anna Marie', clear pink; 'Bismark', pale blue; 'Blue Jacket', deep blue; 'Blushing Dolly', cherry-blossom pink; 'Carnegie', pure white; 'City of Haarlem', primrose yellow; 'Delft Blue', porcelain blue; 'Gipsy Queen', salmon; 'Jan Bos', crimson red; 'King of the Blues', indigo blue;

'Lady Derby', shell pink; 'L'Innocence', ivory white; 'Lord Balfour', rosy violet; 'Myosotis', pale blue; 'Orange Boven', orange-pink; 'Ostara', bright blue; 'Pink Pearl', deep rose; 'Princess Irene', deep pink; 'Princess Margaret', rosy pink; 'Prince Henry', clear yellow; 'Queen of the Pinks', rosy pink; 'Salmonetta', salmon-pink; 'Sky Jacket', rich blue; 'Wedgwood', clear blue; and 'Yellow Hammer', creamy yellow. (See photo.)

Iris pumila (attica) (miniature dwarf eupogon iris) 4–9 in Sun Zones 3–9
   FLOWERING SPAN: Mid-April to mid-May
   NATURAL COLOR: Blue, violet, white, yellow, red
   DISTRIBUTION: Central Europe to southern Russia and Asia Minor

The American Iris Society has recently unscrambled much of the confusion surrounding recent iris categories and now places the rhizomatous *I. pumila* (along with others) under the heading of miniature dwarf bearded iris of the eupogon or "true bearded" grouping. The society defines this category as including plants under 10 in tall with leaves shorter than the flower stalk and blossoms 2–3 in across. The other five horticultural divisions of eupogon are: standard dwarf, intermediate, miniature tall, border, and standard tall bearded. These are described in the May calendar of bloom.

Many of the *pumila* types are fragrant, and all normally produce several unbranched flower stalks from each rhizome when fully established. Attractive as rock garden bedding or front-of-the-border accents, the plant enjoys a sunny, well-drained, sandy-clay soil with average moisture. Enrich the soil before planting with compost, humus, or peat moss, and include a light application of a fertilizer low in nitrogen. Because this perennial quickly spreads outward, it needs regular and frequent division and replanting to maintain its flowering potential. Divide the clumps right after blossoming is done (no later than September), reduce the fan of erect foliage by ⅔ with sharp clippers or a knife, salvage only the plumpest and healthiest rhizomes—divide large clumps cleanly with a knife—and replant in a deeply prepared, sunny location. After spreading out the roots in the planting hole, barely cover the top of the rhizome with soil, and water well until new growth starts. Mulch lightly the first winter to prevent heaving. Various leaf diseases are disfiguring, but the chief pest is the iris borer, which requires a carefully programmed series of controls to overcome. Always discard any mushy rhizomes or foliage when discovered since the mushiness indicates that the iris borer has already eliminated the plant.

The many attractive cultivars are far too numerous to list here. Consult the catalogs of iris growers for the widest selection and newest colorings. (See photo.)

Iris verna (dwarf iris, violet iris) 3–6 in Semishade Zones 6–9
   FLOWERING SPAN: Late April to June
   NATURAL COLOR: Violet-blue

DISTRIBUTION: Pennsylvania to Georgia, west to Kentucky

Although this rhizome is fussy about adapting to a new location with ease, its 3-in-wide flowers with an orange-gold crest are showy, and in mild regions the 3–8-in fan of foliage is evergreen. It performs well from semishade to shade where the soil is constantly moist, acid, and humusy. Division in early spring or after flowering is recommended, and there are no special pests or diseases. If it proves too difficult to establish, the *I. cristata* of May blooming is a reasonably close substitute.

Leucojum aestivum (summer snowflake, giant snowflake) 10–14 in Semishade Zones 4–10

FLOWERING SPAN: Late April to mid-May

NATURAL COLOR: White

DISTRIBUTION: Central and southern Europe

Producing more foliage than flowers in typical growth, this bulb displays bright green, 9–12-in straplike leaves ½ in wide. The taller flower stalks carry 2–8 ¾-in, drooping, bell-shaped florets with noticeable green dotting along the rims. It prefers heavy clay soil near water but can adapt to any rich, constantly moist garden location in semishade. Divide overcrowded groupings when the foliage withers by midsummer, but avoid unnecessary transplanting since the bulb dislikes being moved. No pests or diseases bother it. The robust cultivar 'Gravetye' (sometimes marketed as 'Gravetye Giant') can stretch to 20 in and carry 9 florets.

Leucojum vernum (spring snowflake) 6–12 in Semishade Zones 4–9

FLOWERING SPAN: Early April to May

NATURAL COLOR: White

DISTRIBUTION: Central Europe

This species carries only one, possibly 2, bell-like, ¾-in flowers tipped with green or yellow-green on slender stems rising from deep green, shiny, ½-in-wide straplike leaves that can elongate up to 9 in when grown well. Thriving in rich, well-drained, damp meadows, it self-seeds readily. Diseases and insect pests are infrequent. The variety *carpathicum* normally has two flowers per stem. This bulb is often confused with the May-blooming *Galanthus* but differs by having all its floral parts the same length. (See photo.)

Mertensia virginica (Virginia bluebell, bluebells, cowslip) 18–24 in Semishade Zones 3–9

FLOWERING SPAN: Early April to mid-May

NATURAL COLOR: Pink, aging to blue-violet

DISTRIBUTION: New York to Tennessee and Alabama, west to Kansas

Broad, lanceolate, 5–6-in, pale green leaves surround erect flower stalks heavy with clusters of 1-in funnel-shaped, bluish, nodding blossoms and pink buds. They have a modest fragrance. Naturalizing readily in moist, cool, acid, humusy woodlots or semishaded borders, the plant disappears completely to dormancy by midsummer and is probably better interplanted with ferns to eliminate the blank spot it leaves. Seeding is more reliable than chancy attempts at dividing the chunky roots. Bothersome pests and diseases are unknown. The cultivar 'Alba' has white flowers, while 'Rubra' carries deep pink ones.

Muscari armeniacum (Armenian grape-hyacinth) 6–9 in Sun Zones 3–8
  FLOWERING SPAN: Mid-April to mid-May
  NATURAL COLOR: Deep violet
  DISTRIBUTION: Northeastern Asia Minor
    Scented like ripening grapes, these tiny, clustered, white-rimmed florets densely line erect flower spikes above a fleshy clump of 6–8 semiprostrate, ¼-in leaves that originally appeared the previous autumn and persisted—reasonably unscathed—through the winter. Easily colonized by self-seeding, this adaptable bulb grows in any moist, light, average soil from full sun to light shade. By early summer all the foliage has disappeared and old groupings can then be safely separated and replanted. Plant new bulbs in autumn. Diseases and pests are unimportant. There are several cultivars: 'Blue Spike', flax blue, cauliflowerlike, double-flowered, late-blooming; 'Early Giant', deep cobalt blue, early; and 'Heavenly Blue', rich sky blue. (See photos.)

Muscari botryoides (common grape-hyacinth) 6–12 in Sun Zones 3–8
  FLOWERING SPAN: Mid-April to mid-May
  NATURAL COLOR: Pale blue
  DISTRIBUTION: Central and southern Europe to Caucasus Mountains
    Less vigorous than *M. armeniacum,* which it closely resembles, *M. botryoides* is odorless and carries only 2–4 leaves. Culture is the same for both. The cultivar 'Album' is pure white but slower to colonize, while 'Caeruleum' is bright blue. (See photo.)

Muscari comosum (plumosum) (tassel hyacinth) 12–18 in Sun Zones 3–8
  FLOWERING SPAN: Late April to June
  NATURAL COLOR: Purplish blue
  DISTRIBUTION: Mediterranean Europe, North Africa
    Unusual in having between 20–30 purple-blue, upright, sterile florets at the top of each stalk and 20–70 pendant, greenish brown, fertile florets below, *M. comosum* succeeds in sun or light shading on any moist, average-fertility location. The bulb self-seeds readily. Plant new colonies in the autumn, but you can divide and replant overcrowded groupings right after the foliage fades away in midsummer. Pests and diseases are no problem. The cultivar 'Monstrosum' is showier

with all-sterile, feathery, mauve-blue flower heads and 1-in-wide leaves which flop in disarray. The cultivar 'Plumosum' is similar in appearance to 'Monstrosum' but has reddish purple coloring. (See photo.)

Muscari latifolium 9–12 in Sun Zones 3–8
FLOWERING SPAN: Mid-April to mid-May
NATURAL COLOR: Violet-blue
DISTRIBUTION: Asia Minor
　　　Vividly contrasting in flower coloring, this bulb produces just a solitary, 1½-in-wide leaf up to a foot long. The blossom has pale lilac blue, sterile top florets above dark purplish blue fertile ones. Its culture is the same as for *M. armeniacum.*

Muscari tubergenianum (Tubergen grape-hyacinth) 6–12 in Sun Zones 3–8
FLOWERING SPAN: Late April to June
NATURAL COLOR: Bright blue
DISTRIBUTION: Northwestern Iran, eastern Turkey
　　　A durable performer with dense clusterings of both bright blue upper florets and lighter blue lower ones, this bulb has the alternate name of "Oxford and Cambridge" in some circles. Its 2–3 straplike, ½-in-wide leaves are deep green and up to 10 in long. Grow as *M. armeniacum.*

Narcissus (daffodil) 4–8 in Sun Zones 3–8
FLOWERING SPAN: Early April to June
NATURAL COLOR: Yellow, white, bicolor
DISTRIBUTION: Europe, North Africa
　　　From the continuing worldwide interest in hybridizing these popular bulbs during the past 150 years, it was inevitable that *Narcissus* would eventually become a category of confusing identifications. To bring order to the over 10,000 wild and hybridized types, the Royal Horticultural Society of London was appointed in 1955 by the Fourteenth Horticultural Congress to become the official international authority. The society finally devised a series of divisions for a current total of 12. With the exception of Division 10, each division includes only the flowers which are of a cultivated, not wild, origin. Further separation of classes within the divisions aids identification as well, and only the flower's appearance—not its height, size, or blooming time—provides its location in these listings.
　　　Each narcissus has 2 major parts to its flower. First, a ring of 6 flattish petals (more precisely today: *tepals*) adjacent to the stalk is collectively called the *perianth*. Attached to it, and projecting forward around the stamens and pistil, is another petal group called the *corona,* which is also labeled the *cup, crown,* or *trumpet.* It is the color and length of this corona which separates individual flowers into the main divisions.

Classification of Cultivated Narcissus

DIVISION 1: Trumpet Narcissus

DEFINITION: Single-flowered with the length of the cup or trumpet equal to or longer than that of the perianth segments

CLASS A: All parts yellow

EXAMPLES: 'Dutch Master', golden yellow with a fringed mouth of the trumpet; 'Golden Harvest', golden yellow, early; 'Golden Top', primrose yellow perianth with a canary yellow trumpet; 'King Alfred', rich yellow, today the most widely grown type; 'Little Gem', clear yellow, miniature; 'Rembrandt', golden yellow, large-flowered; and 'Unsurpassable', deep gold, very large.

CLASS B: Perianth white, trumpet yellow

EXAMPLES: 'General Patton', ivory white perianth with a canary yellow, ruffled trumpet, early; 'Little Beauty', white perianth with soft yellow trumpet, miniature; 'Music Hall', deep gold trumpet with a white perianth; 'Spellbinder', trumpet greenish yellow maturing to an almost white interior; and 'Trippie Wicks', lemon yellow trumpet with a fringed mouth and a white perianth.

CLASS C: All white or almost white

EXAMPLES: 'Beersheba', pure white; 'Mount Hood', pure white perianth with a cream trumpet fading to pure white; 'Mrs. E. H. Krelage', sulphur-white perianth and trumpet; and 'W. P. Milner', sulphur-white perianth and trumpet, miniature.

DIVISION 2: Large-cupped Narcissus

DEFINITION: Single-flowered with the cup measuring from ⅓ to nearly the length of the perianth segments

CLASS A: Yellow perianth, cup colored same or darker than the perianth

EXAMPLES: 'Aranjuez', soft yellow perianth with cup of deep yellow margined with rich orange-red; 'Carbineer', bright yellow perianth with an orange cup; 'Carlton', entire flower soft yellow; 'Delibes', soft yellow perianth with an orange-rimmed gold cup; 'Fortissimo', gold perianth with a deep red-orange cup; 'Fortune', yellow perianth with a coppery red cup, tall; 'Largo', primrose yellow perianth with a ruffled, orange cup; 'Scarlet Elegance', yellow perianth with an intensely red cup; and 'Yellow Sun', uniformly golden yellow.

CLASS B: White perianth, cup colored same or darker than the perianth

EXAMPLES: 'Duke of Windsor', pure white perianth with a broad, flat, orange-red cup; 'Flower Record', creamy white perianth with a flat yellow cup edged with red, multiplies readily; 'John Evelyn', pure white perianth with a flat apricot cup, frilled; 'Mercato', pure white perianth with a yellow cup edged in orange; and 'Professor Einstein', clear white with a flat deep red-orange cup.

CLASS C: All white, cup colored same or very pale

EXAMPLES: 'Ice Follies', white perianth with a flat, yellowish white cup fading to white; 'Iceland', pure white perianth with a very pale apricot cup; and 'Jules

Verne', creamy white perianth with a pale yellow cup, early.

CLASS D: Yellow perianth, paler cup

EXAMPLES: 'Binkie', entire flower opening clear sulphur yellow, then cup fades to amost white.

NOTE: Division 2 includes the pink *Narcissus* cultivars. Most are seedlings from the original type, 'Mrs. R. O. Backhouse', and often fail to exhibit pink coloration until the flower is fully developed and starting to decline.

EXAMPLES: 'Louise de Coligny', pure white perianth with an apricot-pink trumpet, good fragrance; 'Pink Rim', white perianth with a cup of creamy white edged in rose; 'Mrs. R. O. Backhouse', ivory white perianth with a slim trumpet of clear apricot; 'Rosy Sunrise', white perianth with a trumpet of salmon-apricot outside and pale yellow inside; and 'Salome', white perianth with a gold-banded, coral-pink cup.

DIVISION 3: Small-cupped Narcissus

DEFINITION: Single-flowered with the cup measuring less than ⅓ of the perianth segments

EXAMPLES: 'Amor', creamy white perianth with a flattened, ruffled, orange-rimmed cup; 'Barret Browning', creamy white perianth with a bright red cup; 'Edward Buxton', soft yellow perianth with a flat yellow cup edged in orange; 'Jezebel', perianth deep red-gold with a reddish cup; 'La Riante', pure white perianth and a deep red cup; 'Polar Ice', snowy white perianth with a greenish white cup; and 'Pomona', white perianth with a sulphur yellow cup margined in red.

DIVISION 4: Double Narcissus

DEFINITION: Single-flowered with double blossoms

EXAMPLES: 'Coral Strand', mix of white and coral; 'Duet', mix of ivory and deep yellow; 'Golden Ducat', all yellow (the double 'King Alfred'); 'Ice King', mix of white, cream, and yellow (the double 'Ice Follies'); 'Mary Copeland', outer petals creamy white with a center mix of orange and red; 'Mrs. William Copeland', mix of white and yellow, very full; 'Petit Four', mix of white and apricot; 'Rosy Cloud', mix of cream and apricot-pink (the double 'Mrs. R. O. Backhouse'); 'Tahiti', mix of yellow and orange-red; 'Texas', mix of golden yellow with bright orange; 'Twink', creamy yellow mixed with golden orange; 'Van Sion', yellow with greenish streaks; and 'White Lion', creamy white with a yellow center.

DIVISION 5: Triandrus Narcissus

DEFINITION: Clusters of 2–6 flowers per stem, generally white, with a bowl-shaped cup

EXAMPLES: 'Liberty Bells', lemon yellow throughout; 'Moonshine', creamy white throughout; 'Silver Chimes', pure white perianth with a pale yellow cup; 'Thalia', pure white throughout with backturned petals; and 'White Marvel', white throughout with a very double cup.

DIVISION 6: Cyclamineus Narcissus

DEFINITION: Single-flowered, drooping blossoms, perianth segments curve backward noticeably, cup thin with a fringed mouth

EXAMPLES: 'February Gold', golden yellow throughout; 'February Silver', silvery white throughout; 'Jack Snipe', creamy white perianth with an orange-yellow cup; 'Jenny', white throughout; 'March Sunshine', deep yellow, dwarfed; 'Peeping Tom', deep golden yellow throughout, long-lasting; and 'Tête-à-Tête', yellow perianth with an orange cup, dwarfed.

DIVISION 7: Jonquilla Narcissus (often sold as "Jonquil" types)

DEFINITION: Clusters of 2–6 flowers per stem, generally yellow, showing noticeable fragrance

EXAMPLES: 'Baby Moon', all lemon yellow; 'Cherie', perianth ivory with a small, pink-flushed cup; 'Golden Sceptre', golden yellow throughout; 'Sugarbush', white perianth with a lemon yellow, white-rimmed cup; 'Suzy', canary yellow perianth with an orange cup; 'Trevithian', pale lemon yellow perianth with a darker yellow cup; and 'Waterperry', white perianth with a light yellow cup which becomes pink at maturity.

DIVISION 8: Tazetta Narcissus

DEFINITION: Clusters of 4–8 small flowers per stem, perianth generally white, fragrant

EXAMPLES: 'Cheerfulness', white perianth with a fully double, creamy white center with some yellow shading; 'Cragford', creamy white perianth with a dark orange cup; 'Geranium', pure white perianth with an orange-scarlet cup; 'Grand Soleil d'Or', yellow perianth with an orange cup, very fragrant; 'Orange Wonder', white perianth with an orange-red cup; 'St. Agnes', pure white perianth with a citron yellow cup; and 'Yellow Cheerfulness', yellow throughout.
NOTE: None of the paperwhite Tazetta types of indoor forcing will survive planting outdoors except in the very warmest zones.

DIVISION 9: Poeticus Narcissus

DEFINITION: Single-flowered, perianth usually white, cup short and yellow with a wavy, red-edged border, fragrant

EXAMPLES: 'Actaea', snowy white perianth with a canary yellow cup edged in bright red; 'Margaret Mitchell', pure white perianth with a soft yellow cup rimmed in red; and 'Old Pheasant's Eye', white perianth with a yellow cup edged in orange-red, late.

DIVISION 10: Species, Wild Forms, Wild Form Hybrids

DEFINITION: All botanical species and their wild variations

EXAMPLES: *N. bulbocodium* var. *citrinus*, 6 in, pale citron yellow; *N. bulbocodium* var. *conspicuus*, 4 in, dark yellow; *N. canaliculatus*, 6 in, white perianth with a gold cup, cluster-flowering; *N. minor,* 6 in, perianth lighter than the deep yellow trumpet; *N. triandrus,* 8 in, pure white; and *N. watieri,* 5 in, pure white.

DIVISION 11: Split-cup Narcissus (commercially sold as "Orchid," "Collar," or "Butterfly" types)
DEFINITION: Corona splits for at least ⅓ its length into 6 separate parts which form a flared collar against the perianth
    EXAMPLES: 'Baccarat', light yellow perianth with a deep yellow, ruffled, split cup; 'Cassata', white perianth with a split cup of lemon yellow fading to white; 'Evolution', white perianth with a yellow split cup; 'La Argentina', white perianth with a white split cup striped in orange and yellow; 'Orangery', white perianth with a pink-and-yellow-speckled split cup of orange; 'Parisienne', creamy white perianth with a ruffled, deep orange split cup; 'Pearlax', white perianth with a flat, soft rose cup; 'Split', white perianth with an ivory split cup; and 'White Butterfly', creamy white perianth with a white split cup streaked in yellow and green.

DIVISION 12: Miscellaneous Narcissus
DEFINITION: All which do not fit into any other division. The hybrids of varying, intermediate shapes, such as hoop-petticoat styles, are placed here.

Blooming times of the various narcissus vary with each locality and with the type of spring weather experienced, but the progression normally follows this order: the cyclamineus and species of Divisions 6 and 10 often appear by late March or early April; the trumpets of Division 1 and the large-cupped of Division 2 soon follow; the small-cupped of Division 3, the doubles of Division 4, the triandrus of Division 5, and the split-cups of Division 11 begin by mid-April, while the especially fragrant jonquilla, tazetta, and poeticus of Divisions 7, 8, and 9, complete the sequence by late April.

Growing these bulbs is uncomplicated. Since they tolerate a wide range of soils and do well in light shading, they can be incorporated into any garden space. They prosper and colonize best, however, in fertile, humusy, well-drained locations which are moist or even wet in spring and are then moist to dry in summer. Avoid sun-baked, generally dry sites as well as those near highly competitive roots of vigorous, shallow-rooted trees and shrubs. Fertilize annually *after* blossoming to promote a strong bud for the following year and use a dressing of bonemeal or a balanced, low-nitrogen fertilizer. Avoid any use of fresh manure since it creates disease problems.

Retain all the foliage until it naturally withers. The bulb needs the leaves to produce the elements for the next season of flowering. Any grassy areas set with narcissus should be left unmowed until early July. To disguise the fading leaves in borders, plant later-blooming perennials with spreading foliage nearby. Knotting or plaiting the leaves may be decorative, but it is both a chore and a time-waster since it does nothing to hasten the drying of the foliage.

Occasionally the larva of the narcissus fly burrows through the bulb to cause rot; destroy all infected bulbs quickly. Fusarium rot can also be troublesome since it causes mushiness in stored bulbs. Again, discard such bulbs speedily. All in all, these reliable perennials are very adaptable and usually unbothered by major problems.

All narcissus resent drying out, and because they have only a short resting period, install new groupings as early as they appear in nurseries during early autumn. Division of overcrowded clumps means separating right after flowering and before the foliage has completely withered (or else you will not locate them). Retain all the leaves when transplanting and reset quickly since they still need to produce a large volume of roots for effective flowering in the next season. Keep well-watered until the foliage is completely gone. Fertilize transplants with diluted liquid rather than granular types to avoid scorching the disturbed roots. (See photos.)

Omphalodes verna (creeping forget-me-not) 6–8 in Semishade Zones 5–9
FLOWERING SPAN: Mid-April to June
NATURAL COLOR: Bright blue
DISTRIBUTION: Europe
Easily naturalized, this slow-creeping perennial carries forget-me-not-like flowers in delicately branched, loose sprays above broad, heart-shaped, 3-in-long leaves. A cool, moist, average, woodsy soil suits it, although it will readily accept the dry shading from many deciduous shrubs. Division in either spring or autumn is the preferred propagation method. Diseases and pests are of no concern. The cultivar 'Alba' has white blossoms.

Ornithogalum nutans (nodding star-of-Bethlehem) 9–12 in Sun Zones 4–9
FLOWERING SPAN: Mid-April to late May
NATURAL COLOR: Greenish white
DISTRIBUTION: Southern and central Europe, southwestern Asia, eastern United States
Tall, slender, ¼-in-wide leaves, which can stretch to 2 ft in length, surround spikes of nodding, 1½-in, star-shaped florets of jade green edged in white. Unaffected by dryness since it likes a light, sandy soil with full sun, the plant also tolerates light shading readily. Foliage disappears right after flowering. Because it self-seeds with great abandon, it can easily become invasive. Any new colonies should be planted in the autumn, and there are no special pests or diseases.

Pachysandra procumbens   (Allegheny pachysandra, Allegheny spurge)   8–10 in
Semishade   Zones 5–9
FLOWERING SPAN: Early April to mid-May
NATURAL COLOR: Purplish to greenish white
DISTRIBUTION: Kentucky to Louisiana and Florida

Far different from its Japanese relative, *P. terminalis,* this ground cover plant has dull green, semipermanent foliage on long stalks and is usually flattened to the ground in winter and into early spring. The prostrate, 3-in leaves allow the slender, 5–6-in flower stalk of feathery-looking, narrow flowers to be more noticeable, however. Spreading slowly in rich, humusy, moist soil with semishade to shade, it propagates easiest by simple division. There appear to be no important pests or diseases.

Pachysandra terminalis   (Japanese pachysandra, Japanese spurge)   6–10 in   Semishade
Zones 4–8
FLOWERING SPAN: Mid-April to mid-May
NATURAL COLOR: Greenish white
DISTRIBUTION: Japan

A popular evergreen ground cover for shaded locations, especially beneath trees, this glossy-leaved perennial adapts to a wide variety of soil conditions and light intensities, yet constant exposure to full sun or arid growing conditions will turn the rich green foliage yellowish and scorched at the margins. The terminal flower spikes of clustered, narrow blossoms are not produced in any uniform or showy quantity. Its long, fleshy stem carries a close bunching of 2-in, jagged-edged leaves and tends to sprawl. Once established it makes a dense cover because of its vigorous, runner-type growth habit. Few bulbs or other perennials can long exist with any strength when interplanted with it, yet large-leaved *Hosta* cultivars make a good showing.

Although tolerant of dryness for reasonable periods, this perennial thrives in rich, moist, humusy, acid soil with semishade to shade. Either spring division or summer stem cuttings make propagation simple, but for greater flowering effect in the future, take cuttings only from stems which have previously blossomed. Pests are normally unproblematic, but wilt disease can occasionally destroy sizeable areas of a bed. The cultivar 'Green Carpet' shows greater hardiness, glossier foliage, and more compact growth. A slower-growing cultivar, 'Variegata', is attractive with cream margins and veining on the leaves, but it flowers sparsely. It needs consistent shading to maintain its color contrast. (See photos.)

Phlox × *procumbens*   3–9 in   Sun   Zones 4–9
FLOWERING SPAN: Late April to June
NATURAL COLOR: Bright purple
ORIGIN: Horticultural hybrid of *P. stolonifera* × *P. subulata*

From a dark green mat of 1-in glossy foliage appear prolific, dense clusters of ¾-in flowers on wiry stems. Thriving on dry sites, it likes sun or light shading and good drainage in an average soil. Division is the usual propagation method, and insects and diseases seem to avoid it. The cultivar 'Folio-variegata' has yellow-striped foliage which offers a somewhat startling color combination at bloom, while 'Rosea' has rose pink flowers and green leaves.

Phlox subulata (setacea) (moss phlox, moss pink, mountain phlox)   3–5 in   Sun   Zones 2–9

FLOWERING SPAN: Mid-April to mid-May
NATURAL COLOR: Pink, magenta, white
DISTRIBUTION: New York to Michigan, south to Maryland

Remarkably hardy, this mossy-looking ground cover's 1-in, needlelike, evergreen leaves form a dense mat, especially on low-fertility, dry, gritty, well-drained soils which are either neutral or alkaline. The loose clusters of ½-in, flat, fragrant blossoms have shallowly notched petals and cover the entire foliage on a well-grown specimen. Use in sunny rock gardens, plant walls, or borders for dramatic color displays. Shear back halfway after flowering to promote compactness, then topdress lightly with compost or humus for thrifty, new growth. Division in early spring, using only nonwoody stems, or summer stem cuttings propagate it readily. Root nematodes can be a serious pest: destroy any affected plants. Mildew may also prove troublesome in times of extended summertime heat. The large list of cultivars is superior to the parent: 'Alexander's Aristocrat', deep pink; 'Alexander's White', pure white; 'Brilliant', deep rose; 'Blue Hills', sky blue; 'Camla', salmon-pink; 'Emerald Blue', light blue; 'Emerald Pink', rose-pink; 'G. F. Wilson', pale lavender-blue; 'Intensity', cerise; 'Millstream Daphne', clear pink; 'Scarlet Flame', bright scarlet; 'Schneewitchen', white, small-flowered; 'Vivid', rich pink; and 'White Delight', white, large-flowered. (See photo.)

Polemonium reptans (humile) (creeping Jacob's ladder)   8–18 in   Semishade   Zones 3–9

FLOWERING SPAN: Mid-April to July
NATURAL COLOR: Pale blue to bluish white
DISTRIBUTION: New Hampshire to Alabama and Georgia, west to Oklahoma and Minnesota

Attractive, fernlike, compound foliage of 6–19 leaflets up to 2 in long is dark green and appears early in the spring in heavy tufts, but the plant does not creep. The weak, flowering stems, however, sprawl easily, especially in hot, humid weather, and give the appearance of the plant's enlargement. Bell-like, ¾-in flowers in generous clusters fill the stems. The plant naturalizes readily by self-seeding and is at home in rock gardens with half shade, good drainage, and a consistently moist, average soil. Division in early spring or autumn, along with summer stem cuttings, propagates it readily if self-seeding is not adequate. While insects and diseases are of no concern, snails often feed on all parts of the plant. The cultivar 'Album' has white blossoms, while 'Blue Pearl' makes a strong-stemmed clump with deeper blue flowers. (See photo.)

Primula auricula (alpina, lutea) (auricula) 6–8 in Semishade Zones 3–8
FLOWERING SPAN: Late April to June
NATURAL COLOR: Clear yellow
DISTRIBUTION: Central European Alps

From an evergreen rosette of light green, thick, wide, 2–4-in leaves rise sturdy flower stalks with generous heads of 1-in, fragrant blossoms. The leaves are covered with a granular, grayish spotting called "meal," which is characteristic of many *Primula* species. The flower cultivars available today are a far cry from the dwarfed original of the mountains, since hybridizing has produced every imaginable shade and mix of yellow and red, including some with double flowers plus a darker "eye" in contrast. Precise cataloging here is not possible with so many new improvements constantly offered by growers.

All primulas require a cool site along with a rich, well-drained, moist, acid soil improved with humus or compost regularly. In severe winter areas mulch lightly to prevent heaving of the shallow roots. While they often naturalize freely along woodlot streams in semishade, they also adapt to sunnier garden locations if kept consistently moist or even wet. Division immediately after flowering or careful separation of the offsets at the base of the parent gives assured results for a particular color combination. Seed germinates easily as soon as it is ripe but assures some color novelties and perhaps little resemblance to the parent's coloring. Pests are unfortunately many and include aphids, flea beetles, spider mites, slugs, and snails. Botrytis and "damping off" diseases can also be destructive. (See photo.)

Primula denticulata (cashmiriana, cachemiriana)   (Himalayan primrose)   8–12 in
Semishade Zones 4–8
FLOWERING SPAN: Mid-April to late May
NATURAL COLOR: Purple, lilac, white
DISTRIBUTION: Himalaya Mountains

Even before the lancelike, crinkly, 3–4-in, new leaves develop, this perennial from India produces dense, 2-in, globose flower heads of ½-in florets with yellow eyes. The emerging foliage can elongate to a foot after bloom, and the light green leaves show a conspicuous dusting of yellow-white flecks, or meal. The foliage grows in a heavy bunching manner but, unfortunately, becomes unattractive by midsummer, especially if the weather is hot and humid. Culture is the same as for *P. auricula,* and it will tolerate even wet, muddy sites as long as wintertime drainage is excellent. Pests and diseases are also the same as for *P. auricula.* A few cultivars are known: 'Alba', pure white with yellow eyes; 'Rosea', pink-toned; and 'Snowball', entirely white. (See photo.)

Primula × polyantha (polyanthus) 8–12 in Semishade Zones 3–8
  FLOWERING SPAN: Late April to June
  NATURAL COLOR: White, pink, red, maroon, mauve, lavender, purple
  ORIGIN: Horticultural hybrid of *P. veris, P. elatior,* and *P. vulgaris*
      Since the 17th century, this type has been by far the most popular because of
  its large, flat clusters of fragrant blossoms in a myriad of colorings, all with a
  yellow eye. Its dark green, crinkled, 4–6-in foliage is reasonably evergreen in
  many growing areas. Its culture is identical to that for *P. auricula,* but summertime shading is important here to forestall serious attacks of red spider mites. The
  cultivar list is too prolific to catalog here, so consult the listings of specialty
  growers for the widest selections and newest introductions. (See photo.)

Primula sieboldii (Siebold primrose) 8–12 in Semishade Zones 4–8
  FLOWERING SPAN: Late April to June
  NATURAL COLOR: Purple, rose red, white
  DISTRIBUTION: Japan, northeastern Asia
      Generous clumps of scalloped, light green, wrinkled, hairy leaves up to 8 in
  in length almost overwhelm this primula's slender flower stalks. Clusters of 6–10
  deeply indented, 1½-in florets with a white eye are showy and have a crepe-paper
  texture. The foliage disappears entirely by midsummer, exposing the creeping
  rootstock for easy division. This species is far more tolerant of drought and extra
  sunlight than any other, yet the general cultural rules listed for *P. auricula* still
  apply for the best results. The cultivar 'Alba' is pure white, while the 'Barnhaven
  Strain' selections offer more color variety and sturdiness.

Primula veris (officinalis) (cowslip) 4–12 in Semishade Zones 5–8
  FLOWERING SPAN: Late April to June
  NATURAL COLOR: Bright yellow
  DISTRIBUTION: Central Europe, British Isles, western Asia
      Tubular clusters of sweet-scented, nodding, ½-in flowers cover the soft
  green, wrinkled, hairy foliage of this evergreen perennial. While not nearly as
  showy as *P. × polyantha,* it recently has been hybridized to produce some double-
  looking blossoms and a wider color selection. These plants have not been given
  broad distribution, however, except for the cultivar 'Judy', which is pale yellow
  with double-appearing, hose-in-hose flowers, that is, one set of petals is inside
  another set and projects forward from it.

Primula vulgaris (acaulis, hybrida) (English primrose) 4–6 in Semishade Zones 5–8
  FLOWERING SPAN: Late April to June
  NATURAL COLOR: Yellow, cream, blue, purple
  DISTRIBUTION: Western and southern Europe, British Isles
      This well-known perennial, popular since the time of Shakespeare, has indi-
  vidual, ½-in flowers appearing on slender, hairy stems directly above dark green,
  crinkled, 8–10-in-long evergreen foliage. Although it tolerates more sun and

heavier clay soils than other species, the general culture under *P. auricula* should be followed. Recent hybridizing has evolved some pure white, pure blue, and other showy combinations, including pure red and even double-flowering specimens, but they have not yet received wide distribution here. All sorts have darker-colored eyes. In general, the variety name *hortensis* is applied to these cultivated variations, although cultivar names are often listed in catalogs, too.

Pulmonaria angustifolia (azurea) (cowslip lungwort) 8–12 in Semishade Zones 3–8
FLOWERING SPAN: Late April to June
NATURAL COLOR: Bright blue
DISTRIBUTION: Eastern Europe
Resembling the flower shape and coloring of earlier-blooming *Mertensia*, the pulmonarias are both dwarfer and more pronouncedly blue as their pink buds mature. This species has spreading clumps of 12-in, hairy, lancelike, all-green leaves with weak-stemmed clusters of drooping, small flowers useful in shaded rock gardens, borders, and as ground cover under deciduous shrubs. It enjoys a rich, moist, light-textured soil and will accept more sunlight if kept consistently moist at all times. Division in early summer, followed by regular and copious watering, is the simplest propagation method. Seed sown in midsummer also works well but produces variable color results. There are no disfiguring diseases or insect nuisances, but slugs can be occasionally troublesome. Several cultivars are available: 'Azurea', intensely blue, 10 in; 'Johnson's Blue', gentian blue, 8 in; and 'Rubra', rose-violet, 10 in. (See photo.)

Pulmonaria montana (rubra) 12–18 in Semishade Zones 3–9
FLOWERING SPAN: Late April to June
NATURAL COLOR: Dark red, violet
DISTRIBUTION: Mountains of southeastern Europe
The pale, all-green foliage emerges after the flowers, which develop from ¾-in, reddish buds. The 5–6-in leaves are covered with soft hairs and remain attractive through the season. Its culture is the same as for *P. angustifolia*. The cultivar 'Salmon Glow' has large clusters of vibrant, salmon-pink blossoms.

Pulmonaria officinalis (Jerusalem sage, Jerusalem cowslip) 8–12 in Semishade Zones 3–9
FLOWERING SPAN: Late April to June
NATURAL COLOR: Bluish violet
DISTRIBUTION: Europe
In this species the deep rose flower bud fades to a bluish violet ½-in blossom. The bristle-haired, 2–4-in leaves are light green with conspicuous silvery white mottling. Quick to enlarge in the cool, moist, woodsy, shaded locations it

favors, these foliage mounds remain consistently attractive after flowering is complete. Its culture is the same as for *P. angustifolia*. The cultivar 'Sissinghurst White' offers clear white flowers.

Pulmonaria saccharata   (Bethlehem sage)   8–18 in   Semishade   Zones 3–8
   FLOWERING SPAN: Late April to mid-June
   NATURAL COLOR: Reddish violet, occasionally white
   DISTRIBUTION: Southeastern France, Italy
      The dark green, oval leaves up to 12 in long of *P. saccharata* are noticeably flecked with irregular silver spots, while the buds and ¾-in flowers are both reddish violet. Cultivate as for *P. angustifolia*. The cultivar 'Alba' is 15 in with white flowers and marbled leaves; 'Argentea' is only a foot high with blue-toned blossoms; 'Mrs. Moon' is dwarfed at 10 in with pink buds and gentian blue flowers; 'Pink Dawn', 12 in, carries pink buds and blossoms; and 'Roy Davidson', 12 in, has sky blue flowers. (See photo.)

Sanguinaria canadensis   (bloodroot, red puccoon)   6–9 in   Semishade   Zones 3–8
   FLOWERING SPAN: Mid-April to mid-May
   NATURAL COLOR: White
   DISTRIBUTION: Southeastern Canada to Florida, west to the Mississippi River
      Tightly rolled, rounded but deeply lobed, 8-in leaves with silver undersides act as a slender sheath for the single, 8-petaled, emerging flowers of this interesting perennial. Best grown in a moist, woodsy, light-textured soil with shade, it accepts more sun if kept consistently moist. By early summer the foliage disappears, and late summer division of the dormant roots, which have reddish yellow sap, provides easy propagation. There are no problems with pests or diseases. The double-flowered cultivar 'Multiplex' ('Plena') is superior for showiness with up to 50 petals in a rounded head and longer durability. (See photos.)

Trillium grandiflorum   (white wake-robin, snow trillium)   12–18 in   Shade
Zones 3–8
   FLOWERING SPAN: Late April to June
   NATURAL COLOR: White
   DISTRIBUTION: Quebec to the Carolinas, west to Missouri
      From a single collar of 3 broad, pointed leaves up to 5 in long held high above the ground emerges a solitary, heavy-petaled, showy, 3-in, waxy flower which ages to dull rose from white. There is much natural variation in flower coloring, especially when they appear in large drifts and can easily interbreed. Its fruit is a greenish white berry almost an inch long. Preferring a rich, deep soil that is consistently moist, acid, and cool in well-shaded woodlots, this colonizing perennial can tolerate semishade if kept consistently moist or even wet. Division

of the thick rhizomes in late summer is the best propagation method since seed requires three years to produce a flowering plant. Rust is the chief disease problem, but there are no insect nuisances. This is the easiest and showiest of all trilliums for garden culture, and because of its wide distribution in nature, expect dwarfed, double-flowered, and bizarrely colored novelties to occur. On the Pacific Coast, *T. ovatum (californicum)* is very similar in all aspects. (See photos.)

Trillium nivale (snow trillium, dwarf white trillium) 4–6 in Shade Zones 3–9
FLOWERING SPAN: Mid-April to mid-May
NATURAL COLOR: White
DISTRIBUTION: Western Pennsylvania to Minnesota, south to Missouri and Nebraska
The leaves of this scarce wildflower are only 2 in long, and the flower carries 1½-in petals marked in purple. Its culture is the same as for *T. grandiflorum,* except that it prefers a more neutral soil, which can be managed by adding some garden limestone to the plant bed in spring or autumn if the soil is acid.

Trillium sessile (toadshade) 9–12 in Shade Zones 4–9
FLOWERING SPAN: Mid-April to June
NATURAL COLOR: Brown-purple
DISTRIBUTION: Western New York to Missouri, south to Georgia, Mississippi, and Arkansas
The long-pointed, solitary flower of *T. sessile* sits directly on the whorl of red-spotted, very broad, 4-in green leaves. Natural variation occasionally produces some greenish yellow flowers. Its culture is the same as for *T. grandiflorum.* The cultivar 'Rubrum' carries red-purple blossoms. A West Coast species, *T. chloropetalum (sessile* var. *californicum),* is very similar in form but larger in all aspects.

Trillium undulatum (painted trillium) 12–18 in Semishade Zones 3–9
FLOWERING SPAN: Late April to June
NATURAL COLOR: White with magenta markings
DISTRIBUTION: Southeastern Canada to South Carolina and Georgia, west to Tennessee
Undoubtedly the showiest trillium, this perennial is very particular about what it wants if it is to endure. It thrives naturally in acid, cool, moist locations which are almost boggy and often appears under mature stands of hemlock set next to mountain pools. Tolerant of more sun than other species, it accepts garden situations when kept constantly moist on a humusy, woodlot soil out of the warmest heat of the day. The 1½-in white flowers are similar to those of *T. grandiflorum,* except that the center of each of its three wavy petals is streaked with

magenta. The 7-in leaves are bluish green. Propagate the same as for *T. grandiflorum.* Mice sometimes feed on the rhizomes in winter. Do not collect trillium flowers with foliage since the few leaves are essential to the future life of any plant.

Tulipa (tulip) 2–32 in Sun Zones 3–8

FLOWERING SPAN: Mid-April to June

NATURAL COLOR: Every conceivable coloring and mix of coloring

DISTRIBUTION: Mediterranean Europe, northern Africa, Asia Minor, and China for the botanical species; Europe for the hybridization of the many cultivated types

Parallel with the nomenclature difficulties described under *Narcissus,* the myriad forms of *Tulipa* in cultivation were confused and misrepresented until an international agreement was reached about creating an authorized catalog. The first official register of named tulips was published in 1915 by the Royal General Bulbgrowers' Society of Holland. Constantly updated and revised, the current list includes over 4,000 names separated into 15 divisions according to flowering sequence and the shape of the blossom. The first 11 divisions cover all the cultivated tulips, and each division is further placed into one of 3 sections: early, midseason, and late. The 4 remaining divisions describe the wild species— normally called "botanicals"—and their hybrids. As commercial breeding continues to create new introductions, additional divisions are very likely.

A listing of the wild species of divisions 12–15 follows this April grouping, and the May-flowering tulips are separately treated in that month.

Classification of Cultivated Tulips

April Flowering Sequence

EARLY (Mid-April to early May)

1. SINGLE EARLY (Horticultural hybrid of *T. gesneriana* × *T. suaveolens*)

DESCRIPTION: Single cup, 10–18 in, usually fragrant

EXAMPLES: 'Bellona', 14 in, deep yellow, large; 'Christmas Marvel', 12 in, cherry pink; 'Couleur Cardinal', 12 in, velvety crimson with an outside grayish sheen; 'Diana', 12 in, white; 'Generaal de Wet', 12 in, bright orange with scarlet striping, yellow center; 'Ibis', 12 in, dark pink; 'Keizerskroon', 13 in, bright red with a wide, deep yellow edge, large; 'Pink Beauty', 14 in, deep rose with a white blush; 'Prince Carnival', 15 in, red-orange with yellow streaks; 'Prince of Austria', 15 in, bright orange-red outside, brilliant scarlet inside; 'Princess Irene', 12 in, salmon-orange with reddish streaks; and 'White Hawk', 12 in, pure white.

2. DOUBLE EARLY (Known since the 17th century as a chance mutation or "sport")
DESCRIPTION: Wide-opening cup with many rows of petals, 10–12 in, slight fragrance, resembles the shape of a double peony
EXAMPLES: 'All Gold', 11 in, bright yellow; 'Bonanza', 11 in, carmine-red edged with yellow; 'Carlton', 11 in, bright scarlet; 'Dante', 11 in, deep red; 'Electra', 10 in, carmine-red shading to light violet; 'Golden Victory', 12 in, golden yellow; 'Goya', 11 in, light orange-red with a yellow base; 'Marechal Niel', 11 in, soft orange-yellow; 'Mr. van der Hoeff', 11 in, deep orange-red; 'Peach Blossom', 11 in, bright rosy pink; 'Scarlet Cardinal', 11 in, bright scarlet, early; 'Schoonoord', 11 in, pure white; 'Wilhelm Kordes', 11 in, orange-yellow flushed red; and 'Willemsoord', 11 in, carmine-red with a white edge.

MIDSEASON (Late April to mid-May)

3. MENDEL (Horticultural hybrid of 'Duc van Tol' × Darwin)
DESCRIPTION: Large, single cup, 14–24 in, not as sturdy as Triumph, which has largely supplented it commercially
EXAMPLES: 'Athleet', 18 in, pure white; 'Her Grace', 20 in, white with a flush of cerise red; 'High Society', 20 in, orange with a brighter orange edge; 'Olga', 18 in, violet-red with a white edge; 'Orange Wonder', 22 in, bronzy orange with a scarlet flush and a deep yellow edge; 'Pink Trophy', 18 in, pink with a rose flush; 'Remagen', 18 in, deep pink; 'Sulphur Triumph', 22 in, soft yellow; and 'White Sail', 18 in, creamy white.

4. TRIUMPH (Horticultural hybrid of Single Early × Darwin)
DESCRIPTION: Large, single cup, 18–26 in, heavy-textured flower, sturdy stem, carries colored margins usually not found on other types, blooms after Mendel
EXAMPLES: 'Apricot Beauty', 18 in, orange-rose outside, rich apricot inside with a green base; 'Arabian Mystery', 18 in, purple with a silvery white edge, long-lasting; 'Attila', 18 in, light purple; 'Aureola', 26 in, bright red with a deep yellow edge; 'Bing Crosby', 20 in, scarlet; 'Blizzard', 20 in, pure white; 'Bruno Walter', 26 in, light orange; 'Crater', 20 in, bright scarlet; 'Denbola', 22 in, cerise-red with a creamy white edge; 'First Lady', 26 in, violet-red, long-lasting; 'Garden Party', 18 in, white with a wide, vividly rose edge; 'Golden Melody', 18 in, deep yellow; 'Jimmy', 18 in, carmine-rose blending to orange; 'Kansas', 20 in, snowy white; 'Kees Nelis', 18 in, deep red edged in orange-yellow; 'La Suisse', 24 in, vermilion with a yellow base; 'Madame Spoor', 20 in, mahogany red with a yellow edge; 'Madame Spoor's Favorite', 18 in, light yellow with a vermilion edge; 'Makassar', 22 in, deep yellow; 'New Design', 18 in, silvery pink with a deeper pink edge, foliage edged in lilac; 'Nivea', 26 in, pure white; 'Orange Sun', 26 in, pure orange; 'Orange Wonder', 20 in, bronzy orange with a scarlet flush; 'Pax', 18 in, pure white; 'Peerless Pink', 18 in, clear pink; 'Princess Beatrix', 22 in, scarlet with an orange flush and a deep yellow edge; 'Reforma', 18 in, sulphur

yellow; 'Rose Beauty', 22 in, creamy white with a deep rose edge; 'Sulphur Glory', 22 in, sulphur yellow; 'Tambour Maitre', 24 in, deep red with a yellow base, long-lasting; 'Telescopium', 24 in, violet-rose; and 'Yellow Present', 18 in, canary yellow.

5. DARWIN HYBRID (Horticultural hybrid of *T. fosteriana* × Darwin)

DESCRIPTION: Very large, single cup, 24–28 in, strong stem, brilliant colorings, long-lasting, blooms with or slightly after Triumph

EXAMPLES: 'Apeldoorn', 24 in, cherry red with a black base; 'Apeldoorn's Elite', 24 in, bright scarlet with a pale mauve flush and a black base, yellow edge; 'Beauty of Dover', 24 in, soft yellow with a salmon flush outside, golden yellow inside with a black base; 'Daydream', 24 in, soft apricot; 'Diplomate', 24 in, vermilion with a green-yellow base, large; 'Dover', 26 in, vivid red with a dark blue base; 'Dutch Fair', 24 in, rich yellow flamed scarlet with a black base; 'Elizabeth Arden', 26 in, deep salmon-pink flushed violet; 'Empire State', 24 in, vivid scarlet with a yellow base; 'General Eisenhower', 26 in, orange-red with a vivid black base, creamy white edge; 'Golden Apeldoorn', 24 in, golden yellow with a black base; 'Golden Parade', 24 in, bright yellow; 'Golden Springtime', 26 in, clear golden yellow, large; 'Gordon Cooper', 24 in, carmine with a red edge; 'Gudoshnik', 28 in, sulphur yellow with a flush of red and a blue-black base, large, no uniformity of color; 'Holland's Glory', 26 in, orange-scarlet with a black base; 'Ivory Floradale', 24 in, ivory yellow with carmine spots; 'Jewel of Spring', 28 in, sulphur yellow with a faint red edge, very large and long-lasting; 'Koningin Wilhelmina', 24 in, scarlet with a yellow rim; 'London', 26 in, bright scarlet; 'My Lady', 28 in, salmon with a bronzy green base; 'Oranjezon', 24 in, bright orange; 'Parade', 26 in, scarlet with a black base; 'President Kennedy', 26 in, rich yellow with an orange flush and a red rim; 'Spring Song', 26 in, vivid red flushed with orange and a white base; 'Striped Apeldoorn', 24 in, yellow with red stripes; 'Vulcano', 28 in, carmine, large, long-lasting; and 'Yellow Dover', 26 in, soft yellow with a black base.

Successfully raising tulips is a simple process. Preferring open, sunny locations and moist, porous soil of average fertility, either acid or alkaline, they excel where drainage is excellent. Fortify for prolonged performance with humus or compost dug deeply beforehand into the planting bed, together with bonemeal. Avoid using fresh manure near tulips since it promotes the spread of infectious diseases. Well-rotted, aged manure is considered safe. Late planting in autumn, unlike *Narcissus,* suits the bulb well, and in the warmest zones 8 weeks of prior cold storage (in the refrigerator) is essential for reliable blooming. This artificial cold simulates most of the span of a northern winter.

Tulips repeat annual flowering better if the site chosen is sun-baked and reasonably dry during summer dormancy—a throwback to their original conditions in nature. Expect subdivision of the bulb as a natural condition in gardens, so that by the third season the majority will be weak-flowered or even "blind" and uneven in effect. Hot, humid summer heat in the warm zones often exhausts tulips completely after one season, making this bulb more of an annual than a perennial. In any location, a tulip showing spring growth of a single, broad leaf will never blossom again, and the bulb should be discarded. It is usually non-productive to use tulip offset bulbs for propagation; leave that detail to the experts. The low cost of tulips encourages complete rebedding every few years.

Retaining all the foliage until it shrivels fully is important to the future flowering of this bulb, as is the prompt removal of any forming seed capsules, which have no usefulness for gardeners and drain energy. Mask the withering foliage with nearby spreading leaves from other perennials, including ferns tolerant of sun. When collecting flowers for use indoors, pick stems with no more than one leaf. Cutting leafless stems is even more helpful to the plant.

Tulips will bloom well even in the light spring shading from deciduous trees and tall shrubs nearby but will flower somewhat later than normal. The potentially invasive root systems of these large plants, however, can quickly debilitate the bulb, and less root-competitive areas are better choices to insure repeat blooming of reasonably uniform size.

Cultivated tulips can be seriously disfigured at any stage of growth by a sooty fungus called *Botrytis tulipae,* which is spread mainly by aphids. Plants showing black, sooty mush on any part should be quickly dug and discarded into the trash, along with any fallen petals, since this disease moves rapidly, particularly in wet, humid weather. With serious infections, delay replanting tulips in the same area by at least 3 years. Mice occasionally gnaw at the buried bulbs through tunnels made in the garden by the insect-eating mole, and gophers can be just as troublesome. Even with these handicaps, tulips have an assured place in garden displays since millions of new bulbs are planted every autumn. (See photos.)

Tulipa aucherana (Aucher tulip) 2–8 in Sun Zones 4–9
> FLOWERING SPAN: Late April to mid-May
> NATURAL COLOR: Clear rose with a yellow center
> DISTRIBUTION: Northern Iran and Syria
> Suitable for rock garden accent, this miniature species has 2–5 prostrate, narrow green leaves and 1-in, star-shaped flowers ranging from deep rose to almost-white. The outer petals carry a thin, greenish yellow stripe. Provide full sun, average-fertility soil with good drainage, and dry dormant conditions in summer. There are no known pests or diseases. This plant is often incorrectly listed in catalogs as a form of *T. humilis* (ground tulip).

Tulipa clusiana (lady tulip) 8–12 in Sun Zones 4–9
> FLOWERING SPAN: Mid-April to early May
> NATURAL COLOR: White with broad streaks of crimson on outside of petals

DISTRIBUTION: Iran, Iraq, Afghanistan, southeastern Europe

Cultivated since the 17th century, this bulb produces a long-tapered, 2-in flower above ½-in, linear foliage that can stretch in length to 10-in. The blossom is white inside with a deep purple base and opens to its starlike shape only in sunny weather. Provide a well-drained, warm location in full sun. Pests and diseases are not troublesome. The wavy-leaved variety *chrysantha* from northwest India is all-yellow inside and cerise red outside. It is generally listed in catalogs now as the cultivar 'Tubergen's Gem'. Both types colonize well if left undisturbed. (See photos.)

Tulipa eichleri (Eichler tulip) 6–8 in Sun Zones 4–8
> FLOWERING SPAN: Mid-April to early May
> NATURAL COLOR: Bright scarlet with a black base
> DISTRIBUTION: Northwestern Iran, Turkestan

Readily colonizing, this conspicuous, sharp-pointed flower opens to a 4-in spread above 4–5 wide, grayish green leaves up to 8 in long. The foliage is occasionally bordered in red. Brilliantly glossy inside and out, the center of the flower has a black, yellow-edged base. Full sun, average-fertility soil with quick drainage, and summertime dryness are its preferences. Pests and diseases are unknown. The cultivar 'Excelsa' has larger blossoms, while 'Maxima' is also larger-flowered but blooms a bit later. (See photo.)

Tulipa fosteriana (Foster tulip) 8–12 in Sun Zones 3–7
> FLOWERING SPAN: Early April to May
> NATURAL COLOR: Bright scarlet with a black base
> DISTRIBUTION: Central Asia

By far the showiest and largest of all the wild tulips, this Division 13 bulb produces very wide-petaled flowers which open to an 8-in spread. Its over-scaled blossom size promotes its use in sunny borders rather than as a rock garden accent. The 3–4 large leaves are up to 8 in long, floppy, and grayish green. The glossy sheen of the inner flower is noticeably blotched at the base with black markings. Pests and diseases are uncommon, and the bulb enjoys summertime dryness on an average soil with good drainage.

Taller cultivars with a constantly expanding color range are now readily available: 'Candela', soft golden yellow; 'Cantata', vermilion; 'Easter Parade', pure yellow flushed with bright red on the outside; 'Golden Eagle', deep yellow with red markings on the outside; 'Orange Emperor', true orange without pink overtones; 'Pink Empress', soft pink with pencil markings of green on the outside; 'Princeps', orange-scarlet, late; 'Purissima' ('White Empress'), pure white throughout; 'Red Emperor' ('Madame Lefeber'), bright vermilion; 'Solva', rosy pink; 'Yellow Empress' ('Golden Empress'), golden yellow; 'White Emperor', creamy white; and 'Zombie', carmine-red with cream edges. (See photo.)

Tulipa greigii 6–10 in   Sun   Zones 3–7

FLOWERING SPAN: Early April to May

NATURAL COLOR: Scarlet

DISTRIBUTION: Central Asia

Distinguished by its novel foliage coloring, this broad-flowered tulip of Division 14 opens to 5 in wide with petals more pointed than *T. fosteriana* and with a yellow center marked in black. Its broad, gray-green leaves are 3 in wide and up to 8 in long, conspicuously streaked or spotted with deep purple, an attractive bonus not found on any other tulip type. Sensitive to high heat, this dependable bulb prefers a sunny, well-drained average site and wants very dry conditions in dormancy. Botrytis disease, discussed earlier in the general *Tulipa* essay, is a problem.

An extensive list of cultivars, taller and with a wide color range, is promoted in all catalogs: 'Cape Cod', 14 in, orange-red, edged in yellow outside, inside bronzy yellow striped with scarlet; 'Donna Bella', 14 in, cream with a soft carmine outside, creamy yellow inside with a black base and large scarlet blotches; 'Dreamboat', 11 in, deep salmon inside and out blending into amber yellow at the base; 'Golden Day', 14 in, red outside with a yellow edge, inside lemon yellow with red streaks; 'Goldwest', 12 in, clear yellow throughout; 'Miskodeed', 12 in, outside apricot-pink, inside lemon yellow; 'Orange Elite', 14 in, apricot, edged in orange outside, orange with deep green streaks inside and a yellow base; 'Oriental Splendor', 16 in, scarlet with a lemon yellow border inside and out, oversized; 'Pandour', 10 in, pale yellow with red streaks; 'Perlina', 10 in, rosy red with a lemon yellow base inside and out; 'Plaisir', 10 in, red and white stripes outside, inside white with a broad center streak of red and a bright yellow base: 'Red Riding Hood', 7 in, scarlet inside and out with a conspicuous black center and deep brown-purple leaf streaking, very dependable; 'Royal Splendor' ('Margaret Herbst'), 18 in, vermilion inside and out; and 'Zampa', 12 in, primrose yellow with a flush of red. (See photo.)

Tulipa kaufmanniana (waterlily tulip) 4–8 in   Sun   Zones 3–8

FLOWERING SPAN: Early April to May

NATURAL COLOR: Yellowish white to pale yellow with pink on the outer petals

DISTRIBUTION: Southern Russia

Compact in habit, this species from Division 12 resembles a waterlily by opening its 6-in-wide flower almost flat in full sun. Nicely adaptable for rock gardens and borders, the robust bulb naturalizes readily on well-drained, average-fertility sites which are dry in summertime. The 3–5 broad leaves can elongate to 10 in and are somewhat gray-green. Hybrids created with it have brown-mottled foliage. Pests are no bother, but botrytis disease can be a hazard.

A sizeable range of attractive cultivars exist: 'Alfred Cortot', 8 in, deep scarlet with a coal black center, foliage mottled purple; 'Ancilla', 4 in, rosy red exterior with a red-tinged, white interior; 'Caesar Franck', 8 in, bright crimson exterior edged bright yellow, deep yellow interior; 'Concerto', 12 in, sulphur white with a black, yellow-edged base; 'Daylight', 8 in, scarlet with a black, yellow-striped base; 'Fritz Kreisler', 8 in, salmon-pink edged in soft yellow; 'Gaiety', 4 in, white with rosy red stripes outside, creamy white inside; 'Gold Coin', 8 in, scarlet with a golden edge; 'Heart's Delight', 8 in, carmine-red outside with a rose edge, soft rose with a yellow base inside, foliage mottled; 'Shakespeare', 7 in, blend of orange, yellow, and salmon-pink with a deep yellow base; 'Stresa', 8 in, golden yellow exterior with a red-orange border, inside deep yellow with red markings; and 'Vivaldi', 8 in, clear yellow outside with red shadings, interior yellow with a crimson ring at the base, leaves green but mottled with dark streaks. (See photo.)

Tulipa kolpakowskiana 6–10 in Sun Zones 3–7
FLOWERING SPAN: Mid-April to May
NATURAL COLOR: Soft yellow
DISTRIBUTION: Southern Russia, eastern Turkestan

Tapered and graceful 2-in flowers rise above 2–4 narrow, crinkle-edged, prostrate leaves up to 6 in long. The outside flower color is olive green with a broad streak of pinkish red; the interior is entirely pale yellow. Culture is the same for *T. kaufmanniana* without a concern for botrytis disease. (See photo.)

Tulipa linifolia (slimleaf tulip) 4–6 in Sun Zones 4–8
FLOWERING SPAN: Late April to mid-May
NATURAL COLOR: Bright scarlet with a black blotch inside
DISTRIBUTION: Southern Russia, Turkestan

Vibrantly colorful and late in this group for blooming, this species has a slender, 1½–2-in flower attractive in rock gardens or borders. The slightly gray, linear foliage is 4–6 in long and carries a faint red edge. These leaves are arranged in a rosette around the flower stalk. Its lancelike petals are spaced in sets of slightly unequal length and end inside at a black or dark purple base. Cultivate the same as for *T. kaufmanniana,* but *T. linifolia* has no botrytis problems. A rich yellow counterpart is *T. batalini* for size and shape, and some botanists believe it may actually be a variant of *T. linifolia.*

Tulipa praestans (leatherbulb tulip) 9–15 in Sun Zones 3–8
FLOWERING SPAN: Mid-April to early May
NATURAL COLOR: Brick red
DISTRIBUTION: Central Asia

Multiple-flowering with up to 5 cup-shaped, 2½-in blossoms on a stout stem, this tulip creates a showy rock garden accent or border feature. Reliably hardy, it has foliage similarities to *T. fosteriana* with 5–6 broad leaves up to 10 in in length, long-pointed, and slightly gray. Cultivate the same as for *T. kaufmanniana* but be alert here for botrytis disease. The natural color is difficult to incorporate in gardens, but the cultivar 'Fusilier' is bright scarlet and preferred. (See photo.)

Tulipa pulchella (dwarf Taurus tulip) 4–5 in Sun Zones 5–8
FLOWERING SPAN: Early to late April
NATURAL COLOR: Deep pinkish crimson to purple
DISTRIBUTION: Asia Minor

Two or 3 olive green, slender leaves with purple tips stretch to 6 in and surround a globular, flat-opening, 1-in flower on a short stalk. The blossom's exterior is either gray or gray-green, while the yellowish interior ends in a purplish black center. At times 2–3 flowers emerge from one bulb. It prefers a warm, well-drained location of average fertility in full sun but may require winter mulching in cold areas. There are no special pest or disease problems. The cultivar 'Humilis' has violet-pink flowers; 'Pallida' is white with a deep blue inside blotch; 'Persian Pearl' is entirely magenta-rose; and 'Violacea' displays purple-red blossoms. (See photo.)

Tulipa tarda (dasystemon) (Kuenlen tulip) 4–6 in Sun Zones 4–8
FLOWERING SPAN: Late April to mid-May
NATURAL COLOR: Canary yellow and white blend
DISTRIBUTION: Eastern Turkestan

Clusters of noticeable, starlike flowers crowd the slender stems of this easily colonized bulb for use in rock gardens, edgings, and borders with bright sun, average fertility, and reasonably dry dormant conditions. Its 2-in flowers open widely—but only on sunny days—and may be up to 7 on a stem. The exterior is greenish white while the interior is glossy yellow blending to a white tip. Its 4–7 almost-prostrate, narrow leaves can be up to 6 in long. Readily seeding itself to form colonies, this tulip has seed capsules which elongate to create attractive dried accents for indoors. There are no problems with pests or diseases. (See photo.)

Tulipa turkestanica (biflora var. *turkestanica)* 6–8 in Sun Zones 5–8
FLOWERING SPAN: Early April to May
NATURAL COLOR: Ivory white
DISTRIBUTION: Turkestan

The 1¼-in, starlike flowers have a reddish exterior, a creamy white interior ending in an orange base, and appear in branched ascent of up to 7 on a slender stalk. They do not open, however, on overcast days. The narrow, gray-green leaves cluster at the base and may elongate up to half a foot. Colonizing well, it enjoys the same culture as *T. tarda.* (See photo.)

Tulipa whittallii (Spartan tulip) 8–12 in Sun Zones 5–7
  FLOWERING SPAN: Mid-April to early May
  NATURAL COLOR: Bright orange
  DISTRIBUTION: Greece, western Turkey
    Distinctively colored with a greenish buff exterior and a vividly orange interior ending in a dark green base, this star-shaped flower opens to a 4-in spread. Its 3–4 narrow, red-margined leaves can expand up to 8 in in length. A good colonizer when provided with the same conditions as *T. tarda,* it has no particular diseases or pests. Some botanists include it as a form of *T. orphanidea* or *T. hageri,* both of which bloom later.

Vinca minor (common periwinkle, myrtle) 4–6 in Sun Zones 4–9
  FLOWERING SPAN: Late April to late May
  NATURAL COLOR: Violet-blue
  DISTRIBUTION: Europe
    Shallow-rooted and a suitable companion for vigorous bulb collections such as *Narcissus,* this thin-stemmed, evergreen creeper makes a showy display of 1-in, trumpet-shaped flowers appearing for weeks from the axils of the ¾-in, deep green, glossy leaves. It blossoms best with sun for at least ¾ of the day and accepts shading well but with a loss of flower production. Best grown in a consistently moist, humusy soil with excellent drainage, it also tolerates moderate dryness without problem. Its prostrate stems root at the joints in loose soil, making propagation simple by easy division at almost any time. Summer stem cuttings are also very workable. Pests and diseases are not problematic. A number of attractive cultivars exist: 'Alba', white; 'Atropurpurea', purple but sparse; 'Bowlesii' ('La Grave'), the best for vigor, durability, productivity, and flower size; 'Flore Pleno', double, scant-flowering; 'Miss Jeckyll's White', smaller in all respects, slow-growing, 1 in tall, few flowers; 'Multiplex', double, purple, scant-flowering; and 'Variegata', leaf margins and veins yellowish, modest flower production. (See photos.)

Viola blanda (sweet white violet) 3–6 in Semishade Zones 3–9
  FLOWERING SPAN: Late April to June
  NATURAL COLOR: White
  DISTRIBUTION: Quebec to Georgia and Louisiana
    In either cool, moist, fertile woodlots or the heavy, wet soil of meadows, this sweetly fragrant perennial displays easy adaptability. The ½-in, narrow, smooth blossoms have a noticeable purple streak on the central petal. The foliage is heart-shaped, glossy, almost hairless, and about an inch wide. Growing in tufts, it is easily transplanted when young. Divide older plants in early spring and discard any woody parts. Like any *Viola,* this species can be prone to many pests, such as aphids, red spider mites, caterpillars, nematodes, slugs, and the violet sawfly,

together with leaf spot and root rot diseases. But these afflictions are not common to all growing areas or prevalent in every season.

Viola cornuta (horned violet) 5–8 in Sun Zones 5–8
FLOWERING SPAN: Late April to September
NATURAL COLOR: Violet
DISTRIBUTION: Spain, Pyrenees Mountains
A durable, long-flowering perennial for well-drained, humusy sites which do not become sun-baked, it has a multitude of 1½-in, erect flowers rising from a tuft of oval leaves slightly hairy on the undersides. If cut back severely after the main blooming and then fertilized and watered well, a second flowering should be almost as profuse. The plant dislikes intense heat and open, wet winters but can accept light shading. Division in early spring, seeding, or stem cuttings in late summer all propagate it satisfactorily. Pest and disease problems are the same as for *V. blanda.* Hybridization has greatly improved the color range, flower size, and length of bloom, yet cultivars tend to diminish in vigor due to overproduction of flowers. Among the popular cultivars are: 'Apricot', bronzy apricot; 'Andross Gem', dull gold and blue; 'Arkwright Ruby', ruby red, fragrant; 'Chantreyland', clear apricot, large-flowered; 'Jersey Gem', deep violet-blue, large; 'Lord Nelson', violet-purple; 'Purple Heart', purple with a yellow center, 12 in tall; 'Scottish Yellow', lemon yellow; 'White Perfection', pure white, large; and 'Yellow Vixen', soft yellow. (See photo.)

Viola odorata (sweet violet, florist's violet) 3–6 in Semishade Zones 5–8
FLOWERING SPAN: Mid-April to June
NATURAL COLOR: Deep violet
DISTRIBUTION: Europe, North Africa, Asia
This sweet-scented, stemless, ½-in flower grows in low tufts and carries a shovel-shaped central petal. The plant enlarges by sending out slender runners and enjoys a moist, humusy site. This species is better propagated by division, since seeding often produces some murky colorings. Bothersome pests and diseases are listed under *V. blanda.* These cultivars are available: 'Double Russian', purple, double, late; 'Rosina', deep rose, tall, very fragrant; 'Royal Robe', deep violet-blue, 8 in tall, highly scented; and 'White Wonder' ('White Czar'), white with faint yellow and purplish streaks.

Viola palmata (early blue violet) 3–6 in Semishade Zones 4–8
FLOWERING SPAN: Mid-April to June
NATURAL COLOR: Violet-purple
DISTRIBUTION: Massachusetts to northern Georgia, west to Minnesota
The fingered, hairy leaves of this stemless plant are deeply lobed into 5–11

segments with the middle one the widest. Its ¾-in, bearded flowers have a pale yellow center. Adaptable to either dry, open, alkaline woodlots or fertile meadows with some shade, it propagates generously by self-seeding. Pests and diseases are listed under *V. blanda.*

Viola pubescens (downy yellow violet) 8–12 in Semishade Zones 3–8
FLOWERING SPAN: Mid-April to mid-May
NATURAL COLOR: Pale yellow
DISTRIBUTION: Nova Scotia to North Carolina, Georgia, and Mississippi, west to Oklahoma and North Dakota

The 3-in, rounded foilage has stems downy with soft hairs, but the flower stalks are often hairless and leafless. The petals are tapered to a sharp point. Enjoying a rich soil in dry woodlots, *V. pubescens* can be propagated readily by either division or seeding. Potentially disfiguring insects and diseases are given under *V. blanda.* The variety *eriocarpa (V. pensylvanica)* is rarely even 6 in tall and is almost hairless on all parts.

Viola sororia (papilionacea) (woolly blue violet) 3–6 in Semishade Zones 4–8
FLOWERING SPAN: Mid-April to June
NATURAL COLOR: Light to deep violet
DISTRIBUTION: Eastern United States

This commonest of all native violets is at home in a variety of moist woodlots or meadows and has wide-spreading, soft-bearded side petals which shade to white or yellowish green at the center. Northern-grown plants normally have smaller flowers than those grown in southerly locations. The cultivar name 'Alba' is commonly used for any of the white-flowered forms. All have dull green, triangular, 2–4-in leaves stretching almost as tall as the flower stalks and in robust profusion. Division is the simplest propagation technique, yet this species delivers such voluminous seeding as to be considered a nuisance in many locations. The diseases and pests provided under *V. blanda* apply here as well. Additionally, a true variety, *priceana,* with gray-lilac petals which are noticeably veined in violet-blue, thrives from New England westward to Wyoming. Commonly referred to as "Confederate violet," it can be just as invasive from overseeding as its parent. (See photos.)

Viola tricolor (European wild pansy, Johnny-jump-up) 4–12 in Sun Zones 4–8
FLOWERING SPAN: Late April to mid-June, sporadically all summer
NATURAL COLOR: Mix of yellow, purple, white
DISTRIBUTION: Europe, northern Asia, eastern United States

A valuable parent of the large-flowered garden pansy of cultivation, this easily grown plant is a prolific self-seeder in rich, moist soil with either full sun or light shading. Its behavior can be that of a perennial, a biennial, or even an annual in any location. The color blend of the ¾-in blossoms creates an appealing facelike appearance. The upper leaves are heart-shaped while the lower ones are rounded. The soft, brittle stems elongate without much prop strength and usually flop over with age to create a wide-spreading but tangled mass. Although the pests and diseases listed for *V. blanda* are potential problems, this very vigorous plant is rarely bothered by anything but its own overproduction. (See photo.)

May

WHITE

Ajuga reptans cvs.
Anemone alpina
Anemone canadensis
Anemone sylvestris
Anemonella thalictroides
Aquilegia alpina cvs.
Aquilegia caerulea cvs.
Aquilegia chrysantha cvs.
Aquilegia × hybrida
Arenaria verna
Arisaema triphyllum var.
  stewardsonii
Armeria maritima cvs.
Aster alpinus cvs.
Astrantia major
Baptisia leucantha
Cerastium arvense
Clintonia umbellulata
Convallaria majalis
Cornus canadensis
Corydalis nobilis
Cypripedium candidum
Dianthus × allwoodii cvs.
Dicentra formosa cvs.
Dicentra spectabilis cvs.
Dodecatheon meadia
Dryas octopetala
Endymion hispanicus cvs.

Endymion non-scriptus cvs.
Epimedium grandiflorum cvs.
Epimedium × youngianum
Erigeron glaucus cvs.
Galax urceolata
Galium odoratum
Geranium sanguineum cvs.
Hedyotis caerulea
Hutchinsia alpina
Iberis saxatilis
Iberis sempervirens
Iris bearded cvs.
Iris cristata cvs.
Iris gracilipes cvs.
Iris tectorum cvs.
Jeffersonia diphylla
Lamium maculatum cvs.
Linum perenne cvs.
Lychnis viscaria cvs.
Myosotis sylvatica cvs.
Ornithogalum umbellatum
Paeonia lactiflora cvs.
Paeonia officinalis cvs.
Papaver alpinum
Phlox divaricata cvs.
Phlox stolonifera cvs.
Podophyllum hexandrum
Podophyllum peltatum

Polemonium caeruleum var.
  lacteum
Polygonatum multiflorum
Polygonatum odoratum
Potentilla tridentata
Primula japonica cvs.
Ranunculus aconitifolius
Ranunculus amplexicaulis
Saxifraga virginiensis
Sedum acre cvs.
Silene caroliniana
Silene quadrifida
Sisyrinchium angustifolium
  cvs.
Smilacina racemosa
Symphytum officinale
Thalictrum aquilegifolium cvs.
Tiarella cordifolia
Tiarella wherryi
Tradescantia × andersoniana
  cvs.
Tulipa cvs.
Veronica chamaedrys cvs.
Veronica gentianoides cvs.
Veronica latifolia
Veronica pectinata cvs.
Veronica repens cvs.
Viola canadensis
Xerophyllum asphodeloides

YELLOW

Alchemilla mollis
Anemone alpina var.
  sulphurea
Aquilegia caerulea cvs.
Aquilegia chrysantha
Aquilegia × hybrida
Clintonia borealis
Corydalis lutea
Cypripedium calceolus var.
  pubescens
Doronicum cordatum
Doronicum pardalianches

Doronicum plantagineum
Dryas octopetala
Epimedium pinnatum var.
  colchicum
Epimedium × versicolor cvs.
Geum quellyon cvs.
Hypoxis hirsuta
Iris bearded cvs.
Iris pseudacorus
.Lithospermum canescens
Papaver alpinum
Patrinia triloba

Polygonatum biflorum
Polygonatum commutatum
Potentilla anserina
Potentilla argentea
Ranunculus aconitifolius cvs.
Ranunculus acris
Ranunculus ficaria
Ranunculus montanus
Ranunculus repens
Sedum acre
Sisyrinchium angustifolium
  cvs.

Symphytum grandiflorum
Thermopsis montana
Trollius asiaticus
Trollius europaeus

Trollius japonicus
Tulipa cvs.
Uvularia grandiflora
Uvularia perfoliata

Uvularia sessilifolia
Viola hastata
Viola lutea
Waldsteinia fragaroides

_____ O R A N G E _____

Epimedium × warleyense
Geum × borisii
Geum quellyon cvs.
Iris bearded cvs.

Papaver alpinum
Trollius europaeus cvs.
Tulipa cvs.

_____ R E D _____

Aquilegia caerulea cvs.
Aquilegia formosa cvs.
Aquilegia × hybrida
Armeria maritima cvs.
Armeria plantaginea cvs.
Asarum europaeum
Dianthus × allwoodii
Dianthus deltoides cvs.
Dianthus gratianopolitanus
    cvs.

Dicentra formosa cvs.
Dicentra spectabilis
Dodecatheon meadia cvs.
Epimedium × rubrum
Epimedium × versicolor
Geranium sanguineum
Geum quellyon
Geum rivale cvs.
Geum triflorum
Iris bearded cvs.

Paeonia lactiflora cvs.
Paeonia officinalis cvs.
Paeonia tenuifolia
Papaver rupifragum
Primula japonica
Tiarella cordifolia cvs.
Tradescantia × andersoniana
    cvs.
Tulipa cvs.

_____ P I N K _____

Aethionema coridifolium
Aethionema grandiflorum
Aethionema × warleyense
Ajuga genevensis cvs.
Anemonella thalictroides
Aquilegia caerulea cvs.
Aquilegia × hybrida
Armeria maritima cvs.
Armeria plantaginea cvs.
Aster alpinus cvs.
Astrantia major cvs.
Dianthus × allwoodii
Dianthus deltoides
Dianthus gratianopolitanus
Dianthus plumarius

Dodecatheon meadia
Endymion hispanicus cvs.
Endymion non-scriptus cvs.
Erigeron glaucus cvs.
Geranium endressii
Geranium maculatum
Geranium sanguineum var.
    prostratum
Iris bearded cvs.
Iris gracilipes
Lamium maculatum cvs.
Lychnis viscaria cvs.
Myosotis alpestris cvs.
Myosotis sylvatica cvs.

Paeonia lactiflora cvs.
Paeonia officinalis cvs.
Phlox pilosa
Phlox stolonifera
Podophyllum hexandrum
Primula rosea
Silene caroliniana
Symphytum officinale
Thalictrum aquilegifolium
Tradescantia × andersoniana
    cvs.
Tulipa cvs.
Veronica pectinata cvs.
Veronica repens cvs.

_____ P U R P L E / L A V E N D E R _____

Ajuga reptans cvs.
Aquilegia × hybrida
Armeria plantaginea
Aster alpinus
Camassia cusickii
Campanula elatines
Campanula poscharskyana
Corydalis bulbosa
Cypripedium acaule
Dianthus deltoides

Dicentra formosa
Dodecatheon meadia
Dodecatheon pulchellum
Epimedium grandiflorum cvs.
Erigeron glaucus cvs.
Geum rivale
Hedyotis caerulea
Hedyotis purpurea
Ipheion uniflora
Iris bearded cvs.

Iris pallida
Iris tectorum
Lamium maculata
Lathyrus vernus
Lychnis viscaria
Phlox pilosa
Phlox stolonifera
Sisyrinchium douglasii
Symphytum officinale
Thalictrum aquilegifolium
Tiarella cordifolia cvs.

Tradescantia × andersoniana
   cvs.

Tulipa cvs.
Viola pedata

Viola sagittata

_____ B L U E _____

Ajuga genevensis
Ajuga pyramidalis
Ajuga reptans
Amsonia tabernaemontana
Aquilegia alpina
Aquilegia caerulea
Aquilegia × hybrida
Aster alpinus cvs.
Baptisia australis
Camassia quamash
Camassia scilloides
Endymion hispanicus

Endymion non-scriptus
Geranium endressii cvs.
Hedyotis caerulea
Ipheion uniflora cvs.
Iris bearded cvs.
Iris cristata
Jeffersonia dubia
Linum narbonense
Linum perenne
Mazus reptans
Myosotis scorpioides
Myosotis sylvatica

Phlox divaricata cvs.
Phlox stolonifera cvs.
Polemonium caeruleum
Sisyrinchium angustifolium
Symphytum officinale cvs.
Tradescantia × andersoniana
Veronica chamaedrys
Veronica gentianoides
Veronica latifolia cvs.
Veronica officinalis
Veronica pectinata
Veronica repens

_____ B I C O L O R _____

Aquilegia caerulea
Aquilegia formosa
Aquilegia × hybrida
Arisaema triphyllum
Corydalis nobilis

Dianthus × allwoodii
Dianthus deltoides
Epimedium grandiflorum
Epimedium pinnatum
Epimedium rubrum

Epimedium × warleyense
Iris bearded cvs.
Paeonia lactiflora cvs.
Tulipa cvs.

(Photos for May are between pages 96 and 97.)

_____ T H E   P L A N T S _____

Aethionema coridifolium (Iberis jucunda) (Lebanon cress) 8–10 in Sun Zones 5–8
   FLOWERING SPAN: Mid-May to mid-June
   NATURAL COLOR: Rosy lilac to pink
   DISTRIBUTION: Mountains of southern Turkey and Lebanon
      Cooperative plants for hot, dry locations in sunny rock gardens and plant
   walls, these are close relatives of *Iberis*. Fragrant, dense, terminal flower heads
   appear on stiff, upright stems with ½-in, blue-green, fleshy leaves. As with *Iberis*,
   shear back hard after flowering to maintain its compactness. Enjoying light, sandy
   soil and full sun, it does best in an alkaline condition (add ground limestone to the
   planting bed in acid areas). Mainly evergreen in very mild areas, it needs either
   consistent snowfalls or light mulching in cold sections to prevent excessive stem
   dieback. It resents transplanting when established and should be propagated
   either by seeding in the spring or by summer stem cuttings. There are no disease
   or pest problems. (See photo.)

Aethionema grandiflorum (Persian stone cress)   10–12 in   Sun   Zones 5–8
   FLOWERING SPAN: Late May to late June
   NATURAL COLOR: Deep pink
   DISTRIBUTION: Iran, Iraq, Turkey
      Similar to but later-blooming and slightly taller than *A. coridifolium,* this species has 1½-in, loosely spaced, blue-green leaves. Culture is the same for both.

Aethionema × warleyense (Warley stone cress)   4–6 in   Sun   5–9
   FLOWERING SPAN: Mid-May to mid-June
   NATURAL COLOR: Deep rosy pink
   ORIGIN: Horticultural hybrid of *A. armenum × A. grandiflorum*
      Nonfragrant, this plant forms a wide-spreading, low mat when it is content with its surroundings. With ¼-in flowers and blue-green leaves tightly compressed on the stem, it is a sterile hybrid and can be reproduced only by summer stem cuttings. Cultivate as for *A. coridifolium.*

Ajuga genevensis (alpina, rugosa) (Geneva bugle)   3–8 in   Sun   Zones 4–9
   FLOWERING SPAN: Mid-May to mid-June
   NATURAL COLOR: Bright blue
   DISTRIBUTION: Europe, Asia Minor
      Bright green, upright, 3-in leaves form rounded mats and surround the erect flower stalks in bright sun or light shade. Noncreeping, this species enjoys a dry, average-fertility soil, either acid or alkaline. Propagate by spring division only. It has no insect pests, but crown rot can be troublesome at times. Several cultivars of note are available, but it is botanically unclear where they officially belong; some botanists choose *A. reptans.* They are: 'Brockbankii', dark blue, short; 'Bronze Beauty', deep blue, bronzed leaves; 'Crispa', wavy foliage, bright blue; 'Metallica', bronzed leaves, bright blue flowers; 'Pink Beauty', delicate pink flowers; 'Rosea', rosy pink, durable flowers; and 'Variegata', leaves mottled in creamy white. (See photo.)

Ajuga pyramidalis   8–12 in   Sun   Zones 4–9
   FLOWERING SPAN: Mid-May to mid-June
   NATURAL COLOR: Deep blue
   DISTRIBUTION: Europe
      Rich, dark green, oval, 4-in leaves form a compact, noncreeping pyramid topped with erect flower stalks on tall stems. Preferring full sun or light shade in consistently moist locations of average fertility, the plant's appearance is improved by cutting off the old flowers right after bloom. Division in spring or early autumn is the most practical propagation method, and crown rot is the main disease problem. Insects do not appear to bother it. The cultivar 'Metallica Crispa' is just 6 in tall and carries purplish brown, wavy leaves with a metallic glint. (See photo.)

Ajuga reptans (repens) (carpet bugle) 4–8 in Sun Zones 4–9
FLOWERING SPAN: Mid-May to mid-June
NATURAL COLOR: Violet-blue
DISTRIBUTION: Europe

Invasively expanding in any but hot, dry, sun-baked locations, this ground cover perennial has a vigorous habit in either full sun or deep shade (where it flowers only sparsely) and can readily dominate adjacent lawns if left unchecked. Its upright, small-flowered blossoming comes out of ground-level rosettes of 2-in, flat but wavy-margined, oblong leaves. Simple division in spring or early autumn is the best propagation method. There appear to be no pests or diseases of consequence. The list of cultivars, which are more compact and slightly less invasive, is sizeable (but there is still botanic disagreement about whether they belong here or with *A. genevensis*): 'Alba', light green leaves and creamy white flowers, not overly hardy; 'Atropurpurea', bronzy purple foliage with dark purplish blue flowers; 'Bronze Beauty', bronze-purple leaves, purple flowers; 'Burgundy Glow', pink-green leaves with cream margins and wine red new growth, blue flowers; 'Multicoloris' ('Rainbow'), mix of green, white, red, and yellow in the leaves, deep blue flowers; 'Rubra', deep bronze to purple foliage, purple-red flowers; and 'Variegata' ('Albovariegata'), mix of cream and gray-green leaves, blue flowers, slow-growing, needs some shading since the foliage scorches easily in full sun. (See photo.)

Alchemilla mollis (lady's mantle) 12–24 in Sun Zones 3–8
FLOWERING SPAN: Late May to late June
NATURAL COLOR: Greenish yellow
DISTRIBUTION: Mountains of eastern Europe, Asia Minor

Novel in foliage appearance and undoubtedly one of the better species for sustained interest, this hardy perennial has gray-green, oval-to-round, scallop-edged, 6-in-wide leaves densely covered with soft hairs. Vigorous when established in bright sun to light shading, it produces great quantities of tiny flowers in loose, floppy clusters on tall stalks, which can later be cut and dried for indoor use. The plant is also highly regarded for the unusual ability of the foliage to hold attractively poised water droplets after a shower. Cultivate in a moist, well-drained soil of average fertility and divide either in early spring or autumn. Division usually takes care of propagation. It appears to be unbothered by pests or diseases. (See photo.)

Amsonia tabernaemontana (willow amsonia, blue star) 24–36 in Semishade
Zones 5–9
FLOWERING SPAN: Late May to late June
NATURAL COLOR: Pale blue
DISTRIBUTION: Southeastern United States

Dense terminal clusters of ½-in, star-shaped flowers appear atop slender stems with many thin, smooth, dull-surfaced, willowlike, 3–6-in leaves which can turn a soft gold in the autumn. Useful in moist, average-fertility locations from shrub border to wild garden with moderate sun or moderate shading, this durable perennial forms attractive clumps and often self-seeds with abandon. Spring division or summer stem cuttings also work well for propagation. Pests and diseases are not troublesome. A similar species native to the Midwest called *A. illustris* carries leathery, shiny foliage and should be grown with the same cultural conditions. (See photo.)

Anemone alpina (Pulsatilla alpina) (alpine anemone) 12–18 in Sun Zones 4–8
  FLOWERING SPAN: Early May to June
  NATURAL COLOR: White
  DISTRIBUTION: Mountains of Europe
    From woolly buds come 2–3-in daisylike flowers which begin cup-shaped and then open flat above a heavy clump of fernlike, much-divided, rich green foliage. The exterior of the blossom is often tinted bluish purple, while the center cluster of stamens is bright gold. Its long, feathery seedheads, similar to those of the April *A. pulsatilla,* become the better propagation method when ripe since the thick root system is deep and taplike. Established plants resent relocation, so choose a permanent site when first adding them to the garden. This perennial likes full sun in a moist, well-drained, neutral soil on the gravelly side. There is one variety, *sulphurea,* with 2-in sulphur yellow flowers. Neither is bothered with pests or diseases.

Anemone canadensis (pensylvanica) (meadow anemone) 12–24 in Semishade
  Zones 3–8
  FLOWERING SPAN: Early May to mid-July
  NATURAL COLOR: White
  DISTRIBUTION: Southeastern Canada to Maryland, west to Missouri and New Mexico
    Broad, 1-in petals surround a bright mass of yellow stamens on this prolific bloomer. With 1–3 upturned flowers per stem, this very hardy perennial produces a basal clump of deeply cut, dark green leaves. In moist to wet locations of average soil in semishade or moderate sun, the thin, brown rhizomes ramble along enthusiastically—perhaps invasively—and can be divided at any time. Diseases and pests present no handicaps.

Ànemone sylvestris (snowdrop anemone) 9–18 in Semishade Zones 4–8
  FLOWERING SPAN: Early May to July
  NATURAL COLOR: White
  DISTRIBUTION: Central and eastern Europe into Sweden and Siberia

Solitary, fragrant, 1½–3-in blossoms with yellow stamens are long-blooming on this attractive species, and the 5-parted leaves have hairy undersides. The creeping rootstock expands readily when provided with a moist, well-drained, humusy location. Fresh seed is the better propagation method. Cultivars worth looking for are: 'Flore Pleno' with double flowers and 'Grandiflora' with larger blossoms. None has pest or disease problems. (See photo.)

Anemonella thalictroides (rue anemone) 6–8 in Semishade Zones 4–8
FLOWERING SPAN: Early May to mid-June
NATURAL COLOR: White, pink
DISTRIBUTION: Maine to Florida, west to Oklahoma
Closely related to *Anemone,* this one-species genus has a set of greatly compounded, 1-in basal leaves on black, wiry stems. The 1½-in flower has 5–10 petals around a mass of golden stamens. If cut back right after flowering, it usually reblooms. Provide a moist, sandy soil, and the fingerlike tubers can be separated for propagation at any time after the first blooming. Curiously, these rootstocks are safely edible. There are no particular pest or disease difficulties. The cultivar 'Rosea' carries red-toned flowers.

Aquilegia alpina (alpine columbine) 12–18 in Sun Zones 3–8
FLOWERING SPAN: Late May to late June
NATURAL COLOR: Light to dark blue or blue and white bicolor
DISTRIBUTION: Alps of Switzerland
Long-spurred, nodding, 2-in flowers, several to a stalk, appear with 3-parted, widely spaced leaflets above a neat clump of foliage. It wants a well-drained, sandy, consistently moist soil in full sun or light shading. Spring or autumn division, along with seeding, work equally well for propagation. Crown rot and mildew can be serious diseases, while root borer and leaf miner are often disfiguring insect problems. The few cultivars include: 'Alba', pure white throughout, and 'Atroviolacea', deep purplish blue.

Aquilegia caerulea (Colorado columbine) 24–30 in Sun Zones 3–8
FLOWERING SPAN: Mid-May to late June
NATURAL COLOR: Blue and white bicolor
DISTRIBUTION: Rocky Mountains (Colorado state flower)
Long-spurred in blue, these 2-in, erect flowers are a bicolor of sky blue and white on thin stalks and make a noticeable accent in sunny borders. This species, however, is highly color-variable in culture and may turn out to be only an off-lavender. The basal clump of foliage—and perhaps even the entire plant—may go completely dormant in very hot summers. Cultivate as for *A. alpina.* Cultivars include: 'Alba', white, which does not come true with seeding; 'Citrina', lemon yellow; 'Cuprea', coppery red; and 'Rosea', pink or red, often double-flowered.

Aquilegia chrysantha (golden columbine) 36–42 in Sun Zones 3–9
FLOWERING SPAN: Mid-May to late July
NATURAL COLOR: Deep yellow
DISTRIBUTION: New Mexico, Arizona, northwestern Mexico
    Long-lasting, slender-spurred, 2–3-in flowers on freely branching stalks rise above the clump of ground foliage. Hardy and long in bloom, this columbine contributes a bright addition to sunny borders or woodlot edges. Its culture is the same as for *A. alpina.* Several cultivars are known: 'Alba', white; 'Alba-plena', pale yellowish white, double; 'Flore Pleno', deep yellow, double; 'Grandiflora Sulphurea', deep cream; and 'Nana', golden yellow, 18 in tall.

Aquilegia formosa (Sitka columbine) 24–36 in Sun · Zones 3–9
FLOWERING SPAN: Mid-May to mid-June
NATURAL COLOR: Yellow and red bicolor
DISTRIBUTION: Northern California to Alaska, east to Montana and Utah
    Larger-flowered and taller than its April-blooming cousin, *A. canadensis,* this hardy perennial has thin, gray-green, divided leaves and pendant, long-spurred blossoms on openly branched stalks. Its culture is the same as for *A. alpina.* A few cultivars exist: 'Nana', shell pink, dwarfed; and 'Rubra Plena', all-red, double.

Aquilegia × *hybrida* 18–36 in Sun Zones 4–9
FLOWERING SPAN: Late May to July
NATURAL COLOR: Crimson, pink, purple, yellow, blue, white, bicolors
ORIGIN: Horticultural hybrid of *A. caerulea, A. canadensis, A. chrysantha, A. formosa,* and *A. longissima* for long-spurred forms and of *A. vulgaris* for short-spurred forms
    These popular hybrids produce 3–4-in, mostly long-spurred flowers in bright and unusual colorings for a lengthy time on much-branched stalks. Delicate colors endure longer if given light shading during the heat of the day. Only division ensures color duplication, although seed bought from reliable dealers usually provides good propagation results, too. Do not collect and plant garden-gathered seed since it gives highly erratic results. New and outstanding cultivar strains in various mixed colorings include: 'Langdon's Rainbow', 30 in, very long spurs; 'McKana Giants', 36 in, extra-large blossoms in rare colorings; 'Mrs. Scott Elliott Hybrids', 24 in, long-spurred; and 'Spring Song', 30 in, long-spurred, almost-double, large blooms set closely on the stem. Individual color cultivars are: 'Crimson Star', 24 in, crimson and white; 'Rose Queen', 36 in, soft rose and white; 'Royal Purple', 24 in, deep purple; and 'Snow Queen', 30 in, pure white. A very double, 24-in form combining red, pink, and green colorings is 'Nora Barlow'. Culture for all is given under *A. alpina.* (See photo.)

Arenaria verna (caespitosa) (moss sandwort) 1–2 in Sun Zones 4–8
 FLOWERING SPAN: Late May to mid-July
 NATURAL COLOR: White
 DISTRIBUTION: Spain to northern Russia
   Pancakelike, this flat film of ½-in, bright green, mosslike foliage becomes nicely dotted with tiny but noticeable pinhead-sized flowers for a lengthy time. It is, however, a highly variable species when cultivated. It enjoys either sun or semishade on well-drained but moist locations of average fertility. Use it as a filler between stepping stones, but water regularly in hot, dry summers to preserve the very shallow roots. Division in spring is simple and the better propagation method. There are no pest or disease problems. An erratically varied cultivar, 'Aurea', has the potential of yellow-green foliage. (See photo.)

Arisaema triphyllum (Indian Jack-in-the-pulpit, Indian turnip) 18–30 in Semishade Zones 5–9
 FLOWERING SPAN: Late May to late June
 NATURAL COLOR: Green with purple stripes
 DISTRIBUTION: Northeastern Canada to Florida, west to Minnesota and Texas
   Unusually shaped and colored, this stately wildflower has 2 large, 8-in green leaves widely divided into 3 lancelike segments. The 6-in, hooded blossom stands erect with an enveloping spadix (the pulpit) around a 3-in, brown-spotted spathe (Jack), which later becomes a showy cluster of scarlet, berrylike fruit as the foliage disappears by midsummer. It wants a humusy, moist, rich soil and is best propagated by seed. The flat-topped, round corm is difficult to locate when spring-dormant. Where spring frost lingers, protect the tender, emerging foliage from damage by mulching its location the previous autumn. Insect pests and diseases are uncommon, but slugs enjoy the foliage and chipmunks relish the red seeds. A later-blooming variety, *stewardsonii,* carries more noticeable, greenish white flowers. (See photo.)

Armeria maritima (sea pink, thrift) 4–8 in Sun Zones 3–9
 FLOWERING SPAN: Mid-May to July
 NATURAL COLOR: Lilac pink to white
 DISTRIBUTION: Northwestern Europe, Iceland
   Dense, grasslike cushions of bright green, narrow, 4-in foliage produce many 1-in, globular heads of tightly packed florets attractive to hummingbirds. Neat as an edging in sunny locations with light, well-drained soil, this plant requires division every 3–4 years since the center part becomes bare from age. Fresh seed also works readily for propagation. There are no pests or diseases of consequence. Several cultivars exist: 'Alba', glistening white, 4 in; 'Dusseldorf Pride', carmine red, 8 in, for Zones 5–9; 'Laucheana', crimson, 4–6 in; and 'Vindictive', deep pink, 6–8 in. (See photo.)

Armeria plantaginea (montana) (plantain thrift) 18–24 in Sun Zones 6–9
   FLOWERING SPAN: Mid-May to July
   NATURAL COLOR: Lavender
   DISTRIBUTION: Central and southern Europe
      The 4–6-in-long foliage of this species is ¼ in wide and carries tall but bare
   flower stalks topped with globular flowers similar to *A. maritima.* Culture is the
   same for both, but this is a more tender perennial. The cultivar 'Bee's Ruby' is
   bright crimson, while 'Royal Rose' is deep pink.

Asarum europaeum (European wild ginger) 4–6 in Shade Zones 4–8
   FLOWERING SPAN: Mid-May to early June
   NATURAL COLOR: Greenish brown to maroon red
   DISTRIBUTION: Europe
      As an interesting ground cover in shade to semishade on moist, rich, cool,
   humusy woodlots, this glossy-leaved, slow spreader is not cultivated for its
   flowering, which is inconspicuous, but for its thick, deep green, kidney-shaped
   foliage on 5-in fleshy stalks. These leaves are evergreen in most areas but do flat-
   ten to the ground from the weight of heavy snow. Its ½-in, dull-colored, tub-
   shaped blossoms remain well hidden beneath the foliage. Spring division of the
   rootstock is the simplest propagation method, yet generous self-seeding can be
   counted on if it likes its home. The rootstock pieces smell like tropical ginger
   when separated. Pests and diseases seem to avoid this perennial. The North
   American species, *A. virginicum,* is also evergreen with larger leaves, but it is less
   visually attractive for gardens. (See photo.)

Aster alpinus (alpine aster) 3–9 in Sun Zones 3–8
   FLOWERING SPAN: Late May to July
   NATURAL COLOR: Rosy purple
   DISTRIBUTION: Mountains of Europe and Asia
      Daisylike, 2–3-in, sturdy flowers with golden sets of stamens rise well above
   the low mound of pale green, 2-in leaves in sunny, alkaline sites which are well-
   drained in winter. For propagation, summer cuttings, seed, or spring division
   work equally well. There are no known insect pests, but mildew, rust, and wilt
   can be troublesome diseases. Several vibrant cultivars are available: 'Albus',
   cloudy white; 'Beechwood', lavender-blue; 'Coeruleus', soft blue, 15 in; 'Dark
   Beauty', deep violet; 'Goliath', purple-blue, 15 in; 'Roseus', pale rose, 6 in; and
   'Superbus', purple, very showy.

Astrantia major (large masterwort) 18–30 in Sun Zones 4–8
   FLOWERING SPAN: Late May to September
   NATURAL COLOR: Greenish white

DISTRIBUTION: Europe

Long-lasting in flower, this perennial has mostly basal, rounded, 3–6-in, deep green leaves with deeply toothed lobes. Rising out of the foliage are much-branched stalks carrying 1½-in-wide pincushionlike flowers surrounded by leafy white bracts. An average-fertility, moist soil in sun or light shading is suitable, but avoid dry locations. Propagate by spring division or wait for the inevitable self-sown seedlings. Pests and diseases are not troublesome. The cultivars include: 'Margery Fish', soft pink; 'Rosensinfonie', rosy pink; and 'Sunningdale Variegated', greenish white with foliage splotched irregularly in yellow. (See photo.)

Baptisia australis (blue false indigo) 36–72 in Sun Zones 4–8
FLOWERING SPAN: Late May to July
NATURAL COLOR: Indigo blue
DISTRIBUTION: Pennsylvania to North Carolina, west to Tennessee

Generously expansive and showy with bushy foliage similar to its cousins *Lupinus* and *Thermopsis,* this hardy perennial likes a sunny, permanent location in average-fertility soil. Its blue-green, compound leaves have 3-in stalks with 1-in, loosely arranged, pealike florets. Moist, deep, humusy soil suits it best since the plant has long taproots. Careful division in spring is workable for propagation, but seeding is better. There are no pests or diseases worth mentioning. (See photo.)

Baptisia leucantha (prairie false indigo, white false indigo) 36–48 in Semishade
Zones 3–8
FLOWERING SPAN: Late May to July
NATURAL COLOR: White
DISTRIBUTION: Ohio to Minnesota, south to Mississippi and Texas

Fussier to grow than *A. australis,* this perennial wants more shading and consistent, deep moisture to do its best. Here the leaf segments are only 2 in long, but the flower spike stretches often to 24 in and carries 1-in florets. A loose, sandy soil is its preference. Spring division with care (since it has a taproot) or seeding are the usual propagation techniques. Diseases and pests are unknown.

Camassia cusickii 24–36 in Sun Zones 3–8
FLOWERING SPAN: Mid-May to late June
NATURAL COLOR: Pale blue to blue-violet
DISTRIBUTION: Northeastern Oregon

A showy spike with from 30–100 star-shaped florets 1½ in long emerges from a basal ring of gray-green, 1-in-wide leaves up to 18 in in length. The blossoms display noticeably protruding, pale gold anthers. Thriving in sunny, permanent locations where winters are wet and summers dry, this very pungent, clustered bulb can weigh up to half a pound and should be planted in autumn on a moist, average-fertility site as soon as received. Once established, it resents being disturbed. Propagation, then, is best achieved by seed. There are no problematic diseases or insect pests. (See photo.)

Camassia quamash (esculenta) (quamash, common quamash, camosh) 12–36 in Sun Zones 3–8

FLOWERING SPAN: Late May to July

NATURAL COLOR: Pale blue to white

DISTRIBUTION: Northern Oregon, northern Idaho, and western Montana, north to southeastern British Columbia

Once a staple in the diet of Indians from the northwestern United States, this vigorous, onionlike bulb has ¾-in-wide leaves up to 20 in long. Its 5–40 irregularly shaped, starlike, 1-in florets occur on slender spikes, and most of the blossoms open at the same time. Enjoying a fertile, damp site in full sun, it resents disturbance and should be autumn-planted when received in a hole improved for drainage with coarse sand dug into the bottom. Variable trace elements in the soil produce differences in flower coloring. When flowering diminishes after a few years, top-dress the bulbs in early spring with well-rotted manure for improved blossoming. Propagation from seed is the wisest procedure. No diseases or insect pests are bothersome.

Camassia scilloides (fraseri) (eastern camass, wild hyacinth, indigo squill) 10–18 in Sun Zones 3–8

FLOWERING SPAN: Early May to June

NATURAL COLOR: Pale blue to blue-violet, white

DISTRIBUTION: Southern Pennsylvania to southern Minnesota, south to West Virginia, Georgia, and Texas

Smaller-flowered than *C. quamash,* these florets are broadly star-shaped with golden stamens and are more closely set on the spike. The green foliage is ½ in wide and up to a foot long. Preferring fertile, moist sites in sun or semishade, this onionlike bulb should be installed in late summer or early autumn. Seed should be sown as soon as it is ripe. Bothersome insects or diseases are uncommon, but field mice find the bulbs attractive and can be highly destructive.

Campanula elatines (garganica) (Adriatic campanula) 3–6 in Sun Zones 5–9

FLOWERING SPAN: Late May to September

NATURAL COLOR: Pale blue-violet

DISTRIBUTION: Adriatic Sea environs

Bell-shaped, 5-petaled, numerous, ½-in flowers appear for many months on trailing, thin stems in sunny sites with room to accommodate its vigorous spreading habit. The 1-in gray-green leaves are pointed and shaped like ivy. Simply provide a moist, average soil for quick growth. Expect generous self-seeding as a matter of course, but you can readily divide the plants for propagation in early spring or make summer stem cuttings with a piece of root attached. Slugs have a fondness for the foliage of all *Campanula* species, but insects are not a problem. Rust disease, however, can greatly disfigure the foliage. The hairy cultivar 'Hirsuta' is similar but prefers semishaded locations.

Campanula poscharskyana 6–12 in Sun Zones 5–9
> FLOWERING SPAN: Late May to September
> NATURAL COLOR: Pale blue-violet
> DISTRIBUTION: Northern Yugoslavia
> Very similar to *C. elatines* except that the blossoms are an inch wide on more erect stems, plus the leaves are deeply toothed and shiny green on long stalks. Vigorous in growth and abundant in flowering, this hardy perennial creates large but neat-looking foliage mats on sites with sun to light shade. Gritty, well-drained soil suits it nicely. Spring division, summer stem cuttings, or seed work equally well for propagation. Disease and slug problems are the same as for *C. elatines*. (See photo.)

Cerastium arvense (strictum) (starry grasswort) 4–9 in Sun Zones 3–9
> FLOWERING SPAN: Early May to July
> NATURAL COLOR: White
> DISTRIBUTION: Europe
> Tolerant of very dry conditions, this perennial has pale green to gray-toned, 1-in, narrow leaves on sprawling stems 8–12 in long. It readily forms a vigorous mat on dry, rocky sites—even in pure sand—with full sun or light shading. The flowers are ½ in wide with a noticeable cleft in each petal and carry clustered, bright yellow stamens. Shear off the old flowers right after bloom to promote plant compactness and to stimulate continued blossoming. Either spring or autumn division is the better propagation method. Pests and diseases are of little consequence. The dwarfed cultivar 'Compactum' is not much above 3 in tall and blooms later.

Clintonia borealis (bluebead lily, corn lily) 12–18 in Shade Zones 5–8
> FLOWERING SPAN: Mid-May to early June
> NATURAL COLOR: Greenish yellow
> DISTRIBUTION: Eastern United States
> Thriving best in cool, moist, humusy locations, this wildflower can garden-adapt in very acid, bonemeal-enriched sites with consistent moisture. Its 3–8 bell-

shaped, ¾-in, nodding flowers rise on thin stems out of a clump of handsome foliage. The 2–5 deep green, shiny, 10-in-long, up to 2-in-wide leaves remain attractive all season. Noticeable, bright blue fruiting is a special bonus by autumn. Division of the creeping rootstock in early autumn works better for propagation than seeding (also in early autumn), since you must wait several years for flowering with seed. Diseases and insect nuisances are unknown, but slugs are an occasional problem.

Clintonia umbellulata (speckled wood lily) 8–18 in Shade Zones 6–8
FLOWERING SPAN: Mid-May to early June
NATURAL COLOR: White
DISTRIBUTION: New Jersey, western New York, and eastern Ohio, south to Tennessee and Georgia

Tolerant to conditions less acid, moist, and cool than *C. borealis,* this more tender wildflower has between 10–30 tiny, ½-in blossoms in rounded heads with petals dotted in green and purple. Its fruit is black-toned. The 2–5 broad leaves can stretch to a foot in length. Propagate as for *C. borealis.* It is pest-free.

Convallaria majalis (lily-of-the-valley) 6–8 in Semishade Zones 3–9
FLOWERING SPAN: Mid-May to early June
NATURAL COLOR: White
DISTRIBUTION: Europe, Asia

Remarkably long-lived and adaptable to all degrees of shading, this hardy, vigorous ground cover has been enjoyed since the 16th century for its sweetly fragrant blossoms. These ¼-in, bell-shaped flowers appear on arching stems between the 2 leaves, 3–4-in-wide and up to 6 in tall, which sprout from each "pip" or "eye" of the fleshy, underground rootstock. Thriving in rich, moist, humusy locations in semishade to shade (with reduced flowering), the plant enjoys an annual topdressing in early spring of well-rotted manure or compost enhanced with a dash of balanced fertilizer. When overcrowded, the flower crop diminishes, and division is needed. Carefully separate the dormant plants in very early spring or early autumn and replant in a well-prepared, humusy location. Leaf spot fungus is an occasional problem, but insects are of little concern. Double-flowered, pale pink, and color-margined forms are available but are mere novelties without any special garden appeal. (See photo.)

Cornus canadensis (bunchberry, dwarf cornel) 3–8 in Shade Zones 2–7
FLOWERING SPAN: Late May to mid-June
NATURAL COLOR: White
DISTRIBUTION: Greenland to Alaska and eastern Asia, south to West Virginia and New Mexico

Where conditions are to its liking, this exceptionally hardy, semievergreen ground cover will present an annual display of perky flowers rising singly above a whorl of 3-in leaves. By midsummer the spent flowers turn into clusters of shiny, bright red, persistent fruit, which American colonists considered worthwhile for puddings in the 17th century. Detesting heat and dryness, this perennial thrives in upland woods to form dense mats where the soil is acid, cool, consistently moist, well-drained, and humusy. Its showy "flower" is actually four white, 1½-in bracts (modified leaves) useful in attracting insects for pollinating the minute cluster of greenish yellow true flowers packed into the center of the blossom. Autumn or spring division of the stringy, creeping rootstock is workable but risky for success; collecting solid blocks of sod is better. The best propagation method, even if it is slow for results, is autumn seeding. Pests and diseases are few and far between. (See photo.)

Corydalis bulbosa (fumewort) 4–6 in Sun Zones 5–9
FLOWERING SPAN: Early May to late May
NATURAL COLOR: Rosy purple, white
DISTRIBUTION: Europe, Asia

Closely related to *Dicentra,* especially in its similar-looking blue-green, lacy foliage, this dwarf, tuberous plant has erect clusters of ¾-in, trumpet-shaped backward-turned florets resembling a snapdragon's in early spring. Once bloom is over, it quickly descends into total dormancy by mid-June. Provide a well-drained moist, humusy, slightly acid soil in sun or light shade and be prepared for many self-sown colonies. Division of the small tubers is best done right after flowering; replant quickly to avoid drying out. It appears to have no troublesome pests or diseases. (See photo.)

Corydalis lutea 10–15 in Semishade Zones 5–9
FLOWERING SPAN: Late May to October
NATURAL COLOR: Golden yellow
DISTRIBUTION: Southeastern Europe

Loose sprays of short-stemmed, tubular, ½-in flowers provide a long-lasting accent above lacy foliage. The much-divided, gray-green, 2–3-in leaves are attractive in their own right. Adaptable from semishade to full sun (if kept consistently moist), it does best in well-drained, gravelly soil that is slightly alkaline and thrives next to boulders and in rock plant walls. Often self-seeding prolifically when it enjoys its growing site, its rhizome is difficult to transplant with success except when very small. Pests and diseases are uncommon. (See photo.)

Corydalis nobilis 18–30 in Semishade Zones 3–9
FLOWERING SPAN: Mid-May to mid-June
NATURAL COLOR: Whitish yellow
DISTRIBUTION: Central Asia

Sturdier and more ornamental than many other species of the genus, this perennial is hard to find commercially. The attractive foliage is vivid green with much-incised, wedge-shaped leaflets below dense heads of 20–30 spurred, 1-in, brown-tipped, brownish orange florets. It enjoys a well-drained, humusy soil with reasonable moisture. Full dormancy arrives right after the bloom, when division of the husky, fleshy rhizomes is best handled. Seed may be difficult to germinate. Diseases and pests are not bothersome.

Cypripedium acaule (Fissipes acaulis) (pink lady's slipper, two-leaved lady's slipper, moccasin flower) 8–12 in Semishade Zones 3–8
FLOWERING SPAN: Mid-May to mid-June
NATURAL COLOR: Pinkish purple
DISTRIBUTION: Newfoundland to North Carolina, west to Minnesota

Showy in flower and one of the more widely distributed of our native wood orchids, this challenging plant—like all of its cousins—wants exactly the right growing conditions or it may disappear entirely. The unusual, single, 3–5-in flower stands a foot above 3-in-wide, oblong leaves up to 8 in in length clustered at ground level. The blossom has brownish, thin-pointed top petals and an inflated pouch or "lip" below with a cleft in the middle. Veins in the pouch are usually darker in color.

There is a delicately balanced relationship between this plant and microbes in the soil where it grows naturally. Collecting small plants from one's own property in early spring is less hazardous when each seedling is dug with as much soil as possible clinging to the coarse, stringy, brittle roots. Never take these valuable perennials from the wild because of conservation reasons important to all of us. Protect the dug roots from exposure to wind and sun until replanted, then water heavily and often until the plant is established. Mulch with fallen pine needles after replanting. Seed is very difficult to germinate, and buying nursery-raised seedlings is by far the wiser way to start a new collection or add to an established one.

Sandy, well-drained, acid soil in semishade is preferred. Since the plant accepts deeper shade in summer, planting under deciduous trees is appropriate. Adequate moisture in spring is important, but occasional dryness later usually has no effect on growth. Trying to grow them successfully in gardens creates more anxiety than any infrequent pests or diseases. (See photo.)

Cypripedium calceolus var. *pubescens* (yellow lady's slipper) 10–20 in Semishade Zones 3–9
FLOWERING SPAN: Late May to mid-June
NATURAL COLOR: Bright yellow
DISTRIBUTION: Southeastern Canada to Georgia and Louisiana, west to Arizona and Oregon

The basic species, *C. calceolus* from Eurasia, is rarely cultivated in the United

States, but the variety *pubescens* is commonly offered in nurseries. One of the easiest wood orchids to establish, it has 1–2 flowers on leafy stems with 3-in, chocolate-brown petals above and a clear yellow pouch below. Readily forming large clumps of 6–8-in, hairy, broad leaves in moist, open woods with a neutral, humusy soil, the plant can adapt to richer garden locations successfully in consistently moist, semishaded areas. Lift the clumps in early spring or autumn for simple division. Ease the crowns apart carefully with roots attached, then replant immediately in a prepared bed and water well and often. At times slugs, snails, and fungus diseases can be troublesome. Formerly classified as a species, *C. parviflorum* (small yellow lady's slipper), showing maroon upper petals and noticeable fragrance, is now considered only a variety of *C. calceolus*. Nursery growers tend to lump them together for sale today.

Cypripedium candidum (small white lady's slipper) 8–12 in Semishade Zones 3–9
 FLOWERING SPAN: Late May to mid-June
 NATURAL COLOR: Milky white
 DISTRIBUTION: New York to Kentucky, west to Minnesota and Missouri
  Seemingly just a white form of *C. acaule* at first glance, this flower has a 1-in lip below greenish white, twisted upper petals with crimson veining. The flower stalk is surrounded by 3–5 broad, 5-in-long leaves. Found naturally in bogs and wet meadows, the plant is not common in the wild. It prefers slightly alkaline soil in gardens (add ground limestone to acid locations), semishaded conditions, and, of course, abundant moisture. Do not dig plants from the wild but buy nursery-grown seedlings. Slugs and rodents are occasionally bothersome to some parts of the plant.

Dianthus × *allwoodii* (Allwood pink) 12–15 in Sun Zones 3–8
 FLOWERING SPAN: Late May to September
 NATURAL COLOR: Various blends of pink, red, and white
 ORIGIN: Horticultural hybrid of *D. plumarius* × *D. caryophyllus*
  This very fragrant introduction from the Allwood Brothers nursery in England is a hardy hybrid between the old-fashioned garden pink and the perpetually flowering carnation. With 1–1½-in-wide, double or semidouble blossoms on multibranched stems, this plant is capable of reblooming if the flowers are frequently cut for indoor use or if deadheaded regularly. The compact foliage mound is grayish green with narrow, straplike leaves in pairs along the slender stems. All dianthuses enjoy a well-ventilated and well-drained site in full sun with slightly alkaline soil (add ground limestone to acid locations) enriched with compost or humus. In severe climates, add a light mulch for winter since these are shallow-rooted perennials. Propagate these hybrids by stem layering or by summer stem cuttings; seed will produce variable colorings, especially if it is taken from garden plants. Pests and diseases are not common. There

are many special cultivars: 'Aqua', double, white; 'Doris', semidouble, light pink with a deep pink center; 'Helen', double, deep salmon; 'Her Majesty', double, white; 'Ian', double, rich red, dwarfed; 'Robin', double, bright scarlet; and 'Zing Rose', bright rose. The 'Alpinus Strain' offers single, fragrant, pink-to-red, 6–12-in-tall flowering with continuous bloom until frost. (See photo.)

Dianthus deltoides (maiden pink) 6–18 in Sun Zones 3–9
FLOWERING SPAN: Late May to mid-June
NATURAL COLOR: Reddish purple, rose, and white, all with a crimson center
DISTRIBUTION: Northern Europe
    Variable in flower coloring from plant to plant, *D. deltoides* forms a loose mat of grasslike, evergreen foliage. When in bloom, the plant is fully covered with solitary, ½-in, lightly scented flowers with sharp-toothed petals atop slender stems. Useful in rock gardens, border edges, or in pavement seams, these hardy perennials want good air circulation, full sun, excellent drainage, and a highly alkaline soil. To improve compactness shear back old flowers and some foliage right after blooming, and in very cold areas mulch lightly for winter. This species self-sows easily—perhaps too generously in some gardens—but can also be divided in early spring if the parent is not too old and leggy. Crown rot and root rot are occasionally serious difficulties as are infestations of red spider mites on the leaves during hot, dry summers. A few cultivars exist: 'Albus', pure white; 'Brilliant', double, deep pink; and 'Hansen's Red', bright crimson. (See photo.)

Dianthus gratianopolitanus (caesius) (cheddar pink) 3–10 in Sun Zones 4–9
FLOWERING SPAN: Mid-May to mid-June
NATURAL COLOR: Rosy pink
DISTRIBUTION: Southern Europe, southern British Isles
    Stiff, blue-green, 2-in grassy leaves eventually form large, dense, evergreen mats with this perennial. The solitary, 1-in, spicy-sweet, fringed flowers literally cover the foliage when in bloom. Cultivate as for *D. deltoides*. Spring-sown seed or summer stem cuttings work better than division for propagation. A few cultivars are available: 'Petite', single, bright pink, 3 in tall; 'Rose Queen', double, bright rose, 6 in tall; and 'Tiny Rubies', double, rosy red, 3 in tall. (See photo.)

Dianthus plumarius (grass pink, cottage pink) 6–12 in Sun Zones 4–9
FLOWERING SPAN: Late May to July
NATURAL COLOR: Rose, pink
DISTRIBUTION: Central Europe to Siberia
    Either fringed or deeply toothed, 1½-in, single to semidouble flowers grow in clusters of 2–5 from a tuft of blue-green foliage with thick, recurved leaves. Highly fragrant with a clove scent, this hardy species is long-lived where the soil

is moist, well-drained, and humus-enriched in sunny, open locations. It likes slightly alkaline conditions, however, and acid soil can be modified with yearly applications of ground limestone. For longer blooming deadhead regularly. For compactness and greater vigor, severely cut back the old flower stalks and some foliage right after flowering is completed. Summer stem cuttings are the better propagation method. Pests and diseases are the same as for *D. deltoides.* The cultivar list includes: 'Agatha', semidouble, purplish pink; 'Cyclops', bright red; 'Dinah', rose with a maroon center; 'Evangeline', double, rosy pink; 'Pink Princess', coral-rose; and 'Moon Mist', pure white.

Dicentra formosa (western bleeding-heart) 6–18 in Semishade Zones 3–9
    FLOWERING SPAN: Mid-May to July
    NATURAL COLOR: Rosy purple to white
    DISTRIBUTION: Central California to British Columbia
    Very similar in appearance to the April-blooming *D. eximia,* this species carries heavier, coarser, blue-green foliage. Some say only an expert can separate them properly. Cultivated best in cool, humusy, moist, acid locations with semishade, the plant enjoys an annual topdressing of compost or humus in spring for continued lush growth. In severe climate areas, mulch lightly for winter since it is shallow-rooted. Spring division only is recommended for propagation, and pests or diseases are uncommon. Hybridization has produced some attractive cultivars: 'Adrian Bloom', ruby red, large flower clusters; 'Arrowsmith', creamy white; 'Bountiful', carmine red, sun-loving, repeat bloomer in autumn; 'Luxuriant', cherry pink, sun-tolerant; 'Sweetheart', pure white with constant bloom; and 'Zestful', rosy pink. There is still a lively debate whether these cultivars appropriately belong with this species or with *D. eximia,* but the flowering times should provide a good clue. (See photo.)

Dicentra spectabilis (bleeding-heart) 18–30 in Semishade Zones 3–9
    FLOWERING SPAN: Early May to mid-June
    NATURAL COLOR: Deep rosy red
    DISTRIBUTION: Japan
    Long, arching sprays of 1-in, heart-shaped flowers with white tips gracefully complement the large, grayish green, 9-in-long, much-divided leaves of this popular and hardy perennial. Favoring a light, consistently moist, average-fertility soil in cool semishade, the entire plant will wither into dormancy quickly during long, hot, dry summers. Spring or early autumn division, along with its modest self-seeding, propagate it readily. Disease or insect nuisances are seldom seen. There is now an all-white-flowered cultivar, 'Alba' ('Pantaloons'), which is less vigorous but visually noteworthy. (See photo.)

Dodecatheon meadia (shooting-star) 6–20 in Semishade Zones 4–9
FLOWERING SPAN: Early May to mid-June
NATURAL COLOR: Purple, lavender, pink, white
DISTRIBUTION: Pennsylvania to Alabama, west to eastern Texas and southern Wisconsin

Related to both *Primula* and *Cyclamen,* this wildflower displays a ground rosette of dull green, 1–2-in-wide leaves up to a foot long which are often reddened at the base. The tall flower stalk carries 10–20 dartlike, narrow-petaled, ¾-in flowers varying in color from plant to plant over its wide distribution area. Provide a well-drained, consistently moist, sandy soil high in humus with cool semishade to full shade for sturdy growth. The foliage disappears in midsummer even with seedlings. Autumn division of the dormant rootstock is difficult but possible. Seeding in permanent locations is better, if slow to produce bloom. There are no troublesome diseases or insect pests. Several cultivars are known: 'Album', a graceful white form, and 'Splendidum', with yellow-centered, crimson flowers.

Dodecatheon pulchellum (amethystinum) 6–20 in Semishade Zones 3–9
FLOWERING SPAN: Early May to June
NATURAL COLOR: Magenta to lavender
DISTRIBUTION: Southern Alaska and western Canada to Mexico

With this species the basal cluster of dull green foliage is 10 in at most in length and surrounds a slender flower stalk topped by 3–25 florets, delicate and pendant with sharply recurved petals, suggesting stars. Its culture is the same as for *D. meadia,* but it is fussier. There is an attractive cultivar, 'Album', with entirely white blossoms.

Doronicum cordatum (caucasicum) (Caucasian leopards-bane) 12–24 in Sun
Zones 4–9
FLOWERING SPAN: Early May to mid-June
NATURAL COLOR: Bright yellow
DISTRIBUTION: Southeastern Europe, western Asia

Glossy-green, 3-in, toothed leaves create a mound of spreading foliage from which come sturdy stems and all-yellow, daisylike, 2-in flowers with enduring cutting quality. Useful as a border-edging accent, this perennial is neatly tidy but has the drawback of becoming dormant by early August, leaving a sizeable gap in the garden space. Its preference is for a rich, deep, consistently moist soil in moderate shading. Divide in early spring to forestall the inevitable wilting which occurs with separations made just after flowering. Pests and diseases appear to avoid it. The cultivars are superior to the parent: 'Finesse', 3-in blossoms, late; 'Magnificum', 2½-in blossoms, taller; 'Miss Mason', free-flowering to July with persistent foliage until frost; plus 'Spring Beauty', double, deep yellow flowering, earlier to bloom. (See photo.)

Doronicum pardalianches 30–42 in Sun Zones 4–9
    FLOWERING SPAN: Mid-May to July
    NATURAL COLOR: Canary yellow
    DISTRIBUTION: Europe
        Unusual for this genus, the plant has clusters of 3–5 flowers up to 2½ in wide
    on each stem above a mound of hairy, toothed, winged leaves. Its culture is the
    same as that for *D. cordatum*. This plant may be poisonous.

Doronicum plantagineum 24–42 in Sun Zones 4–9
    FLOWERING SPAN: Mid-May to mid-June
    NATURAL COLOR: Bright yellow
    DISTRIBUTION: Europe
        More appropriate for the back of a garden border due to its coarse foliage,
    this perennial has generous but solitary, 3-in blossoms. Its cultivation and propa-
    gation are the same as for *D. cordatum*. The cultivar 'Harpur Crewe' ('Excelsum')
    grows 5 ft tall, blooms later, and carries 4-in flowers. (See photo.)

Dryas octopetala (mountain avens) 4–6 in Sun Zones 1–6
    FLOWERING SPAN: Late May to July
    NATURAL COLOR: Creamy yellow, white
    DISTRIBUTION: Alaska to Greenland, Eurasia
        This low, evergreen ground cover is extremely hardy and provides an inter-
    esting texture with its thick, crinkly, 1-in leaves with white-haired undersides.
    The wide-spreading, 1-in flowers resemble anemones and later develop into con-
    spicuous, feathery seed plumes. Readily adaptable to rock gardens with full sun or
    light shade, the plant wants an acid, well-drained, modestly moist soil enriched
    with leaf mold or compost. Seed, division, or stem cuttings work equally well for
    propagation. Bothersome insects and diseases are uncommon. The cultivar
    'Minor' has compact growth and dwarfed parts throughout.

Endymion hispanicus (Scilla campanulata) (Spanish bluebell, Spanish squill) 8–18 in
    Semishade Zones 4–9
    FLOWERING SPAN: Late May to mid-June
    NATURAL COLOR: Blue to rosy purple
    DISTRIBUTION: Spain, Portugal, northwestern Africa
        A hardy bulb that colonizes readily in shaded borders and open woodlots,
    this species is larger and more vivid that its relative, *E. non-scriptus*. Unfor-
    tunately, the 10–30 nodding, ¾-in florets crowding the tall stalks are almost
    scentless. Its 5–9 straplike, 1½-in-wide leaves can become perhaps 20 in long. It
    prefers a well-drained, moist, humusy site from semishade to nearly full sun. The
    foliage disappears by midsummer, when the dormant bulbs can be separated for

propagation and quickly replanted. New plantings should be made in autumn. This bulb self-seeds freely and will hybridize with any *E. non-scriptus* planted nearby. Pests and diseases are uncommon. A sizeable number of distinctive cultivars are commonly available: 'Alba', white; 'Alba maxima', white, large florets; 'Excelsior', deep blue, large; 'King of the Blues', deep sky blue; 'Mount Everest', white; 'Myosotis', sky blue; 'Queen of the Blues', purplish blue; 'Queen of the Pinks', deep rosy pink; 'Rosea', rosy pink; and 'White Triumphator', white, large-flowered, taller than the others. (See photo.)

Endymion non-scriptus (Scilla non-scripta)   (English bluebell, harebell)   8–18 in   Semishade   Zones 5–8
FLOWERING SPAN: Mid-May to mid-June
NATURAL COLOR: Violet-blue
DISTRIBUTION: Western Europe
     Similar in appearance to *E. hispanicus,* but not as cold-tolerant, the bulb carries ½-in-wide leaves elongating no more than 18 in at maturity. The bell-shaped, ½-in florets are nicely fragrant and come 4–16 on a stem. The botanical difference between these two closely related speces is that the flowers of *E. non-scriptus* are arranged all on one side of the stalk and have cream-colored anthers, while those of *E. hispanicus* have blue anthers and surround the stalk. Culture for both is identical. The cultivars include: 'Alba', white; 'Caerulea', light blue; 'Cernua', violet-blue with nodding blossoms; 'Lilacina', lilac-blue; and 'Rosea', rosy pink.

Epimedium grandiflorum (macranthum)   (longspur epimedium)   6–12 in   Semishade   Zones 4–8
FLOWERING SPAN: Early May to June
NATURAL COLOR: Violet-red with white spurs
DISTRIBUTION: Japan, Korea, Manchuria
     All *Epimedium* species carry large, compound leaves with thin, heart-shaped leaflets. Usually, the spring foliage is very light green with prominent streaks of red, becoming glossy green by midsummer. In autumn the foliage turns bronzy and may persist—although scorched or even dead—through the winter in its colder growing zones. Where winters are mild, however, the foliage often remains pleasantly green-bronze. The ½-in, delicately shaped flowers have 1-in spurs flaring out from the rear in clusters of 4 on thin, airy stems and have good cutting quality.
     The entire genus does best in semishade with moist, acid, humusy soil, but any species will accept a surprisingly wide range of exposures, soils, and degrees of moisture. Because all species grow rapidly in early spring, divide the thick rootstock in early autumn for propagation. Any plant can be left undisturbed for many years, however, if the growing conditions are favorable and the plant

prospers. Pests and diseases are rare. Flower coloring and flower size are the usual differentiations made among the various look-alike species, and all forms are useful as dependable, attractive ground covers.

Several cultivars of *E. grandiflorum* are known: 'Rose Queen', deep pink with white-tipped spurs; 'Violaceum', light violet throughout; and 'White Queen', entirely white.

Epimedium pinnatum (Persian epimedium) 8–12 in Semishade Zones 4–8
FLOWERING SPAN: Early May to June
NATURAL COLOR: Canary yellow with red-purple spurs
DISTRIBUTION: Northern Iran, Caucasus Mountains
Less dense than other species in its foliage mass and lightly hairy on all its parts, this type spreads sluggishly. Its culture is the same as for *E. grandiflorum*. The variety *colchicum* is brilliantly yellow and is probably the form most found in cultivation today. (See photo.)

Epimedium × *rubrum* 6–12 in Semishade Zones 4–8
FLOWERING SPAN: Early May to June
NATURAL COLOR: Bright crimson with pale yellow to white spurs
ORIGIN: Horticultural hybrid of *E. alpinum* × *E. grandiflorum*
The juvenile foliage of this hybrid is noticeably veined in red, and the 1-in flowers are more abundantly presented and continue a bit longer than in other species. Cultivate as for *E. grandiflorum*, except that this hybrid tolerates more shade. (See photo.)

Epimedium × *versicolor* 9–12 in Semishade Zones 5–8
FLOWERING SPAN: Mid-May to June
NATURAL COLOR: Soft rose with reddish spurs
ORIGIN: Horticultural hybrid of *E. grandiflorum* × *E. pinnatum* var. *colchicum*
Emerging leaves are mottled in red on this form but later turn green. Its 1-in flowers resemble those of *E. pinnatum* with soft yellow petals around a rosy tube of sepals. Robust in growth with consistently attractive foliage, this plant has a cultivar, 'Sulphureum', which is sulphur yellow throughout. Culture is the same as for *E. grandiflorum*.

Epimedium × *warleyense* 9–12 in Semishade Zones 4–8
FLOWERING SPAN: Early May to June
NATURAL COLOR: Coppery red with yellow spurs
ORIGIN: Horticultural hybrid of *E. alpinum* × *E. pinnatum* var. *colchicum*
A novel color breakthrough that some identify as orange in catalogs, this

hybrid has both foliage with a coarse appearance and skimpy general growth. Culture is the same as for *E. grandiflorum.*

Epimedium × youngianum   8–12 in   Semishade   Zones 4–8
   FLOWERING SPAN: Early May to mid-June
   NATURAL COLOR: White to rose
   ORIGIN: Horticultural hybrid of *E. diphyllum × E. grandiflorum*
      These 1-in, drooping blossoms have short spurs and are heavier-textured than those of the other species, and rise above smaller, fine-textured leaves. Cultivate as for *E. grandiflorum.* The best-known and popular cultivar, 'Niveum', is pure white throughout and only 7 in tall, while 'Roseum' is rosy lilac. (See photo.)

Erigeron glaucus (hispidus)   (beach fleabane, seaside daisy)   12–18 in   Sun   Zones 6–10
   FLOWERING SPAN: Early May to mid-June, continual on the Pacific Coast
   NATURAL COLOR: Lilac to violet
   DISTRIBUTION: Coastal southern California to northern Oregon
      Usually evergreen, the sprawling mat has broad, whitened leaves which can elongate to 6 in when grown in full sun. Generous flowering of 1–2-in blossoms with upturned petals around a golden center create a striking rock garden accent on sandy, alkaline soils of good drainage. It adapts well to exposed sites, especially along the shoreline. Propagation is best handled by division only. Insect pests are infrequent, but the "aster yellows" disease can cause stunting or discoloration of the leaves. Its cultivars include: 'Albus', white; 'Elstead Pink', light mauve; 'Roger Raiche', deep purple; and 'Roseus', rosy pink.

Galax urceolata (aphylla)   (wand-flower, beetleweed)   6–24 in   Semishade
   Zones 5–8
   FLOWERING SPAN: Late May to July
   NATURAL COLOR: White
   DISTRIBUTION: Virginia to Georgia
      The glossy evergreen leaves of this perennial have long been used in florists' decorative work because of their size, color, and durability. In the garden the new foliage is bright green but changes later to bronze and remains that color through the winter. The leathery, 3–5-in, rounded leaves occur on long, wiry stalks up to 9 in in length, and the 3-in, narrow flower stems are compactly filled with very tiny blossoms. It likes a moist, cool, acid, humusy soil in semishade to full shade and thrives nicely in conjunction with members of the rhododendron family. Spring or early autumn division is recommended for propagation. Diseases and insect nuisances are not common.

Aethionema coridifolium

Ajuga genevensis
'Metallica'

Ajuga pyramidalis

Ajuga reptans
'Alba'

MAY

Alchemilla mollis

Amsonia tabernaemontana

Anemone sylvestris

Aquilegia × *hybrida*
'Snow Queen'

Arenaria verna

Arisaema triphyllum

Armeria maritima

Asarum europaeum

Astrantia major

Baptisia australis

Camassia cusickii

Campanula poscharskyana

Convallaria majalis

Cornus canadensis (fruit)

Corydalis bulbosa

Corydalis lutea

MAY

Cypripedium acaule

Dianthus × allwoodii
'Doris'

Dianthus deltoides
'Albus'

Dianthus gratianopolitanus

Dicentra formosa
'Luxuriant'

Dicentra spectabilis

Doronicum cordatum
'Miss Mason'

Doronicum pardalianches

Endymion hispanicus

Epimedium pinnatum var. *colchicum*

Epimedium × rubrum

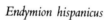

Epimedium × youngianum
'Niveum'

Galium odoratum

Geranium endressii
'Johnson's Blue'

Geranium sanguineum

Geranium sanguineum var. *prostratum*

Geum quellyon
'Lady Stratheden'

Hedyotis caerulea

Iberis sempervirens
'Purity'

Ipheion uniflora

Iris
cultivars (Bearded: Standard Tall)

Iris
'Royal Touch' (Bearded: Standard Tall)

Iris cristata

Iris pseudacorus

Iris tectorum

Lamium maculatum

Lamium maculatum
'Beacon Silver'

Lathyrus vernus

Linum perenne

Myosotis scorpioides

Ornithogalum umbellatum

Paeonia lactiflora (Single)
cultivars

Paeonia lactiflora (Japanese)
cultivar

Paeonia lactiflora (Semidouble) cultivar

Paeonia lactiflora (Double) cultivar

Paeonia officinalis 'Rubra Plena'

Papaver alpinum

Phlox divaricata

Phlox stolonifera

Podophyllum peltatum

Polemonium caeruleum

Polygonatum biflorum

Primula japonica

Ranunculus aconitifolius
'Luteus Plenus'

Ranunculus repens

Smilacina racemosa

Smilacina racemosa (fruit)

Symphytum grandiflorum

Thalictrum aquilegifolium

Thermopsis montana

Tiarella cordifolia

Tradescantia × *andersoniana*

Trollius europaeus

Trollius europaeus
'Orange Princess'

Tulipa (Darwin)
'Aristocrat'

Tulipa (Lily-flowered)
'West Point'

Tulipa (Cottage)
'Unique'

Tulipa (Cottage: Viridiflora Type)
'Court Lady'

Tulipa (Rembrandt)
'Cordell Hull'

Tulipa (Double Late)
'Angelique'

Tulipa (Parrot)
'Estella Rijnveld'

Tulipa (Fringed)
'Maja'

Tulipa mixture

Veronica latifolia
'Crater Lake Blue'

Viola canadensis

Viola hastata

Waldsteinia fragaroides

Galium odoratum (Asperula odorata) (sweet woodruff) 6–8 in Semishade
Zones 4–8
FLOWERING SPAN: Mid-May to mid-June
NATURAL COLOR: White
DISTRIBUTION: Europe, western Asia, North Africa

The dried leaves and stems of this ground cover are fragrant like new-mown hay and have long been used to flavor liqueurs and wines as well as to create durable sachets. Lancelike, 1-in leaves arranged in whorls of 8 are topped by star-shaped, ¼-in blossoms in loose clusters. Best grown in a moist, well-drained, acid, humusy soil from semishade to full shade, it can also tolerate dryness beneath maples if the soil remains fertile and loose. Growth is more rapid with consistent moisture, and the plant may become truly invasive. Spring or early autumn division is the workable propagation technique, and no pests or diseases seem to bother it. Because it is very shallow-rooted, however, the plant can die out in severe climates if there is little winter snow cover. Light mulching can help prevent this. (See photo.)

Geranium endressii 15–18 in Sun Zones 4–8
FLOWERING SPAN: Late May to September
NATURAL COLOR: Rosy pink
DISTRIBUTION: Pyrenees Mountains

Heavy mounds of dull-surfaced, light green, 2–4-in, nicely incised leaves, which color reddish in autumn, are enlivened by generous amounts of showy, 1½-in, saucer-shaped blossoms, two to a stem, at the main flush of bloom. For the rest of the season the flowering is apparent but spotty. Favoring full sun or light shading equally, this hardy, vigorous perennial does well in any consistently moist, well-drained soil of just average fertility. Spring or autumn division, summer stem cuttings, and seeding give similarly good propagation results. Insects appear to shun the plant, but various leaf spot diseases, botrytis disease, and "crinkle" can be handicaps to attractive growth. These cultivars have superior color: 'Johnson's Blue', lavender-blue; and 'Wargrave Pink', deep pink. (See photo.)

Geranium maculatum (wild geranium, wild cranesbill) 12–18 in Semishade
Zones 3–9
FLOWERING SPAN: Late May to July
NATURAL COLOR: Pale rose to deep pink
DISTRIBUTION: Maine to Georgia, west to South Dakota

From a basal cluster of deeply cut, dull green leaves 2–8 in wide, come erect stems bearing loose clusters of 1-in, noticeable, cup-shaped flowers. While not as showy in bloom as other species, the plant is reliable and fits well into wild garden spaces. Any average soil with reasonable moisture in semishade suits it readily, and an annual topdressing with compost or humus keeps it from drying out in summer and also protects its plump, ground-level buds from loss in winter. Spring or autumn division of the stout rhizomes, along with seeding, give good propagation results. Pests are the same as for *G. endressii.* A white form, 'Album', is known but difficult to find in cultivation.

Geranium sanguineum (bloody cranesbill) 12–18 in Sun Zones 4–9
FLOWERING SPAN: Late May to October
NATURAL COLOR: Purplish red
DISTRIBUTION: Europe, western Asia

Vigorous in sunny borders or at the edges of woodlots, this perennial has very hairy, lacy, 7-parted, 4-in leaves and large quantities of saucer-shaped, 1½-in, vivid blossoms all summer. Adaptable to almost any well-drained, moist soil, the foliage turns noticeably red with frost. Division in spring or autumn, plus seeding, work well. Disease problems are listed under G. *endressii.* A scarce white cultivar, 'Album', is 9 in tall and prostrate in habit, while the popular variety, *prostratum,* which was formerly named *lancastriense,* has pale pink blossoming with darker veining, a creeping, carpetlike growth, is only 6–8 in tall, and tolerates drought very well. (See photos.)

Geum × *borisii* 9–12 in Sun Zones 5–9
FLOWERING SPAN: Late May to July, repeats in early autumn
NATURAL COLOR: Orange-scarlet to yellow-orange
ORIGIN: Horticultural hybrid of G. *bulgaricum* × G. *reptans*

Wedge-shaped, 6–8-in, deeply toothed leaves form heavy mounds of bright green foliage close to the ground and surround erect, leafy stems with sprays of showy, double-petaled, nodding, ½-in flowers. Provide a light, rich, moist, and well-drained soil (especially in winter) with full sun or light shading. Protect with a light mulch in severely cold areas. Division in spring or autumn, together with seeding, is the recommended propagation method. Diseases are not problematic, and sow bugs are the prime insect nuisance.

Geum quellyon (chiloense, atrosanguineum) (Chilean avens) 12–24 in Sun Zones 5–9
FLOWERING SPAN: Late May to July, repeats in early autumn
NATURAL COLOR: Scarlet
DISTRIBUTION: Chile

Although this species is not reliably hardy in every locality, its cultivars, which are the plants normally offered by nurseries, are more durable. The flowers are 1½ in across on erect stems above a clump of 3-parted, deeply cut leaves often up to a foot long. Cultivate as for G. × *borisii.* Included with the many cultivars are: 'Dolly North', orange-yellow; 'Fire Opal', single, orange-red, 3-in blossoms; 'Lady Stratheden', semidouble, clear yellow, tall-growing; 'Mrs. Bradshaw', semidouble, ½-in flowers of crimson, tall; 'Prince of Orange', orange-yellow; and 'Princess Juliana', bright orange, tall. Both 'Lady Stratheden' and 'Mrs. Bradshaw' appear to weaken and diminish in quality faster than the others. (See photo.)

Geum rivale (Indian chocolate, purple avens, water avens) 18–24 in Semishade
Zones 3–8
FLOWERING SPAN: Late May to mid-July
NATURAL COLOR: Purple with orange-pink petals
DISTRIBUTION: Eurasia, North America
Drooping, clawlike, ½-in flowers on reddish, unbranched stems rise from a clump of ground-hugging, hairy, 3-parted leaves with noticeable teeth on the margins. It likes a wet meadow or bog in semishade, and spring division or seeding propagate it satisfactorily. Diseases and pests are uncommon. The cultivar 'Leonard's Variety' carries double, coppery rose blossoms.

Geum triflorum (Apache plume, prairie smoke) 9–15 in Semishade Zones 3–8
FLOWERING SPAN: Early May to July
NATURAL COLOR: Purplish red
DISTRIBUTION: Western New York to British Columbia, south to Illinois, Nebraska, and Montana
Unusual in this genus for having feathery, pinnately compound leaves covered with soft hairs, this compact wildflower carries at least 3 drooping, jug-shaped, 2-in flowers on each stalk. The spent blossoms later become 2-in seed panicles resembling miniature feather dusters and can be collected and dried for indoor use. Provide a light, humusy, consistently moist soil and propagate either by division in spring or by seeding. Pest and disease problems are negligible.

Hedyotis caerulea (Houstonia caerulea) (bluets, quaker-ladies) 1–6 in Sun
Zones 4–8
FLOWERING SPAN: Early May to June
NATURAL COLOR: Violet, pale blue, white
DISTRIBUTION: Southeastern Canada to Georgia, west to Arkansas and Wisconsin
Tufts of narrow, dark green, ½-in leaves produce a host of slender flower stalks topped with single, 4-pointed, ½-in blooms showing a deep yellow center. Thriving in moist, well-drained, average soil almost anywhere, the plant probably should be installed only in a wild area since it self-seeds widely and can readily overwhelm a nearby lawn or mulched bed. No pest or disease seems to bother this stalwart plant, nor does semishade. (See photo.)

Hedyotis purpurea (Houstonia purpurea)   6–18 in   Semishade   Zones 4–8
FLOWERING SPAN: Late May to July
NATURAL COLOR: Purple to lilac
DISTRIBUTION: Southern New England to Michigan and Missouri, south to Alabama and eastern Texas

Spear-shaped, 1–2-in leaves form a tuft at ground level with long flower stalks carrying small clusters of ½-in, funnel-shaped blossoms. This perennial enjoys a dry, rocky, acid soil but needs semishade to do its best. Spring division is the only recommended propagation method, and there are no pest or disease problems of concern. There are many local variations of flower color and size throughout its wide native range of distribution.

Hutchinsia alpina   (alpencress)   2–4 in   Semishade   Zones 4–8
FLOWERING SPAN: Mid-May to July
NATURAL COLOR: White
DISTRIBUTION: Mountains of central and southern Europe

As a rock garden ground cover for semishade, this long-flowering perennial has glossy, dark green, 1-in, feathery leaves in basal tufts. Attractive clusters of ⅛-in flowers similar to the April-blooming *Draba sibirica* cover the foliage in its flush of bloom. Best grown in a well-drained alkaline soil with ample moisture, the plant is readily propagated either by seed, summer stem cuttings, or division. Problems with pests or diseases are unknown.

Hypoxis hirsuta (erecta)   (star grass)   9–12 in   Sun   Zones 4–9
FLOWERING SPAN: Late May to August
NATURAL COLOR: Bright yellow
DISTRIBUTION: Maine to Florida, west to Texas

Tufts of narrow, grasslike leaves up to 1 ft long produce clusters of 6-pointed, 1-in, starlike blossoms which can flower well into summer if soil moisture is consistent. The plant prospers in acid, well-drained, sandy soil from sun to semishade. Spring division of the dormant corms is the reliable propagation technique. Diseases and pests are rare.

Iberis saxatilis   (rock candytuft)   3–6 in   Sun   Zones 4–8
FLOWERING SPAN: Mid-May to mid-June
NATURAL COLOR: White
DISTRIBUTION: Southern Europe

Often confused with the more popular *I. sempervirens,* this species has narrower foliage and terminal flowers. Noticeable in rock gardens enjoying full sun, the flat-topped, 1½-in flower heads of this prostrate evergreen appear on twisted stems with ⅛-in, cylindrical leaves. It likes a well-drained, gravelly, alkaline soil but will adapt to an acid condition with ground limestone added to its planting bed annually. The surest propagation method is spring division of reasonably young plants. No special pests or diseases bother it.

Iberis sempervirens (edging candytuft) 9–12 in Sun Zones 4–8
FLOWERING SPAN: Mid-May to mid-June
NATURAL COLOR: White
DISTRIBUTION: Mediterranean Europe

Useful as a shrubby evergreen edging or rock garden accent, the neatly spreading mound of foliage and profuse, side-shoot flowering of this durable perennial is rarely matched for year-long attractiveness. Dark green, 1½-in, elongated leaves are evident all year on slender, arching stems and yet are normally fully masked by the generous springtime bloom from 1½-in-wide, slightly pyramidal flower heads. All species should be sheared back at least ⅓, including foliage, right after flowering to promote compactness. Thriving in full sun or very light shading on well-drained, rich soil, either acid or alkaline, this attractive plant is readily propagated by late summer stem cuttings. Diseases or insect pests are not bothersome.

Many white cultivars are available: 'Autumn Beauty', 8 in, reblooms lightly in autumn; 'Christmas Snow', 6 in, flowers occasionally in autumn and early winter in mild areas; 'Little Gem', 6 in, compact; 'Purity', 8 in, dense, long-flowering, and the most popular form; 'Snowflake', 10 in, showy, compact, and large-flowered; and 'Snowmantle', 10 in, wide-spreading and heavily flowered. (See photo.)

Ipheion uniflora (Brodiaea uniflora) (spring starflower) 6–8 in Sun Zones 5–10
FLOWERING SPAN: Early May to June
NATURAL COLOR: Pale lilac
DISTRIBUTION: Argentina, Uruguay

Solitary, 1-in, trumpet-shaped flowers open into a star design above narrow, grasslike foliage which withers by midsummer. Not always durable, this bulb can potentially increase into large displays from its offshoots where the soil is rich, well-drained, and reasonably moist. It accepts either full sun or light shading equally, and new colonies can be planted during early autumn. Pests and diseases are rare. The cultivar 'Wisley Blue' multiplies with ease and shows violet blossoming with a white center. (See photo.)

Iris "Bearded" hybrids 8–40 in Sun Zones 3–9
FLOWERING SPAN: Early May to mid-June, occasional rebloom in autumn
NATURAL COLOR: All those of the rainbow
ORIGIN: Horticultural hybrids from many sources

As with other plant categories having great appeal for both the commercial grower and the gardener, the horticultural iris has had its share of confusing naming and classification. The American Iris Society has now devised a reclassification system placing the initial emphasis on the 2 main forms of the underground stem: the bulb and the rhizome. Because the rhizomatous iris is the largest division in cultivation, it has been further divided into the bearded, or eupogon, the beardless, or apogon, and the crested, or evansia, groups. A beard is the fuzzy tuft emerging from the blossom throat and continuing down the fall, or downturned petal. It may differ in color from the rest of the flower. The rhizomes of the spring-flowering bearded iris are normally large and fleshy, while those of the early summer beardless iris generally have small rhizomes. Some of the new bearded iris hybrids rebloom in early autumn, opening up a new category of performance that will surely enlarge soon.

The plant height in flower, the blooming time, and the size of the individual blossom are the main determinants used in classifying those iris which are in the eupogon, or "true bearded" category. The 6 horticultural divisions of bearded iris are: miniature dwarf, standard dwarf, intermediate, miniature tall, border, and standard tall. The miniature dwarfs, which bloom mainly in April, are described in that month under *I. pumila*. Culture for all bearded iris is also given under that heading. (See photos.)

Classification of Bearded Iris

STANDARD DWARF
Classified as being 10–15 in tall with leaves nearly as high as the blooms and flowers 3–4 in across; starts blooming in early May.
WHITE: 'Baby Snowflake', 'Moonspinner', 'Small Cloud'
CREAM: 'Baria', 'Blonde Doll', 'Lemon Flare'
YELLOW: 'Brassie', 'Coreop', 'Golden Fare'
YELLOW AND BROWN: 'Centerpiece', 'Lillie-Var'
BLUE: 'Blue Denim', 'Small Sky', 'Small Wonder', 'Tinkerbell'
PURPLE: 'Dark Fairy', 'Pagan Midget'
BLACK: 'Little Grackle'
RED-TONED: 'Royal Thumbprint', 'Velvet Caper'
BLEND: 'Aqua Green', 'Little Witch', 'Sky Torch', 'Spring Mist'

INTERMEDIATE
Classified as being 15–28 in tall with flowers 2–4 in across; starts blooming in mid-May.
WHITE: 'Arctic Flare', 'Cloud Fluff', 'Little Angel'
YELLOW: 'Barbi', 'Butterbit', 'Lime Ripples'
YELLOW AND WHITE: 'Frosty Lemonade', 'Interim'
BLUE: 'Arctic Ruffles', 'Blue Fragrance', 'Moonchild'

LAVENDER: 'First Lilac'
PURPLE: 'Black Magic', 'Elfin Royal', 'Marine Wave'
BLACK: 'Black Hawk', 'Dark Eden'
RED-TONED: 'Maroon Caper', 'Red Orchid', 'Ruby Glow'
PINK: 'Lillipinkput', 'Pink Fancy', 'Pink Reward', 'Sweet Allegro'

MINIATURE TALL

Classified as being 18–26 in tall with flowers 2½ in across on slender, wiry stems; commonly known as "table iris"; starts blooming in late May. The few cultivars are: 'Cherwink', light blue; 'Daystar', white with orange beards; 'Kinglet', yellow; 'Little Helen', white with violet falls; 'Tom Tit', deep blue-violet; and 'Warbler', yellow.

BORDER

Classified as being under 28 in tall with flowers 3–4 in wide appearing 3–4 per stalk and having smaller-scaled blossoms and stems than the tall bearded; starts blooming in late May. Here the cultivar list is also short: 'Black Forest', blue-black; 'Bluet', blue; 'Botany Bay', violet; 'Chocoleto', brown; 'Echoette', white; 'Fairy Jewels', white and gold; 'Glacier Bay', white and blue; 'Little Dude', blue; 'Pagoda', pink; 'Priscilla', white; 'Summer Sunset', apricot; 'Timmie Too', deep violet; and 'Tulare', golden yellow.

STANDARD TALL

Classified as being over 28 in tall with 3–4 blossoms per stalk and 4–8-in-wide flowers; starts blooming by late May. This group is further subdivided: *self*, all one color; *plicata*, veined with a second color; *bicolor*, standards (or upright petals) one color, falls (or downturned petals) another; *bitone*, standards and falls two values of one color; and *blend*, two or more intermixed colors. Cultivars are very numerous and this list is an abbreviated one.

SELF

WHITE: 'Arctic Fury', 'Celestial Snow', 'Cliffs of Dover', 'Helen Hayes', 'Henry Shaw', 'Irish Linen', 'Laced Cotton', 'Poet's Dream', 'Snow Goddess', 'Super White', 'The Citadel'

CREAM: 'Country Cream', 'Crinkled Ivory', 'Paleface', 'Soaring Kite'

LIGHT YELLOW: 'Cool Comfort', 'Golden Anniversary', 'On Target'

DEEP YELLOW: 'Bravado', 'Carolina Gold', 'Front Page', 'Gold Piece'

BUFF TO BROWN: 'Brass Accents', 'Bronze Bell', 'Butterscotch Kiss', 'Carmela', 'Dark Chocolate', 'Gingerbread Castle', 'Olympic Torch'

RED: 'Ahoy', 'Bang', 'Captain Gallant', 'Garnet Royal', 'Rampage', 'Raspberry Ripples', 'Tall Chief'

PINK: 'Garden Party', 'Lynn Hall', 'Mary Randall', 'Picture Pink', 'Pink Fulfillment', 'Rose Flame', 'Spring Charm', 'Taffy Pink'

APRICOT TO ORANGE: 'Apricot Dancer', 'Apricot Lustre', 'Flaming Day',

'Glittering Amber', 'Magnet', 'Orange Crush', 'Orange Frills'

BLUE: 'Blue Luster', 'Blue Raven', 'Demetria', 'Fox Grapes', 'Jean Sibelius', 'Marriott', 'Pacific Panorama', 'Sparkling Waters'

VIOLET: 'Indiglow', 'Jersey Beauty', 'Polka Time', 'Royal Touch', 'Silent Majesty'

ORCHID TO LILAC: 'Alpine Rose', 'Hope Divine', 'Lilac Festival', 'Palais Royal'

BLACK: 'Black Onyx', 'Early Dusk', 'Edenite', 'Licorice Stick', 'Night Deposit', 'Night Owl', 'Night Song'

PLICATA

'Benton Susan', cream with brown; 'Chinquapin', cream with golden brown; 'Dot and Dash', deep purple with white; 'Gene Wild', cream with rose; 'Golden Spice', yellow with brown; 'Loop the Loop', white with violet-blue; 'Memphis Lass', rose with burgundy; 'Moongate', white with blue; 'Tea Apron', white with blue.

BICOLOR

'Arctic Skies', pale blue standards and white falls; 'Baby's Bonnet', white standards and salmon falls; 'Bright Hour', purple standards and white falls; 'Cloverdale', white standards and rosy lilac falls; 'Kahili', pale gold standards and red falls; 'On Parade', beige standards and reddish falls; 'Panay', white standards and green-yellow falls; 'Pretender', yellow standards and dark blue falls; 'Rain Cloud', blue-violet standards and white falls.

BITONE

'Arcady', pale blue tones; 'Braithwaite', lavender and purple tones; 'Helen Collingwood', pale lavender-blue standards and deep purple falls; 'Melodrama', pale blue-violet standards and deep lilac falls; 'Toll Gate', pale yellow tones; 'Viking Admiral', medium blue standards and ice blue falls.

BLEND

'Allaglow', golden brown with blue overtones; 'Gala Madrid', butterscotch gold standards with red falls edged in brown-red and flushed with violet-blue; 'Hindu Wand', chartreuse, yellow, buff, and brown; 'Jungle Bird', violet, rose, and claret; 'Lula Marguerite', pale blue with gold overtones; 'Melbreak', rosy pink with brown overtones; 'Smoke Mist', apricot with mauve overtones; 'Watermelon', bright pink with yellow-green overtones.

Iris cristata (dwarf crested iris, crested iris) 4–9 in Semishade Zones 6–9
FLOWERING SPAN: Early May to June
NATURAL COLOR: Pale lavender-blue, violet, purple
DISTRIBUTION: Maryland to Georgia, west to Oklahoma

Eventually forming wide mats, this creeping perennial has ½-in-wide, flat leaves taller than its blooms, but the tips of the foliage arch backward to show the flowers. The wide-opening, 4-in blossoms have narrow petals crested with showy tufts of hairs in ridges of white or yellow. Thriving in a moist, rich, acid, humusy soil with semishade, the plant accepts more sun if kept consistently moist. Division of the slender rhizomes right after flowering is recommended, and there are no bothersome diseases or pests. A few cultivars exist: 'Alba', pure white, and 'Caerulea', sky blue. (See photo.)

Iris gracilipes (slender iris) 6–15 in Semishade Zones 4–9
FLOWERING SPAN: Late May to mid-June
NATURAL COLOR: Lilac-pink, shaded white
DISTRIBUTION: Japan

Ruffled, wide-petaled blossoms with conspicuous orange crests appear on slender, branched stalks above a heavy clump of ½-in-wide, arching, swordlike foliage. This iris is attractively flowered for wild garden spaces and in woodlots with dappled shading, and its rhizomes divide readily in early spring as the favored propagation method. Pests and diseases are of no concern. A white cultivar, 'Alba', exists but shows less vigor. The American Iris Society carries this species in the evansia, or "crested," subsection.

Iris pallida (*odoratissima*) (orris) 24–36 in Sun Zones 4–9
FLOWERING SPAN: Mid-May to mid-June
NATURAL COLOR: Light lavender-blue
DISTRIBUTION: Southern Tyrol

Highly variable in flower color when cultivated, this is the iris used not only in the making of perfume but also in creating the popular tall, bearded forms we all know and use today. It develops stout stems and almost-evergreen, 1½-in-wide, grayish green leaves up to 2 ft long. The flower buds are covered with a silvery, noticeable sheathing, and the blossoms are pleasantly scented. Provide a well-drained, average-fertility soil with reasonable moisture in sun or light shading. Divide for propagation after flowering. Several of its available cultivars offer unusual foliage coloring: 'Albo-variegata', with leaves striped in white; 'Dalmatica', clear lavender blossoms with larger leaves; and 'Variegata', with foliage noticeably edged in cream. Pests and diseases are rare.

Iris pseudacorus (*bastardii, lutea*) (yellow iris, yellow flag) 36–60 in Sun Zones 3–9
FLOWERING SPAN: Late May to July
NATURAL COLOR: Bright to pale yellow

DISTRIBUTION: Western Europe, North Africa, eastern United States

Naturally at home along watersides and in boggy conditions, this perennial creates generous clumps of coarse-looking, swordlike foliage up to 1½ in wide and as tall as 5 ft. Garden cultivation on drier sites is workable with consistent moisture and humusy soil in sun or light shade. The broad, 4-in flowers are center-marked with prominent brown veins. Early spring or autumn division, along with autumn seeding, gives good propagation results. Problems with diseases or insects are minor. This species is carried as an apogon or "beardless" iris by the American Iris Society. A number of cultivars exist: 'Alba', creamy white; 'Flora Plena', double; 'Gigantea', larger flowers, soft yellow; and 'Variegata', showing leaves with yellow or cream stripes early, turning all-green later. (See photo.)

Iris tectorum (wall iris, roof iris) 12–15 in Sun Zones 5–9
FLOWERING SPAN: Late May to mid-June
NATURAL COLOR: Bright lilac
DISTRIBUTION: Central and southwestern China

Although this hardy, semievergreen plant is actually grown on thatched roofs in the Orient, it does come down to earth well in gardens. The 3-in wavy flowers are wide-opening and appear above thin, 1-ft-long, swordlike foliage 1½ in wide. Tolerant of moderately dry sites and semishade, this rhizomatous plant enjoys the same cultural care as *I. cristata.* There is a less hardy, white cultivar, 'Alba', with noticeable yellow crests. The American Iris Society catalogs them as evansia, or "crested," irises. (See photo.)

Jeffersonia diphylla (twinleaf) 8–10 in Semishade Zones 4–8
FLOWERING SPAN: Late May to mid-June
NATURAL COLOR: White
DISTRIBUTION: Southeastern Canada to Alabama, west to Iowa

Closely resembling *Hepatica* of April in flower appearance, the unusual characteristic of this wildflower is its deeply cleft, 5-in-wide and 3-in-long leaves, which resemble a set of lungs in outline. After the 1-in flowers fade, the foliage continues to elongate. By late summer unique, pear-shaped seed pods appear and persist for the rest of the growing season. Provide a moist, acid, humusy soil and propagate either by seeding or by autumn division of the thick rootstock. Pests and diseases are unknown.

Jeffersonia dubia 6–9 in Semishade Zones 4–8
FLOWERING SPAN: Late May to July
NATURAL COLOR: Light lavender-blue
DISTRIBUTION: Northeastern Asia

This scarce species has 1-in, bowl-shaped flowers and 4-in-wide, heart-shaped leaves with ragged edges. Its culture is the same as for *J. diphylla.*

Lamium maculatum (spotted dead nettle) 8–18 in Semishade Zones 3–9
FLOWERING SPAN: Late May to August
NATURAL COLOR: Pink-purple
DISTRIBUTION: Europe, British Isles, New England to North Carolina

A vigorous, sprawling plant useful as a summer "filler" over beds of earlier spring bulbs, it carries hooded, 1-in flowers in ascending whorls on erect stalks. The 1–2-in crinkled leaves have a central blotch of gray-green to creamy green highlighting the shady locations it calls home. Easily tolerant of drought, the plant accepts just about any soil and light exposure—except full sun. Spring division is the simplest propagation method, although seeding works well, too. Diseases and insect nuisances are uncommon. Its cultivars are superior and less invasive for growth: 'Beacon Silver', not as cold-tolerant but offers mostly silvered foliage and magenta pink flowering; 'White Nancy', foliage mottled in silver with white flowers, accepts more sun in northerly locations (See photos.)

Lathyrus vernus (Orobus vernus) (spring vetchling) 9–18 in Sun Zones 4–9
FLOWERING SPAN: Early May to late May
NATURAL COLOR: Reddish purple
DISTRIBUTION: Europe

Neat in growth and slow to expand, this perennial carries attractive, pinnately compound, semiglossy, long-pointed, 3-in foliage of deep green. The erect flower stalks sport clusters of ¾-in, pealike blossoms which are held above the leaves. Plant in a sunny location on an average-fertility, moist soil, and propagate by early spring division or by seed. The cultivar 'Roseus' has pink flowers, while 'Spring Melody' carries violet-blue ones. Diseases and insects make no important inroads. (See photo.)

Linum narbonense (Narbonne flax) 18–24 in Sun Zones 5–9
FLOWERING SPAN: Late May to late June
NATURAL COLOR: Azure blue
DISTRIBUTION: Mediterranean Europe

A delicate, airy accent for borders or rock gardens with full sun, this somewhat tender perennial has 5-pointed, funnel-shaped, 1½-in flowers with white centers arranged in loose clusters on thin, erect stems. The narrow leaves vary from ¾–1½ in and are bluish green. Grow on a moist, sandy, well-drained soil and propagate by summer stem cuttings or seed because division of the long, tangled roots is chancy. Cutworms and rust disease are its chief afflictions. In severe climates, mulch lightly for winter.

Linum perenne (perennial flax) 18–24 in Sun Zones 5–9
FLOWERING SPAN: Late May to mid-July
NATURAL COLOR: Pale blue
DISTRIBUTION: Europe

Less robust and smaller-flowered than *L. narbonense, L. perenne* has graceful, slender flower stalks with arching tips and all-blue blossoming. These flowers last but a day but are produced in generous quantities for extended bloom. In late summer reduce the foliage by half, including the flower stalks, to prevent plant exhaustion from overblooming. The cultivar 'Alba' has white blossoms, while the variety *lewisii* of western North America is sky blue, grows to almost 3 ft, and accepts semishading. Culture is the same as for *L. narbonense*. (See photo.)

Lithospermum canescens   (hoary gromwell, yellow puccoon)   9–15 in   Sun
Zones 3–8
FLOWERING SPAN: Early May to June
NATURAL COLOR: Orangish yellow
DISTRIBUTION: Southeastern Canada to Georgia, west to Texas
Round, ½-in, noticeable flowers appear in arching sprays above ½-in-wide, willowlike leaves up to 1½ in long. Short, white hairs on the stems and leaves give the plant a grayish cast, accenting the bright flowers. Easy to grow in dry, infertile, acid, sandy, or gravelly soil, it blooms less in rich, moist locations. Seeding or root cuttings are the better propagation techniques since safe division of the long, woody roots is very difficult. Pests and diseases appear to avoid this perennial.

Lychnis viscaria (vulgaris, Viscaria viscosa)   (German catchfly)   12–20 in   Sun
Zones 3–8
FLOWERING SPAN: Late May to July
NATURAL COLOR: Reddish purple, deep purple, purplish pink
DISTRIBUTION: Europe, Turkey, Central Asia, Siberia
Flowering profusely in sun-drenched locations, these blossoms are of a color difficult to incorporate successfully in a mixed border. They seem less strident when planted close to white-flowering plants. Branched stalks with single, flat-faced, 1-in florets rise from tufts of 5-in, grasslike foliage. The stem part beneath the flower is sticky. Withstanding drought and cold well, it prefers a moist, sandy, well-drained location. Self-sown seedlings are rampant and can soon overcrowd small spaces. There are no insect nuisances, but smut disease can be a serious affliction. The cultivars are preferred to the parent: 'Alba', white, long-flowering: 'Rosea', pink; 'Splendens', rosy pink, low; 'Splendens Flore-Pleno', deep pink to magenta, very double, enduring; and 'Zulu', salmon, tall.

Mazus reptans   1–2 in   Semishade   Zones 5–9
FLOWERING SPAN: Late May to July
NATURAL COLOR: Purplish blue
DISTRIBUTION: Himalaya Mountains
As a tidy carpeting between stepping-stones in a shaded garden, this mat of

bright green foliage is attractive even when out of flower. The ¾-in, lobelialike flowers appear in profuse clusters of 2–5 on erect, wiry stems. Rooting readily at each leaf node as it expands, the plant spreads quickly on rich, consistently moist soil. But since it is shallow-rooted, it can fail to survive a cold, unsnowy winter. Light mulching beforehand can help prevent this problem. Division in spring is the simplest propagation method, yet seeding is productive, too. Pests and diseases are uncommon. A white-flowered form is known but rare in cultivation.

Myosotis scorpioides (palustris) (forget-me-not) 6–18 in Sun Zones 3–8

FLOWERING SPAN: Late May to August
NATURAL COLOR: Bright blue
DISTRIBUTION: Europe, Asia, southeastern Canada to Louisiana

In very moist, streamside locations in full sun or dappled shading, the mat-forming habit of this hardy, long-blooming perennial comes into its own. Pinkish buds produce ongoing clusters of ¼-in, rounded blossoms with either yellow, pink, or white eyes above light green, narrow, 2–3-in leaves at ground level. Enjoying a wet, gravelly soil, it will accept garden conditions if kept very moist at all times. Spring division of the creeping rhizomes and summer stem cuttings work better than seeding for propagation. Both mildew and red spider mites on the leaves can be disfiguring. The preferred variety, *semperflorens,* is rich blue, only 8 in tall, and lives up to its name by flowering constantly until early frost. (See photo.)

Myosotis sylvatica (*oblongata*) (garden forget-me-not) 12–20 in Semishade Zones 3–8

FLOWERING SPAN: Late May to August
NATURAL COLOR: Sky blue, occasionally white or pink
DISTRIBUTION: Europe, northern Asia

These noticeable clusters of ⅓-in, rounded flowers can enliven the summer months of any semishaded garden area with reasonably moist, humusy soil. The hairy foliage clump is gray-green, and the stems tend to sprawl. Although this wildflower is perennial in many areas, it often behaves more like a biennial that keeps reseeding itself generously in the same location. Nevertheless, the visual effect of a less dense planting is still very satisfying. Too many growers offer this plant as *M. alpestris* since it is similar-looking when young, but *M. alpestris,* the state flower of Alaska, is shorter in all its parts and rarely cultivated. Mildew and red spider mites are disfiguring to the foliage as with *M. scorpioides.* The many cultivars are: 'Alba', white; 'Compacta', dwarfed; 'Fischeri', bluish pink, low; 'Oblonga Perfecta', early, larger flowers; 'Robusta Grandiflora', vigorous, over-sized blooms; and 'Rosea', pink.

Ornithogalum umbellatum   (star-of-Bethlehem, nap-at-noon) 6–12 in   Sun
Zones 4–10
FLOWERING SPAN: Early May to June
NATURAL COLOR: White
DISTRIBUTION: North Africa, southern France, Asia Minor

Grassy clumps of ¼-in-wide, deep green, narrow leaves up to 1 ft long spread apart to show a central multitude of short-stemmed, 1-in flowers with pointed petals, green-striped exteriors, and pure white interiors. They open fully only on sunny days, however, and even with sun close by early afternoon. Tolerant of light shading, this bulb has an easy tendency to self-seed in all directions annually and can become weedy if left to its own devices. It has no pests or diseases worth noting, and initial plantings can be installed in the autumn. Culture is the same as that for the April-blooming *O. nutans*. (See photo.)

Paeonia lactiflora (albiflora, chinensis) (Chinese peony) 24–48 in Sun Zones 3–8
FLOWERING SPAN: Late May to late June
NATURAL COLOR: White to pink in the wild, myriad variations from hybrids
DISTRIBUTION: Siberia, Tibet, China

If any perennial can be said to be truly long-lived in one place, this is the champion. Thriving clumps 80 years old or more are frequently recorded from many locations throughout the world. The historical record of their cultivation goes back 2000 years. (The tree peony, *P. suffruticosa*, is a perennial with woody stems and is not included here.) With such longevity and visual appeal, peonies deserve close attention to proper placement and correct planting, especially since they are not demanding—only selective. Peonies are fragrant and long-lasting when cut.

New spring growth is often reddish, and its quick enlargement soon produces many tall, unbranched, stout stems with much-divided, sizeable, glossy green leaves along with round flower buds. The weight of foliage and the large-scaled blossoms requires early support with encompassing metal hoops to mitigate the damage from downpours. Since the Chinese peony carries more than one flower bud per stem, the quick removal of side buds—which promotes a larger main bloom—is a matter of personal choice. When left in place, these side buds extend the blooming period. Unless the seed is wanted for propagation purposes, remove all flowering as it fades. The foliage mass continues as an attractive backdrop to other plants and may even offer some autumn coloring in bronze or red. To forestall future disease problems, always cut all current-season foliage to ground level in autumn and destroy it. Do not add it to your compost heap.

All peony types enjoy a well-drained, sandy-clay soil which has never before been used for peony cultivation. Intolerant of heavy shade and the invasive rootings of nearby vigorous shrubs or trees, they grow best in full sun in open bedding. The delicately colored types, however, benefit from light afternoon shading to preserve their tints longer. Thorough and frequent watering in dry summers, along with an annual application of a balanced fertilizer right after flowering, improves future blossoming.

The proper planting technique is important to long life and generous flowering. Either purchase nursery stock or divide old plants by mid-August or September (late October in the southern United States). Choose the best-liked and strongest plants for dividing. Dig an opening around the plant; slit the roots with a sharp spade; lift it from the ground with a spading fork; cut off any broken ends; and replant.

For each new plant excavate beforehand a pit at least 18 in deep and 24 in wide, and discard any rock or hardpan as unsuitable. Pile the acceptable earth to one side and intermix it with generous amounts of humus, moist peat moss, compost, or well-rotted manure—fresh manure is harmful—a pound of bonemeal or superphosphate, plus ground limestone if the soil is very acid. Redeposit this mix into the hole to a depth 10 in below the ground level, water well to settle it thoroughly, then add another 2 in of the dry soil mix to center the new peony roots snugly in place.

These roots are thick and brittle with large, pink-toned, fragile, underground buds or "eyes" close to the top. Cut off cleanly any broken, damaged, or raggedy parts to avoid root rot. Select divisions with at least 3 large buds—bud size varies with the particular hybrid—and place each unit in the middle of the hole with the tip of the lowest bud *no more than* 2 in below the surrounding ground level. If planted deeper, flowering will greatly diminish. Continue to backfill and work the soil carefully by hand between the roots. Water thoroughly and later backfill any depressions. Mulch the first winter to prevent heaving.

Botrytis disease, a sooty fungus afflicting buds and foliage, is a serious problem spread by wind and rain—not by the omnipresent ants on these perennials as long supposed—and requires immediate spraying control as well as discard of all infected plant parts. Scraping away and replacing the first inch or so of the spore-contaminated soil at the stems with fresh, limed topsoil often forestalls future infection. Other diseases are not as troublesome, and insect pests are uncommon.

The ongoing wealth of new hybrids in cultivation increases annually, and thousands of cultivar names are now registered. Blossom appearance is a handy guide for differentiation, and the American Peony Society uses these 4 major descriptions: *single,* having 5 or more large outer petals set around a broad cluster of pollen-bearing stamens; *Japanese* or *anemone,* having 5 or more petals around a center of either non-pollen-bearing staminodes or else a fluffy mass of narrow petals with a coloring similar to or complementary to the main petal hues; *semidouble,* having 5 or more outer petals surrounding broad inner petals intermixed with numerous rings with a prominent center of pollen-bearing stamens; and *double,* having 5 or more outer petals and a center almost fully transformed into heavy clusters of petals from modified stamens.

In the following list of highly regarded cultivars, the general time of bloom is given for each: "E" is early, "M" is midseason, and "L" is late. Color descriptions are also simplified to fit only the main color value. Many hybrids now carry blossoms 8 in in diameter. (See photos.)

Classification of Hybrid Chinese Peonies

WHITE
SINGLE: 'Dunlora' (E), 'Krinkled White' (M), 'Le Jour' (E), 'Requiem' (M)

JAPANESE: 'Ada Priscilla' (M), 'Bride's Dream' (M), 'Cheddar Gold' (M), 'Isani-Gidui' (M), 'Lotus Queen' (M), 'Moon of Nippon' (M), 'Pat Victor' (L)

SEMIDOUBLE: 'Mildred May' (M), 'Miss America' (E), 'Rare China' (M), 'White Rose' (L)

DOUBLE: 'Ann Cousins' (M), 'Avalanche' (M), 'Cheddar Surprise' (M), 'Elsa Sass' (L), 'Festiva Maxima' (E), 'Florence Nicholls' (M), 'George W. Payton' (L), 'Kelway's Glorious' (E), 'Le Cygne' (E), 'Moonglow' (M), 'Mother's Choice' (M), 'Nauvoo' (M), 'Nick Shaylor' (M), 'Ramona Lins' (L), 'The Fleece' (M), 'Victory' (L), 'White Ivory' (M)

LIGHT PINK
SINGLE: 'Dainty' (E), 'Dancing Nymph' (L), 'Dawn Pink' (M), 'Moon Mist' (E), 'Pink Princess' (M), 'Seashell' (M)

JAPANESE: 'Ama-no-sode' (M), 'Rose Valley' (M), 'Tamate-Boku' (L), 'Westerner' (M)

SEMIDOUBLE: 'Flamingo' (M), 'Lady Alexandra Duff' (M), 'Minnie Shaylor' (M), 'Silvia Saunders' (E), 'Zuzu' (M)

DOUBLE: 'Alice Harding' (M), 'Amberglow' (M), 'Ave Maria' (M), 'Chiffon Parfait' (L), 'Florence Ellis' (M), 'Gertrude Cox' (E), 'Hermione' (L), 'La Lorraine' (M), 'Mary Auten' (L), 'Moon River' (M), 'Nancy Dolman' (M), 'Nancy Nicholls' (M), 'Retta' (L), 'Solange' (M), 'Therese' (E), 'Wabash' (M), 'Westhill' (E)

DARK PINK
SINGLE: 'Cinderella' (M), 'Doreen' (M), 'Harriet Olney' (M), 'L'Etincelante' (M), 'Mischief' (M)

JAPANESE: 'Alice Roberts' (M), 'Butter Bowl' (M), 'Filigree' (M), 'Magnolia' (M), 'Sky Pilot' (M)

SEMIDOUBLE: 'Butch' (M), 'Cincinnati' (M), 'Paula Fay' (E)

DOUBLE: 'Doris Cooper' (L), 'Edulis Superba' (E), 'Frances Mains' (M), 'Glory Hallelujah' (L), 'Monsieur Jules Elie' (E), 'Mrs. Franklin D. Roosevelt' (M), 'Mrs. Livingstone Farrand' (L), 'Reine Hortense' (M), 'Sarah Bernhardt' (M), 'Tempest' (M), 'Vivid Rose' (L), 'Walter Faxon' (L)

RED

SINGLE: 'Arcturus' (M), 'Bravura' (E), 'Camden' (M), 'Flame' (E), 'Illini Warrior' (E), 'Kaskaskia' (M), 'Miss Mary' (M), 'Red Key' (M)

JAPANESE: 'Charles Burgess' (M), 'Dignity' (M), 'Fuyajo' (M), 'Gay Paree' (M), 'Hari-Ai-Nin' (M), 'Mount Palomar' (E), 'Nippon Brilliant' (E), 'Nippon Chief' (L)

SEMIDOUBLE: 'Cherry Red' (M), 'Chippewa' (M), 'Firebelle' (E), 'Red Goddess' (M), 'Red Red Rose' (E), 'Rosalie' (M)

DOUBLE: 'Bonanza' (L), 'Carol' (E), 'Dearborn' (E), 'Felix Crousse' (L), 'Felix Supreme' (M), 'Jay Cee' (E), 'Jean E. Bockstoce' (E), 'King Midas' (M), 'Longfellow' (M), 'Philippe Rivoire' (L), 'Renato' (M)

Paeonia officinalis (common peony)   24–36 in   Sun   Zones 3–8

FLOWERING SPAN: Mid-May to early June

NATURAL COLOR: Deep crimson

DISTRIBUTION: France to Hungary to Albania

Similar in foliage and growth habit to *P. lactiflora,* this wild species has been used extensively for hybridizing. Each stalk carries a single, 4–5-in, cup-shaped blossom and coarsely cut, dark green, glossy leaves, somewhat hairy beneath. Because of its time of bloom, it is often referred to as the "Memorial Day peony." Cultivate as for *P. lactiflora* but know that the tuberous roots are more brittle to handle in transplanting. Several cultivars are available; 'Alba Plena', white, double; 'Rosea Plena', bright rose, double; 'Rosea Superba Plena', watermelon pink, double; and 'Rubra Plena', vivid ruby red, double. (See photo.)

Paeonia tenuifolia (fernleaf peony)   15–18 in   Sun   Zones 3–8

FLOWERING SPAN: Early May to late May

NATURAL COLOR: Dark crimson

DISTRIBUTION: Asia Minor, southeastern Europe

The distinction of this species is the greatly divided, lacy foliage and the single, 3-in, cupped blossoms terminally resting on the dark green leaves. It has been used for extensive crossbreeding. Since by late summer all the foliage withers and disappears, plant an identification stake early to help locate established plants for autumn division or transplanting. The creeping, underground rhizome is very brittle. Cultivate as for *P. lactiflora.* There is a longer-lasting, later-flowering, double cultivar, 'Plena' ('Rubra Plena'), as well as a rosy red one, 'Rosea', which is hard to find.

Papaver alpinum (alpine poppy)   4–8 in   Sun   Zones 5–9

FLOWERING SPAN: Mid-May to early June

NATURAL COLOR: White, yellow, orange

DISTRIBUTION: Alps

Because this plant is highly variable, some authorities believe it should be classified under another species name, but there is no agreement about this yet. It acts as a bright accent for rock gardens or sunny borders with its tissue-thin, bowl-shaped, 2-in flowers enhanced by a ring of bright yellow stamens at the center. These flowers stand erect on thin stems above a basal collection of gray-green, finely divided, 1–2-in leaves. As is usual with poppies, the green-encased flower bud is noticeably downturned before it opens. Individual plants are often short-lived but reseed generously if they enjoy their growing conditions. Provide a moist, gravelly soil, well-drained in sun or light shading. Because the roots are slender and very brittle, this plant resents being moved at any stage. Natural seedlings should take care of propagation readily, but they will need to be thinned-out to allow for full growth. Aphids and stem blight are the worst afflictions. (See photo.)

Papaver rupifragum (Spanish poppy) 6–18 in   Sun   Zones 5–9
    FLOWERING SPAN: Late May to July
    NATURAL COLOR: Brick red
    DISTRIBUTION: Spain
    Flat clumps of ground-hugging, gray-green, deeply cut leaves surround tall flower stems with 2–3-in, cup-shaped blossoms. Any sunny, well-drained, average-fertility location in a border will suffice for its growth. Either spring seeding or late summer division of the fleshy roots works well for propagation. Diseases and insect nuisances are uncommon.

Patrinia triloba   12–24 in   Sun   Zones 5–9
    FLOWERING SPAN: Mid-May to late June
    NATURAL COLOR: Golden yellow
    DISTRIBUTION: Japan
    Basal mounds of 3-in, deeply cut, palmately lobed, bright green leaves produce red-brown flower stems and 4-in heads of ¼-in florets. Expanding slowly, this perennial thrives in peaty but well-drained, damp, cool locations with sun to semishade and can be best propagated from seed or spring division. Pests and diseases are inconsequential.

Phlox divaricata (canadensis) (wild sweet William, blue phlox) 9–15 in   Semishade
    Zones 4–9
    FLOWERING SPAN: Mid-May to late June
    NATURAL COLOR: Lavender-blue
    DISTRIBUTION: Southeastern Canada to Georgia and northern Alabama, west to Michigan
    An attractive underplanting for late spring bulbs in a garden or a woodlot,

this slow-creeping wildflower creates a low foliage mat of 2-in green leaves. The long-lasting, loose, terminal clusters of 1-in, flat-petaled blossoms appear on thin stalks, and the plant can be made to bloom longer if the old stalks are removed when finished. It likes a moist but well-drained, humusy site in semishade but will accept more sunshine if the location remains always moist. Summer stem cuttings from one-year-old plants or spring division of 3-year-old clumps is the recommended propagation method. Mildew and drought are its worst enemies. The subspecies *laphamii* has larger, deep blue-violet blossoming and is probably a parent of the new *P.* × 'Chattahoochee' cultivar, which is 10 in tall and carries lavender-blue flowering with red eyes. The cultivar 'Fuller's White' is clear white, while 'Grandiflora' has larger blossoming. (See photo.)

Phlox pilosa (downy phlox) 12–18 in Sun Zones 4–9
    FLOWERING SPAN: Mid-May to late June
    NATURAL COLOR: Reddish lavender to pink
    DISTRIBUTION: Southeastern Connecticut to southern Florida, west to Texas and Wisconsin

    This phlox does not creep and has very narrow, sharp-pointed, 3-in leaves and stiff, down-covered flower stems with blossoms similar to those of *P. divaricata.* Full sun and dryness, plus an acid, sandy, well-drained soil, suit it best, and if the old flower heads are sheared off, the plant normally reblooms in August on a reduced scale. Division or seeding are the recommended propagation methods. No disease or insect is bothersome.

Phlox stolonifera (reptans) (creeping phlox) 5–8 in Semishade Zones 5–8
    FLOWERING SPAN: Early May to June
    NATURAL COLOR: Light purple to rosy pink
    DISTRIBUTION: Pennsylvania to Georgia

    Glossy, rounded, evergreen leaves from ¾–1½ in long form a ground-hugging mat that spreads quickly in a rich, acid, moist, peaty soil with semishade to full shade. Clusters of 1–1½-in, round florets provide a generous springtime showing and then appear intermittently throughout the summer. Plants in full shade offer reduced blossoming. Division of the creeping root mass in early spring or early autumn is the recommended propagation technique. Disease or insect nuisances are not apparent. Several more colorful cultivars are available: 'Blue Ridge', light blue, large-flowered; 'Bruce's White' ('Ariene'), bright white with a yellow eye; 'Cecil Davies', mauve-blue; and 'Lavender Lady', intensely deep mauve. (See photo.)

Podophyllum hexandrum (emodi) (Himalayan mayapple) 12–18 in Semishade
    Zones 4–9
    FLOWERING SPAN: Late May to mid-June
    NATURAL COLOR: White to pale rose

DISTRIBUTION: Himalaya Mountains

A curious plant conspicuous for its leaves and fruit more than for its flowering, this perennial has umbrellalike, 10-in, bronze-red leaves which become fully green by summer. The pink-brown stalks carrying the 2-in, solitary, drooping flower appear beneath this foliage canopy. Each blossom is ragged-petaled with prominent yellow stamens and becomes an edible fruit of brilliant red the size of a hen's egg. Thriving in large colonies in deep, rich, consistently moist woodlots well-endowed with humus or leaf mold, it is usually propagated by fresh seed or spring division of the rhizomes. Pests and diseases are not as troublesome as drought. In severe winter climates it needs protective mulching.

Podophyllum peltatum (mayapple) 12–18 in Semishade Zones 3–9
FLOWERING SPAN: Early May to late May
NATURAL COLOR: Creamy white
DISTRIBUTION: Southeastern Canada to Florida, west to Texas

Either a single, noticeably white-veined leaf on a long stalk or a flowering stem with 2 very broad, palmately divided, dark green leaves emerges from the thick rootstock each spring. Vigorously colonizing in woodlots or garden spaces, it carries a sickeningly sweet (to some), 2-in, single flower poking out from beneath the oversized, 10-in leaves. Its yellowish, 2-in fruit has edible pulp, but all other parts of this plant are considered poisonous. Cultivate as for *P. hexandrum,* except that only autumn division is preferred. (See photo.)

Polemonium caeruleum (sibiricum) (Jacob's-ladder, Greek valerian) 12–36 in Semishade Zones 3–9
FLOWERING SPAN: Early May to July
NATURAL COLOR: Sky blue
DISTRIBUTION: Europe, Asia

Bushy mounds of pinnately compound leaves with 19–27 leaflets about 1 in long are set like the rungs of a ladder and add a pleasant textural pattern of foliage to borders or wildflower areas. The stiffly erect flower stalks carry terminal, loose clusters of nodding, ¾-in, bell-shaped florets with noticeable orange stamens. It grows best on cool, consistently moist, deep, rich, well-drained soil from semishade to full sun. Insects are no bother, but mildew is often troublesome. Spring or autumn division, summer stem cuttings, and seeding work equally well for propagation. The variety *lacteum* has milky white blossoming. (See photo.)

Polygonatum biflorum (canaliculatum) (small Solomon's-seal) 12–36 in Semishade Zones 4–8
FLOWERING SPAN: Late May to mid-June

NATURAL COLOR: Pale yellow to greenish yellow
DISTRIBUTION: New Hampshire to Florida, west to Texas and Nebraska

Zig-zagged, arching, unbranched stems carry double rows—sometimes more—of pendulous, ¾-in, tubular flowers from the axils of the 4-in, pale green leaves. Dark blue or black fruit develops by midsummer. Best placed in acid, semidry but humusy locations with semishade to full shade, this reliable perennial is propagated by either division of the knobby rootstock in early spring or seed. It has no problems with disease or insects. (See photo.)

Polygonatum commutatum (great Solomon's-seal) 48–72 in Semishade Zones 3–8
FLOWERING SPAN: Late May to mid-June
NATURAL COLOR: Greenish yellow to greenish white
DISTRIBUTION: New Hampshire to Florida, west to Mexico and Manitoba

More robust than *P. biflorum,* the leaves of *P. commutatum* are up to 7 in long and 4 in wide, while the 1-in, tubular, pendant flowers frequently appear in clusters of 8 in the leaf axils. Culture of both is the same, except this species has a special preference for consistent moisture. Colonizing easily, especially in shady woodlots, it is attractive with ferns.

Polygonatum multiflorum 24–36 in Semishade Zones 4–8
FLOWERING SPAN: Late May to mid-June
NATURAL COLOR: White to greenish white
DISTRIBUTION: Europe, northern Asia

Here the leaves are bright green, lance-shaped, and up to 6 in long. Flowers are only ½ in in length and have constricted middles. Provide a reasonably moist, neutral to slightly acid, humusy soil, and propagate by division either in early spring or autumn. Nothing appears to bother it.

Polygonatum odoratum (officinale) 12–18 in Semishade Zones 5–8
FLOWERING SPAN: Late May to mid-June
NATURAL COLOR: Greenish white
DISTRIBUTION: Europe, Asia

While other *Polygonatum* species have rounded stems, this one has angled or grooved stems. Its leaves are spearhead-shaped, up to 4 in long, pendant, and not as wavy-edged as the others. The 1-in, fragrant flowers are either solitary or paired. Grow as for *P. multiflorum.* A robust Japanese variety, *thunbergii,* can stretch to 42 in with slightly enlarged parts, while *thunbergii* 'Variegatum' offers noticeably white-edged leaves occasionally thinly striped with white.

Potentilla anserina (silverweed, goose grass) 6–12 in Sun Zones 3–9
FLOWERING SPAN: Late May to August
NATURAL COLOR: Golden yellow

DISTRIBUTION: Europe, Asia, Alaska to Newfoundland, south to California, New Mexico, and New York

Especially attractive for its fernlike, dark green rosettes of pinnately compound foliage with 9–31 leaflets, ½–2 in long and silvered beneath with long, silky hairs, this creeping perennial creates a generous mat from red stems which root where they touch soil. Its solitary, 1-in, rounded flowers present a somewhat sketchy appearance but are ongoing for most of the summer. Preferring a moist, sandy soil of average fertility in full sun, it is propagated by simple division in spring or autumn. Diseases and insects present no problems.

Potentilla argentea (silvery cinquefoil) 4–12 in Sun Zones 3–9
   FLOWERING SPAN: Late May to August
   NATURAL COLOR: Sulphur yellow
   DISTRIBUTION: Europe, Asia, eastern North America

Although not florally distinguished, this long-blooming perennial can establish itself well in dry, sterile situations where little else will grow. Its deep green, palmately compound leaves have 5 1-in. leaflets, densely silvered beneath. The ½-in circular flowers are produced all summer on branched, erect stems rising above the basal foliage. Propagate by spring division. Leaf spot disease is the main difficulty.

Potentilla tridentata (three-toothed cinquefoil) 6–12 in Sun Zones 3–8
   FLOWERING SPAN: Late May to August
   NATURAL COLOR: White
   DISTRIBUTION: Greenland, Wisconsin to Georgia, west to Iowa

The leathery, evergreen, 1½-in, 3-parted, compound leaves of this rapidly creeping perennial often turn slightly orange-red in autumn. Its ½-in, star-shaped flowers appear in clusters on erect stems above the foliage. Adaptable for dry embankments or rock gardens in full sun, it likes an acid, sandy soil and can be propagated easiest by simple division. Pests and diseases seem to avoid it.

Primula japonica (Japanese primrose) 18–24 in Semishade Zones 5–8
   FLOWERING SPAN: Late May to late June
   NATURAL COLOR: Magenta, crimson, white
   DISTRIBUTION: Japan

Unusual for its 3-tiered blossoming of yellow-eyed, 1-in florets in 2–3-in heads, the Japanese primrose is categorized as a candelabra type and blooms for a lengthy period with one whorl of flowers opening above another. The ground-level foliage clump is composed of 8–10-in-long, light green leaves up to 2 in wide. Provide constantly moist, humusy soil in semishade. Like most other primroses, it will accept more sun if its site is kept wet. Self-seeding is usually generous to the point of overcrowding, and because crossbreeding is typical even within its own flowers, expect color variations from seedlings. Diseases are less problematic than red spider mite infestations in hot, dry weather. Cultivars with attractively separate colorings are 'Miller's Crimson' and 'Postford's White'. (See photo.)

Primula rosea 5–18 in Semishade Zones 5–8
    FLOWERING SPAN: Mid-May to mid-June
    NATURAL COLOR: Rosy pink
    DISTRIBUTION: Himalaya Mountains
       This is a primrose which blossoms before the leaves develop fully. Its ¾-in florets have yellow eyes and appear in loose clusters on erect, tall stems above smooth, light green, 4–8-in foliage clumps. Native to streamside locations which are constantly moist to the point of wet, it can adapt satisfactorily to gardens with peaty, very moist soil. Division right after flowering or fresh seed propagates it readily. Slugs, leaf beetles, aphids, and red spider mites are troublesome occasionally in some growing areas, while botrytis disease in hot, humid weather ruins the foliage. The cultivar 'Grandiflora' has larger blossoming. In severe climates, these plants require winter mulching to survive.

Ranunculus aconitifolius (aconite buttercup) 6–24 in Sun Zones 4–8
    FLOWERING SPAN: Mid-May to July
    NATURAL COLOR: White
    DISTRIBUTION: Central Europe
       From a ground-level clump of palmately divided, 3–7-segmented, deep green leaves similar to aconite foliage come tall, slender, branched stems with widely spaced blossoms emerging from reddish buds. In a sunny border to lightly shaded woodlot space that is moist, rich, and well-drained, it flowers long but expands slowly. Count on many self-sown seedlings to appear. Division of the tuberous roots in early spring or autumn is also workable. Insects present no problems, but mildew in hot, humid weather can be troublesome. The cultivar 'Flore-Pleno' has double, rounded flowers, while 'Luteus Plenus' carries double, golden yellow blossoms. (See photo.)

Ranunculus acris (tall buttercup, common buttercup) 8–42 in Sun Zones 5–8
    FLOWERING SPAN: Mid-May to July
    NATURAL COLOR: Bright yellow
    DISTRIBUTION: Europe, Asia, eastern United States, eastern Canada
       The common buttercup of fields and meadows in many parts of the world, its hairy stems and foliage are topped with 1-in, cupped flowers on tall, much-branched stalks. Clump-forming, basal leaves are palmately divided many times

and carry sharp-pointed tips. Cultivate as for *R. aconitifolius*. The preferred cultivar, 'Flore-Pleno', has conspicuously double and very durable flowers, while 'Stevenii' is larger-blossoming.

Ranunculus amplexicaulis (yelloweye buttercup) 3–12 in Sun Zones 4–9
FLOWERING SPAN: Early May to early June
NATURAL COLOR: White
DISTRIBUTION: Pyrenees Mountains, western Alps
The 1-in blossom is wide-petaled and made more conspicuous by a yellow blotch at the center. Its branched flower stems are slender and enclasped by the gray-green, lancelike leaves. It prefers a moist, well-drained, rich soil and can be readily propagated by seeding or spring division. It seems to have no pests or diseases of note.

Ranunculus ficaria (lesser celandine) 2–8 in Sun Zones 4–9
FLOWERING SPAN: Early May to June
NATURAL COLOR: Bright yellow
DISTRIBUTION: Europe, western Asia, eastern United States
The 2-in, heart-shaped, dark green, shiny leaves on elongated stalks form attractive dense mats. Its 1-in, cupped flowers appear on heavy stems and are unusual in having 10–12 petals. Suitable for a wild area or rock garden in sun to nearly semishade on any well-drained, moist, average-fertility soil, it self-seeds generously to the point of crowding. Division of the knobby tubers in early spring or autumn is also effective for propagation. There appear to be no bothersome pests or diseases.

Ranunculus montanus 3–6 in Sun Zones 4–9
FLOWERING SPAN: Mid-May to July
NATURAL COLOR: Bright yellow
DISTRIBUTION: Pyrenees to Caucasus Mountains
A creeping, rock garden perennial with a long period of winter dormancy, it expands slowly to form a low mat of dark green, much-divided foliage topped with 1-in, glistening flowers on short stems. It enjoys a rich but rocky soil with good drainage in sun to semishade. Propagate by division of the stoloniferous rootstock either in early spring or autumn. Insects are not problematic, but mildew in hot, humid weather can spoil the foliage. The cultivar 'Molten Gold' is very floriferous.

Ranunculus repens (creeping buttercup) 8–18 in Sun Zones 4–9
FLOWERING SPAN: Mid-May to July
NATURAL COLOR: Golden yellow
DISTRIBUTION: Europe, Siberia, North America, New Zealand

This wildflower has a sprawling habit with stems that flop over easily. Its dull green leaves are divided into 3 segments and appear on the flower stalks as well as at ground level. The waxy, 1-in blossoms are pointed at the tips. Provide a location in full sun on rich, moist soil. Divide the stoloniferous root mass either in spring or autumn for propagation. Self-seeding is very likely, too. The double-flowered cultivar, 'Pleniflorus' ('Flore-Pleno'), is more attractive. (See photo.)

Saxifraga virginiensis (early saxifrage) 3–12 in Sun Zones 4–8
  FLOWERING SPAN: Early May to mid-June
  NATURAL COLOR: White
  DISTRIBUTION: Southeastern Canada to Georgia, west to Tennessee and Arkansas
    Thick, rounded, gray-green leaves up to 3 in across form a broad rosette at ground level for the erect, hairy stems of the widely branched, 2–3-in flower heads with ¼-in florets. Native to rock clefts and dry, sandy hillsides in full sun, it is an obvious rock garden addition. Offsets, spring division, and seeding propagate it equally well. Diseases are not prevalent, but beetles and aphids disturb the foliage.

Sedum acre (gold moss) 1–3 in Sun Zones 4–9
  FLOWERING SPAN: Late May to mid-June
  NATURAL COLOR: Bright yellow
  DISTRIBUTION: Europe, northern Africa, western Asia
    Perhaps the commonest of all the many *Sedum* species in cultivation, the matlike, dense growth habit of *S. acre* is very useful for ground cover needs on dry, arid, sunny locations—even those with only a thin soil layer over rock outcrops. Dependably hardy, the plant has ¼-in, cylindrical, bright green leaves and star-shaped, ½-in, clustered flowers which can disguise the foliage entirely when in bloom. Propagation means just simple separation of the leaf mats at any time during the growing season. Insect and disease problems are nonexistent. A number of cultivars exist: 'Album', white-flowered; 'Aureum', golden yellow spring foliage, slow-growing; and 'Majus', larger-flowering.

Silene caroliniana (wild pink) 6–8 in Sun Zones 5–8
  FLOWERING SPAN: Early May to July
  NATURAL COLOR: Rose, pink, white
  DISTRIBUTION: New Hampshire to Alabama, west to Missouri
    Dense clumps of narrow, blue-green, 2-in-wide leaves, sticky and hairy, produce flower stems with 1-in, slightly notched blossoms closely clustered at the tip ends. It likes a dry, sandy, acid soil in full sun but will accept modest shading. Careful division of the taproots in spring or autumn, root cuttings, or seeding are the propagation methods. Diseases and insects are not bothersome.

Silene quadrifida (alpestris, Heliosperma alpestre) (alpine silene) 4–12 in Sun
Zones 3–8
    FLOWERING SPAN: Mid-May to mid-July
    NATURAL COLOR: White
    DISTRIBUTION: Eastern Alps to the Balkans
        An attractive, long-flowering rock garden accent, this perennial has tight
clusterings of satiny, ¾-in, 5-petaled, rounded flowers on wiry stems. The
ground-level foliage clump carries lancelike, sticky, 1½-in leaves. Any average-
fertility, sandy, well-drained soil with full sun suits it, and seeding, spring division, or summer stem cuttings equally propagate it. Insects and diseases are of no
concern.

Sisyrinchium angustifolium (blue-eyed grass) 12–18 in Sun Zones 3–8
    FLOWERING SPAN: Mid-May to early June, occasionally in autumn
    NATURAL COLOR: Violet-blue
    DISTRIBUTION: Southeastern Canada to Florida, west to Texas and Minnesota
        Clumps of irislike, flat, ¼-in-wide leaves offer slender flower stalks with
terminal, glossy, gold-centered ¾-in blossoms. These flowers open fully only on
sunny days. The plant spreads readily on acid, sandy, well-drained, average-
fertility soil in bright sun. Dividing the fibrous root mass either in early spring or
autumn is the propagation technique normally followed, and self-seeding is
likely, too. Diseases and insect pests are unknown. The tender Bermuda native, *S.
bermudiana,* might well be tried in mild, southerly garden areas. Its flowers are
similar but darker in color.

Sisyrinchium douglasii (grandiflorum) (purple-eyed grass) 6–12 in Sun Zones 4–8
    FLOWERING SPAN: Mid-May to early June
    NATURAL COLOR: Dark red-purple
    DISTRIBUTION: Northern California to British Columbia
        Attractively flowered, this species unfortunately withers and goes into com-
plete dormancy by late summer, when division can then take place. Cultivate as
for *S. angustifolium.*

Smilacina racemosa (false Solomon's-seal, false spikenard) 18–30 in Semishade
Zones 3–9
    FLOWERING SPAN: Mid-May to early June
    NATURAL COLOR: Creamy white
    DISTRIBUTION: Southeastern Canada to Virginia, west to Missouri
        The zig-zagged, unbranched stems are terminally capped with 6–8-in
feathery clusters of tiny flowers above deep green, pointed leaves 3–6 in long.
Blossoming is followed by large, late-summer clusters of light red, rounded fruit

attractive to several forms of wildlife. Provide a rich, humusy, acid, moist but well-drained soil in semishade to full shade. It colonizes easily but when transplanted will not reflower until the 2nd season. Autumn or spring division of the thick, horizontal rootstock is the better propagation method, although seeding is workable but germination slow. Pests and diseases are not prevalent. (See photos.)

Symphytum grandiflorum (Pulmonaria lutea)   12–15 in   Sun   Zones 3–9
  FLOWERING SPAN: Mid-May to July
  NATURAL COLOR: Creamy yellow
  DISTRIBUTION: Caucasus Mountains
    Readily adaptable to troublesome dry areas, this ground cover plant is neat in appearance and modest in expansion. Its 4-in, deep green, wrinkled, spear-shaped, hairy foliage surrounds taller flower stalks with clusters of ¾-in, tubular florets, which rebloom sparsely when sheared back. Use on average-fertility, arid sites with sun to semishade. Division of the thick rootstock, root cuttings, or seeding all propagate it well. Pests and diseases are uncommon. Its cultivars include: 'Hidcote Blue', reddish buds, blue flowers fading toward white, taller; "Hidcote Pink', pinkish flowers fading to white, taller; and 'Variegatum' with foliage streaked in creamy yellow. (See photo.)

Symphytum officinale   (common comfrey, healing herb, boneset)   24–36 in   Sun   Zones 3–9
  FLOWERING SPAN: Late May to mid-July
  NATURAL COLOR: White, pink, rose
  DISTRIBUTION: Europe, Asia, North America
    Coarse-leaved but durable and long-flowering, this perennial is not for choice border locations but belongs in the background. Its branched, slightly hairy stems carry 3-in, lancelike leaves and clusters of tubular, ½-in, drooping flowers. Cultivate as for *S. grandiflorum,* except that it prefers more soil moisture. The cultivar 'Variegatum' is altogether superior with noticeably creamy white leaf margins and pale blue blossoms.

Thalictrum aquilegifolium   12–36 in   Sun   Zones 5–9
  FLOWERING SPAN: Late May to early July
  NATURAL COLOR: Light to dark purple, pink
  DISTRIBUTION: Europe, northern Asia
    Large, hollow stems produce gray-green, finely divided, compound leaves resembling columbine, plus heavy, terminal heads of feathery, ½-in, long-lasting flowers. Provide a consistently moist, well-drained, humusy soil in sun to light shading, and propagate by division in spring only. Where winters are severe,

mulch lightly. Problems with pests or diseases are uncommon. The cultivars include: 'Album', white; 'Atropurpureum', dark purple; 'Aurantiacum', orange-toned; and 'Roseum', lilac rose. (See photo.)

Thermopsis montana (mountain thermopsis) 18–24 in Sun Zones 3–8
    FLOWERING SPAN: Mid-May to mid-July
    NATURAL COLOR: Bright yellow
    DISTRIBUTION: Washington to Montana, south to Nevada and Colorado
      Erect, hairy stems with 2–4-in, compound, lancelike leaves carry terminal, 6–10-in spikes of showy, sweet pea-shaped flowers. The foliage remains attractive even after blossoming is completed. Install on a moist, well-drained, sandy soil in full sun and be aware this perennial can be invasive from its expanding rootstock in a short time. Seeding is more satisfactory than dividing the deep root mass. Diseases and insect nuisances are not known. (See photo.)

Tiarella cordifolia (foamflower) 6–12 in Semishade Zones 3–8
    FLOWERING SPAN: Early May to June
    NATURAL COLOR: White to reddish white
    DISTRIBUTION: Southeastern Canada to Alabama and Georgia
      A creeping set of underground stems readily makes compact mats of long-stalked, 3-in, heart-shaped, downy, light green leaves. Erect and slender flower stalks carry spikes of ¼-in, star-shaped florets well above the foliage. Install in a cool, moist, humusy, neutral soil with semishade or heavier shading. Best arranged in sizeable masses, it is easily propagated by spring division or by seeding. Diseases and insect pests are infrequent. The cultivars include: 'Purpurea', purple; 'Purpurea Major', wine red; and 'Purpurea Marmorata', maroon with bronze foliage. (See photo.)

Tiarella wherryi (*cordifolia* var. *collina*) 6–12 in Semishade Zones 5–8
    FLOWERING SPAN: Early May to June
    NATURAL COLOR: Creamy white
    DISTRIBUTION: Virginia and Tennessee to Mississippi, Alabama, and Georgia
      Noncreeping, this species has clumps of decorative, heart-shaped, 2–4-in, bronze-green leaves which turn reddish in the autumn. Its flowering is slightly larger than that of *T. cordifolia,* and culture is the same for both.

Tradescantia × andersoniana (virginiana, montana) (spiderwort) 18–30 in Sun Zones 4–9
    FLOWERING SPAN: Early May to July
    NATURAL COLOR: Violet-blue
    ORIGIN: Horticultural hybrid of *T. ohiensis × T. subaspera × T. virginiana*

The straplike, 6–15-in, dull green leaves form grasslike clumps and sprawl erratically once flowering is done. By early August the foliage starts yellowing, and severely cutting back all growth prompts new leaves and possible reflowering in autumn. Its erect, hairy flower stems come generously clustered with terminal, egg-shaped buds and 3-petaled, 1-in florets lasting but a day. The plant seeds itself freely in all directions and can quickly become weedy in borders. Long-lived and long-flowering, this hardy perennial thrives in a reasonably moist, well-drained, average-to-poor soil with sun or light shading. In hot, dry locations provide extra water in summer. Spring division is the only way to ensure duplication of the cultivars since seed can bring much color variation. Any pests or diseases are unlikely. Many cultivars are in the marketplace: 'Alba', white; 'Atrosanguinea', dark red; 'Blue Stone', deep blue; 'Caerulea', bright blue; 'Coccinea', bluish red; 'Congesta', purple; 'Innocence', white; 'Isis', deep blue, 2-in flowers; 'James Stratton', deep blue; 'Purple Dome', bright rosy purple; 'Red Cloud', deep magenta; 'Rubra', deep rosy pink; 'Snowcap', pure white; 'Violacea', purplish blue; and 'Zwanenburg Blue', rich blue. (See photo.)

Trollius asiaticus (Siberian globeflower)   18–24 in   Sun   Zones 3–8
    FLOWERING SPAN: Early May to June
    NATURAL COLOR: Orange-yellow
    DISTRIBUTION: Siberia

Finely divided, bronze-green leaves surround the erect, slender flower stems with their solitary, 1–2-in, globular blossoms. It thrives in very damp locations enriched with peat moss, compost, or humus in sun or light shade. Division of the fibrous rootstock or seeding propagates it readily. Mildew is an occasional nuisance, but insects appear to avoid the plant. The cultivar 'Fortunei' is double-flowered, while 'Giganteus' is taller and more robust.

Trollius europaeus (common globeflower)   12–24 in   Semishade   Zones 2–8
    FLOWERING SPAN: Early May to mid-June
    NATURAL COLOR: Lemon yellow
    DISTRIBUTION: Northern Europe, arctic North America

Compared with *T. asiaticus,* here the globular flower is 2 in wide and carries a darker center, while the foliage is dark green. Cultivation is the same as for *T. asiaticus,* except that it prefers a sandy soil enriched with compost. The cultivars are superior and have more flower substance: 'Earliest of All', soft yellow, dwarfed; 'Loddigesii', deep yellow: 'Orange Princess', bright orange, tall; and 'Superbus', light yellow, tall. Some of these are often listed in nursery catalogs under *T. chinensis* (Chinese globeflower), where authorities seem to believe they botanically belong, but official agreement is lacking. (See photos.)

Trollius japonicus 4–8 in Semishade Zones 3–8
  FLOWERING SPAN: Early May to June
  NATURAL COLOR: Orange-yellow
  DISTRIBUTION: Japan
    Except for its low height, this species is very similar to *T. asiaticus* and requires the same cultivation.

Tulipa (tulip) 18–30 in Sun Zones 3–8
  FLOWERING SPAN: Early May to early June
  NATURAL COLOR: Every imaginable coloring and mix of coloring
  DISTRIBUTION: Horticultural hybrids mostly from European sources
    As with the April-blooming tulips, these are also listed by their sequence of flowering. This section of cultivated tulips falls entirely under the Royal General Bulbgrowers' Society of Holland classification of "Late" and covers the *Darwin, Lily-flowered, Cottage* (including viridiflora and bunch-flowering types), *Rembrandt, Parrot,* and *Double Late.* Fringed tulips are also discussed in this section. Their culture is identical with all the comprehensive recommendations given under the April-flowering tulip listing. (See photos.)

Classification of Cultivated Tulips

May Flowering Sequence

LATE (Early May to early June)
1. DARWIN (Derived from selections of the 19th century Cottage and further hybridized.)
  DESCRIPTION: Large, globular cups squared off at both the base and the top, 24–32 in, satiny texture, intense colorings, sturdy stems
  EXAMPLES:
    MAUVE, LILAC, PURPLE, MAROON: 'Aberdeen', 28 in, silvery mauve; 'Ace of Spades', 24 in, almost black, large; 'Aristocrat', 30 in, violet-rose with white edges; 'Black Forest', 26 in, deep reddish black; 'Black Swan', 28 in, deep maroon with a violet-blue base; 'Bleu Aimable', 24 in, bright lilac-blue; 'Blue Hill', 28 in, amethyst with a white base; 'Blue Perfection', 28 in, lavender-blue with a white base; 'Cum Laude', 28 in, deep violet-blue; 'Demeter', 28 in, plum purple, early; 'Gander', 26 in, pale magenta, early; 'Insurpassable', 28 in, lilac; 'Lafayette', 28 in, purplish violet; 'La Tulipe Noire', 28 in, deep maroon-black with a dark violet center; 'Madame Butterfly', 28 in, pale mauve with a violet flush; 'Pandion', 24 in, purple with silver edges; 'Queen of the Night', 28 in, deep velvety maroon, almost black, large; 'Scotch Lassie', 28 in, deep lavender; 'The Bishop', 28 in, lavender-purple with a blue base, large; and 'William Copeland', 26 in, lilac.

PINK, ROSE, ORANGE: 'Afterglow', 26 in, soft orange; 'Azida', 30 in, rose with a white center, large; 'Cantor' 26 in, coral-pink with a white base; 'Clara Butt', 24 in, bright rosy pink; 'Dillenburg', 24 in, orange–terra-cotta; 'Elizabeth Arden', 24 in, deep salmon-pink; 'Etoile Du Midi', 26 in, rosy pink with a white base, long-lasting; 'Little Queen Bess', 28 in, white with a large flush of rose; 'Mr. van Zyl', 28 in, pink with a white base; 'Perry Como', 24 in, bright strawberry-rose; 'Picture', 26 in, soft rose; 'Pink Supreme', 28 in, soft pink; 'Pride of Zwanenburg', 28 in, salmon-rose, large; 'Princess Elizabeth', 26 in, light rose; 'Queen of the Bartigons', 24 in, salmon-pink with a bluish white base; 'Smiling Queen', 28 in, rose, large, long-lasting; 'Temple of Beauty', 24 in, salmon-rose, flushed orange, large; 'Wilhelm Tell', 28 in, rosy raspberry; and 'William Copeland Rose', 26 in, rosy lilac.

YELLOW: 'Anjou', 26 in, canary yellow with darker yellow edges; 'Golden Age', 28 in, deep yellow with an orange flush, large; 'Golden Niphetos', 28 in, bright gold with a light yellow center, long-lasting; 'Gold Standard', 28 in, pure golden yellow, large; 'Mamasa', 28 in, bright yellow; 'Niphetos', 28 in, lemon yellow, long-lasting; 'Silver Wedding', 28 in, yellow with silvery streaks; 'Sunkist', 26 in, bright, deep yellow; 'Sweet Harmony', 28 in, lemon yellow with ivory white edges; and 'Tarakan', 24 in, bright yellow.

SCARLET, CRIMSON: 'Balalaika', 28 in, deep red with a yellow base, large; 'Charles Needham', 26 in, bright scarlet with a black base; 'City of Haarlem', 28 in, bright scarlet with a dark blue base; 'Eclipse', 28 in, dark red with a violet base: 'Florence Nightingale', 28 in, bright red; 'Flying Dutchman', 27 in, bright red, long-lasting; 'Halcro', 24 in, raspberry red; 'Koblenz', 26 in, deep wine red; 'Margaux', 28 in, deep wine red with a blue base; 'Nobel', 28 in, deep red with a black center; 'Pride of Haarlem', 28 in, scarlet with a blue base; 'Red Master', 28 in, deep crimson with a blue base; 'Renown', 24 in, light red; and 'Scarlett O'Hara', 28 in, bright scarlet with lighter edges.

WHITE: 'Anne Frank', 28 in, pure white; 'Blizzard', 28 in, translucent white; 'Duke of Wellington', 28 in, white with a creamy white base; 'Glacier', 26 in, pure white; 'Jeanne d'Arc', 26 in, ivory white, long-lasting; 'Snowpeak', 28 in, pure white, large; 'White Elephant', 28 in, white with a flush of icy green; and 'White Giant', 26 in, white, large.

2. LILY-FLOWERED (Derived from hybridizing *T. retroflexa* and Cottage.)
   DESCRIPTION: Slender, urn-shaped with long, curving petals turning outward, 22–28 in, long-lasting, blooming with the Darwin
   EXAMPLES: 'Aladdin', 22 in, scarlet with narrow yellow edges; 'Alaska', 26 in, clear yellow; 'Ascona', 26 in, pale yellow fading to white; 'Ballade', 22 in, reddish purple edged in white; 'Beverly', 24 in, orange; 'Captain Fryatt', 24 in, reddish purple; 'China Pink', 26 in, satin pink with a white base; 'Elegans Alba', 24 in, white with narrow crimson edges; 'Gisela', 28 in, pure rose; 'Golden Duchess', 28 in, golden yellow; 'Inimitable', 26 in, golden yellow, large; 'Kiruna', 26 in, deep ruby red, long-lasting; 'Lilac Time', 26 in, deep lavender with white edges;

'Mariette', 25 in, deep rose, very long-lasting; 'Philemon', 22 in, creamy yellow; 'Queen of Sheba', 26 in, ruby red with yellow edges; 'Red Shine', 26 in, glowing, ruby red; 'West Point', 26 in, deep yellow with elongated petal points; 'White Triumphator', 26 in, white; and 'Yellow Triumphator', 26 in, soft yellow.

3. COTTAGE (Named for types found in 19th-century English and French cottage gardens and later hybridized; also listed in catalogs as *Single Late.*)

DESCRIPTION: Long, egg-shaped, mostly pastel or light-colored, 18–30 in, sturdy stems. Included in this category are the *viridiflora,* or "green," types as well as the *bunch-flowering,* or multiple-blossom forms with as many as 3 blossoms per stem. All bloom with Darwin and Lily-flowered.

EXAMPLES:

WHITE: 'Albino', 25 in, pure white; 'Carrara', 22 in, white, cup-shaped; 'Ivory Glory', 26 in, ivory white, egg-shaped; 'Maureen', 28 in, large, translucent white; 'Sigrid Undset', 30 in, creamy white, long-lasting; and 'White City', 27 in, pure white.

YELLOW: 'Asta Nielsen', 24 in, creamy yellow outside, bright yellow inside; 'Belle Jaune', 28 in, deep yellow outside, bright yellow inside; 'Blushing Bride', 26 in, creamy white with carmine red banding, long-lasting; 'Bond Street', 26 in, bright yellow flushed with orange; 'Elsie Eloff', 28 in, bright yellow; 'Golden Harvest', 28 in, lemon yellow; 'Golden Measure', 28 in, deep yellow; 'Mongolia', 28 in, soft yellow; 'Mother's Day', 28 in, citron yellow, late; 'Mrs. John T. Scheepers', 26 in, clear yellow, large; 'Princess Margaret Rose', 23 in, canary yellow with orange-red edges; 'Queen of Spain', 27 in, pale yellow flushed pink; and 'Scaramouche', 27 in, bronze with a yellow flush and clear yellow edges.

RED, ROSE, PINK: 'Advance', 29 in, bright orange-red with a silvery sheen; 'Chappaqua', 28 in, violet-rose outside, interior reddish rose with a yellow center; 'City of Alkmaar', 28 in, bright cerise; 'Dido', 28 in, salmon-rose with orange-yellow edges; 'General De La Rey', 27 in, salmon with a creamy white base, large; 'Halcro', 26 in, carmine, large, long-lasting; 'Majestic', 27 in, bright orange-scarlet with a black base; 'Marjorie Bowen', 28 in, salmon-rose; 'Marshal Haig', 28 in, brilliant scarlet with a yellow base; 'Mirella', 28 in, deep salmon; 'Northern Queen', 25 in, white with wide pink edges; 'Oriental Queen', 24 in, bright red with a greenish base; 'Palestrina', 22 in, salmon-pink flushed with rose; 'Renown', 26 in, light red; 'Rosy Wings', 26 in, bright apricot-pink; and 'Unique', 28 in, white with broad streaks of carmine, long-lasting.

VIRIDIFLORA: 'Angel', 20 in, white with greenish feathering; 'Artist', 18 in, blend of rose, yellow, purple, red, and green, long-lasting; 'Court Lady', 20 in, white with dark green feathering; 'Formosa', 18 in, greenish yellow with green feathering, late; 'Golden Artist', 18 in, blend of yellow and green; 'Greenland', 22 in, deep rose with wide green feathering, long-lasting; 'Hummingbird', 20 in, yellow with green feathering, large; 'Pimpernel', 18 in, carmine red with light green feathering; and 'Viridiflora Praecox' ('Green Knight'), 18 in, pale green with yellow edges.

BUNCH-FLOWERING: 'Claudette', 24 in, white with red edges; 'Georgette', 18 in, clear yellow with later-developing red edges; 'Kuekenhof', 24 in, clear scarlet, large; 'Madame Mottet', 24 in, bright rose with lighter edges; 'Monsieur Mottet', 24 in, creamy white with a pale pink flush; 'Orange Bouquet', 26 in, orange-red with a pale yellow base outside, interior bright red with a bright yellow base; 'Rose Mist', 26 in, rich pink; and 'Wallflower', 24 in, deep brown with a yellow base.

4. REMBRANDT (Derived from virus-infected bulbs since the 17th century; sometimes listed in catalogs as *Broken.*)

DESCRIPTION: Striped or streaked with brown, bronze, black, red, pink, or purple on either red, white, or yellow backgrounds, 24–30 in, blooming with Darwin and Cottage, limited availability today due to lack of popular appeal.

EXAMPLES: 'Absalon', 26 in, yellow feathered with coffee brown; 'American Flag', 30 in, deep red with broad, white feathering and a blue base; 'Cordell Hull', 24 in, carmine with white feathering; 'Madame de Pompadour', 24 in, white with lilac-purple feathering; 'May Blossom', 24 in, creamy white with purple feathering; 'Union Jack', 25 in, ivory white feathered with raspberry red and a white base; and 'Victor Hugo', 24 in, white with cherry red feathering.

5. PARROT (Known in a limited number of offerings since the 17th century, many current types are chance mutations or "sports" of Darwin.)

DESCRIPTION: Fringed, scalloped, laciniated, or wavy petals, very large, often weak-stemmed (avoid windy sites), 18–28 in, light green foliage, blooming with Darwin.

EXAMPLES: 'Black Parrot', 27 in, purple-black; 'Blue Parrot', 28 in, lilac-blue and bronze outside, purple inside; 'Caprice', 24 in, violet-rose; 'Discovery', 28 in, soft rose; 'Doorman', 24 in, cherry red with deep yellow edges, large; 'Estella Rijnveld', 20 in, white with red streaks; 'Fantasy', 26 in, salmon-rose feathered with green; 'Faraday', 26 in, scarlet; 'Ivory Parrot', 28 in, creamy white; 'James V. Forrestal', 22 in, orange-red with yellow edges, large; 'Muriel', 28 in, clear violet-blue; 'Orange Favorite', 23 in, bright orange flushed green with a yellow base; 'Orange Parrot', 20 in, deep bronze-orange, late; 'Parrot Wonder', 28 in, cherry red, large; 'Professor Roentgen', 20 in, rose with lemon yellow overlay and green streaks, large; 'Red Champion', 24 in, carmine; 'Sunshine', 18 in, golden yellow; 'Texas Flame', 20 in, bright yellow flushed with carmine and a green base; 'Texas Gold', 20 in, clear yellow with bright red, narrow edges; 'Van Dyck', 28 in, bright rose, large; and 'White Parrot', 23 in, white flushed with green.

6. DOUBLE LATE (Also known as "Peony-flowered" because of their form.)
  DESCRIPTION: Large cups filled with many rows of petals, 20–25 in, blooms as Darwin and Cottage fade, prone to flower loss in strong wind or storm due to very stiff stems.
  EXAMPLES: 'Angelique', 20 in, pale pink; 'Brilliant Fire', 22 in, bright red; 'Carnival de Nice', 20 in, pale ivory with red stripes and cream-edged foliage; 'Elite', 22 in, red with broad white edges; 'Eros', 24 in, rich rose, large; 'Gerbrandt Kieft', 22 in, deep red edged with white, large; 'Gold Medal', 20 in, deep gold; 'Grand National', 22 in, creamy yellow; 'Lilac Perfection', 22 in, deep lilac-blue; 'Mount Tacoma', 25 in, pure white, large; 'Nizza', 22 in, soft yellow with red feathering; 'Orange Triumph', 22 in, orange-red with deep yellow edges; 'Symphonia', 25 in, cherry red; 'Vincent van Gogh', 22 in, wine red edged with yellow and creamy yellow; 'White Lady', 22 in, pure white; and 'Wirosa', 20 in, wine red edged in cream.

  Another group of commercially available hybridized tulips known as "fringed" deserves mention for its visual appeal and late bloom.

FRINGED (Also known as "Orchid" in catalogs.)
  DESCRIPTION: Resembling Darwin in general shape, but petal tips are finely cut and tend to fade lighter than the main color for a "frosted" effect. 18–28 in, blooming with the Double Late.
  EXAMPLES: 'Bellflower', 20 in, rose with a blue-tinged, white base; 'Blue Heron', 18 in, lilac-blue; 'Bridal Veil', 18 in, pure white; 'Burgundy Lace', 28 in, rich wine red; 'Fancy Frills', 26 in, rosy pink blending to cream; 'Fringed Apeldoorn', 20 in, cherry red; 'Fringed Elegance', 18 in, blended yellows with red flecks; 'Fringed Lilac', 26 in, lilac; 'Humor', 26 in, purple-violet; 'Maja', 24 in, pale yellow with a bronze base; 'New Look', 28 in, creamy yellow flushed with pink; and 'Swan Wings', 26 in, pure white.

Uvularia grandiflora (bellwort, merrybells) 12–30 in Shade Zones 3–8
  FLOWERING SPAN: Mid-May to mid-June
  NATURAL COLOR: Lemon yellow
  DISTRIBUTION: Southeastern Canada to Tennessee, west to Oklahoma and Minnesota
  While hardy and vigorous, this wildflower is only modestly noticeable in bloom. Its blossoms conspicuously droop beneath the rich green, lancelike, 3–5-in leaves with soft hairs on the undersides. These narrow, 1½–2-in, twisted, bell-shaped flowers appear early and seem to grow from the centers of the wrap-around leaves. Provide a rich, slightly acid to alkaline, moist, humusy soil in full to half shade. Propagate by careful division of the thick, creeping rootstock. There are no problematic diseases or pests.

Uvularia perfoliata (strawbell) 6–24 in Shade Zones 3–9
FLOWERING SPAN: Mid-May to mid-June
NATURAL COLOR: Pale yellow
DISTRIBUTION: Quebec to northern Florida, west to northern Louisiana and Ohio
   Similar in growth habit and general appearance to *U. grandiflora,* the thinner stems of *U. perfoliata* carry 1½-in flowers and 3-in leaves entirely smooth on both sides. Culture is identical except that this species shows a greater liking for acid soil.

Uvularia sessilifolia (Oakesiella sessilifolia) (wild oats) 6–15 in Shade Zones 4–8
FLOWERING SPAN: Mid-May to mid-June
NATURAL COLOR: Greenish yellow
DISTRIBUTION: Southeastern Canada to Alabama, west to South Dakota and Arkansas
   Smaller and more delicately shaped than the other *Uvularia* species discussed here, the flowers are only 1 in long and the 3-in leaves are oval. Its culture is the same as for *U. grandiflora.*

Veronica chamaedrys (germander speedwell, angel's-eye) 12–18 in Sun Zones 4–9
FLOWERING SPAN: Late May to late June
NATURAL COLOR: Bright blue
DISTRIBUTION: Northern and central Europe, Asia, North America
   Slender, erect flower stalks with large, star-shaped, clustered florets carrying a noticeable white eye appear above a creeping mat of mostly evergreen, thick, hairy, 1½-in leaves. Enjoying any moist, average-fertility soil in sun to light shade, it is easily propagated by simple division in spring or early autumn. Insects are no bother, but leaf spot disease can spoil the foliage. The cultivar 'Alba' has white blossoming.

Veronica gentianoides (gentian speedwell) 6–24 in Sun Zones 5–9
FLOWERING SPAN: Early May to June
NATURAL COLOR: Pale blue
DISTRIBUTION: Asia, Crimea, Caucasus Mountains
   Tufts of smooth, somewhat thick, 2–3-in, glossy, deep green leaves form a heavy mat of durable summertime foliage. The erect flower stalks tower above the leaves and create conspicuous bloom from ½-in, cup-shaped florets in numerous loose clusters. Cultivate the same as for *V. chamaedrys.* Several cultivars are available: 'Alba', pure white'; 'Nana', pale blue, dwarfed; 'Pallida', porcelain blue; and 'Variegata', with leaves streaked in creamy white.

Veronica latifolia (teucrium)   (Hungarian speedwell)   18–30 in   Sun   Zones 4–9
FLOWERING SPAN: Late May to July
NATURAL COLOR: Bright lavender-blue
DISTRIBUTION: Central and southern Europe
    Slender spikes of long-blooming, ½-in florets are surrounded by narrow, hairy, lancelike, ¾-in, dark green leaves. The plant enjoys a well-drained, moist, average-fertility soil in sun to light shade and has no particular pest or disease problems. Propagate by division in either early spring or autumn. Several attractive cultivars are available: 'Blue Fountain', 15 in, rich blue; 'Crater Lake Blue', 12 in, purplish blue, compact; and 'Royal Blue', 18 in, medium blue. (See photo.)

Veronica officinalis   (common speedwell, gypsyweed)   6–12 in   Shade   Zones 4–9
FLOWERING SPAN: Mid-May to mid-July
NATURAL COLOR: Pale blue
DISTRIBUTION: Europe, Asia, southeastern Canada to Tennessee
    Prostrate, hairy, creeping stems root where they touch and form a durable, evergreen mat in densely shaded areas where little else will grow. The leaves are hairy, elliptical, and 2 in long, while spikes of bell-shaped, ¼-in florets make an ongoing flower display. Any moist, average-fertility soil is suitable from full to half shade, and propagation is simplest by separating any of the rooted stems. Pests and diseases are uncommon.

Veronica pectinata   2–3 in   Sun   Zones 4–9
FLOWERING SPAN: Early May to mid-June
NATURAL COLOR: Deep blue
DISTRIBUTION: Asia Minor
    Prostrate and creeping easily, this woolly-leaved rock garden plant has gray-green, evergreen foliage ½ in long and carries short spikes of ¼-in florets with white centers. Agreeable to sun or light shade, it grows in almost any soil or exposure without difficulty. Division is the simplest propagation method, and it is not bothered by diseases or pests. The cultivar 'Alba' has white blossoming, while 'Rosea' has rosy pink flowers.

Veronica repens   (creeping speedwell)   ½–1 in   Sun   Zones 6–9
FLOWERING SPAN: Early May to June
NATURAL COLOR: Pale blue
DISTRIBUTION: Corsica, Spain
    Although never heavily flowered, the mosslike, shining, ½-in foliage looks attractive in its own right as a prostrate ground cover, especially between stepping stones in sun to light shade. It prefers a moist, sandy soil and requires extra watering in very dry weather. The infrequent ¼-in flowers appear in small

clusters on wiry stems. Division is recommended for propagation in early spring, and there are no difficulties with pests or diseases. The cultivar 'Alba' is white-flowered, and 'Rosea' has pink blossoms.

Viola canadensis (Canada violet, tall white violet) 3–12 in Semishade Zones 3–8

FLOWERING SPAN: Early May to July

NATURAL COLOR: White

DISTRIBUTION: Southeastern Canada to Alabama, west to Arizona, Oregon, and Washington

Thriving best in cold areas, the solitary, long-enduring, ½-in flowers emerge from the leaf axils and are often flushed with violet on the outsides. Its 2–4-in leaves are heart-shaped, long-pointed, and serrated on the margins. Preferring cool, moist, humusy locations, the husky, fibrous rootstock is difficult to divide when mature, and seed is the better propagation method. Transplant seedlings when dormant either in early spring or late autumn. Nothing troublesome appears to bother it. (See photo.)

Viola hastata (halberd-leaved violet) 4–10 in Semishade Zones 5–9

FLOWERING SPAN: Early May to mid-June

NATURAL COLOR: Lemon yellow

DISTRIBUTION: Pennsylvania to Florida

Showy when massed in moist, humusy woodlots, the solitary, terminal, ½-in, violet-tinged flowers come from a cluster of wedge-shaped, 2–4-in, toothed leaves often splotched with silver markings. Division is the preferred propagation technique. Diseases and pests are uncommon. (See photo.)

Viola lutea 2–10 in Semishade Zones 4–8

FLOWERING SPAN: Early May to June

NATURAL COLOR: Bright yellow

DISTRIBUTION: Central Europe

Heavily flowered when grown in moist, humusy woodlots with semishade, this low-growing mat of spearhead-shaped, 2-in foliage is compactly neat. The upper 2 petals of the blossoms are occasionally purple. Propagate the slender rhizomes by division in early spring or autumn. There are no troublesome diseases or insects.

Viola pedata (birdsfoot violet, pansy violet, crowfoot violet) 3–6 in Sun
Zones 4–9

FLOWERING SPAN: Mid-May to mid-June

NATURAL COLOR: Lilac

DISTRIBUTION: Maine to Florida, west to Texas and Minnesota

The showy, 1-in blossoms abundantly appear on sun-drenched, dry locations prior to the full emergence of the finely divided, 2-in, green foliage resembling a bird's footprint. Typically, the 2 upper flower petals are velvety, dark violet with 3 pale lilac, lower ones surrounding a noticeably gold center. Requiring excellent drainage at all times, it grows best on acid, rocky, or sandy locations of low fertility. Seeding and dormant root cuttings work best for propagation, and there are no disease or insect nuisances. The blossoms of variety *lineariloba* are entirely pale bluish purple.

Viola sagittata (arrow-leaved violet) 2–4 in Semishade Zones 3–8
FLOWERING SPAN: Mid-May to mid-June
NATURAL COLOR: Violet-purple
DISTRIBUTION: Maine to Georgia, west to eastern Texas and Minnesota

Lancelike or arrow-shaped, 2-in leaves surround the long-stalked, 1-in-wide, white-centered flowers. Noninvasive, this wildflower likes moist, humusy sites in semishade to light shading. Propagate by seeding, division, or offsets. Pests and diseases are unlikely.

Waldsteinia fragaroides (barren strawberry) 3–8 in Semishade Zones 4–8
FLOWERING SPAN: Early May to June
NATURAL COLOR: Bright yellow
DISTRIBUTION: Southeastern Canada to Georgia, west to Minnesota

The plant's 3 deeply lobed, glossy, bright green, 2-in leaflets greatly resemble the true strawberry and form attractive tufts of evergreen in winter. Clusters of ¾-in, 5-petaled flowers appear above the foliage on slender stems but produce no edible fruit. Suitable for either dry or moist locations in semishade, this perennial tolerates a wide variety of soil conditions without difficulty. Division of the rhizomes propagates it best, and this can be done safely at any time the plant is not blooming. Pests and diseases are uncommon. (See photo.)

Xerophyllum asphodeloides (turkeybeard, mountain asphodel) 24–60 in Semishade
Zones 6–9
FLOWERING SPAN: Mid-May to July
NATURAL COLOR: Yellowish white
DISTRIBUTION: New Jersey to Georgia, west to Tennessee

From a ground-hugging mass of numerous, 12-in, wiry, gray-green, grasslike leaves comes a tall, stout spike topped by a 6–12-in, cylindrical head of star-shaped, ¼-in florets of conspicuous showiness, fragrance, and durability. Best grown in semishade to light shade on moist, sandy, acid soils, it requires careful division of the long taproots in early spring for that propagation technique. Seeding is easier, and moving the small seedlings to permanent locations requires taking intact roots. It is not bothered by any special diseases or insect pests.

June

---------- WHITE ----------

Achillea ageratifolia
Achillea clavennae
Achillea ptarmica
Anemone virginiana
Antennaria dioica
Anthericum liliago
Aquilegia flabellata cvs.
Aruncus dioicus
Asphodelus albus
Astilbe × arendsii
Campanula carpatica cvs.
Campanula glomerata 'Alba'
Campanula latifolia 'Alba'
Campanula persicifolia cvs.
Campanula portenschlagiana
    var. alba
Catananche caerulea cvs.
Centaurea montana cvs.
Centranthus ruber cvs.
Cerastium biebersteinii
Cerastium tomentosum
Chrysanthemum coccineum
Chrysanthemum × superbum
Clematis recta
Coronilla varia

Delphinium × belladonna
Delphinium elatum cvs.
Delphinium grandiflorum
Dianthus barbatus
Dianthus × latifolius cvs.
Dictamnus albus
Digitalis lanata
Digitalis purpurea
Eremurus himalaicus
Filipendula purpurea cvs.
Filipendula ulmaria
Filipendula vulgaris
Gypsophila repens
Helianthemum
    nummularium cvs.
Hesperis matronalis cvs.
Heuchera × brizoides
Heuchera sanguinea cvs.
Heuchera villosa
Iris × 'Dutch Hybrids'
Iris cvs.
Leontopodium alpinum
Leontopodium leontopodiodes
Lewisia rediviva

Lilium cvs.
Lilium candidum
Lilium martagon var. album
Lupinus × 'Russell Hybrids'
Lychnis coronaria cvs.
Lychnis flos-cuculi
Monarda didyma cvs.
Papaver orientale cvs.
Paradisea liliastrum
Penstemon × gloxinoides
Platycodon grandiflorus
Polemonium boreale cvs.
Saponaria ocymoides cvs.
Saxifraga cotyledon
Saxifraga paniculata
Scabiosa caucasica cvs.
Scabiosa columbaria
Sedum pulchellum
Sedum telephioides
Shortia galacifolia
Shortia uniflora
Sidalcea candida
Valeriana officinalis
Verbascum × hybridum

---------- YELLOW ----------

Achillea filipendulina
Achillea tomentosa
Alstroemeria aurantiaca
Anthemis marschalliana
Anthemis tinctoria
Aquilegia longissima
Aquilegia skinneri
Cephalaria gigantea
Chrysogonum virginianum
Coreopsis auriculata
Coreopsis grandiflora
Coreopsis lanceolata
Digitalis grandiflora
Digitalis lanata
Digitalis lutea
Gaillardia × grandiflora cvs.

Genista sagittalis
Helianthemum nummularium
Hemerocallis lilioasphodelus
Hemerocallis thunbergii
Hieracium villosum
Iris × 'Dutch Hybrids'
Kniphofia tuckii
Lilium cvs.
Lilium hansonii
Linum flavum
Lotus corniculatus
Lupinus × 'Russell Hybrids'
Lysimachia nummularia
Lysimachia punctata
Lysimachia vulgaris
Meconopsis cambrica

Oenothera fruticosa
Oenothera missouriensis
Oenothera tetragona
Opuntia humifusa
Potentilla argyrophylla
Potentilla atrosanguinea cvs.
Primula bulleyana
Saxifraga aizoides
Saxifraga paniculata cvs.
Sedum aizoon
Sedum rosea
Sedum sexangulare
Sempervivum cvs.
Thermopsis caroliniana
Verbascum chaixii
Verbascum × hybridum

ORANGE

Alstroemeria aurantiaca
Aquilegia skinneri
Helianthemum
    nummularium cvs.
Hemerocallis middendorffii

Iris × 'Dutch Hybrids'
Lilium canadense
Lilium cvs.
Papaver orientale
Potentilla atrosanguinea cvs.

Primula bulleyana
Saxifraga aizoides
Trollius ledebourii

RED

Alstroemeria aurantiaca cvs.
Astilbe × arendsii
Centaurea montana cvs.
Centranthus ruber
Chrysanthemum coccineum
Dianthus alpinus cvs.
Dianthus barbatus
Dianthus × latifolius
Euphorbia griffithii
Gaillardia × grandiflora
Helianthemum

    nummularium cvs.
Heuchera × brizoides
Heuchera sanguinea
Incarvillea mairei
Lewisia rediviva
Lilium cvs.
Lupinus × 'Russell Hybrids'
Lychnis chalcedonica
Lychnis coronaria
Lychnis flos-cuculi
Lychnis flos-jovis

Malva alcea
Monarda didyma
Papaver orientale
Penstemon barbatus
Penstemon × gloxinoides
Phlox carolina
Potentilla atrosanguinea
Primula × bullesiana
Saponaria ocymoides cvs.
Sidalcea malviflora
Silene virginica

PINK

Allium ostrowskianum
Astilbe × arendsii
Centaurea dealbata cvs.
Chrysanthemum coccineum
Coronilla varia
Delphinium elatum cvs.
Dianthus alpinus
Dianthus barbatus
Dianthus × latifolius cvs.
Digitalis × mertonensis
Eremurus robustus
Erigeron speciosus cvs.
Filipendula purpurea
Filipendula rubra
Gypsophila repens cvs.
Helianthemum
    nummularium cvs.

Heuchera × brizoides
Heuchera villosa
Lewisia cotyledon
Lewisia tweedyi
Lilium cvs.
Lupinus × 'Russell Hybrids'
Lychnis coronaria cvs.
Lychnis flos-jovis
Lythrum virgatum
Malva alcea
Monarda didyma cvs.
Papaver orientale cvs.
Penstemon barbatus cvs.
Penstemon × gloxinoides
Phlox carolina
Phlox maculata
Platycodon grandiflorus cvs.

Polygonum bistorta
Primula × bullesiana
Saponaria ocymoides
Saxifraga paniculata
Sedum pulchellum
Sedum telephioides
Sempervivum cvs.
Shortia uniflora
Sidalcea malviflora
Silene schafta
Stachys byzantina
Stachys grandiflora cvs.
Valeriana officinalis
Verbascum × hybridum
Veronica incana cvs.
Veronica prostrata cvs.
Veronica spicata cvs.

PURPLE/LAVENDER

Allium christophii
Allium cyaneum
Allium karataviense
Anchusa azurea cvs.
Campanula glomerata
Campanula latifolia
Campanula persicifolia
Centaurea dealbata
Centaurea gymnocarpa
Delphinium elatum cvs.
Delphinium grandiflorum

Dictamnus albus cvs.
Digitalis purpurea
Dipsacus sativus
Dodecatheon jeffreyi
Erigeron speciosus
Hesperis matronalis
Incarvillea delavayi
Iris × 'Dutch Hybrids'
Iris sibirica
Lilium martagon
Lupinus polyphyllus

Lupinus × 'Russell Hybrids'
Lychnis flos-jovis
Monarda didyma cvs.
Nepeta × faassenii
Penstemon × gloxinoides
Phlox carolina
Phlox maculata
Platycodon grandiflorus
Polemonium boreale
Primula beesiana
Primula × bullesiana

Salvia × *superba*
Saxifraga paniculata cvs.
Scabiosa columbaria
Scabiosa graminifolia

Sedum pulchellum
Sedum rosea
Stachys grandiflora
Thymus × *citriodorus*

Valeriana officinalis
Verbascum × *hybridum*
Veronica incana cvs.

_____ B L U E _____

Allium caeruleum
Anchusa azurea
Aquilegia flabellata
Campanula carpatica
Campanula glomerata cvs.
Campanula latifolia cvs.
Campanula persicifolia cvs.
Campanula portenschlagiana
Campanula rotundifolia

Catananche caerulea
Centaurea montana
Clematis integrifolia
Delphinium × *belladonna*
Delphinium elatum cvs.
Delphinium grandiflorum
Iris × 'Dutch Hybrids'
Iris sibirica cvs.
Lupinus polyphyllus

Lupinus × 'Russell Hybrids'
Platycodon grandiflorus
Polemonium boreale
Scabiosa caucasica
Scabiosa graminifolia
Veronica incana
Veronica prostrata
Veronica spicata

_____ B I C O L O R _____

Aquilegia flabellata cvs.
Cypripedium reginae
Dianthus barbatus
Erigeron speciosus
Iris × 'Dutch Hybrids'

Kniphofia tuckii
Lilium cvs.
Lupinus × 'Russell Hybrids'
Papaver orientale cvs.
Penstemon × *gloxinoides* cvs.

Primula beesiana
Primula × *bullesiana*
Sempervivum cvs.
Verbascum × *hybridum*

(Photos for June are between pages 160 and 161.)

_____ T H E   P L A N T S _____

Achillea ageratifolia   4–8 in   Sun   Zones 4–8
     FLOWERING SPAN: Early June to July
     NATURAL COLOR: White
     DISTRIBUTION: Northern Greece

Daisylike, 1-in flowers stand above the ground clumps of woolly, silvery green, lancelike, 1½-in foliage on this drought-resistant plant. Any average-fertility, well-drained, moderately moist soil in full sun is suitable. Division in spring or autumn readily propagates it, but seeding is also workable. There are no pests or diseases. The variety *aizoon* has larger blossoming.

Achillea clavennae (silver yarrow)   4–10 in   Sun   Zones 3–8
     FLOWERING SPAN: Late June to August
     NATURAL COLOR: White

DISTRIBUTION: Southern Alps

A mounding perennial with trowel-like, cleft leaves 1½ in long covered with white, silky hairs, it displays loose clusters of ¾-in, daisylike blossoms. Thriving in bright sun on sandy, average-fertility soil of an alkaline nature, the plant is best propagated by simple division. Occasionally, stem rot and rust disease bother it, but insects are of no concern. The earlier-blooming and slightly larger perennial, *Chrysanthemum isabellinum,* is very often mistaken for this plant, resembling it closely.

Achillea filipendulina (eupatorium) (fern-leaf yarrow) 36–48 in Sun Zones 3–9
FLOWERING SPAN: Mid-June to September
NATURAL COLOR: Mustard yellow
DISTRIBUTION: Caucasus Mountains, Asia Minor

Attractive, gray-green, feathery leaves up to 10 in long—but in size progressively reduced upward toward the flowers—surround stiffly erect stems capped by flat-topped, 5-in-wide clusters of tightly packed, tiny florets. Stripped of leaves, the cut flower stalks can easily be dried for winter bouquets. All yarrows dislike wet, poorly drained sites and this species is no exception in liking full sun, average-fertility soil, and good drainage. Because of the flower head size, this plant may need some staking in windy locations. Although it accepts drought readily, it prefers reasonable moisture at all times for the best flower production. Seeding, spring division, and summer stem cuttings all propagate it well. Stem rot is a problem at times, but insects normally avoid the pungent foliage. The cultivars are superior: 'Coronation Gold', 36 in, bright mustard yellow, 3-in flower heads; 'Gold Plate', 48 in, golden yellow, 6-in flower heads, late-blooming; and 'Parker's Variety', 42 in, bright yellow, 4-in flower heads less dense than 'Gold Plate'. (See photo.)

Achillea ptarmica (sneezewort, sneezeweed) 12–24 in Sun Zones 2–8
FLOWERING SPAN: Early June to September
NATURAL COLOR: White to greenish white
DISTRIBUTION: Europe, British Isles, Asia, eastern North Africa

Apt to become rangy, straggling, and invasive in its natural form (a trait less likely with the cultivars), this very hardy species has an ongoing flower response worth inclusion in the cutting garden. The narrow, dark green, 1–4-in leaves are almost entire (without indentations to the outline) below much-branched flower heads with ball-shaped, ½-in blossoming. Its dried roots were once used as homemade snuff, which accounts for the "sneeze" part of its name. Any moist, well-drained, average-fertility soil in bright sun suits it, and propagation is better by either seeding or spring division. Stem rot is an occasional nuisance, but insects are uncommon. All of the double-flowered cultivars are superior: 'Angel's Breath', 24 in; 'Perry's White', 24 in with ¼-in florets; 'Snowball', 14 in with ½-in florets; and 'The Pearl', 24 in, cultivated since 1900 for its ½-in, very double florets and sparkling whiteness. (See photo.)

Achillea tomentosa (woolly yarrow) 2–10 in   Sun   Zones 3–8
    FLOWERING SPAN: Early June to September
    NATURAL COLOR: Canary yellow
    DISTRIBUTION: Europe, western Asia
       The deeply cut, fernlike foliage is conspicuously woolly, gray-green, and forms ground cover matting in full sun on dry, sandy sites. Its 1–2-in-wide, dense clusters of tiny florets bloom all summer. Propagate by spring division, summer stem cuttings, or seeding. Pests and diseases appear to shun it. The cultivar 'Aurea' has deeper yellow blossoming. (See photo.)

Allium caeruleum (azureum) 18–30 in   Sun   Zones 3–8
    FLOWERING SPAN: Late June to late July
    NATURAL COLOR: Sky blue
    DISTRIBUTION: Asia
       A tightly composed, 2-in, globular flower head rises well above the straplike, narrow foliage at ground level. Cultivate the same as for *A. christophii.*

Allium christophii (albopilosum) (stars of Persia) 6–30 in   Sun   Zones 4–8
    FLOWERING SPAN: Late June to late July
    NATURAL COLOR: Deep lilac
    DISTRIBUTION: Iran to Asia Minor
       One of the largest and most conspicuous of the *Allium* species when in flower, the bulb produces globular, 8–10-in blossoming. The ½-in, silver-coated, starlike florets are later worthwhile as dried seedheads for indoor decoration. The ½-in-wide, gray, strap leaves are hairy beneath and stretch up to 18 in in length. Provide a light, average-fertility, moist location with good drainage, and install new plantings in the autumn. Propagate as for *Narcissus.* Diseases and insect pests are uncommon, but in severe climates add a winter mulch. (See photo.)

Allium cyaneum 6–12 in   Sun   Zones 4–9
    FLOWERING SPAN: Mid-June to mid-July
    NATURAL COLOR: Violet, purplish blue
    DISTRIBUTION: China
       The 1–3 linear leaves are only ⅛ in wide, and the blossom heads are 1½ in across with loose clusters of star-shaped florets. Useful as a sunny rock garden accent, this bulb dislikes constantly moist sites and grows best in sandy, average-fertility soil with excellent drainage. Install these slender, distorted bulbs in the autumn. Pests and diseases are unknown.

Allium karataviense 6–10 in   Sun   Zones 4–8
    FLOWERING SPAN: Early June to mid-July
    NATURAL COLOR: Pale mauve

DISTRIBUTION: Turkestan

Grown almost as much for its long-lasting, sizeable foliage as for its showy flower head, the bulb has twin, 4-in-wide leaves that are gray-green, mottled in purple, and 1 ft long. Its 4–8-in, round flower head stands stiffly erect. Plant new bulbs in the autumn in full sun on a well-drained, average-fertility location. Diseases and insects are not bothersome, but in cold areas provide a winter mulch for protection. (See photo.)

Allium ostrowskianum 6–12 in Sun Zones 4–9
FLOWERING SPAN: Mid-June to mid-July
NATURAL COLOR: Purplish pink
DISTRIBUTION: Turkestan, central Asia

Increasing quickly in sunny, summer-dry locations, this bulb has ½-in florets in dense, rounded heads almost 3 in wide. Its 2–3 narrow green leaves remain at ground level. Divide overcrowded colonies as soon as the foliage disappears, and install new plantings in autumn. There are no bothersome pests or diseases. This species is sometimes considered by authorities as only a color variant of *A. oreophilum,* which is purple and similar in size but just 4 in tall when flowering.

Alstroemeria aurantiaca (Peruvian lily) 30–36 in Sun Zones 6–10
FLOWERING SPAN: Mid-June to mid-July
NATURAL COLOR: Orange, yellow
DISTRIBUTION: Chile

Not always hardy or reliable in the north, this unusual, showy plant has fleshy, brittle roots which produce no top growth during the first year following spring or early autumn installation. Established plants greatly resent disturbance. Its 4-in, narrow, lancelike, gray-green leaves sparsely line the heavy stem which terminates in a loose cluster of 2-in, lilylike florets spotted with red. Tolerant of full sun in cool climates, it needs semishade in hot areas. Best installed in a protected, south-facing border with well-drained, sandy, humusy, moist soil annually enriched with either compost or rotted manure, the roots should be heavily mulched in very cold sections. The cultivar 'Aurea', 30 in, is mostly gold-colored; 'Dover Orange', 36 in, is a rich orange-red; and 'Lutea', 30 in, is bright yellow. (See photo.)

Anchusa azurea (italica) (Italian bugloss, Italian alkanet) 36–60 in Sun Zones 3–8
FLOWERING SPAN: Mid-June to mid-July
NATURAL COLOR: Bright blue
DISTRIBUTION: Mediterranean Europe

Tall and erect in habit, this bushy, pyramidal plant is somewhat coarse with lancelike, hairy, silvery leaves often 18 in in length. Its forget-me-not, ¾-in flowers appear on much-branched stems for a very distinct garden emphasis. Grow in a deep, fertile, moist soil but know it dislikes sogginess, especially in winter. Propagate by spring seeding or division. There are no important insect pests or diseases. The list of cultivars includes: 'Dropmore', 36 in, cobalt blue; 'Little John', 18 in, deep blue; 'Loddon Royalist', 36 in, royal purple; and 'Royal Blue', 36 in, intense blue.

Anemone virginiana (thimbleweed) 2–18 in Semishade Zones 4–8
  FLOWERING SPAN: Mid-June to August
  NATURAL COLOR: White to greenish white
  DISTRIBUTION: Southeastern Canada to South Carolina, west to Kansas
    Up to 3 noticeable, 1–1½-in flowers rise above rounded, glossy, dark green, deeply incised leaves and display a wide ring of golden stamens. Best grown in moist, acid, humusy locations with dappled light, it also produces an elongated, cylindrical seedhead which gives it its common name. Only spring division is recommended, and there are no diseases or insects of note.

Antennaria dioica (pussytoes) 3–10 in Sun Zones 4–8
  FLOWERING SPAN: Early June to July
  NATURAL COLOR: Pinkish white
  DISTRIBUTION: Europe, northern Asia, northern North America
    While not distinguished by its erect flowering in small, rounded heads, the creeping foliage mat has an easy adaptability for hot, dry, sunny spots. The silvery green leaves are a woolly white beneath and 1 in long in a dense rosette. Removing the spent flowering keeps the plant decorative longer. Seeding or spring division suit it equally for propagation, and there are no pests or diseases of consequence. The cultivar 'Tomentosa' has especially decorative, woolly leaves.

Anthemis marschalliana (biebersteiniana) 5–12 in Sun Zones 4–9
  FLOWERING SPAN: Early June to July
  NATURAL COLOR: Bright yellow
  DISTRIBUTION: Caucasus Mountains
    Useful in sunny rock gardens as a bright accent, its glistening, much-cut, silvery foliage spreads neatly in dense mounds and displays solitary, 1-in, daisylike flowers on thin stems. Accepting sun or light shading, it enjoys a moist, well-drained, average-fertility soil and can be divided in spring or propagated by seeding. Insects and diseases appear to avoid it.

Anthemis tinctoria (golden marguerite) 24–36 in Sun Zones 5–9
  FLOWERING SPAN: Mid-June to September
  NATURAL COLOR: Golden yellow

DISTRIBUTION: Central and southern Europe, western Asia

The lacy foliage is green and noticeably aromatic when bruised. Its 1½-in, daisylike blossoms are solitary and appear on stiff stems over a long span, but overproduction exhausts the plant perhaps within 2 years. Cutting back severely in late summer to produce more basal growth often keeps the plant healthy. Requiring no annual fertilizing to succeed, this plant enjoys a dry, well-drained, average-fertility soil and can be propagated readily by spring division or stem cuttings in summer. Nothing but overbloom seems to bother it. The cultivars offer greater color variation but do not propagate from garden-collected seed if you want exact duplicates. The list includes: 'Grallagh Glory' ('Beauty of Grallagh'), 30 in, deep yellow, large-flowered; 'Grallagh Gold', 30 in, deep orange-gold; 'Kelwayi', 30 in, bright yellow; 'Moonlight', 18 in, pale yellow; 'Mrs. E. C. Buxton', 24 in, lemon yellow; and 'Pale Moon', 24 in, light yellow fading to ivory. (See photo.)

Anthericum liliago (St. Bernard's lily) 18–30 in Sun Zones 4–9
FLOWERING SPAN: Mid-June to August
NATURAL COLOR: White
DISTRIBUTION: Southern Europe

Reasonably simple to grow well, the tuberlike rhizomes require a full season after initial planting to reestablish the large root system it needs for blooming. Basal clumps of narrow, reedlike foliage up to 1 ft long surround the solitary flower stalk with its 15–20 star-shaped, 1-in, fragrant florets with conspicuous golden stamens. Disliking hot, dry locations, it needs a rich, moist, sandy, humusy soil with abundant water when in bloom. Careful division in early spring of crowded clumps is recommended, and new plantings should be made in autumn. Pests and diseases are not evident.

Aquilegia flabellata (akitensis, japonica) (fan columbine) 12–18 in Sun Zones 3–9
FLOWERING SPAN: Early June to July
NATURAL COLOR: Lavender-blue
DISTRIBUTION: Japan

A skimpy collection of pale green leaves with grayish hairs surrounds the erect flower stalks carrying waxy, nodding, 1½-in, wide-petaled blooms ending in short, gracefully curved, lilac spurs. This perennial grows best in sun or light shade on a moist, sandy, well-drained soil and is propagated either by seeding or by careful spring division of young plants. Any older specimen is best left undisturbed. Crown rot and mildew are troublesome at times along with root borer and leaf miner. The variety *pumila,* which may be the cultivar 'Nana Alba' to some authorities, has bluish white flowering on 6-in stems. The blue-and-white bicolor cultivar 'Nana' rarely reaches 1 ft. (See photo.)

Aquilegia longissima (longspur columbine) 18–30 in Sun Zones 3–9
    FLOWERING SPAN: Late June to August
    NATURAL COLOR: Pale yellow
    DISTRIBUTION: Western Texas to Mexico
       Parent of many of the long-spurred cultivars seen today, this wildflower has greatly divided, thin leaves with somewhat silvery undersides. Its typical flower sports exceptionally long and slender spurs which stretch from 4–6 in with a graceful curve. The plant likes a very moist, humusy soil and full sun. Careful division in early spring is workable but not always successful. Nursery plants sold under this name are more likely to be *A. chrysantha,* which is very similar but deeper yellow in coloring.

Aquilegia skinneri 18–30 in Sun Zones 3–8
    FLOWERING SPAN: Mid-June to August
    NATURAL COLOR: Greenish yellow
    DISTRIBUTION: New Mexico
       Well-shaped with thin, divided leaves and nodding, 1½-in flowers ending in bright red spurs, this plant enjoys full sun and a moist, sandy, average-fertility soil. Propagate only by seeding. Pests and diseases are not important. The cultivar 'Flore-Pleno' carries double flowering.

Aruncus dioicus (sylvester, Spiraea aruncus) (goatsbeard) 48–72 in Semishade
    Zones 4–9
    FLOWERING SPAN: Early June to July
    NATURAL COLOR: Creamy white
    DISTRIBUTION: Europe, Asia, North America
       Useful as a tall background planting in a shaded border or woodlot, this sizeable perennial has foot-long, feathery, terminal plumes of many tiny florets above much-divided and much-branched, large, rough-surfaced leaves of medium green. Bees are highly attracted to the blossoms. Thriving in consistently moist, humusy, well-drained soil, it propagates best by division of the deep rootstock, yet seeding gives good results, too. Pests and diseases are no bother. The 3-ft cultivar 'Kneiffii' has finely dissected leaves and is hardy into Zone 3. (See photo.)

Asphodelus albus (asphodel) 30–48 in Sun Zones 5–9
    FLOWERING SPAN: Mid-June to mid-July
    NATURAL COLOR: White, pale buff pink
    DISTRIBUTION: Portugal to Greece
       Starry, ¾-in blossoms with brown-veined petals appear in great quantities on the erect, unbranched flower stalk for several weeks above a collection of straplike leaves which often stretch to 1 ft in length. Tolerant of light shading, the

large, fleshy tubers prefer a light, sandy, well-drained soil, and in severe climates need a winter mulch. Autumn division is recommended for overcrowded colonies. Pests and diseases are uncommon.

Astilbe × *arendsii*   12–24 in   Semishade   Zones 4–8
    FLOWERING SPAN: Early June to mid-July
    NATURAL COLOR: White, pink, red
    ORIGIN: Horticultural hybrid of many *Astilbe* species and subspecies
    Although individual cultivars have showy flower plumes of varying size, fullness, and coloring, the semiglossy, feathery, compound foliage is common to all and attractive in its own right. Shallow-rooted but vigorous, it quickly depletes the soil in its location and requires division every 3rd season to maintain vigor. The plant prefers an acid, moist, very humusy, well-drained (especially in winter) site and will adapt to full sun when supplied with consistently moist conditions. It offers greater usefulness, however, for shaded areas needing color enhancement. Some red cultivars keep their strong coloring when dried if picked when a silvery sheen appears on most of the florets. None is prone to troublesome diseases or pests.
    The list of cultivars is extensive, and since many originated from German growers, the names reflect that origin: 'Bonn', rich, bright pink; 'Cattleya', rosy pink, 36 in, Zones 3–7; 'Deutschland', white, dwarfed, early; 'Düsseldorf', deep salmon-pink; 'Emden', light rose; 'Erica', rose, tall; 'Etna', deep red; 'Europa', clear pink; 'Fanal', deep garnet red; 'Federsee', carmine red, drought-tolerant; 'Feuer', deep red; 'Gladstone', white; 'Irrlicht', pale rose fading to near-white; 'Koblenz', bright red; 'Mainz', deep rose; 'Peach Blossom', light salmon-pink; 'Queen Alexandra', light rose; 'Red Sentinel', scarlet, late; 'Rheinland', clear pink; and 'White Gloria', white, tall. (See photos.)

Campanula carpatica (turbinata)   (tussock bellflower)   8–15 in   Sun   Zones 3–9
    FLOWERING SPAN: Early June to September
    NATURAL COLOR: Bright violet-blue
    DISTRIBUTION: Eastern Europe, Carpathian Mountains
    Readily expanding into large mats of light green, lancelike, 1½-in foliage in full sun to light shading, this long-blooming, hardy perennial produces masses of 1½-in, cup-shaped, up-facing flowers on erect, wiry stems. It thrives on cool, moist, rich, well-drained soil and is easily propagated by spring division. Unfortunately, it also has a tendency to self-seed indiscriminately beyond its immediate area and can become weedy. Slugs and rust disease are often bothersome. Many attractive cultivars are available: 'Blue Carpet', clear blue; 'Blue Clips', clear blue, profuse flowering, 8 in tall; 'China Doll', lavender-blue, large-blossomed, compact, 8 in; 'Cobalt', deep blue; 'Riverslea', dark blue, 2–3-in-wide flowers; 'Turbinata', purplish blue with gray-green leaves, 6 in tall; 'Wedg-

wood', pale blue-violet; 'Wedgwood White', pure white, 8 in high; 'White Carpet', white, generous flowering; and 'White Star', white, 8 in tall, profuse blossoming. (See photo.)

Campanula glomerata (clustered bellflower) 12–24 in Sun Zones 3–9

FLOWERING SPAN: Early June to mid-July

NATURAL COLOR: Deep violet

DISTRIBUTION: Europe, British Isles, Iran, Siberia

Heavy terminal clusters of 1-in, up-facing, funnel-shaped florets dominate the hairy, 2–3-in, long-stalked, spearheadlike leaves of this showy perennial. Cultivate as for *C. carpatica.* Several varieties are known including: *acaulis,* 4 in tall with very large blossoms, and *dahurica,* 12 in high with 3-in-wide flower clusters. The cultivar list includes: 'Alba', white; 'Joan Elliott', 18 in, deep violet; and 'Superba', 36 in, deep violet-blue in large clusters.

Campanula latifolia (macrantha) (great bellflower) 36–48 in Sun Zones 3–9

FLOWERING SPAN: Mid-June to August

NATURAL COLOR: Bluish purple

DISTRIBUTION: Europe, Asia, New England

Easily grown in sun to semishade, the 8-in flower spikes are lined with 1-in, bell-shaped blossoms showing noticeably recurved petals above coarse-looking, 6-in, spearhead-shaped foliage. Provide a moist, deep, fertile, well-drained soil and propagate either by spring division of the thick roots or by summer stem cuttings. Several cultivars are available: 'Alba', off-white, 48 in tall; 'Brantwood', violet-purple, 48 in tall; 'Gloaming', pale lilac-blue; and 'Macrantha', 60 in, with darker, larger florets.

Campanula persicifolia (amabilis, grandis) (willow bellflower, peachbells) 24–36 in Sun Zones 3–9

FLOWERING SPAN: Early June to mid-July

NATURAL COLOR: Violet

DISTRIBUTION: Europe, northeastern Asia, North Africa

The 6–8-in foliage is dark green, glossy, and narrow in a basal tuft. The erect, unbranched flower stalks carry 1½-in, cup-shaped florets with several usually open at one time. Cultivate the same as for *C. latifolia.* Many cultivars exist: 'Alba Superba', white, large-flowered; 'Bernice', powder blue, double-blossomed; 'Blue Gardenia', rich blue, double-flowered; 'Moerheimii', white, double, 2–3-in-wide flowering; 'Percy Piper', deep blue; 'Snowdrift', white; 'Telham Beauty', porcelain blue, 2–3-in flowers, 48 in tall; and 'Wirral Blue', rich blue, double-flowered. (See photo.)

Campanula portenschlagiana (muralis) (Dalmatian bellflower)   4–8 in   Sun
Zones 5–9
FLOWERING SPAN: Early June to August
NATURAL COLOR: Light purple-blue
DISTRIBUTION: Yugoslavia

Abundant in flowering, this creeping perennial forms neat but large mats of shiny green, kidney-shaped, 1½-in leaves—possibly evergreen in mild areas—with ½–¾-in, up-facing, star-shaped blossoms. It likes any average-fertility, well-drained soil that is not too dry and accepts light shading. Spring division is the simplest propagation method. Rust disease, slugs, and snails may be problematic at times. The variety *alba* carries white flowering. (See June photo of *Gypsophila repens*.)

Campanula rotundifolia (bluebell, harebell)   6–12 in   Sun   Zones 3–9
FLOWERING SPAN: Mid-June to September
NATURAL COLOR: Bright violet-blue
DISTRIBUTION: Europe, Siberia, North America

Widely distributed, this hardy, durable plant has very narrow, 1½–3-in foliage in grassy tufts. The rounded leaves of its species name exist at ground level and are infrequent. It branched, wiry, flower stalks have 1-in, drooping, bell-shaped blossoms for a lengthy period. Growing best in rich, well-drained, moist soil, it adapts readily to sunlit ledge openings or plant walls. It seeds easily beyond its borders with the potential for becoming weedy. Division or summer stem cuttings also propagate it well. The plant is unbothered by diseases or insects of consequence. Its cultivar 'Olympica' has intensely blue, larger flowers on a compact, 12-in form.

Catananche caerulea (Cupid's dart, blue cupidone)   18–24 in   Sun   Zones 4–9
FLOWERING SPAN: Mid-June to September
NATURAL COLOR: Lavender-blue
DISTRIBUTION: Mediterranean Europe

Although it offers a colorful accent in gardens, its favored use is as a durable dried flower cut at any time in the season. The very narrow, gray-green, lightly hairy leaves appear in a clump at the base of the tall flower stems with their 2-in, many-petaled, flattish blossoms much-incised at the edges. It prefers a well-drained, light, semidry soil in full sun. Early spring division is best, but summer stem cuttings and seeding also propagate it easily. The cultivar 'Alba' has white blossoms; 'Bicolor' has flowers with white edges; and 'Blue Giant' is larger-flowered with deep blue centers and medium blue edges.

Centaurea dealbata   (Persian cornflower)   18–30 in   Sun   Zones 4–9
FLOWERING SPAN: Early June to August
NATURAL COLOR: Rosy purple to pink
DISTRIBUTION: Caucasus Mountains

Feathery, coarsely toothed leaves with silvery undersides may elongate beyond 1 ft, and the erect flower stems produce 2–3-in, solitary terminal blossoms with ragged edges much like its annual relative, bachelor's-button. Any average-fertility, light soil on the dry side satisfies it in full sun, and either spring or autumn division is acceptable. Rust and "yellows" diseases can disfigure the foliage but are not annual problems. Insects appear to avoid it. The cultivar 'John Coutts' (which may be a hybrid, some think, of *C. hypoleuca*) displays bright pink-purple blossoms with a noticeable, yellow center; 'Rosea' has more-silvery foliage and rosy pink flowering; while the vigorous 'Steenbergii' is long-blooming with gray-green leaves and purplish red blooms with white centers. This cultivar has an invasive root system. (See photo.)

Centaurea gymnocarpa   (velvet centaurea, dusty miller)   18–24 in   Sun   Zones 9–10
FLOWERING SPAN: Late June to August
NATURAL COLOR: Rosy violet
DISTRIBUTION: Capri

Limited to growing only in the very warmest areas, this perennial is raised primarily for its neat clumps of very silvered, feltlike foliage. The 1½-in flowers are insignificant and are mostly hidden by the ferny leaves. Useful as a low, trimmed hedge, it enjoys the same general culture as *C. dealbata*.

Centaurea montana   (mountain bluet, mountain knapweed)   12–20 in   Sun   Zones 3–9
FLOWERING SPAN: Mid-June to September
NATURAL COLOR: Bright purple-blue
DISTRIBUTION: Central Europe

The 5–7-in foliage is rough-surfaced, green, and lance-shaped, but juvenile leaves are normally hairy and whitened. The ragged-edged, 3-in, feathery, rounded flowers have very narrow petals far more widely spaced than those of *C. dealbata*. Spreading quickly by underground stems, as well as by prodigious self-seeding, the plant has floppy stems and needs staking in areas of high wind. Propagation by division can take place either in spring or autumn. The cultivar 'Alba' is white; 'Caerulea' is blue; and 'Rubra' is rosy red. (See photo.)

Centranthus ruber (Kentranthus ruber, Valeriana ruber)   (red valerian, Jupiter's beard)   24–36 in   Sun   Zones 4–8
FLOWERING SPAN: Mid-June to September

NATURAL COLOR: Deep crimson to pale red

DISTRIBUTION: Europe, British Isles, North Africa

Durable and long-blooming, this compact perennial has 3–4-in, gray-green, lancelike foliage with terminal, 3-in clusters of tiny florets, nicely perfumed. Provide a sandy, humusy, moist, well-drained location that is slightly acid or neutral in sun or light shading. Shear off the initial flowering to promote additional blooms. Division or seeding will propagate it equally well. The cultivar 'Albus' is white-flowered, and 'Roseus' carries uniformly rosy blossoming. (See photo.)

Cephalaria gigantea (tatarica) (yellow cephalaria) 60–72 in Sun Zones 3–9

FLOWERING SPAN: Late June to August

NATURAL COLOR: Pale yellow

DISTRIBUTION: Caucasus Mountains

Although loosely open in general outline, the plant is showy when flowering with 2-in, scabiosalike, round-faced blossoms on widely branched stems carrying slightly hairy, pinnately divided, lancelike foliage. Very undemanding about soil type but preferring full sun, it has no known pests or diseases. It propagates easiest by self-seeding and may become invasive.

Cerastium biebersteinii (Taurus cerastium) 4–12 in Sun Zones 3–9

FLOWERING SPAN: Early June to July

NATURAL COLOR: White

DISTRIBUTION: Asia Minor

Useful in sunny rock gardens or as a broad edging, the heavy mat of creeping foliage is neat in appearance and conspicuous with narrow, 2-in, woolly, silvered leaves. Bell-shaped, ½-in flowers appear generously. Any average-fertility soil that is well-drained, including pure sand, is acceptable. Shear back heavily for greater compactness after flowering. It is without problems.

Cerastium tomentosum (columnae) (snow-in-summer) 6–12 in Sun Zones 3–8

FLOWERING SPAN: Early June to July

NATURAL COLOR: White

DISTRIBUTION: Mountains of Italy

Spreading easily on hot, rocky slopes in full sun, this shallow-rooted, creeping plant has narrow, ½-in, lancelike, woolly gray, mostly persistent leaves on prostrate stems. Its loose sprays of ¾-in, bell-like flowers carry notched petals. Cut back severely after blooming for greater compactness and new growth. Tolerant of any average-fertility, semidry soil in sun to light shading, it is easily propagated by spring division. Self-seeding may prove generous, too. Nothing bothers it. The cultivar 'Silver Carpet' is 8 in high and has more-silvery foliage, while 'Yo-Yo' grows 10 in tall with greater blossoming. (See photo.)

Chrysanthemum coccineum (roseum, Pyrethrum roseum) (pyrethrum, painted daisy, persian insect flower) 12–24 in Sun Zones 4–9
FLOWERING SPAN: Early June to mid-July
NATURAL COLOR: Carmine red, pink, white
DISTRIBUTION: Iran, Caucasus Mountains

Thin, feathery, 3-in, deep green foliage clumps produce slender-stemmed, unbranched flower stalks topped with showy, 2–3-in daisylike blossoms with bright yellow centers. It thrives on well-drained, moist, sandy soil in full sun but may need extra summer watering if the season is dry. Where winters are severe, provide a light mulch. Fibrous-rooted, it divides easily in early spring or late summer for propagation, and seeding works well, too. Aphids and red spider mites, along with mildew and rust disease, are occasionally problematic. Many cultivars exist in both the single and double forms: 'Brenda', bright cerise, single; 'Carl Voight', white, double; 'Crimson Giant', cerise, single, tall; 'Eileen M. Robinson', salmon-pink, single; 'Helen', soft rose, double; 'James Kelway', scarlet, single; 'Madeleine', bright pink, double; 'Robinson's Mix', mostly tones of red and pink, single; 'Robinson's Pink', medium pink, single; 'Vanessa', rosy carmine, double; 'Victoria', ruby red, single; and 'Snowball', white, double. (See photo.)

Chrysanthemum × superbum (maximum) (shasta daisy, Pyrenees chrysanthemum) 12–36 in Sun Zones 5–9
FLOWERING SPAN: Mid-June to September
NATURAL COLOR: White
ORIGIN: Horticultural hybrid of *C. lacustre × C. maximum*

Conspicuously showy and well-liked for cutting, this yellow-centered, 3–4-in-wide flower is daisylike on heavy stems above deep green, glossy, narrow leaves up to 10 in long. Provide a rich, well-drained, constantly moist location conditioned beforehand with ground limestone (except in an alkaline soil) and divide before the 3rd year to promote continued vigor. Removing the exhausted flowering regularly encourages longer bloom time. Single types enjoy full sun, but doubles appear to do better in some shade. Spring division, summer stem cuttings, and seeding all prove satisfactory for propagation. Aphids and verticillium wilt are the main afflictions. Cultivar selections now offer a wider range of blossom forms: 'Aglaya', 24 in, frilled edges, 3-in blooms, the most double of all; 'Alaska', 24 in, single, 2-in blooms; 'Cobham Gold', 18 in, creamy white, 3-in blooms, double, Zones 6–9; 'Little Miss Muffett', 14 in, semidouble, 3-in blooms, late; 'Majestic', 24 in, single, 4–6-in blooms; 'Mayfield Giant', 42 in, single, 3-in blooms; 'Snowcap', 15 in, single, 3-in blooms, compact; 'Thomas Killen', 18 in, semidouble, 5-in blooms; and 'Wirral Supreme', 30-in, double, 4-in blooms, adaptable to wider growing conditions. (See photo.)

Chrysogonum virginianum (goldenstar) 4–10 in Semishade Zones 5–9
  FLOWERING SPAN: Early June to October
  NATURAL COLOR: Bright yellow
  DISTRIBUTION: Pennsylvania to Florida, west to Louisiana
  Five-petaled, 1-in, daisylike flowers on long, hairy stalks arise almost continually from the leaf axils of this one-species wildflower. It thrives on any moist, humusy, average-fertility, acid-to-neutral soil in semishade to full sun—if kept constantly moist in more light. The oval, hairy, 1–3-in leaves are scalloped on the margins, and the foliage may be fully evergreen in very mild growing areas. Division of the creeping rootstock is possible at any time during the growing season for propagation. There are no troublesome diseases or pests. (See photo.)

Clematis integrifolia 24–36 in Sun Zones 3–8
  FLOWERING SPAN: Mid-June to August
  NATURAL COLOR: Indigo blue
  DISTRIBUTION: Southern Europe, Asia
  Nonclimbing, this herbaceous clematis is sun-loving and presents 1-in, solitary, bell-shaped flowers with noticeably twisted petals. Its dark green, undivided, 2–4-in leaves are widely spaced on thin, sprawling stems which require staking or at least nearby support from other plants. The plant grows easily on any moist, average-fertility soil and can be left undisturbed for many years. Propagation is by spring division, summer stem cuttings, and seeding. Blister beetles and tarnished plant bugs are often bothersome, but diseases are not prevalent. The cultivar 'Hendersonii' is lavender-blue with a longer flowering period. Some authorities believe it is more closely related to *C.* × *eriostemon*.

Clematis recta (ground clematis) 24–48 in Sun Zones 3–8
  FLOWERING SPAN: Mid-June to August
  NATURAL COLOR: White
  DISTRIBUTION: Southern Europe
  Large, terminal sprays of starry, 1-in, fragrant florets appear above feathery, pinnately compound foliage with 1½-in leaflets on rambling, ground-hugging stems. Like *C. integrifolia,* it needs staking or other plant support to show off the blossoming. Culture is the same for both. The variety *mandshurica* is superior with more vigor, greater height, and more flowering from additional axillary clusters. The rare cultivar, 'Plena', carries double flowers, while 'Purpurea' displays coppery purple foliage. (See photo.)

Coreopsis auriculata 12–24 in Sun Zones 4–9
  FLOWERING SPAN: Early June to mid-July
  NATURAL COLOR: Orange-yellow

DISTRIBUTION: Virginia to Florida and Mississippi

The 2-in, daisylike flower has the typical ragged petal edges of the genus, but the simple, 5-in leaves have a pair of protuberances or "ears" at right angles to the main leaf blade. Readily adaptable to any well-drained, average-fertility soil in sun to light shade, it can be propagated with ease by spring division or seeding. Mildew is an occasional nuisance, but insects do not bother it. The dwarf cultivar, 'Nana', has 1–1½-in, golden yellow blossoms on thin, 8–12 in stems and deep green, semiglossy, often-persistent foliage forming thick mats useful in rock gardens or as border edgings. (See photo.)

Coreopsis grandiflora   18–24 in   Sun   Zones 5–9
FLOWERING SPAN: Early June to August
NATURAL COLOR: Bright yellow
DISTRIBUTION: Florida to New Mexico, north to Kansas and Missouri

The orange-centered flowers are 1½–3-in wide, and the lancelike, 3-in leaves are entire—not indented—and run up the stem. It grows well on dry, infertile sites and should not be fertilized in garden locations. Although short-lived from overblooming, it self-seeds generously to fill any gaps by the next season. Its worst affliction is mildew. Several cultivars are available: 'Goldfink', 9 in, deep yellow; 'Sunburst', 30 in, semidouble; 'Sunray', 24 in, compact, double, very drought-tolerant. Whether these hybrids belong here or under *C. lanceolata* is still debated by botanists. (See photo.)

Coreopsis lanceolata   12–24 in   Sun   Zones 5–9
FLOWERING SPAN: Early June to September
NATURAL COLOR: Golden yellow
DISTRIBUTION: Michigan to Florida, west to New Mexico

Similar in appearance to *C. grandiflora,* this commonly seen species has flowers only 2 in wide with somewhat brownish centers. The narrow, hairy, 2–6-in foliage is mostly at ground level. Culture is the same for both, but *C. lanceolata* is longer-lived and can be propagated by spring division. (See photo.)

Coronilla varia   (crown vetch)   12–24 in   Sun   Zones 3–9
FLOWERING SPAN: Mid-June to October
NATURAL COLOR: Pinkish white
DISTRIBUTION: Europe, northeastern United States

Rampantly invasive, this weedy ground cover has its best use as a hardy and durable planting on dry, steep embankments in full sun where not much else will grow. Its fernlike, compound, 2-in leaves appear generously on straggly, trailing stems, and the terminal heads of ½-in, pealike flowers are attractive throughout the summer. This plant self-seeds in tremendous amounts, however, and soon invades all nearby bedding. The roots grow deep and resist division. There are no problematic pests or diseases, but the plant itself might become the real nuisance if not carefully located. The cultivar 'Penngift', developed by the Pennsylvania State University for highway planting use, has solid pink blossoming. (See photo.)

Cypripedium reginae (hirsutum, spectabile) (showy lady's slipper) 18–30 in Semishade Zones 3–9
FLOWERING SPAN: Early June to July
NATURAL COLOR: White with pink-purple shading
DISTRIBUTION: Newfoundland to New Jersey, west to Missouri and Minnesota
      Unusually shallow-rooted for *Cypripedium,* it needs a plentiful supply of leaf mold or humus around its base at all times. The broad, 9-in-long, stem-clasping leaves are entirely hairy and can cause a nuisance rash in some people. The 1–3 pouched blossoms are 3 in wide and long. Culture is the same guesswork as with the May-flowering *C. acaule,* except that this plant prefers almost boggy conditions and a neutral-to-alkaline soil.

Delphinium × *belladonna* 36–48 in Sun Zones 3–9
FLOWERING SPAN: Mid-June to mid-July
NATURAL COLOR: Dark to light blue, white
ORIGIN: Horticultural hybrid of *D. elatum* × *D. grandiflorum*
      Openly branched flower stalks provide many slender spikes of 1½–2-in florets with 1-in spurs. The finely divided foliage is 3–5-in long, deeply cleft, and sharply toothed on the margins. Because this hybrid lacks a central flowering spike, it rarely needs staking but does prefer good air circulation to forestall mildew. As with many of the new types, the plants dwindle to insignificance within a few years and need to be replaced. Cut back the old stalks after bloom for potential repeat flowering in the autumn. Install in a well-drained, moist, sandy, alkaline soil (add ground limestone where soil is acid) in sun or light shade. Propagate by spring division or seeding. Mildew, black spot disease, and crown rot are problems in wet, humid weather, while red spider mites are bothersome pests in hot, dry times. Where winters are severe, apply a light mulch to prevent heaving.
      Many cultivars are available: 'Bellamosa', dark blue; 'Casa Blanca', pure white; 'Cliveden Beauty', deep turqouise; 'Lamartine', vivid gentian blue; and 'Sapphire', delicate, pale blue. The 'Connecticut Yankee Strain' is a much-branched, bushy form with the same color range but shorter to 24–30 in and more wind-proof.

Delphinium elatum (alpinum) 36–84 in Sun Zones 3–9
FLOWERING SPAN: Mid-June to late July
NATURAL COLOR: Blue-purple

DISTRIBUTION: Europe to Siberia

Densely packed florets on tall spikes characterize this well-liked perennial. The group has been so hybridized, however, that clear identification of individuals is no longer a simple task. All grow best in cool areas, need regular fertilizing for quality flowering, but can be devastated by attacks from slugs and snails. Otherwise, cultivate as for D. × belladonna with the added requirement of thinning-out the emerging spring stalks to 3–4 since the root system cannot maintain more at these potential heights. Each plant of this species is distinguished by a set of deeper-colored and contrasting sepals, or "bee" for its appearance, in the middle of each floret. The tall, mostly double-flowered 'Pacific Hybrid' mixture offers named cultivars: 'Astolat', pink; 'Black Knight', deep violet-blue; 'Blue Bird', medium blue; 'Cameliard', lavender-blue; 'Galahad', pure white; 'Guinevere', lavender-pink; 'King Arthur', royal purple; and 'Summer Skies', light blue. The English cultivars from Blackmore, Langdon, and Wrexham are also showy but are normally available here only from seed. (See photo.)

Delphinium grandiflorum (chinense)   12–30 in   Sun   Zones 3–9

FLOWERING SPAN: Late June to August

NATURAL COLOR: Blue to violet

DISTRIBUTION: Siberia, China

Although plants of this species are short-lived, seedlings often can bloom the same year from spring-sown seed. The 1½-in, long-spurred florets are loosely arranged on much-branched, slender, fuzzy stems having stalked lower leaves and unstalked, or sessile, upper ones. Culture is the same as for D. × belladonna. The named cultivars include: 'Azure Fairy', sky blue; 'Blue Butterfly', deep blue; 'Blue Elf', medium blue, dwarfed; 'Blue Mirror', gentian blue; 'Cambridge Blue', rich blue; and 'White Butterfly', pure white. (See photo.)

Dianthus alpinus   3–8 in   Semishade   Zones 4–8

FLOWERING SPAN: Early June to mid-July

NATURAL COLOR: Rosy pink

DISTRIBUTION: Eastern Alps

Unusual as a *Dianthus* by preferring shading, the plant has faintly scented, solitary, 1-in, rounded blossoms speckled in white with a small, central ring of deep crimson. They rise on slender stems from a bright green mat of very narrow, 1½-in leaves. Full flowering can mask the foliage entirely. Drainage must be excellent, and the sandy soil it prefers highly alkaline. Topdress with humus or leaf mold yearly to prevent the center of the clump from dying out. Propagate by division right after flowering or take summer stem cuttings. Crown rot and red spider mites are the most problematic afflictions. This species is the parent of the more desirable hybrid, D. × allwoodii, which blooms in May.

Dianthus barbatus (sweet William) 12–24 in Sun Zones 4–9
FLOWERING SPAN: Early June to mid-July
NATURAL COLOR: Crimson, scarlet, pink, white, often intermixed
DISTRIBUTION: Central and southern Europe, Russia, China
 Individual seedlings are actually biennial (requiring 2 seasons to blossom), but the generous self-seeding which results from an initial planting gives the effect of perennial bedding. The 4-in, dark green, lance-shaped leaves appear on stout, erect flower stems which terminate in 3–6-in, rounded clusters of lightly scented, dense blossoming. The flowers are long-lasting when cut. Although separate colorings are available, the plants easily interbreed to a mongrel mixture with weakened stems and will need eventual replacement. Cultivate as for *D. alpinus.* (See photo.)

Dianthus × *latifolius* (button pink) 10–15 in Sun Zones 5–9
FLOWERING SPAN: Early June to August
NATURAL COLOR: Rose to dark red
ORIGIN: Horticultural hybrid of uncertain parentage
 Prolific in flowering, these plants often exhaust themselves so quickly that only annual division in early spring assures permanence in the garden. The 1-in, single, semidouble, or double, nicely scented blossoms appear 1–6 in clusters and resemble florists' carnations. The stiff, gray-green, 2–3-in, linear leaves are at ground level but not on the erect stems. Provide a rich, sandy, modestly moist soil and winter-mulch in cold areas. The cultivars include: 'Beatrix', double, salmon-pink; 'Furst Bismark', rosy red; 'Raven Rock Red', crimson; and 'Silver Mine', white.

Dictamnus albus (fraxinella) (gas plant, dittany) 24–36 in Sun Zones 3–9
FLOWERING SPAN: Mid-June to mid-July
NATURAL COLOR: White
DISTRIBUTION: Southern Europe to China
 Durably permanent once established, this hardy, one-species perennial has deep roots which adjust well to modest drought and resent relocation except when very young. Terminal flower stalks are 3–4 in wide with many citron-scented, irregularly shaped, 1–2-in florets loosely spaced. The attractive, thick, deep green, pinnately compound leaves have up to 11 lancelike leaflets 3 in long and a pronounced lemon odor when bruised. Some people can develop a nuisance rash from any contact with the foliage. The blossom's volatile fragrance oils can be ignited, supposedly, on quiet, sultry evenings, but this curious bonus obviously has limited appeal. Preferring a rich, moderately moist, heavy soil to do its best, it propagates from careful division in spring. There are no pest or disease problems, but the seed is considered poisonous. The variety *caucasicus,* also white, is a bit larger in every respect, while the cultivar 'Purpureus' has mauve-purple

flowering, and 'Rubra' displays rosy purple ones. The star-shaped seed pods of any are collectible for dried, indoor uses. (See photo.)

Digitalis grandiflora (ambigua) (yellow foxglove) 24–30 in Semishade Zones 4–9
FLOWERING SPAN: Early June to mid-July
NATURAL COLOR: Pale yellow
DISTRIBUTION: Europe, western Asia

At times behaving like a biennial, the plant has long, erect, slender flower stalks with drooping, 2-in, tubular florets marked inside with brown. Early removal of the entire spent stalk usually stimulates some autumn reflowering. The 6–8-in, lancelike leaves are broad, toothed, and carry downy hairs beneath. It enjoys a moist, sandy, acid soil enriched with humus in semishade but will accept more sun if kept consistently moist. Propagate by spring division or by seeding. There are no troublesome insects, yet slugs and snails can be destructive. Mildew and leaf spot disease are the other difficulties. The cultivar 'Canary Bird' has much brighter coloring. (See photo.)

Digitalis lanata (Grecian foxglove) 24–36 in Semishade Zones 4–9
FLOWERING SPAN: Late June to late July
NATURAL COLOR: Creamy yellow to white
DISTRIBUTION: Southeastern Europe, northeastern United States

The tall, nodding flower spikes are densely covered with 1½-in, tubular florets with brown or purple veining and many fine hairs. The lancelike, smooth, 3–5-in leaves are gray-green. Cultivate the same as for *D. grandiflora*.

Digitalis lutea 24–36 in Semishade Zones 4–9
FLOWERING SPAN: Mid-June to mid-July
NATURAL COLOR: Pale yellow
DISTRIBUTION: Southwestern and central Europe, northwestern Africa

Similar in general appearance to *D. grandiflora*, the plant is much more graceful-looking and self-seeds freely. Cultivate the same as for *D. grandiflora*.

Digitalis × mertonensis 24–36 in Semishade Zones 5–9
FLOWERING SPAN: Mid-June to August
NATURAL COLOR: Coppery pink
ORIGIN: Horticultural hybrid of *D. grandiflora × D. purpurea*

This hybrid is unusual in that seed produces all duplicate plants. The foliage is 8–12 in long and 3–4 in wide at the base and gives a coarse appearance. The stout flower stalks carry tubular florets up to 2½ in long with brown spotting, and they benefit from shading during late afternoon. Cultivate the same as for *D. grandiflora*.

Digitalis purpurea (common foxglove) 24–48 in Semishade Zones 4–9
FLOWERING SPAN: Mid-June to mid-July
NATURAL COLOR: Purple, pink, white
DISTRIBUTION: Western Mediterranean region and northwestern United States
  Often behaving more like a biennial than a perennial, this commonest of all foxgloves usually self-seeds prodigiously to keep a patch of itself always present. The 2-in, dark-spotted, tubular flowers appear on only one side of the stout stem above a basal clump of wide, 8–12-in-long, wrinkled, deep green leaves. Mildew on the foliage is common where air circulation is sluggish. Provide a rich, light, moist soil and propagate only by seeding. The 'Excelsior' and 'Shirley' strains from England are superior with a wide range of desirable colorings, blossoming entirely encircling the flower stalk, and upthrust florets. (See photo.)

Dipsacus sativus (fullonum) (fuller's teasel) 48–72 in Sun Zones 4–8
FLOWERING SPAN: Mid-June to early July
NATURAL COLOR: Pale lilac
DISTRIBUTION: Europe, North Africa, Middle East, and northwestern United States
  Coarse in appearance and useful only as background in a wild garden, the dense clusters of tiny flowers on prickly stems later become a thimble-shaped seedhead 4 in tall. The stiff, closely set scales of this fruiting body were once used extensively in earlier centuries for teasing the nap of woolen cloth. Grow from seed in any moist, average-fertility soil and do not fret about pests or diseases. Obviously, the seedheads, when dried, make interesting decorations indoors. (See photo.)

Dodecatheon jeffreyi (tetandrum) (Sierra shooting-star) 8–24 in Semishade Zones 5–9
FLOWERING SPAN: Early June to mid-July
NATURAL COLOR: Rosy purple to pale pink, occasionally white
DISTRIBUTION: Alaska to California, Idaho, and Montana
  With this species the 1½-in, linear leaves rise almost 20 in and surround the erect flower stalk with its 3–18 florets almost 1 in in size. Provide a constantly moist, well-drained, average-fertility soil in semishade to full shade, preferably on a cool site. Seeding produces the best propagation results since the tangled rootstock is difficult to divide successfully. Pests and diseases are uncommon.

Eremurus himalaicus (Himalayan desert candle) 60–84 in Sun Zones 6–8
FLOWERING SPAN: Late June to late July
NATURAL COLOR: White
DISTRIBUTION: Himalaya Mountains
  Strikingly impressive in bloom, this perennial has a solitary, 3–4-in-wide

flower stalk or "candle" composed of many tiny, starlike florets. Unfortunately, the dormant flower bud is not always dependably hardy in cooler zones. Its 3-in-wide, persistent, thick, twisted leaves form a basal clump and can elongate well beyond a foot. The plant needs full sun, a location protected from high wind, and perfect drainage at all times. Provide a sandy, rich soil fertilized generously each spring and water well in dry seasons. Winter mulching is necessary in cold areas, but it must be porous and not hold moisture itself, or the flower bud may still be lost. Seed is difficult to germinate, and although the brittle, fleshy roots are troublesome to divide without damage, division is still the better propagation method. Insects avoid it because of a natural repellent covering on all the flower parts; diseases are unknown. This is a challenging plant with a rewarding flower display for the patient gardener.

Eremurus robustus (giant desert candle) 72–108 in Sun Zones 6–9
    FLOWERING SPAN: Late June to August
    NATURAL COLOR: Salmon pink
    DISTRIBUTION: Central Asia
       Even more dramatic in bloom than *E. himalaicus,* the evergreen leaves of this species are up to 48 in long and bright green. It requires the same fussy care.

Erigeron speciosus 12–30 in Sun Zones 2–9
    FLOWERING SPAN: Mid-June to August
    NATURAL COLOR: Lilac
    DISTRIBUTION: British Columbia to Oregon, Arizona, and New Mexico, east to western South Dakota
       Dependably hardy and vigorous, the plant has smooth, lancelike, 3–6-in leaves surrounding branched flower stalks carrying 1½-in daisylike blossoming. It prefers a light, sandy, well-drained soil in sun or light shade and can be readily reproduced by division in spring or autumn. When established, it tends to self-seed readily. Insects are no bother, but "aster yellows" disease can stunt and disfigure all growth. This species is a parent of the *E.* × *hybridus* cultivars with July bloom.

Euphorbia griffithii (Griffith spurge) 24–36 in Sun Zones 5–9
    FLOWERING SPAN: Mid-June to mid-July
    NATURAL COLOR: Orange-red
    DISTRIBUTION: Eastern Himalaya Mountains
       Sturdy, erect stems carry semiglossy, lancelike, 4-in leaves with reddish midveins. Its terminal, loose flower heads are surrounded by showy, reddened bracts (modified leaves) in the same manner of its cousin, the poinsettia. Slowly expanding from creeping rhizomes, the plant prefers a well-drained, reasonably

moist, modestly fertile site in full sun or light shading. Propagate by spring division and forget about insect or disease nuisances. The cultivar 'Fireglow' is brighter in color. (See photo.)

Filipendula purpurea (Spiraea palmata) (Japanese meadowsweet) 24–48 in Semishade Zones 6–9
FLOWERING SPAN: Late June to September
NATURAL COLOR: Carmine pink
DISTRIBUTION: Japan
   Perhaps the handsomest of this genus, the plant has pinnately compound leaves with the terminal leaflet 4–8 in wide and carrying 5–7 clefts with sawtooth edges. Flowering is terminal with fluffy, flat-headed clusterings of ¾-in, fragrant florets on crimson stems. Provide a very moist, deep, rich soil in semishade, but the plant will accept more sun if kept wet. Propagate by spring division only. Diseases and insects are of no concern. The cultivars include: 'Alba', white but rare in cultivation; 'Elegans', 15 in, white blossoms with red stamens; and 'Nana', 10 in, pink, long-lasting.

Filipendula rubra (Spiraea lobata) (queen-of-the-prairie) 24–108 in Semishade Zones 3–9
FLOWERING SPAN Mid-June to mid-July
NATURAL COLOR: Deep pink
DISTRIBUTION: Pennsylvania to Michigan and Iowa, south to Georgia, Kentucky and Illinois
   Bold, foot-long, feathery plumes of modestly fragrant, ¼-in florets strikingly dominate the dark green, 4–8-in, compound, lobed leaves of this special wildflower. Cultivate the same as for *F. purpurea*. The cultivar 'Venusta' is only 48 in tall with deep rose flowering. (See photo.)

Filipendula ulmaria (Spiraea ulmaria) (queen-of-the-meadow, European meadowsweet) 24–72 in Semishade Zones 3–9
FLOWERING SPAN: Mid-June to August
NATURAL COLOR: Creamy white
DISTRIBUTION: Europe, western Asia, North America
   Similar in general appearance to *F. rubra,* the scented flowers appear in dense panicles with foliage whitened on the undersides. Culture is the same for both. The cultivar 'Aureo-variegata' has yellow-streaked leaves, while 'Plena' has double flowers but is prone to mildew. (See photo.)

Filipendula vulgaris (hexapetala, Spiraea filipendula) (dropwort) 24–36 in Sun Zones 3–9
FLOWERING SPAN: Early June to mid-July

NATURAL COLOR: Creamy white

DISTRIBUTION: Europe, western Asia, Siberia

An attractive, basal clump of narrow, fernlike, pinnately compound leaves, up to 18 in long, surrounds slender but stiff flower stalks with many ¾-in florets clustered into 4-in-wide, flat groupings. Preferring sun or light shade and a moderately moist, rich, well-drained soil, it can be propagated readily either by division in spring and autumn or by seeding. Insects appear to avoid it, but mildew can be widespread in hot, humid weather. The double-flowered cultivar 'Flore-Pleno' grows only 12–15 in high, while 'Grandiflora' has creamy yellow blossoming. (See photo.)

Gaillardia × *grandiflora* (blanket flower) 18–36 in Sun Zones 3–9

FLOWERING SPAN: Mid-June to late September

NATURAL COLOR: Red with yellow tips

ORIGIN: Horticultural hybrid of *G. aristata* × *G. pulchella*

The 3–4-in-wide, daisylike flowers appear on slender, noticeably hairy stems with somewhat thick, lance-shaped, 8–10-in leaves in a basal clump. The raised, central disc of fertile flowers is surrounded by flattened or crinkly petals with noticeable, color-contrasting tips. Grow in borders or wild areas with full sun on a well-drained, rich, light soil. Tolerant of drought, the plant will develop crown rot and excessive foliage in heavy, clayey, consistently moist locations. Propagate by spring division, spring root cuttings, late summer stem cuttings, or seeding. Hybridization has produced some interesting cultivars: 'Baby Cole', 8 in, compact; 'Burgundy', 36 in, narrow-petaled, wine red; 'Dazzler', 36 in, golden yellow with a maroon center; 'Goblin', crimson with cream tips, 12 in; 'Sun God', 24 in, entirely yellow; and 'Wirral Flame', 30 in, deep orange-red throughout. The 'Monarch Strain' is robust, grows to 48 in, and has a variable range of colorings from yellow to orange to deep red. (See photo.)

Genista sagittalis (prostrate broom) 2–8 in Sun Zones 5–9

FLOWERING SPAN: Early June to July

NATURAL COLOR: Vivid yellow

DISTRIBUTION: Central and southeastern Europe, western Asia

As prostrate as a green pancake, this evergreen ground cover is unique for its flattened, ⅓-in-wide, winged stems and very few actual leaves. Those that do exist are oval, up to ¾ in long, and deciduous, so that the "evergreen" designation is one of persistent *stems,* closely overlapped at ground level, not foliage. A near-relative of *Cytisus,* the true broom, this plant produces showy and abundant flowering on erect stalks with clusters of pealike florets. Provide full sun on a sandy, modestly moist, average-fertility soil with good drainage. Older plants resent division or transplanting, so propagate either by seeding or by making summer stem cuttings with a heel of old wood attached. Pests and diseases are uncommon. (See photo.)

Gypsophila repens (dubia) (creeping gypsophila) 2–6 in Sun Zones 3–9
FLOWERING SPAN: Late June to September
NATURAL COLOR: Pinkish white
DISTRIBUTION: Pyrenees and Alps mountains

A hardy, vigorous creeper in the exposed, dry, rocky locations it likes, the spreading, bluish green, grasslike foliage is topped by graceful clusterings of ¼-in, bell-shaped florets. Any alkaline, well-drained, modestly fertile soil is satisfactory. Propagate by division in spring, summer stem cuttings, or seeding. Pests and diseases are inconsequential. The cultivar 'Rosea' has rosy pink blossoming. (See photo.)

Helianthemum nummularium (chamaecistus) (sun rose, rock rose) 9–18 in Sun Zones 5–9
FLOWERING SPAN: Early June to July
NATURAL COLOR: Bright yellow
DISTRIBUTION: Europe

Loosely sprawling, the plant has 1–2-in, narrow, gray-green leaves and terminal clusters of 1-in, saucer-shaped blossoms with frosted edges on crepe-paper-thin petals. Thriving on alkaline, well-drained, dry, sandy, and gravelly locations, it should be cut back heavily after bloom to induce reflowering again in autumn. Spring division, summer stem cuttings, and seeding all work well for propagation. Diseases and insects are not bothersome, but in severe climates mulch lightly for winter. Cultivars abound: 'Apricot Queen', apricot, dense foliage; 'Ben Afflick', orange-yellow; 'Ben Hope', pinkish crimson; 'Ben Ledi', crimson; 'Ben Nevis', yellowish orange; 'Buttercup', golden yellow with gray foliage; 'Fire Dragon', orange-red; 'Gold Nugget', deep yellow, double; 'Jubilee', yellow, double; 'Lemon Queen', bright yellow, double; 'Mrs. Earle', red, double; 'Mrs. Mould', salmon-pink with silvery foliage; 'Rose Peach', peach-pink; 'The Bride', white with gray foliage; and 'Wisley Pink', clear pink with gray foliage. (See photo.)

Hemerocallis lilioasphodelus (flava) (lemon daylily, lemon lily) 24–36 in Sun Zones 4–9
FLOWERING SPAN: Early June to July
NATURAL COLOR: Lemon yellow
DISTRIBUTION: Eastern Siberia to Japan

Individual blossoms of any daylily last just one day, but the tall, leafless flower scapes (blooming stems) rising out of the center of the large mound of arching, narrow foliage carry many buds. In this species the deep green leaves are ¾ in wide and 18–24 in long at ground level. The weak scapes have 6–9 modestly fragrant of lemon, 4-in-wide, bell-shaped blossoms. All daylilies grow well and expand nicely for many years in the same location if the soil is moist, well-

Achillea filipendulina
'Gold Plate'

Achillea ptarmica
'The Pearl'

Achillea tomentosa

Allium christophii

Allium karataviense

Alstroemeria aurantiaca
cultivar

Anthemis tinctoria
'Kelwayi'

Aquilegia flabellata var. *pumila*

Aruncus dioicus

Astilbe × *arendsii*
'Erica'

Astilbe × *arendsii*
'Red Sentinel'

Astilbe × *arendsii*
'White Gloria'

Campanula carpatica
cultivars

Campanula persicifolia

Centaurea dealbata
'Steenbergii'

Centaurea montana

Centranthus ruber

Cerastium tomentosum

Chrysanthemum coccineum
'Robinson's Mix'

Chrysanthemum × *superbum*

Chrysogonum virginianum

Clematis recta

Coreopsis auriculata
'Nana'

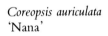

Coreopsis grandiflora
'Sunray'

Coreopsis lanceolata

Coronilla varia

Delphinium elatum
'Galahad'

Delphinium grandiflorum
cultivar

Dianthus barbatus

Dictamnus albus
and *D. albus*
'Rubra'

Digitalis grandiflora

Digitalis purpurea
'Shirley Strain'

Dipsacus sativus (late)

Euphorbia griffithii
'Fireglow'

Filipendula rubra

Filipendula ulmaria

Filipendula vulgaris

Gaillardia × *grandiflora*

Genista sagittalis

Gypsophila repens (left) and
Campanula portenschlagiana

Helianthemum nummularium
'Mrs. Earle'

Hemerocallis lilioasphodelus

Hemerocallis middendorffii

Hesperis matronalis

Heuchera × *brizoides*
'Coral Cloud'

Incarvillea delavayi

Iris × 'Dutch Hybrids'

Iris sibirica
cultivars

Iris sibirica
'Flight of Butterflies'

Kniphofia tuckii

Leontopodium alpinum

Lilium (Asiatic Hybrids: Upright)
'Enchantment'

Lilium (Asiatic Hybrids: Upright)
'Avalon'

Lilium (Asiatic Hybrids: Outward-facing)
'Jasper'

Lilium (Asiatic Hybrids: Pendant)
'Citronella Strain'

Lilium canadense

Lilium candidum

Lilium hansonii

Lilium martagon

Linum flavum
'Compactum'

Lupinus × 'Russell Hybrids'

Lychnis chalcedonica

Lychnis coronaria

Lysimachia nummularia

Lysimachia punctata

Monarda didyma

Monarda didyma
'Granite Pink'

Oenothera fruticosa

Papaver orientale
cultivar

Papaver orientale
'Beauty of Livermore'

Penstemon × *gloxinoides*
'Prairie Fire'

Phlox carolina
'Miss Lingard'

Platycodon grandiflorus
'Mariesi'

Potentilla argyrophylla

Salvia × *superba*
'East Friesland'

Sedum aizoon

Sedum sexangulare

Sempervivum arachnoideum

Sempervivum
cultivars

Shortia galacifolia

Sidalcea malviflora
'Elsie Heugh'

Stachys byzantina

Thermopsis caroliniana

Trollius ledebourii

Valeriana officinalis

Veronica prostrata

Veronica spicata
'Red Fox'

drained, and of average fertility and loose texture. Spring or autumn division is the simplest propagation method for any daylily, yet seed will also work if you have patience for the first bloom. Normally this stalwart plant is unbothered by either insects or diseases, although thrips occasionally mottle the leaves or warp the flower buds in some areas. The cultivar 'Major' is taller with deep yellow coloring. (See photo.)

Hemerocallis middendorffii   12–15 in   Sun   Zones 3–9
   FLOWERING SPAN: Mid-June to mid-July
   NATURAL COLOR: Golden orange
   DISTRIBUTION: Eastern Siberia, northern China, Korea, Japan
       This species has 1-in-wide foliage up to 24 in long, brown-tipped buds, and fragrant, 3-in-long blossoms. Cultivate the same as for *H. lilioasphodelus*. This plant has a surprisingly easy adaptation for growing and blooming well under and near large deciduous plants in either full sun or dappled light. (See photo.)

Hemerocallis thunbergii   24–36 in   Sun   Zones 3–9
   FLOWERING SPAN: Mid-June to mid-July
   NATURAL COLOR: Lemon yellow
   DISTRIBUTION: Japan
       Similar in general appearance but more vigorous and later-blooming than *H. lilioasphodelus,* this plant also carries 4-in, fragrant blossoms, but on a scape that is thicker and flattened about 6 in from the top. Culture is the same for both. Some growers offer this species erroneously as *H. citrina,* which is taller, has a larger flower, but opens only at night.

Hesperis matronalis   (dame's rocket, sweet rocket)   24–36 in   Sun   Zones 3–9
   FLOWERING SPAN: Mid-June to August
   NATURAL COLOR: Purple, lilac
   DISTRIBUTION: Central and southern Europe, North America
       The 4-petaled florets in pyramidal heads and the 4-in, lancelike leaves somewhat resemble summer phlox, but there is no botanical association. Nicely scented—and strongest in early evening—the showy flowering has been appreciated for centuries and can be extended significantly by removing the faded blossoms before they turn to seed. It enjoys a moist, well-drained, alkaline, average-fertility soil in sun to light shade but will adapt to lesser conditions satisfactorily. Not always long-lived, the plant is best propagated by seeding in spring, and new seedlings develop quickly. Cutworms are often troublesome as is a stunting disease spread by aphids. The cultivar 'Alba-plena' is white, double, very fragrant, and superior, but it is temperamental to grow successfully. (See photo.)

Heuchera × *brizoides*   12–30 in   Sun   Zones 3–9
  FLOWERING SPAN: Mid-June to September
  NATURAL COLOR: Red, pink, white
  ORIGIN: Horticultural hybrid of *H. sanguinea* × *H. micrantha* × *H. americana* (possibly)

   Recently introduced for gardens, the plant is far showier in bloom than the popular *H. sanguinea* and will likely supplant it shortly. Both are very hardy and durable. It forms a dense foliage mound at ground level of 2–3-in, rounded, sometimes cleft, deep green leaves which normally persist year-round in zones with moderate winters. The wiry flower stalks appear in quantity and stretch well above the foliage with terminal, loose sprays of ½-in, bell-shaped florets of great durability and long-lasting cutting quality. Grow in a moist, well-drained, humusy soil in sun or light shading and propagate by spring division of the gnarled rootstock or by seeding. Divide every 3–4 years to promote continued vigor. Mulch lightly for winter in severe climates to prevent heaving of the shallow roots. Diseases are rare, but mealybugs can be problematic at times.

   The cultivar list is impressive and originated for the most part in England: 'Chatterbox', pink, large-flowered; 'Coral Cloud', coral-pink; 'Firebird', rich scarlet; 'Freedom', rosy pink; 'Garnet', deep rose; 'Green Ivory', greenish white; 'June Bride', pure white, large-flowered; 'Pluie de Feu', bright red; 'Queen of Hearts', bright salmon; 'Scintillation', bright pink; and 'White Cloud', creamy white. (See photo.)

Heuchera sanguinea   (coral bells)   12–20 in   Sun   Zones 3–9
  FLOWERING SPAN: Mid-June to September
  NATURAL COLOR: Bright crimson
  DISTRIBUTION: New Mexico, Arizona, northern Mexico

   This is the red-flowered parent of the hybrid *H.* × *brizoides* group offered by most growers today. Remarkably long-flowering, the profusion of slim stems on an established plant carry hundreds of bell-shaped, ¼–½-in florets in airy, terminal panicles. The bronze-green basal leaf mass is formed of kidney-shaped or rounded, 1–2-in, crinkled leaves with color-contrasted veining. Provide a rich, well-drained, moist soil in full sun or modest shade and propagate as for *H.* × *brizoides*. Both the cultivars 'Alba' and 'Virginalis' are white forms.

Heuchera villosa   (hairy alumroot)   12–36 in   Sun   Zones 6–9
  FLOWERING SPAN: Mid-June to August
  NATURAL COLOR: White to pinkish white
  DISTRIBUTION: Virginia to Georgia, west to Tennessee

   The deeply cleft, sawtooth-edged, deep green foliage is attractive throughout the growing season and is often covered with small, reddish hairs. Long, wiry, leafless stems carry heavy clusters of ⅛-in, bell-shaped florets for most of the summer. Culture is the same as for *H.* × *brizoides* with perhaps a greater tolerance for dry, rocky sites. The plant combines interestingly as a look-alike foliage companion with *Tiarella* species.

Hieracium villosum (shaggy hawkweed) 12–24 in Sun Zones 3–8
   FLOWERING SPAN: Mid-June to August
   NATURAL COLOR: Golden yellow
   DISTRIBUTION: Southern Europe
      The most modestly behaved of the hawkweeds, known for their capricious spreading, *H. villosum* offers oval, silvery, hairy, 2–3-in leaves in a noticeably tidy basal clump. White-haired flower stalks provide a background sheen for the 1–4 scented, 2-in blossoms resembling the dandelion. It succeeds in any well-drained, average-fertility soil with full sun and propagates well either by spring division or by seeding. Insects and diseases are uncommon.

Incarvillea delavayi (hardy gloxinia) 12–24 in Sun Zones 5–9
   FLOWERING SPAN: Mid-June to mid-July
   NATURAL COLOR: Rosy purple
   DISTRIBUTION: China
      Conspicuous, 2–3-in-wide, trumpet-shaped, yellow-throated blossoms somewhat resembling gloxinia often appear in small clusters before the full appearance of the leaves. The glossy, dark green, pinnately compound foliage can become almost 1 ft long. Not always hardy in the colder limits of its range, it should be winter-mulched heavily in severe climates. Provide a deep, sandy, humusy, constantly well-drained site with ample moisture during flowering. Where summer heat is normally high and constant, plant in a semishaded location. Seeding is far more dependable for propagation than dividing the long taproots. Except for slugs, pests and diseases are not common. (See photo.)

Incarvillea mairei 9–12 in Sun Zones 4–9
   FLOWERING SPAN: Mid-June to mid-July
   NATURAL COLOR: Rosy red
   DISTRIBUTION: China
      The 3–4-in-wide blossoms are larger than in *I. delavayi,* and the foliage leaflets are fewer. Cultivation is the same for both plants. The cultivars 'Bees Pink' and 'Frank Ludlow' are brighter in coloring and only 6–8 in high.

Iris × 'Dutch Hybrids' (Dutch iris) 12–18 in Sun Zones 6–8
   FLOWERING SPAN: Mid-June to mid-July
   NATURAL COLOR: White, yellow, blue, purple, mostly with contrasting colors

ORIGIN: Horticultural hybrids between *I. xiphium, I. tingitana,* and *I. filifolia*

Although a tender bulb, this iris is hardier than either the English or Spanish iris in most of the United States. Producing the familiar "florists' iris" of commerce, it enjoys any moist, well-drained, average-fertility soil in bright sun and benefits from a loose mulch in winter in cold areas. The initial planting of the small bulbs should be in autumn, and expect some narrow, tubular, gray-green foliage to emerge soon after. This new growth persists in good condition through the winter and elongates further in spring. Divide overcrowded colonies by late summer after the foliage dies. Diseases and insects are not bothersome.

The cultivar list is impressive: 'Blue Champion', bright blue with yellow falls; 'Blue Giant', deep indigo blue; 'Blue River', blue bitone; 'Bronze Queen', bronze-purple with deep yellow falls; 'Canary Bird', bright yellow; 'Delft Blue', blue bitone; 'Heracles', a smoky blend; 'Imperator', solid blue with gold blotches on the falls; 'Joan of Arc', white with yellow blotches on the falls; 'King of the Blues', deep blue; 'Lemon Queen', citron yellow; 'Lilac Queen', lilac with white falls; 'L'Innocence', pure white; 'Melody', white with yellow falls; 'Menelik', blue with white falls; 'Orange King', deep orange; 'Wedgwood', light blue with yellow streaks; and 'White van Vliet', ivory white. (See photo.)

Iris sibirica (Siberian iris) 24–36 in Sun Zones 3–9

FLOWERING SPAN: Early June to July

NATURAL COLOR: Deep violet with a white center

DISTRIBUTION: Central Europe, Russia

Cooperatively adapting to almost any site, this very hardy member of the rhizomatous apogon or "beardless" iris group has dense clumps of erect, narrow foliage with quantities of slender flower stalks bearing up to a half dozen 2–3-in-wide blossoms. They make durable cut flowers. Most at home in a moist, acid, humusy soil, the plant will accept heavier, drier sites and modest shading as well. Early spring or autumn division of the fibrous roots is the simplest propagation method, but rebloom in quantity may take 2 growing seasons. Divide every 3–4 years to maintain flower productivity. Diseases and pests are few and far between.

A sizeable number of cultivars are available: 'Blue Brilliant', rich blue; 'Blue Mere', violet-blue; 'Blue Moon', medium blue; 'Caesar's Brother', deep, velvety purple; 'Congo Drums', deep bluish violet; 'Cool Springs', pale violet-blue'; 'Ellesmere', vivid royal blue; 'Eric the Red', reddish magenta, tall; 'Flight of Butterflies', violet-blue, small-flowered; 'Helen Astor', pinkish purple, dwarfed; 'Perry's Blue', sky blue; 'Purple Mere', deep violet-purple; 'Royal Ensign', reddish blue bicolor; 'Showy Egret', white; 'Sky Wings', pale blue; 'Snow Crest', white; 'Snow Queen', white; 'Tealwood', bluish purple; 'Tycoon', deep violet-blue; and 'White Swirl', white with a faint yellow throat. (See photos.)

Kniphofia tuckii   48–60 in   Sun   Zones 6–9
>   FLOWERING SPAN: Mid-June to August
>   NATURAL COLOR: Sulphur yellow, edged in red
>   DISTRIBUTION: South Africa

Showy and long-lasting in flower, this exotic perennial has 3–4-in, swordlike foliage, 12–18 in long in a basal clump. The leafless blossom spikes carry drooping, tubular, ½-in florets tightly clustered in 5–6-in terminal displays. Reasonably hardy in its colder limits, it still requires loose winter mulching to survive. Install in a well-drained, sandy, not overly rich location out of high wind. Although best left undisturbed when established, it can be spring-divided for propagation, but separating the long, ropelike rootstock requires careful digging. Insects are less problematic than leaf spot disease. (See photo.)

Leontopodium alpinum (Gnaphalium leontopodium)   (edelweiss)   6–12 in   Sun
Zones 4–8
>   FLOWERING SPAN: Early June to mid-July
>   NATURAL COLOR: White
>   DISTRIBUTION: Alps, Pyrenees, and Carpathian mountains

Familiar in song and story, but not commonly planted in the United States for unknown reasons, the plant is a rock garden asset in sunny areas. The pencil-wide, slender, silver-gray foliage appears in ground-level clumps with clusters of 1½-in blossoms made noticeable by several woolly leaf bracts surrounding the tiny, yellowish white flowers with a star outline. Best grown in an alkaline soil that is sandy and very well-drained, it needs moisture during spring but dryness in winter. When established, it slowly expands by underground stems. Seeding is the only reliable propagation technique. Nothing unusual bothers it except air pollution, which darkens the silvery foliage. (See photo.)

Leontopodium leontopodiodes (sibiricum)   6–15 in   Sun   Zones 4–8
>   FLOWERING SPAN: Early June to mid-July
>   NATURAL COLOR: White
>   DISTRIBUTION: Siberia

In this species the flowers are almost twice the size of *L. alpinum* and appear singly on the stems, while the foliage is more erect and narrow. Both need the same culture.

Lewisia cotyledon (finchiae)   8–12 in   Semishade   Zones 3–6
>   FLOWERING SPAN: Early June to mid-July
>   NATURAL COLOR: Pink, white with red striping
>   DISTRIBUTION: Mountains of southern Oregon and northern California

Related botanically to the summer annual, *Portulaca,* this showy and evergreen wildflower has thick, fleshy, ground-level rosettes of tongue-shaped, wavy margined leaves 2–3 in long. The branched flower stalks carry many 1-in blossoms with 8–10 petals striped in tones of red. Useful in shaded rockeries, it likes a cool, gritty, absolutely well-drained soil enriched beforehand with acid leaf mold. Propagation is either by seeding or offsets (called "pups") prior to flowering. Neither diseases nor insects are troublesome.

Lewisia rediviva (bitterroot) 2–4 in Sun Zones 3–8
FLOWERING SPAN: Mid-June to August
NATURAL COLOR: Deep rose, white
DISTRIBUTION: Mountains of British Columbia to northern California, east to Colorado and Montana
     The 1-in, chalice-shaped flowers of this deciduous plant (the state flower of Montana) appear only when the needlelike, 2-in foliage retreats into summer dormancy. Provide a rocky, well-drained site in sun which is very dry in summer. Division of the dormant, fleshy, red roots, which once were an American Indian food staple, by late summer is the better method for propagation, although seeding, if slow, gives good results as well. It seems unbothered by diseases or insect pests.

Lewisia tweedyi 4–8 in Sun Zones 3–8
FLOWERING SPAN: Early June to mid-July
NATURAL COLOR: Salmon-pink
DISTRIBUTION: Mountains of central Washington and southern British Columbia
     A fussy plant to grow well, *L. tweedyi* is a strikingly attractive evergreen with 2-in, shimmering blossoms striped in yellow above glossy, 3–4-in, lancelike, basal foliage. Subject to crown rot easily, it requires excellent drainage at all times in a gritty, acid soil with full sun to light shade. Propagate by removing offsets, but dust the cuts with fungicide to forestall rot. Oddly, the flowers need hand pollination to set seed in gardens. Insects, at least, present no special problems.

Lilium (lily) 24–96 in Sun Zones 4–8
FLOWERING SPAN: Mid-June to mid-September
NATURAL COLOR: White, yellow, red, orange, pink, plus many mixtures
DISTRIBUTION: Northern Hemisphere
     Unique in blossom form, fragrance, height, and bulb type, the stately lily has maintained a historical association for 4,000 years with every culture of the North Temperate Zone. As symbols of royalty, religion, and purity, the clusters of sizeable and pleasing flowers have been given featured status in every art form for centuries. The proper classification of the newest hybrids became confused and unwieldy, however, and it took the joint effort of the Royal Horticultural Society in Great Britain and the North American Lily Society to evolve standards for the current horticultural system of 9 divisions based on the ancestral or geographical origin and the form of the blossom.

The June-flowering hybrids of Divisions 1, 2, and 3 are listed below. Divisions 4, 5, and 6, which flower in July, and Division 7 of August are discussed in their respective months. Division 8, all hybrids not provided for in any previous division, and Division 9, all true, wild species and their botanical varieties, follow the main listings.

Classification of Hybrid Lilies

June-blooming Hybrid Lilies

DIVISION 1: Asiatic hybrids: from 24–60 in tall with 4–6-in blossoms. Having the earliest flowering, these are further subdivided into: (a) upright-blossoming, mostly stem-rooting; (b) outward-facing, mostly stem-rooting; and (c) pendant, usually with elongated pedicels (individual flower stalk).

UPRIGHT-FLOWERING EXAMPLES (many are listed as Mid-Century Hybrids in catalogs): 'Avalon', white with purple spotting; 'Cinnabar', crimson; 'Connecticut King', bright yellow with a green center; 'Destiny', lemon yellow; 'Enchantment', deep orange; 'Golden Chalice', deep yellow; 'Harmony', bright orange; 'Joan Evans', golden yellow; 'Tangelo', light orange; and 'Vermilion Brilliant', bright red.

OUTWARD-FACING EXAMPLES: 'Bingo', vivid red; 'Centurion', bright red-orange; 'Gold Shell', bright yellow; 'Jasper', rose and salmon-pink; 'Paprika', rusty red; and 'Sara Marshall', wine red.

PENDANT-FLOWERING EXAMPLES: 'Burgundy Strain', red shades; 'Citronella Strain', yellow shades; 'Connecticut Yankee', spotless salmon-orange; 'Harlequin Jewels', pastels of ivory, buff, salmon, pink, rose, lilac, and purple; and 'Southern Belles', rosy pink.

DIVISION 2: Martagon hybrids: From 36–72 in tall with 3–4-in, heavy-textured blossoms. Having the characteristics of *L. martagon* and *L. hansonii:* small, pendant flowers with recurved tips; stem-rooting.

EXAMPLES: 'Achievement', yellowish white; 'Dalhansonii', purple-brown and mahogany red; and 'Paisley Strain', orange, yellow, white, brown, purple, and lavender colorings and blends.

DIVISION 3. Candidum hybrids: From 36–48 in tall with 4–5-in blossoms. Having the characteristics of *L. candidum* and *L. chalcedonicum:* sharply recurving petals and wide, trumpet-shaped flowers; stem-rooting.

EXAMPLE: *L. testaceum* (Nankeen lily), apricot-yellow, the first recorded hybrid lily.

Relatively easy to grow well and enduring for many years, the lily has a distinctive bulb with no outer skin or tunic covering its overlapping scales, which are actually modified, underground leaves. The round or egg-shaped bulb can be from 2–6 in wide with white, pink, yellow, or brown scales either loosely or tightly attached. Fleshy, somewhat fragile roots come with each bulb and need careful handling to prevent breakage and drying out. Some lilies produce roots only from the bottom of the bulb, while others produce roots both from the bottom and the top of the bulb along the underground part of the stem. Install lilies having only basal rooting at shallow depths in the autumn, but plant those developing additional stem roots only in the spring and at greater depths. Because lilies are dormant for just a brief period, always replant bulbs immediately on receipt or right after garden division. Thoroughly water new installations, even if it is raining, say the experts, to stimulate quick, new rooting.

With the exception of at least the swamp-tolerant *L. superbum* and *L. canadense,* all lilies want excellent drainage throughout the year. Plant in raised beds if surface water moves sluggishly through lily areas. The majority are best installed in a rich, sandy, acid soil deeply improved beforehand with generous amounts of humus, compost, moist peat moss, or leaf mold. Top-dress annually in the spring with several inches of humusy mulching to keep the roots cool and add ongoing nourishment. Avoid applying fresh manure since it fosters disfiguring diseases.

Fertilize with a balanced mixture lightly both before and after the blossoming to improve vigor. Most lilies are sun-lovers, but all dislike windswept and low-elevation locations. Stake the heavy-blossoming or very tall kinds early to forestall stem breakage from gusting winds or downpours. Frequent and thorough watering at flowering, if normal rainfall is scant, gives better bloom. Lilies dwindle into minor assets if planted too close to the moisture-seeking roots or shading from nearby vigorous shrubs and trees. They should be initially installed with this concern in mind.

All of the lancelike foliage, whether singly set or in whorls on the stem, is essential to future flowering and the general livelihood of the bulb. When cutting blossoms for decoration, always leave at least ⅔ of the leaves on the plant since no new foliage reforms to compensate for the loss. Unless wanted for propagation, the quick-forming seed capsules are a drain on the bulb's energies and are best removed early.

Propagating lilies is relatively simple and possible in several ways: seed, bulb scale, offset bulb, and stem bulbil. Divide overcrowded and sparse-flowering colonies after the foliage yellows for the season, but do not expect generous reblooming until the roots have again become fully established.

Insects rarely create nuisances of themselves for lilies, but aphids are now known to carry a viral mosaic disease which seriously mottles the foliage and greatly distorts the blossoming. Infected plants require immediate and complete discard into the trash. Do not replant in the same site for several years. Where the air remains long-stagnant and constantly moist, another disease, *Botrytis elliptica,* can also destroy the foliage and flowers. Mice and gophers relish the bulbs, and protecting them requires the extra work of encasing each bulb in a loose-fitting wire mesh wrapping shaped with enough room to allow for future bulb enlargement. (See photos.)

Lilium canadense (canadense var. *flavum)*   (Canada lily, wild yellow lily, meadow lily) 36–60 in   Semishade   Zones 4–8

FLOWERING SPAN: Late June to August

NATURAL COLOR: Bright orange-yellow to red

DISTRIBUTION: Southeastern Canada to Virginia, west to Ohio and Kentucky

Adaptable to wet, boggy soils of low meadows with tall grasses and shrubs, the bulb is most unusual in not requiring excellent drainage to survive and prosper. Nodding or down-turned, 2–3-in flowers resembling pagoda roofs appear on sturdy stems in loose, open clusters of 6–10 florets with yellow exteriors and orange, dark-spotted interiors. Its 2–3-in, lance-shaped leaves appear in regularly spaced whorls up the stem. Tolerant of full sun if kept wet and heavily mulched, the bulb adapts better to open, acid woodlots with normal moisture and fertility. Propagate by seed or scales and install the base-rooting, new colonies in early autumn. No bothersome pests or diseases are known. The cultivar 'Coccineum' carries orange-red flowers with yellow-spotted centers. (See photo.)

Lilium candidum (album)   (Madonna lily)   36–72 in   Sun   Zones 4–8

FLOWERING SPAN: Mid-June to mid-July

NATURAL COLOR: White

DISTRIBUTION: Balkans, Lebanon, Israel, southern Europe

As the oldest lily of all in cultivation—perhaps 3,500 years—the flowers have an attractive, heady fragrance, and the bulb exhibits a surprising tolerance for alkaline soils. The 4-in upturned blossom clusters are trumpet-shaped with yellow throats and carry noticeable, golden stamens along with reddened pedicels. The heavy flower stalks are lined with very small leaf bracts. Its garden performance is oddly capricious at times for unclear reasons. Provide a rich, limed, well-drained location in full sun and a soil cover *not to exceed* an inch over the bulb top since it is not stem-rooted. Keep the mulch cover thin as well. No other lily has this unusual requirement. Seed is rarely fertile, and therefore scales or bulb offsets are the usual methods for propagation. Early autumn planting only is recommended for initial colonies, but overcrowded groups can be transplanted when the foliage fades. Expect a rosette of winter-hardy foliage to emerge soon after planting. Diseases and insect nuisances are described in the preceding essay on *Lilium.* The variety *salonikae* blooms earlier, has wavy bottom foliage, more open-petaled flowering, and carries green—not reddish—pedicels for the blossoms. (See photo.)

Lilium hansonii (Japanese turk's-cap lily) 36–60 in Semishade Zones 4–8
FLOWERING SPAN: Mid-June to mid-July
NATURAL COLOR: Orange-yellow
DISTRIBUTION: Korea, Japan, and adjacent Siberia
    Preferring semishade but cooperatively adaptable to sunnier locations when kept consistently moist, this spicily fragrant lily accepts a wide range of soils, including limed ones, to become a special garden asset. Clusters of 2-in, pendant, star-shaped florets appear on arching stems and show thick, waxy, recurved petals spotted noticeably in brown. The 4–5-in leaves are in whorls. These bulbs increase readily in a humusy, light, moist location and can be propagated best by offsets or scales. Diseases and pests are not common. This is a stem-rooting bulb for spring planting. (See photo.)

Lilium martagon (turk's-cap lily, martagon lily) 36–72 in Semishade Zones 4–8
FLOWERING SPAN: Early June to July
NATURAL COLOR: Rosy purple
DISTRIBUTION: Most of Europe, western Asia, Mongolia
    This bulb produces up to 50 waxy, drooping, 2–3-in blossoms on purplish stems with dark green, 3–6-in, sometimes hairy leaves. The scent, unfortunately, is disagreeably strong. The plant grows well in any light, moist, well-limed soil with semishade but adapts to more sun when kept very moist in the growing season. Where it enjoys its location, it can naturalize. Scales and offsets propagate it faster than seeding, and new plantings should be made in spring since it is a stem-rooting bulb. Pests and diseases are unimportant. The variety *album* has pure white flowers on green stems; *cattaniae* is deep purple-red and unspotted; *hirsutum* is purplish pink and shorter. (See photo.)

Linum flavum (golden flax) 12–24 in Sun Zones 5–9
FLOWERING SPAN: Mid-June to mid-July
NATURAL COLOR: Golden yellow
DISTRIBUTION: Europe
    Similar in general appearance to the May-blooming species except for coloring, the culture is the same for all. A dwarfed cultivar 'Compactum' is only 6 in tall, while 'Cloth of Gold' attains a height of 9 in. (See photo.)

Lotus corniculatus (bird's-foot trefoil) 4–18 in Sun Zones 5–8
FLOWERING SPAN: Mid-June to September
NATURAL COLOR: Bright yellow
DISTRIBUTION: Temperate zones of Europe and Asia
    Generally sprawling in habit, the plant is a vigorous creeper useful for covering dry, infertile embankments with full sun, yet it can easily become weedy

in fertilized, moist garden locations. Terminal clusters of 8–10 sweet pealike, ½-in florets occur throughout the summer above tiny, 3-parted, compound leaves. Propagate either by spring division or by seeding. Pests and diseases are unimportant.

Lupinus polyphyllus   24–60 in   Sun   Zones 4–7
FLOWERING SPAN: Mid-June to September
NATURAL COLOR: Deep blue, reddish blue, violet
DISTRIBUTION: California to British Columbia

Generous quantities of sturdy flower spikes up to 8 in long appear terminally on tall stalks above palmately compound, 2–5-in green leaves with 12–18 narrow leaflets. Preferring a cool, acid site in full sun, but tolerant of light shade, the sweet pealike blossoms appear for extended periods where the soil is rich, deep, moist, and excellently drained. Resenting transplanting once established, it is best propagated by seed. Mildew and stem rot are serious afflictions, along with aphid infestations and slug damage. Many named types are known in various colorings, but these have generally been replaced in nurseries by the superior *L.* × 'Russell Hybrids', and this species may be one of the parents.

Lupinus × 'Russell Hybrids' (Russell hybrid lupine)   36–48 in   Sun   Zones 4–7
FLOWERING SPAN: Mid-June to September
NATURAL COLOR: Blue, purple, white, yellow, orange, red, pink, and bicolors
ORIGIN: Horticultural hybrid of uncertain parentage

These long flower stalks are normally covered by 18–24 in of crowded, 1-in, sweet pealike florets in a rainbow of colorings. Water deeply in dry times and mulch heavily to conserve soil moisture longer. Remove the spent flower stalks early to encourage further bloom. Not long-lived beyond 4 years in one location, the plant can be propagated either by spring seeding or by early spring, basal stem cuttings with a portion of root attached. The general appearance is similar to that of *L. polyphyllus,* and the culture is the same for both. Neither adjusts to alkaline soils. (See photo.)

Lychnis chalcedonica (Maltese-cross, Jerusalem cross, scarlet lightning)   18–24 in   Sun
   Zones 3–9
FLOWERING SPAN: Mid-June to August
NATURAL COLOR: Vivid scarlet
DISTRIBUTION: Northern Russia, Siberia

Terminal heads of 10–50 closely packed, ¾-in, notched florets resembling crosses appear on somewhat hairy stems above dull green, lancelike, 2–4-in leaves. Blossoming is extended by removing faded flowers early. Provide a well-drained, sandy, average-fertility soil in full sun or light shading and expect moderate drought tolerance. Spring or autumn division, along with seeding, propagates it readily. Insects are not troublesome, but smut disease causes disfigurement. The cultivars include: 'Alba', white; 'Grandiflora', flaming scarlet, larger blossoms; 'Plena', scarlet, double-flowered; 'Rosea', rosy red, double, tender; and 'Salmonea', salmon-rose. (See photo.)

Lychnis coronaria (Agrostemma coronaria) (rose campion, mullein pink) 12–36 in Sun
   Zones 3–9
   FLOWERING SPAN: Mid-June to mid-July
   NATURAL COLOR: Vivid cerise
   DISTRIBUTION: Southeastern Europe, central Asia, northwestern Africa
      Distinguished by oblong, 4-in, white-woolly leaves and silvery flower stalks, the solitary, 1-in, round blossoms appear on wide-branching stems. Not very long-lived, the plant self-seeds generously each year to fill in any gaps. Cultivate the same as for *L. chalcedonica,* except that this species tolerates poorer, drier conditions well. The cultivar 'Alba' has white flowering; 'Atrosanguinea' is dark red; and 'Abbotswood Rose' is vivid magenta. (See photo.)

Lychnis flos-cuculi (ragged robin, cuckoo flower) 12–36 in Sun Zones 3–9
   FLOWERING SPAN: Mid-June to September
   NATURAL COLOR: Deep rose, white
   DISTRIBUTION: Europe, Quebec to Pennsylvania
      Narrow, 3–4-in, lancelike, widely spaced leaves on slender stems surround quantities of terminal, serrated blossoms throughout most of the summer. It grows readily on any moist, average-fertility soil and can be reproduced by seeding, division, or summer stem cuttings. Nothing seems to pester it.

Lychnis flos-jovis (Agrostemma flos-jovis) (flower-of-Jove) 12–36 in Sun Zones 3–9
   FLOWERING SPAN: Mid-June to August
   NATURAL COLOR: Pink, carmine, purple
   DISTRIBUTION: Alps
      The broad, 3-in foliage is gray-green and appears as a basal rosette. The ½-in florets are tightly packed in terminal heads of 4–10 parts and continue for a long period. Readily adaptable to any well-drained, moist, average-fertility soil in full sun to light shading, the plant is propagated by either division or seeding. There are no diseases or insect nuisances.

Lysimachia nummularia (moneywort, creeping Jenny, creeping Charlie) 1–2 in
   Semishade Zones 3–9
   FLOWERING SPAN: Early June to August
   NATURAL COLOR: Deep yellow

DISTRIBUTION: Northern Europe, British Isles, eastern North America

Remarkably adaptive to any moist soil and almost any light condition, this quick-growing, sometimes invasive ground cover produces quantities of cup-shaped, ½-in flowers on short, erect stems above deep green, ¾-in, rounded leaves. Propagate by simple division in spring or early autumn and by summer stem cuttings. Pests and diseases are infrequent. The cultivar 'Aurea' carries bright yellow foliage, less bright in deep shading. (See photo.)

Lysimachia punctata (yellow loosestrife) 18–48 in Semishade Zones 4–9
FLOWERING SPAN: Mid-June to mid-July
NATURAL COLOR: Bright yellow
DISTRIBUTION: Central and southern Europe, United States

This plant is unusually arranged in that both the 3–4-in, lancelike leaves and the 1-in, star-shaped blossoms alternate in clustered whorls all along the slender, erect stems. Its exuberant growth can quickly turn invasive due to far-reaching underground stems, especially in rich, moist locations. Preferring some shade, it adapts to full sun if kept wet. Division in spring or autumn, plus seeding, propagates it easily. White fly infestations and stem rot are occasional problems. (See photo.)

Lysimachia vulgaris (garden loosestrife) 36–60 in Sun Zones 3–9
FLOWERING SPAN: Mid-June to mid-July
NATURAL COLOR: Golden yellow
DISTRIBUTION: Europe, Asia, North America

Its hairy stems are somewhat sticky and carry dull green, pointed leaves either in pairs or whorls. The showy, terminal clusters of cup-shaped, 1-in flowers are erect and occasionally edged in red. Found wild in wet, streamside locations, it adjusts well to moist, average-fertility garden soil in bright sun or light shade. Seeding or simple division reproduces it easily, and pests or diseases are not troublesome.

Malva alcea (mallow, hollyhock mallow) 36–48 in Sun Zones 4–9
FLOWERING SPAN: Late June to September
NATURAL COLOR: Deep rose, pink
DISTRIBUTION: Europe, eastern United States

Downy, deepy cleft, 2–3-in, light green leaves on erect, stiff stems are topped by clusters of long-lasting, 2–3-in, bowl-shaped, notched flowers. Several blossoms are normally open at one time. Adaptable to almost any soil and tolerant of drought and high heat, this perennial can be left undisturbed indefinitely. Seeding, division, and summer stem cuttings propagate it equally. While it has no diseases of note, the Japanese beetle has a fondness for the blossoms. The preferred variety *fastigiata* is more erect, deeper-colored, and carries 3-in flowers.

Meconopsis cambrica (Welsh poppy)   12–24 in   Semishade   Zones 6–9
   FLOWERING SPAN: Mid-June to mid-July
   NATURAL COLOR: Lemon yellow
   DISTRIBUTION: Western Europe
      The attractive foliage clump has hairy, light green, deeply cut, 6–8-in, lancelike leaves and 2½-, round, papery-thin flowers on slender stems. Provide a moist, humusy, well-drained soil, and propagate either by spring division or by seeding—but the seed must be fresh for good germination. Nothing seems to pester its growth. The cultivar 'Aurantiaca' has orange flowering, while 'Flore-Pleno' carries very double, yellow blossoming with conspicuous scarlet veining.

Monarda didyma (beebalm, Oswego tea)   18–36 in   Sun   Zones 4–9
   FLOWERING SPAN: Mid-June to September
   NATURAL COLOR: Bright scarlet
   DISTRIBUTION: New England to Georiga, west to Tennessee
      Ragged-edged, round, 3-in heads of many slender, tubular florets appear at the tips of this vigorous, quick-growing perennial's squared, hollow stems. The rough-haired, 4-in, toothed, bronze-green leaves are spearhead-shaped and aromatic like mint when bruised. (The plant is related to *Mentha,* or mint, as evidenced by its squared stems.) It grows easily on any moist, well-drained, average-fertility soil in either sun or light shading and is propagated easiest by simple division in spring. Insects appear to avoid it, but both mildew and rust disease are destructive to the foliage. The cultivars are superior: 'Adam', 30 in, bright red; 'Cambridge Scarlet', 26 in, crimson, large-headed; 'Croftway Pink', 36 in, clear rosy pink; 'Granite Pink', 30 in, pink; 'Mahogany', 36 in, deep red-brown; 'Prairie Glow', 30 in, salmon-red; 'Prairie Night', 36 in, violet-purple; 'Snow White', 24 in, white; and 'Violet Queen', 36 in, lavender-violet, mildew-resistant. All are attractive to both hummingbirds and hummingbees, which are a bit larger than the bumblebees but with the speed of the hummingbirds. (See photo.)

Nepeta × faassenii (pseudo-mussinii) (Persian catmint)   12–24 in   Sun   Zones 3–8
   FLOWERING SPAN: Early June to August
   NATURAL COLOR: Soft lavender
   ORIGIN: Horticultural hybrid of *N. mussinii × N. nepetella*
      Useful as a billowy, rampant ground cover, especially when positioned to cover the dying foliage of spring bulbs, this quick-spreading perennial enjoys full, hot sun on a well-drained, sandy, average-fertility soil. The silvery gray, 1¼-in, lancelike leaves have a minty aroma when crushed (like *Monarda,* it is also related to true mint) and are topped by a profusion of trumpet-shaped, ½-in, florets in branched clusters. Cut back all growth heavily after the first bloom for repeat flowering in autumn. Only spring division is workable for propagation

since this is a sterile hybrid. Rust disease on the foliage is an occasional nuisance, but insects give it wide berth.

The cultivar 'Six Hills Giant' is 24 in high with aromatic, grayish leaves and violet-blue, sterile blossoming. The cultivars 'Blue Wonder', 15 in, lavender-blue, and 'White Wonder', 12 in, white-flowered, are often listed with *N.* × *faassenii* as well, yet some authorities contend they rightly are related only to *N. mussinii,* which has just minor appeal today.

Oenothera fruticosa (sundrops)   12–24 in   Sun   Zones 4–9
   FLOWERING SPAN: Early June to mid-July
   NATURAL COLOR: Bright yellow
   DISTRIBUTION: Eastern United States
      Highly variable in appearance from region to region, the erect, woody stems and 1–3-in, lancelike leaves are normally covered with noticeable, soft hairs. Its day-blooming, 1–2-in, cup-shaped flowers appear in terminal clusters and bloom for a lengthy time. Shallow-rooted but tolerant of some dryness, it thrives on any moist, well-drained, average-fertility soil in full sun or light shading. Stem leaves generally turn reddish in the autumn, but the ground-level, evergreen rosette of flattened foliage becomes bronzed. Spring division only is recommended for propagation. Occasionally white fly infestations occur in very dry weather, but diseases are of little concern. This plant is commonly confused when young with *O. tetragona,* which blooms a few weeks later and is taller. (See June photo and July photo of *Gypsophila paniculata.*)

Oenothera missouriensis (macrocarpa)   (Ozark sundrop, Missouri primrose) 9–18 in
   Sun   Zones 4–9
   FLOWERING SPAN: Mid-June to August
   NATURAL COLOR: Lemon yellow
   DISTRIBUTION: Missouri and Kansas to Texas
      Flowering from late afternoon to nighttime, the plant carries fragrant, 5-in, funnel-shaped blossoming emerging from noticeably long-tapered, red-streaked buds. The hairy, 4–6-in, lance-shaped, glossy, deep green leaves appear on weak, trailing stems. Best grown in full sun, it enjoys excellent drainage on a deep, rich, alkaline soil that is only moderately moist. For propagation spring division is the preferred method. Stem rot and white fly invasions are the chief problems.

Oenothera tetragona (fruticosa var. *youngii)*   18–36 in   Sun   Zones 4–9
   FLOWERING SPAN: Mid-June to August
   NATURAL COLOR: Lemon yellow
   DISTRIBUTION: Eastern United States
      Found native in the same general areas as its look-alike, but shorter, O.

fruticosa, this daytime-blooming species has cup-shaped, 1½-in blossoms appearing in long-lasting terminal clusters on reddish stems with linear foliage up to 8 in long. Cultivate the same as for *O. missouriensis* but know that too much fertilizing produces foliage in excess with a reduction in flowering. The variety *fraseri* of the southern Appalachian Mountains has blossoms up to 2½ in wide, while *riparia* is exceptionally long-flowering with oversized blooms. The popular cultivar 'Fireworks' has bright red budding, stands but 1 ft high, and displays large, golden yellow blooms along with leathery, bronze-green leaves; 'Yellow River' is 24 in tall with lemony, 2-in flowers.

Opuntia humifusa (compressa)   10–15 in   Sun   Zones 5–10
FLOWERING SPAN: Mid-June to mid-July
NATURAL COLOR: Chrome yellow
DISTRIBUTION: Massachusetts to Florida, west to eastern Texas and north to Montana

In sandy or rocky, well-drained, sunny locations, this hardy cactus thrives. It has thick, oval, 6-in sections joined end to end and carries very few spines. Frilly, 3–4-in blossoms appear in dense clusters and are followed by 1½-in, purplish fruit that is not palatable. The small, red-brown hairs on the smooth stem parts detach easily and can work themselves under the skin to produce an annoying inflammation. Wear heavy gloves when breaking off a pad for reproduction purposes. These root well in barely moist sand. Diseases and insects are not common, but the plant itself is becoming invasive in its southern range on open, infertile land. The cultivar 'Arkansas Yellow' is generous with its flowering.

Papaver orientale (bracteatum)   (oriental poppy)   24–48 in   Sun   Zones 3–8
FLOWERING SPAN: Early June to July
NATURAL COLOR: Scarlet with a blackened base
DISTRIBUTION: Southwestern Asia

Conspicuous in flower, the plant carries 6–12-in-wide blossoms with crinkly, tissue-paper-thin petals on hairy, erect stems easily distorted by heavy rain or even the flower weight. Blossom interiors are enhanced by a tall, broad ring of black stamens. When collecting flowers for arranging, first sear the cut end with flame to stop the flow of milky sap and then plunge the stems into a deep bucket of warm water to harden-off for a few hours. The greatly cleft, 12-in, silvery green leaves are hairy and rough-textured in sizeable clumps at ground level. All foliage disappears soon after flowering is completed, leaving obvious openings in borders. However, new leaves, greatly reduced in size, reappear by late summer. Position poppies so that some other perennial can provide foliage cover for the bare spots when the poppy goes into dormancy. Its deep taproots need a cool, well-drained, average-fertility site, and the flowers resent very high humidity when blooming. Root cuttings are the easiest and best propagation method. Make these during late summer dormancy. Stem blight and aphid infestations are the worst problems but are not always annual difficulties.

A large list of desirable cultivars exists: 'Beauty of Livermore', 30 in, deep red; 'Glowing Embers', 30 in, orange-red; 'Helen Elizabeth', 30 in, light salmon-pink; 'Indian Chief', 30 in, dark red; 'Marcus Perry', 30 in, orange-red; 'Mrs. Perry', 36 in, salmon-pink; 'Perry's White', 30 in, pure white; 'Pinnacle', 30 in, white with an orange-red rim; 'Princess Louise', 36 in, bright salmon-pink; 'Raspberry Queen', 30 in, vivid raspberry red; 'Salome', 30 in, rosy pink; 'Show Girl', 36 in, bright pink; 'Springtime', 36 in, white with a pale pink border; and 'Sultana', 30 in, peach-pink. (See photos.)

Paradisea liliastrum (Anthericum liliago) (St. Bruno's lily, paradise lily) 18–24 in Sun Zones 5–9
FLOWERING SPAN: Mid-June to mid-July
NATURAL COLOR: White
DISTRIBUTION: Mountains of southern Europe

This nonbulbous member of the lily family has a more refined appearance than its close relative, *Anthericum liliago,* which blooms at the same time. Its fleshy tubers produce attractive, 24-in, sedgelike foliage and erect, thin stems of trumpet-shaped, 1¼-in, scented florets with golden stamens. The blossoms are arranged on only one side of the stalk. Provide a moist, very fertile, humusy, well-drained location. Divide the brittle tubers in autumn or else seed for reproduction. Two seasons are needed for divided plants to rebloom in strength. Diseases and insect nuisances are not usual. The cultivar 'Major' is taller with larger florets.

Penstemon barbatus (Chelone barbata) 36–48 in Sun Zones 3–8
FLOWERING SPAN: Mid-June to mid-July
NATURAL COLOR: Bright scarlet
DISTRIBUTION: Utah to Mexico

Pendant, 1-in, tubular blossoms with a yellow lower lip are widely spaced on slender, erect stems along with smooth, deep green, narrow, 6-in leaves. The plant enjoys a very well-drained, moist, average-fertility soil with full sun in northerly areas but more shading in the very hot southern zones. Spring division or seeding propagate it readily. Crown rot is its chief difficulty, and mulching with small stones may help to correct the problem. The cultivar 'Rose Elf' is 18 in tall with coral-rose coloring and extended bloom.

Penstemon × *gloxinoides* 24–30 in Sun Zones 5–10
FLOWERING SPAN: Mid-June to September
NATURAL COLOR: Red, pink, lavender, white
ORIGIN: Horticultural hybrid of *P. cobaea* × *P. hartwegii*

Botanists agree this is not a valid scientific name, but no one has yet derived a more accurate one, and so it continues in use. With this plant the tubular florets are 2 in long and appear in heavy clusters. Removing the faded flower stalks prolongs bloom. Culture is identical with that for *P. barbatus,* but few of its cultivars are reliably hardy in all zones. Available cultivars are: 'Firebird', 18–24 in, crimson, tender; 'Holly's White', 24 in, white with a pink overcast; 'Indian Jewels', 18–24 in, mixed colorings; 'Midnight', 24 in, deep purple; and 'Prairie Fire', 30 in, coral red. (See photo.)

Phlox carolina (suffruticosa) (thick-leaf phlox)　24–42 in　Sun　Zones 4–9
FLOWERING SPAN: Early June to mid-July
NATURAL COLOR: Pink, rose, purple
DISTRIBUTION: North Carolina to northwestern Florida, west to Mississippi and Missouri

The 4–5-in, high-headed clusterings of ¾-in florets make a long-lasting display which can be extended by removing faded blossoms before they set seed; smaller flower heads from the leaf axils at the top soon emerge. The thick, glossy, 4–5-in, slender-pointed leaves are a visual asset and are less susceptible to mildew than other species, especially on consistently moist sites. Grow in a well-drained, airy, average-fertility location enriched liberally with compost, humus, or peat moss. Spring or autumn division and top stem cuttings made in summer propagate it well. When grown too dry, the plant develops red spider mite infestations and has greater susceptibility to mildew. The salmon-pink cultivar 'Gloriosa' is superior for coloring, while 'Miss Lingard', pure white, is an outstanding addition to any garden. Some authorities believe 'Miss Lingard' belongs with *P. maculata,* which has a white wild form, instead of with *P. carolina,* which does not. (See photo.)

Phlox maculata (wild sweet William, meadow phlox)　24–48 in　Sun　Zones 3–9
FLOWERING SPAN: Early June to late July
NATURAL COLOR: Reddish purple, pink, white
DISTRIBUTION: Connecticut to North Carolina, west to Iowa

This species is rarely cultivated today, but its cultivars are much admired. The fragrant, 5–6-in flower heads appear on purple-spotted stems with 2–4-in, very smooth, glossy, slender leaves ending in points. Use the same culture as for *P. carolina.* Its cultivars include: 'Alpha', soft, rosy magenta; 'Omega', white with a pale violet overcast and violet eyes; and 'Rosalinde', purplish pink to magenta with vigorous, 48-in stems.

Platycodon grandiflorus (glaucus) (balloon flower)　18–30 in　Sun　Zones 3–9
FLOWERING SPAN: Mid-June to late July
NATURAL COLOR: Blue, lilac, white

DISTRIBUTION: Eastern Asia

Slow in spring to produce any new growth, this showy, one-species plant may benefit from prior marking to indicate its location. The slender, erect stems become floppy and need support when flowering and carry gray-green, spearhead-shaped, 2–3-in leaves. The stems are topped by clusters of unusual, puffed budding resembling small balloons, and these open into 2½-in-wide, saucerlike stars. Sear the milky stems with flame after cutting for indoor use. Provide a well-drained, consistently moist, sandy soil of average fertility in sun or light shading. Propagation by seed is better than attempting to disentangle the deep, brittle roots of established plants. Pests and diseases are uncommon. The list of cultivars is generous: 'Albus', white; 'Apoyama', medium blue, dwarfed; 'Mariesi', 18 in, blue, white, or pink-toned; 'Mother of Pearl', pale pink; 'Shell Pink', pale pink; and 'Snowflake', semidouble, white. (See photo.)

Polemonium boreale (humile, richardsonii) (skunkleaf Jacob's-ladder) 6–9 in Semishade Zones 2–7
FLOWERING SPAN: Early June to July
NATURAL COLOR: Pale blue to purplish blue
DISTRIBUTION: Arctic regions

Undeniably hardy, the plant is well-adapted for rock gardens with some shade as well as for naturalized areas. Its ½-in, bell-shaped florets have golden stamens and appear in clusters at the tops of hairy stems with compound foliage showing 13-23 wedge-shaped leaflets. Cultivate the same as for the May-blooming *P. caeruleum*. The cultivar 'Album' has all-white blossoms.

Polygonum bistorta (snakeweed, bistort) 12–20 in Sun Zones 3–9
FLOWERING SPAN: Mid-June to August
NATURAL COLOR: Pale pink
DISTRIBUTION: Northern Europe, Asia

The 10-in basal foliage is wide and docklike with moderately wavy, toothed edges. Erect, branches stems carry dense, 3-in spikes of tiny florets which persist for a lengthy time. It prefers a damp, fertile site in sun to light shade in its northern range and more shading where summer heat is consistently high. Pests and diseases are rare. The cultivar 'Superbum' is noteworthy with more size in all its parts and more vivid coloring.

Potentilla argyrophylla 24–36 in Sun Zones 5–9
FLOWERING SPAN: Early June to mid-July
NATURAL COLOR: Bright yellow
DISTRIBUTION: Himalaya Mountains

The distinctive, strawberrylike foliage of 3 palmately compound, sharp-toothed leaflets is probably more interesting than the plant's 1-in, saucer-shaped flowering on loosely arranged, silky stems. The undersides of the leaves are coated with silver. Thriving in full sun with only moderate soil moisture, the plant adapts to any soil from poor and dry to average and damp. Spring division and autumn basal cuttings propagate it well. Leaf spot disease is the chief nuisance. (See photo.)

Potentilla atrosanguinea (ruby cinquefoil)   12–18 in   Sun   Zones 5–9
    FLOWERING SPAN: Mid-June to August
    NATURAL COLOR: Dark purplish red
    DISTRIBUTION: Himalaya Mountains
       Very similar in general appearance to *P. argyrophylla* except for its height, the divided foliage on this shorter species is less silvery and slightly larger. Culture for both is identical. The cultivar list includes: 'Etna', deep crimson; 'Firedance', rich red with a wide yellow border; 'Gibson's Scarlet', deep red; 'Monsieur Rouillard', coppery red, double; 'William Rollisson', reddish orange, semidouble; and 'Yellow Queen', bright yellow with a red center, dwarfed.

Primula beesiana (Bee's primrose)   18–24 in   Semishade   Zones 5–8
    FLOWERING SPAN: Mid-June to mid-July
    NATURAL COLOR: Rosy purple
    DISTRIBUTION: China
       Similar to the May-flowering *P. japonica* by having candelabrum-type blossoming in tiers, the ¾-in florets of *P. beesiana* are distinguished by noticeable gold eyes and blunt, lancelike, 9-in, deciduous foliage. Best grown in a cool, very moist—almost boggy—soil well-enriched with humus or compost, this showy perennial is afflicted with red spider mites when the soil and the air are too dry for long periods. Propagate either by simple division in spring or by making root cuttings after flowering. It benefits from a winter mulching in colder regions.

Primula × *bullesiana*   18–24 in   Semishade   Zones 5–8
    FLOWERING SPAN: Mid-June to mid-July
    NATURAL COLOR: Cream, orange, rose, pink, purple, mauve, deep red
    ORIGIN: Horticultural hybrid of *P. beesiana* × *P. bulleyana*
       Here is a rainbow-colorful addition to any garden in semishade. Grow as for *P. beesiana,* which it closely resembles.

Primula bulleyana (Bulley's primrose)   24–30 in   Semishade   Zones 5–8
    FLOWERING SPAN: Mid-June to August
    NATURAL COLOR: Deep yellow, reddish orange

DISTRIBUTION: China

A rosette of paper-thin, 5–14-in leaves with red midribs gives rise to a stout flower stalk with 5–7 tiers of heavily crowded, 1-in blossoms. Cultivate the same as for *P. beesiana*.

Salvia × *superba (nemorosa)* 24–48 in Sun Zones 4–9
FLOWERING SPAN: Late June to September
NATURAL COLOR: Bright violet
ORIGIN: Horticultural hybrid of *S. sylvestris* × *S. villicaulis*

Ornamental for a long time, the 12–15-in flower stalks carry clusters of sterile, ½-in, tubular florets above rough-textured, 2–3-in gray-green, oblong leaves. The stems are erect, reddened, and squarish (like other members of the mint family). Any average-to-poor soil, well-drained and dry, suits it well. Fertilizing is not necessary. Division in spring or autumn, plus seeding, reproduces it readily. White fly and red spider mites attack the foliage, but diseases are not common. Several cultivars are available, among them: 'East Friesland', 24 in, purple, and 'May Night', 24 in, deep violet-blue. Both are marketed under many other species names. (See photo.)

Saponaria ocymoides (rock soapwort) 4–8 in Sun Zones 3–8
FLOWERING SPAN: Mid-June to August
NATURAL COLOR: Deep pink
DISTRIBUTION: Southwestern and central Europe

When you see "wort" attached to a common name, it is Old English for "plant," and in this case it indicates "a plant with soapy sap" which may have once been used for washing. Its vigorous, creeping mat of ½-in, semievergreen foliage produces a total cover of loosely arranged, ¼-in, star-shaped flowers in full sun and a well-drained site. Adaptable to infertile and very sandy locations, it is easily propagated by seeding or rootstock divisions in spring. There are no disease or insect problems. The cultivar list includes: 'Alba', pure white; 'Rosea', bright rose; 'Rubra Compacta', rich pink, dwarfed; and 'Splendens', deep crimson, larger-flowered. Shearing back heavily right after bloom encourages compactness.

Saxifraga aizoides (yellow mountain saxifrage) 2–6 in Semishade Zones 2–7
FLOWERING SPAN: Mid-June to August
NATURAL COLOR: Yellow, orange
DISTRIBUTION: Europe, Asia, arctic North America

Decidedly hardy, this slow-creeping wildflower has narrow, 1-in, thick, entire leaves in green or reddish green. The high-branched, terminal, often solitary flowers have red-spotted, widely spaced petals and prominent stamens. Easy to grow in moist, average-fertility soil with good drainage, it dislikes hot, dry summers. Division at almost any time is workable, yet seeding is just as productive, if slower. Occasionally, aphids and rust disease are bothersome. The cultivar 'Atrorubens' has orange-red blossoms.

Saxifraga cotyledon 6–24 in Semishade Zones 3–7
FLOWERING SPAN: Early June to mid-July
NATURAL COLOR: Pinkish white
DISTRIBUTION: Mountains of Europe
A robust, cold-tolerant plant with 3-in, spoon-shaped, grayish leaves up to 4 in wide, it carries large, airy panicles of fragrant, ¾-in florets. It enjoys a well-drained, sandy, humusy, moist location, and division in spring or seeding propagates it readily. Aphids and rust disease are just as bothersome as for *S. aizoides*. The cultivar 'Caterhamensis' has red-spotted, white flowers and stretches to 36 in, while 'Icelandica' grows even taller to 48 in and carries bronzed, leathery foliage.

Saxifraga paniculata (aizoon) 3–12 in Semishade Zones 2–7
FLOWERING SPAN: Mid-June to August
NATURAL COLOR: Creamy white
DISTRIBUTION: Europe, Asia, arctic North America
Highly variable in its wide range of distribution, this perennial has a dense rosette of toothed, 1-in, thick, leathery leaves with silvery encrustations of lime attractively evident. Its open sprays of ½-in, bell-shaped flowers endure for a long time. Cultivate the same as for *S. cotyledon*. Many cultivars are available: 'Atropurpurea', rosy purple; 'Baldensis', ash-gray foliage, white flowering, 2–3 in tall; 'Flavescens', lemon yellow; 'Lutea', creamy yellow; 'Paradoxa', white flowers, bluish foliage; 'Rosea', bright pink; and 'Rosularis', white, generous bloom, incurved leaves.

Scabiosa caucasica (scabious, pincushion flower) 18–24 in Sun Zones 3–8
FLOWERING SPAN: Mid-June to September
NATURAL COLOR: Light blue
DISTRIBUTION: Caucasus Mountains
The 2–3-in, round flowers have wavy petals and somewhat resemble a daisy, but the center is a raised mound of prominent, protruding stamens, giving a pincushion effect when fully developed. The blooms appear on thin, erect stems above 3–4-in, linear, basal leaves with greatly cleft, pinnate-looking upper foliage. It enjoys a consistently moist, well-drained, moderately fertile, alkaline to neutral soil (add ground limestone annually to acid locations) in full sun. The plant is intolerant of constant high heat and humidity. Propagate by spring divi-

sion only, and divide every few years to maintain constant vigor. Slugs are the main difficulty. Remove faded flowers quickly to extend the blooming time, and protect with a lightweight, dry, winter mulch in cold areas. The cultivars are more interesting than the parent: 'Alba', pure white; 'Blue Perfection', lavender-blue; 'Clive Greaves', mauve; 'Miss Willmott', white; and 'Moerheim Blue', medium blue. All are durable as cut flowers.

Scabiosa columbaria 18–24 in Sun Zones 5–9
FLOWERING SPAN: Mid-June to September
NATURAL COLOR: Bluish purple, occasionally pink or white
DISTRIBUTION: Europe, Asia, North Africa
The 1½-in, globular flowers of this species appear on very hairy stems above gray-green, greatly divided, somewhat fuzzy leaves. Average-fertility soil, not too rich, with moderate moisture and good drainage is suitable. Divide only in spring to propagate, and forget about disease or insect problems. A protective winter mulch is helpful in the colder zones of its range.

Scabiosa graminifolia 8–12 in Sun Zones 5–9
FLOWERING SPAN: Mid-June to September
NATURAL COLOR: Pale blue to lilac
DISTRIBUTION: Southern Europe
Its silvery, linear foliage is grasslike and forms a low mound. Stiff flower stems carry dense heads of round, 2-in blossoms for a lengthy period. Useful as a neat border edging, its cultural requirements are the same as for *S. caucasica*. The cultivar 'Pinkushion' carries lilac-pink flowering.

Sedum aizoon (maximowiczii, woodwardii) 12–18 in Sun Zones 4–9
FLOWERING SPAN: Mid-June to August
NATURAL COLOR: Yellow to orange
DISTRIBUTION: Siberia, Japan
A multitude of erect stems carry broad, 2–3-in, light green, thin, shiny leaves with coarsely toothed edges and terminate in 2–3-in, flat-headed clusters of ½-in, starry blossoms. All sedums prefer full sun but will accept light shading. Provide a sandy, humusy, well-drained soil and expect no problems from insects or diseases. Late summer division is the preferred method of propagation. The cultivar 'Floribunda' is taller. (See photo.)

Sedum pulchellum 3–9 in Semishade Zones 5–8
FLOWERING SPAN: Early June to mid-July
NATURAL COLOR: Rosy purple, pink, white

DISTRIBUTION: Eastern United States

Novel in its liking for more shading than other *Sedum* species, this perennial also prefers a moist soil at all times. Flowering, however, is irregular, and when it does occur will be as 3–9-in, graceful sprays of ½-in florets underlaid with leafy bracts. The 1-in, grayish, cylindrical, linear leaves are unpaired on trailing stems which easily root to form a wide mat. The foliage colors red, brown, and purple in autumn. Division is the simplest propagation technique in spring, and there are no problematic pests or diseases.

Sedum rosea (roseroot) 4–12 in Sun Zones 3–9
FLOWERING SPAN: Mid-June to August
NATURAL COLOR: Yellow, greenish yellow, reddish purple
DISTRIBUTION: Arctic regions to the temperate northern latitudes

Terminal, dense clusters of ¼-in, upright florets appear above a crowded collection of 1–2-in, gray-green, linear leaves circularly set on thick, stems. Its name does not come from the flower coloring but for the surprising scent of rosewater from cut or bruised stems and rootstock. Cultivate the same as for *S. aizoon*. The variety *integrifolia* is dwarfed with purplish flowers.

Sedum sexangulare (boloniense) 2–4 in Sun Zones 4–9
FLOWERING SPAN: Early June to July
NATURAL COLOR: Deep yellow
DISTRIBUTION: Europe, southwestern Asia

Resembling *S. acre* of May when in flower, the dense foliage of this species is crisply spiral from closely-set, grayish to bronze-green, ¼-in leaves. Useful as a compact ground cover, its simple needs are the same as for *S. aizoon*. At times nurseries offer this plant incorrectly as *S. opsinifolium,* which is no longer valid. (See photo.)

Sedum telephioides (Allegheny stonecrop) 6–18 in Sun Zones 5–8
FLOWERING SPAN: Early June to August
NATURAL COLOR: Flesh pink, white
DISTRIBUTION: North Carolina to Illinois

Here the 1½–2-in leaves are paired, thick, and smooth-edged. Its pyramidal flower heads generally reach 2 in wide on erect, tall stems. Care for it the same as for *S. aizoon*.

Sempervivum cultivars (houseleek, hen-and-chickens, live-forever) 1–24 in Sun Zones 5–9
FLOWERING SPAN: Mid-June to August
NATURAL COLOR: Purplish rose, pink, greenish yellow, yellow, many blends

DISTRIBUTION: Mountains of Europe and northern Africa

Its scientific name translates to "live forever," and this close relative of *Sedum* seems to do just that. Practically indestructible when provided with full sun and excellent drainage, the typically compact rosettes of fleshy, small leaves multiply readily in any light, sandy soil from offsets that appear (like baby chicks) from beneath the bottom leaves of the parent plant. Star-shaped flowering develops in large, overscaled clusters atop heavy stalks rising from the center of the leaf whorl. After flowering, the rosette slowly dies to be replaced shortly by a younger neighbor.

Houseleeks form solid mats of evergreen foliage, and while none needs fertilizing to do well, each appreciates a light mulching of moist peat moss or compost worked around the base of the plant by midsummer. Highly adaptable to even a thin soil layer and the driest conditions, the plant suffers only occasionally from crown rot or foliage rust diseases. Separation of the shallow-rooted offsets can be done at any time during the growing season, yet seeding also works well for propagation. You can definitely expect self-seeding with some of the forms, but know that not all natural seedlings bloom—for unclear reasons.

The hundreds of available species and cultivars offered today are now completely muddled botanically, and pinpointing specific recommendations seems a futile exercise here. Offered widely by nurseries and by specialist growers (where ordering by mail brings no greater assurance of correct identity), these plants are perhaps best selected personally by eye appeal for the colorful foliage alone, which ranges from red, pink, purple, and blue to brown, gray, and green, usually blended together in some combination. The leaf rosette spread can be from ¼ in to 1 ft across, and all types hardy for any area readily intermingle. If any one form can be touted, *S. arachnoideum* (cobweb houseleek, spiderweb houseleek) is a winner with its bright pink flowering and silver strands of webbing overlaid throughout the tight-clustered rosette. It is commonly available and unmistakable in its appearance. (See photos.)

Shortia galacifolia (Oconee-bells) 4–8 in Shade Zones 4–8
FLOWERING SPAN: Early June to July
NATURAL COLOR: Pinkish white
DISTRIBUTION: Mountains of Virginia to Georgia

Attractive in all seasons for its glossy, evergreen foliage, this choice wildflower produces solitary, 1-in, heavily fringed blossoms on 6–8-in stems above rounded, scallop-edged, 2–3-in leaves, which normally turn bronze in autumn if exposed to sun. Readily adaptable to shaded woodlots favoring rhododendrons and azaleas, it can eventually form large mats where the soil is acid, moist, well-drained, humusy to a high degree, and cool. Spring division of the creeping rootstock is recommended as the better propagation method since seed requires years of patience to develop into flowering plants. Pests and diseases are uncommon. (See photo.)

Shortia uniflora (Nippon-bells) 4–8 in Shade Zones 4–8
FLOWERING SPAN: Early June to July
NATURAL COLOR: White, pale pink
DISTRIBUTION: Japan

Similar in general appearance to *S. galacifolia,* this species is not so easily cultivated and appears to want more moisture and cooler conditions to succeed. The fringed blossoms are usually 1½-in wide above heart-shaped, wavy-edged, evergreen, 2–3-in leaves turning red in autumn. The cultivar 'Grandiflora' has showier flowers about 2 in wide.

Sidalcea candida 24–36 in Sun Zones 5–9
FLOWERING SPAN: Early June to mid-July
NATURAL COLOR: White
DISTRIBUTION: Southern Wyoming to Colorado, Utah, and New Mexico

The 3-in, heart-shaped leaves are deeply divided into as many as 7 segments and are widely spaced between palmately divided leaves on the same plant. The 5-petaled blossoms are ¾-in long and heavily clustered up 5-in flower spikes. Removing faded blossoms early extends the length of flowering appreciably. It does well in any moist, well-drained, average-fertility soil in full sun, and propagates easily by division in spring or autumn and by seeding. Diseases and insects are not troublesome.

Sidalcea malviflora (prairie mallow, miniature hollyhock, checkerbloom) 18–48 in
Sun Zones 5–9
FLOWERING SPAN: Mid-June to August
NATURAL COLOR: Crimson to pale pink
DISTRIBUTION: Oregon, California

The parent species is seldom cultivated today, having been supplanted by the improved colorings and increased branching from hybridization. A long-lasting, showy perennial for any sunny garden border, its very sturdy, hollyhocklike flower spikes are crowded with 1-in, bowl-shaped, notched blossoms above 3-in, finger-cut leaves. Promptly removing the old flower stalks extends the blooming time and also promotes new basal growth for successful overwintering. Not especially fussy about soil, it thrives on a rich, well-drained site with reasonable moisture in either sun or light shading and is rarely bothered by pests or diseases. Spring division is the best propagation method. The cultivar list offers attractive options: 'Brilliant', 30 in, deep rose; 'Croftway Red', 36 in, very deep pink; 'Elsie Heugh', 30 in, light pink; 'Loveliness', 30 in, shell pink; 'Reverend Page Roberts', 48 in, light pink; 'Rose Queen', 48 in, rosy pink; 'Sussex Beauty', 30 in, clear pink; 'Wensleydale', 48 in, rosy red; and 'William Smith', 36 in, bright salmon-pink, pyramidal in outline. (See photo.)

Silene schafta 3–6 in Sun Zones 3–8
  FLOWERING SPAN: Mid-June to October
  NATURAL COLOR: Bright rosy pink
  DISTRIBUTION: Caucasus Mountains
    Dependable and simple to grow well, this compact species has ½-in, light green, narrow, hairy leaves at ground level arranged in rosettes. It produces myriad 1-in, pinwheel-like blossoms with notched ends. Thriving in any sandy, humusy soil with full sun or light shading, it reproduces easily from spring or autumn division, summer stem cuttings, or seeding. There are no particular problems with diseases or insect pests.

Silene virginica (fire pink) 24–36 in Semishade Zones 3–8
  FLOWERING SPAN: Early June to August
  NATURAL COLOR: Bright crimson
  DISTRIBUTION: New Jersey to Minnesota, south to Oklahoma and Georgia
    Vividly colorful in flower, the plant has 2-in, 5-parted, rounded blossoms with notched petals arranged in loose clusters on sticky, branched stems above a basal clump of smooth, dark green, 3–4-in, paddle-shaped leaves. Best grown in a moist, sandy, humusy soil with semishade, it accepts full sun if kept very moist. Reproduce by spring division, root cuttings, or seeding. Pests and diseases are not usual.

Stachys byzantina (olympica, lanata) (woolly betony, lamb's-ears) 12–30 in Sun
  Zones 3–9
  FLOWERING SPAN: Mid-June to August
  NATURAL COLOR: Purplish pink
  DISTRIBUTION: Turkey, southwestern Asia
    Welcomed primarily for its thick, velvety, silvered foliage, the plant carries tall spikes of dull-colored flowers which perhaps deserve early removal. The elliptical, 3–4-in, gray-white leaves are heavily felted with long, silky hairs and are the display part of the plant. It enjoys bright sun on any average-fertility, well-drained site and can readily be propagated by division or seeding. Insects are no problem but stem rot can be devastating in hot, humid areas. The sterile cultivar 'Silver Carpet', 18 in, is nonflowering and quickly makes a dense, ornamental ground cover. (See photo.)

Stachys grandiflora (macrantha, Betonica grandiflora, B. macrantha) 12–18 in Sun Zones
  3–9
  FLOWERING SPAN: Mid-June to August
  NATURAL COLOR: Deep violet
  DISTRIBUTION: Caucasus Mountains

Durable and sturdy, this perennial has whorls of closely set flowers on erect, squared stems, much like its cousin, mint. The thick, wrinkled, hairy, broadly lancelike, 2–3-in leaves form a good-sized basal clump of foliage. Provide full sun and an average-fertility, well-drained site. Propagate by spring division or by seeding. There are no important pests or diseases. The cultivar 'Robusta', 24 in tall, has rosy pink flowers; 'Rosea' has pink ones; and vigorous 'Superba' carries purplish violet blossoms.

Thermopsis caroliniana (Carolina lupine) 36–60 in Sun Zones 3–9
  FLOWERING SPAN: Mid-June to mid-July
  NATURAL COLOR: Bright yellow
  DISTRIBUTION: North Carolina to Georgia
  Slender spikes of closely packed, conspicuous, sweet pealike florets up to 10 in tall rise well above the hairy, 3-in, palmately compound leaves. Provide a deep, fertile, well-drained location with sun to light shading. Better produced by seed, it can possibly be divided in very early spring, but expect mixed success. Nothing bothers it. (See photo.)

Thymus × *citriodorus* (lemon thyme) 4–12 in Sun Zones 4–9
  FLOWERING SPAN: Mid-June to August
  NATURAL COLOR: Pale lilac
  ORIGIN: Horticultural hybrid of *T. pulegiodes* × *T. vulgaris*
  Familiar to most for the aromatic foliage, this evergreen creeper has a strong lemon scent when bruised. Best grown in full sun with dry, very infertile soil and good drainage, it has ½-in, lancelike foliage that suffers little damage from diseases or insects. Spring division is the easiest propagation method. There are several cultivars: 'Argenteus', foliage with silvery streaks; 'Aureus', foliage golden; and 'Silver Queen', foliage downy and gray with a narrow, white border. All of these require some winter protection in the cold areas of its range.

Trollius ledebourii (Ledebour globeflower) 24–36 in Semishade Zones 4–8
  FLOWERING SPAN: Mid-June to mid-July
  NATURAL COLOR: Deep orange
  DISTRIBUTION: Eastern Siberia
  Similar to the earlier-blooming *Trollius* species in appearance, this one has larger blooms up to 2½ in wide and nicely extends the blooming period for the entire group. Cultivate as for the May-flowering *T. asiaticus.* Its cultivar 'Golden Queen' has bright orange-yellow coloring and a 48-in height. (See photo.)

Valeriana officinalis   (common valerian, garden heliotrope)   24–48 in   Sun
    Zones 4–8
    FLOWERING SPAN: Late June to August
    NATURAL COLOR: Pink, lavender, white
    DISTRIBUTION: Europe, western Asia, Canada, northeastern United States
        The roots of this perennial have been used for centuries in the manufacture
    of perfumes, and the delightfully scented flower heads offer much garden appeal.
    Dense, pyramidal clusters of tiny florets carry the odor of heliotrope and appear
    terminally, as well as axially, on hollow-stemmed stalks with compound, fernlike
    leaves of 7–10 leaflets. Locate in a very moist, well-drained, average-fertility soil
    and propagate by division or seeding. Diseases are uncommon, but black aphids
    can distort the foliage and flowering. The cultivar 'Alba' is pure white; 'Coccinea'
    deep red; and 'Rubra' medium red. (See photo.)

Verbascum chaixii   24–36 in   Sun   Zones 4–8
    FLOWERING SPAN: Late June to late August
    NATURAL COLOR: Pale yellow
    DISTRIBUTION: Southern and central Europe
        White-woolly stems carry 6-in, gray-green, wavy margined, coarse-toothed
    foliage. Slender flower spikes have many rounded, 1-in flowers with purplish red
    centers in bloom at one time. It prefers a reasonably moist and well-drained,
    average-fertility soil in full sun and will quickly disappear from a wet, cold loca-
    tion. Seeding or root cuttings propagate it equally, and there are no problems
    with pests or diseases. The cultivar 'Album' is white with a mauve eye.

Verbascum × *hybridum*   36–48 in   Sun   Zones 5–9
    FLOWERING SPAN: Late June to September
    NATURAL COLOR: White, yellow, pink, lavender
    ORIGIN: Horticultural hybrid of *V. phoeniceum* and others
        Although short-lived, it is attractive with boldly erect, narrow stalks of 1-in,
    saucer-shaped florets, generally enhanced with color-contrasted centers, in
    bloom for a long time. It has both a ground-level rosette of foliage as well as stem
    leaves, and both are very hairy, gray-green, 3–4 in long, and spearhead-shaped.
    Provide a very well-drained, moderately fertile soil with full sun for the best
    growth. Taking root cuttings in early spring is the only workable propagation
    method since garden-collected seed produces highly variable results with these
    hybrid plants. Unbothered by diseases or insect pests, its cultivars are not always
    locally available: 'C. L. Adams', deep yellow; 'Cotswold Gem', reddish yellow
    with a purple center; 'Cotswold Queen', gold; 'Gainsborough', canary yellow;
    'Mont Blanc', white with gray foliage; and 'Pink Domino', rosy pink with a
    purple center.

Veronica incana (woolly speedwell) 12–24 in   Sun   Zones 4–8
    FLOWERING SPAN: Mid-June to August
    NATURAL COLOR: Violet-blue
    DISTRIBUTION: Northern Asia, Russia
       Veronica species with summertime blooms are easily recognized for their tall, long-lasting flower spikes, which make excellent cut blossoms. Even though the bloom is erratically produced, the 8-in spikes of ¼-in florets add a showy color accent. The 2–3-in, lance-shaped, silvery gray foliage is highly regarded even out of flower. It needs a fertile, humusy, well-drained soil in sun to light shade and is easily propagated by simple division in spring or autumn. Insects and diseases are rarely bothersome. The cultivar list includes: 'Barcarolle', rosy pink and dwarfed at 10 in tall; 'Blue Sheen', light blue; 'Candidissima', pale blue; 'Glauca', deep blue; 'Minuet', 15 in, soft pink; 'Rosea', medium pink; and 'Saraband', deep violet.

Veronica prostrata (*rupestris*) 6–8 in   Sun   Zones 5–8
    FLOWERING SPAN: Early June to July
    NATURAL COLOR: Deep blue
    DISTRIBUTION: Europe
       Occasionally invasive, the creeping foliage mat of 1¼-in, deep green, lancelike leaves is enhanced by a brief but vividly colorful display of ½-in, cup-shaped flowers with prominent stamens on erect, wiry stems. Culture is the same as for *V. incana*. Its cultivars include: 'Alba', white; 'Heavenly Blue', medium blue; and 'Rosea', pink. (See photo.)

Veronica spicata (australis) (spike speedwell) 12–18 in   Sun   Zones 3–8
    FLOWERING SPAN: Mid-June to August
    NATURAL COLOR: Bright blue or pink
    DISTRIBUTION: Northern Europe, Asia
       One of the most-admired for tall showiness, this species has vivid spikes of ¼-in florets on densely crowded, branched stalks above 1–2-in, narrow, wavy-edged, toothed, rich green foliage. It needs the same culture as *V. incana*. Several noteworthy cultivars exist: 'Blue Charm', 18 in, lavender-blue; 'Blue Peter', 18 in, medium blue; 'Icicle', 24 in, clear white; and 'Red Fox', 12 in, deep pink. (See photo.)

July

---------------------------------- WHITE ----------------------------------

Achillea millefolium
Alcea rosea
Allium rosenbachianum cvs.
Anthericum ramosum
Aster linarifolius cvs.
Astilbe simplicifolia
Calluna vulgaris cvs.
Campanula lactiflora
Chelone glabra
Cimicifuga racemosa
Coreopsis rosea cvs.
Deschampsia caespitosa
Echinacea purpurea cvs.
Eryngium yuccifolium

Eupatorium rugosum
Euphorbia corollata
Filipendula camtschatica
Galega officinalis cvs.
Galtonia candicans
Gaultheria procumbens
Gentiana asclepiadea cvs.
Gypsophila acutifolia
Gypsophila paniculata
Hibiscus moscheutos
Hosta tokudama
Iris ensata
Lathyrus latifolius cvs.
Lilium cvs.

Lilium auratum
Lilium regale
Lobelia cardinalis cvs.
Lysimachia clethroides
Malva moschata cvs.
Mentha spp.
Phlox paniculata cvs.
Physalis alkekengi
Physostegia virginiana cvs.
Sedum album
Sedum hispanicum
Veronica longifolia cvs.
Yucca filamentosa
Yucca flaccida

---------------------------------- YELLOW ----------------------------------

Achillea millefolium cvs.
Aconitum lycoctonum
Alcea rosea
Allium flavum
Arnica montana
Cassia marilandica
Centaurea macrocephala
Centaurea ruthenica
Coreopsis verticillata
Erigeron aureus
Gentiana lutea

Helianthus decapetalus
Helianthus × multiflorus
Heliopsis helianthoides
Hemerocallis citrina
Hemerocallis × hybrida
Inula ensifolia
Inula hookeri
Inula orientalis
Iris ensata cvs.
Ligularia dentata
Ligularia przewalskii

Lilium cvs.
Lilium pardilinum cvs.
Rudbeckia fulgida
Rudbeckia laciniata
Ruta graveolens
Sedum kamtschaticum
Sedum reflexum
Senecio cineraria
Solidago × hybrida
× Solidaster luteus
Thalictrum speciosissimum

---------------------------------- ORANGE ----------------------------------

Asclepias tuberosa
Belamcanda chinensis
Erigeron aurantiacus
Hemerocallis fulva

Hemerocallis × hybrida
Lilium cvs.
Lilium bulbiferum var.
   croceum

Lilium pardalinum
Lilium philadelphicum

---------------------------------- RED ----------------------------------

Achillea millefolium cvs.
Alcea rosea
Calluna vulgaris cvs.
Delphinium cardinale
Echinacea purpurea
Hemerocallis × hybrida

Hibiscus moscheutos
Iris ensata cvs.
Lilium cvs.
Lilium bulbiferum
Lilium lancifolium cvs.
Lilium superbum

Lobelia cardinalis
Lythrum salicaria cvs.
Phlox paniculata cvs.
Potentilla nepalensis cvs.
Sedum spurium cvs.

PINK

Achillea millefolium cvs.	Gypsophila paniculata cvs.	Lythrum salicaria cvs.
Allium cernuum	Hemerocallis × hybrida	Lythrum virgatum cvs.
Allium pulchellum	Hibiscus moscheutos	Macleaya cordata
Alcea rosea	Iris ensata cvs.	Malva moschata
Aster linarifolius cvs.	Lathyrus latifolius	Mentha spp.
Bletilla striata	Lilium cvs.	Phlox paniculata cvs.
Calluna vulgaris	Limonium latifolium cvs.	Physostegia virginiana cvs.
Dianthus superbus	Lobelia cardinalis cvs.	Potentilla nepalensis
Erigeron × hybridus	Lycoris squamigera	Sedum spurium cvs.

PURPLE / LAVENDER

Aconitum henryi cvs.	Echinacea purpurea cvs.	Limonium latifolium cvs.
Allium aflatunense	Erigeron × hybridus	Liriope spicata
Allium giganteum	Galega officinalis	Lycoris squamigera
Allium rosenbachianum	Hemerocallis × hybrida	Lythrum salicaria
Allium sphaerocephalum	Hosta crispula	Lythrum virgatum
Anemonopsis macrophylla	Hosta fortunei	Mentha spp.
Aster × frikartii	Hosta sieboldiana	Phlox paniculata cvs.
Astilbe chinensis	Hosta undulata	Salvia pratensis
Briza media	Hosta ventricosa	Teucrium chamaedrys
Calluna vulgaris cvs.	Iris ensata	Thalictrum rochebrunianum
Coreopsis rosea	Lathyrus latifolius	Veronica longifolia cvs.
Deschampsia caespitosa	Lavandula angustifolia cvs.	
Dianthus superbus	Liatris spicata	

BLUE

Aconitum × bicolor cvs.	Echinops sphaerocephalus	Iris ensata cvs.
Aconitum napellus	Eryngium alpinum	Lavandula angustifolia
Campanula lactiflora	Eryngium amethystinum	Limonium latifolium
Campanula sarmatica	Gentiana asclepiadea	Salvia farinacea
Echinops humilis	Gentiana septemfida	Veronica longifolia cvs.

BICOLOR

Aconitum × bicolor	Hibiscus moscheutos	Lilium auratum
Echinacea purpurea cvs.	Iris ensata cvs.	Phlox paniculata cvs.
Hemerocallis × hybrida	Lilium cvs.	

Achillea millefolium
'Red Beauty'

Alcea rosea

Alcea rosea
'Chater's Double'

Allium giganteum

Allium pulchellum

Allium sphaerocephalum

Asclepias tuberosa

Aster × frikartii
'Wonder of Staffa'

Astilbe chinensis
'Pumila'

Calluna vulgaris
cultivars

Calluna vulgaris
'Camla'

Calluna vulgaris
'Peter Sparkes'

Centaurea macrocephala

Cimicifuga racemosa

Coreopsis verticillata

Coreopsis verticillata
'Moonbeam'

Echinacea purpurea
'Bright Star'

Echinops humilis

Eryngium alpinum

Eryngium yuccifolium (late)

Galtonia candicans

Gaultheria procumbens

Gentiana septemfida

Gypsophila paniculata 'Rosy Veil'
and *Oenothera fruticosa*

Hemerocallis fulva

Hemerocallis fulva
'Kwanso'

Hemerocallis × *hybrida*
'Temple Bells'

Hemerocallis × *hybrida*
cultivar

Hemerocallis × *hybrida*
cultivar

Hemerocallis × *hybrida*
cultivar

Hemerocallis × *hybrida*
cultivar

Hemerocallis × *hybrida*
cultivar

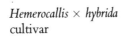

Hemerocallis × *hybrida*
cultivar

Hibiscus moscheutos

Hibiscus moscheutos
'Southern Belle Series'

Hosta crispula

Hosta crispula

Hosta fortunei
'Albo-picta'

Hosta sieboldiana

Hosta undulata

Hosta ventricosa

Iris ensata
'Geihan'

Lathyrus latifolius

Lathyrus latifolius

Lavandula angustifolia

Liatris spicata

Ligularia dentata
'Desdemona'

Ligularia przewalskii
'The Rocket'

Lilium (Longiflorum Hybrids)
'Holland's Glory'

Lilium (Aurelian: Chinese Trumpet)
'Black Dragon Strain'

Lilium (Aurelian: Chinese Trumpet)
'Royal Gold'

Lilium (Aurelian: Sunburst)
'Bright Star'

Lilium auratum
cultivars

Lilium lancifolium

Lilium pardalinum

Lilium regale

Lilium superbum

Lilium superbum

Limonium latifolium

Lobelia cardinalis

Lysimachia clethroides

Lythrum salicaria
'Morden's Pink'

Macleaya cordata

Macleaya cordata

Phlox paniculata
cultivars

Phlox paniculata
cultivars

Phlox paniculata
cultivars

Phlox paniculata
'Charlotte'

Physalis alkekengi

Physostegia virginiana
'Rosy Spire'

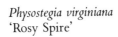

Physostegia virginiana
'Summer Snow'

Physostegia virginiana
'Variegata'

Rudbeckia fulgida

Ruta graveolens

Sedum album

Sedum kamtschaticum

Sedum reflexum

Sedum spurium
'Dragon's Blood'

Sedum spurium
'Coccineum'

Senecio cineraria

Solidago × *hybrida* cultivar

Solidago × *hybrida* cultivar

× *Solidaster luteus*

Thalictrum rochebrunianum

Veronica longifolia

Veronica longifolia var. *subsessilis*

Yucca filamentosa and *Calluna vulgaris*

Yucca filamentosa

Yucca filamentosa
'Golden Sword'

THE PLANTS

Achillea millefolium (common yarrow, milfoil)   12–36 in   Sun   Zones 3–8
FLOWERING SPAN: Early July to September
NATURAL COLOR: Off-white, occasionally reddish
DISTRIBUTION: Europe, British Isles, western Asia, North America

The parent plant is generally considered only an invasive weed without garden appeal, but its cultivars are much admired and used. The narrow, lancelike, 6–8-in foliage is divided pinnately many times and has an airy appearance as a ground-level clump. The flat-topped, 2–3-in terminal clusters of minute florets appear on erect stems carrying some leaves. Any average-fertility, well-drained soil in full sun is workable, and the plant accepts dry conditions well. Spring division is the easiest propagation method, although summer stem cuttings are an alternative. Mildew and stem rot are occasional problems during extended periods of humid, overcast, hot weather. Some of the superior cultivars are: 'Cerise Queen', bright cerise, 18 in; 'Crimson Beauty', 18 in, bright red; 'Fire King', 18 in, deep red, silvery foliage; 'Red Beauty', 18 in, rosy red; and 'Rosea', 24 in, soft rosy pink. A recent group of hybrids created from *A. millefolium* and *A. taygetea,* called the 'Galaxy Series,' offers tones of pink, salmon, red, and yellow. Some of these have been given individual cultivar names. (See photo.)

Aconitum × *bicolor (stoerkianum)*   24–42 in   Semishade   Zones 3–8
FLOWERING SPAN: Mid-July to September
NATURAL COLOR: White, edged in blue
ORIGIN: Horticultural hybrid of *A. napellus* × *A. variegatum*

Attractive for a long time in foliage and flower, the dark green, 2–3-in, deeply cut, glossy leaves have 5–7 toothed divisions. The helmetlike, almost-closed, 1-in florets are loosely arranged on branched, wandlike flower stalks. These blossoms are the *only* plant part not considered poisonous to humans. If the juices of the roots, leaves, or seeds enter an open wound—or if any of these parts is mistakenly eaten—the consequences are life-threatening. Avoid using this perennial where inexperienced children could be tempted to experiment with the foliage or seed. Every *Aconitum* species is just as poisonous, and gardeners should wear gloves when handling this genus.

The plant thrives in a rich, moist, humusy soil with semishade but has an aversion to being disturbed once established. Nevertheless, propagation is manageable, if risky, by careful division of the tuberous, turniplike roots in early spring or late autumn—or it can also be accomplished by fully matured seed. Crown rot, verticillium wilt, and mildew are often serious disease afflictions, but insects appear to be wary of the plant, perhaps with just cause. The cultivar list includes: 'Bressingham Spire', 36 in, violet-blue, long-flowering, and 'Newry Blue', 48 in, deep blue.

Aconitum henryi (autumnale) (autumn monkshood) 36–72 in Semishade Zones 3–8
FLOWERING SPAN: Late July to September
NATURAL COLOR: Deep blue-purple
DISTRIBUTION: Northern China
This species carries 2–6-in, glossy, dark green leaves with 3–5 deep clefts and neatly serrated edges. Its hooded blossoms are hairless, up to 1 in long, and set loosely on slender, much-branched stalks held well above the foliage. It requires the same culture as *A.* × *bicolor*. The cultivar 'Spark's Variety' has violet-blue coloring, thinner leaves, and very slender stems. These are both poisonous plants.

Aconitum lycoctonum (wolfsbane) 36–48 in Semishade Zones 3–8
FLOWERING SPAN: Early July to September
NATURAL COLOR: Creamy yellow
DISTRIBUTION: Northern Europe
The plant has narrowly tubular flowers with a pinched appearance on slightly elongated stalks projecting from the flower stem. The leaves are 6–8 in long and cut with 5–7 lobes. Cultivate as for *A.* × *bicolor*.

Aconitum napellus (English monkshood, helmet flower, soldier's cap) 36–48 in Semishade Zones 3–8
FLOWERING SPAN: Mid-July to September
NATURAL COLOR: Violet-blue
DISTRIBUTION: Northern Europe
Ornamentally popular, this species is the most poisonous of the group and the source of the medicinal drug aconite. It offers 2–4-in, deeply cut, dark green leaves with the lobes further divided into 3 lacy segments. Its 1½-in, helmet-like blossoms have a visor or beak and appear on sturdy, erect, much-branched stems. Cultivate as for *A.* × *bicolor*. Quick removal of the spent blooms often produces a 2nd, smaller reflowering. There is an almost-white cultivar, 'Albus', and a pink-toned one, 'Carneum', which requires cool growing conditions for its best coloring. Much of the nursery material offered today as this species is actually *A. henryi*.

Alcea rosea (Althaea rosea) (hollyhock) 60–96 in Sun Zones 3–9
FLOWERING SPAN: Early July to September
NATURAL COLOR: White, pink, purple, occasionally yellowish
DISTRIBUTION: Asia Minor
Cultivated in Europe with appreciation since the 16th century, this stately and showy perennial has 3–5-in, saucer-shaped blossoms on erect, stout stems and large-scaled foliage. Flowering begins at the bottom of the stalk and proceeds upward for a lengthy period. Usually 18–24 in of the stem is in bloom at one time.

The base leaves are 6–8 in wide, oval with wavy edges, hairy, and coarse-looking. The foliage is prone to very serious injury from several rust and leaf spot diseases, while Japanese beetles relish the blossoms. Because the plant is tap-rooted and resents transplanting, seeding in early summer followed by careful transplanting of the seedlings to their permanent locations early the following spring is the best method for propagation. Although not long-lived, an established plant self-seeds widely to fill in any gaps. Several hybrid improvements are available with these cultivars: 'Begonia-flowered', having pastel, fringed, single blossoms; 'Chater's Double', mostly double-flowered and only 72 in tall; 'Majorette', double, lacy blooms, pastels; and 'Powder Puffs', 60–84 in high, fully double in an impressive set of novel colors. (See photos.)

Allium aflatunense   30–60 in   Sun   Zones 3–8
FLOWERING SPAN: Early July to August
NATURAL COLOR: Light violet
DISTRIBUTION: Central Asia

This 2½-in bulb produces 3-in, globular flower heads with many tiny florets opening into star shapes above 6–8 gray-green straplike leaves ½ in wide. Make initial plantings in early autumn on a sunny site with average-fertility but well-drained, sandy-textured soil. Propagate as for *Narcissus*. Diseases and pests are not common, but in severe climate areas mulch for winter. The cultivar 'Purple Sensation' has larger, violet-purple flowers.

Allium cernuum (recurvatum)   (nodding onion, wild onion)   12–24 in   Sun   Zones 3–8
FLOWERING SPAN: Early July to August
NATURAL COLOR: Light rose, occasionally white
DISTRIBUTION: Rocky slopes of southeastern Canada to South Carolina, west to British Columbia and California

The small bulb produces open-headed, domed clusters of ¼-in florets on elongated stalks plus narrow, linear foliage in a basal clump. Its flowering is pendulous from a bend in the stem just below the blossom. This is a very hardy, adaptable, easy-to-grow perennial, and its culture is the same as for *A. aflatunense*. The closely related species *A. stellatum* of the central United States has completely erect flower stems and deeper-colored blossoms.

Allium flavum   12–24 in   Sun   Zones 3–9
FLOWERING SPAN: Mid-July to mid-August
NATURAL COLOR: Bright yellow
DISTRIBUTION: Southern Europe, Turkey

Loose, 2-in-wide heads of pendulous, ¼-in, bell-shaped florets terminate the slender, erect stems of this dependable bulb. Its grasslike foliage is no more than ⅛ in wide. Cultivate the same as for *A. aflatunense*.

Allium giganteum   36–72 in   Sun   Zones 5–8
    FLOWERING SPAN: Early July to August
    NATURAL COLOR: Violet
    DISTRIBUTION: Central Asia
    Probably the tallest flowering *Allium,* the bulb produces arching, 18-in-long, 1–2-in-wide, gray-green, straplike leaves. Its 4–8-in globular flower is composed of many ⅛-in, star-shaped florets and makes a unique, sizeable indoor decoration when dried after flowering is finished. Care for this large bulb as for *A. aflatunense.* (See photo.)

Allium pulchellum   12–24 in   Sun   Zones 3–8
    FLOWERING SPAN: Mid-July to mid-August
    NATURAL COLOR: Reddish violet to rose
    DISTRIBUTION: Southern Europe, western Asia
    A group of 3–4 narrow, ⅛-in-wide leaves surround an erect, slender stem topped with a loose flower head carrying tiny, pendulous florets. Culture for this small bulb is the same as for *A. aflatunense.* Some growers occasionally market this plant as *A. flavum* 'Pumilum Rosea', which is an invalid name. (See photo.)

Allium rosenbachianum   18–30 in   Sun   Zones 4–8
    FLOWERING SPAN: Mid-July to mid-August
    NATURAL COLOR: Purplish violet
    DISTRIBUTION: Turkestan
    Similar in leaf appearance to *A. aflatunense,* this species has a stout flower stalk topped by a solitary, decorative, 4–5-in globe of many small florets. It needs the same culture as *A. aflatunense.* A white cultivar, 'Album', is known but not readily available.

Allium sphaerocephalum   (roundheaded garlic)   12–24 in   Sun   Zones 3–8
    FLOWERING SPAN: Early July to August
    NATURAL COLOR: Reddish purple
    DISTRIBUTION: Europe, western Asia, North Africa
    The flower head is not round but noticeably egg-shaped, 2–3 in long, and appears on a very slender stem above grayish green foliage not more than 1/16 in wide. It often seeds freely to become weedy in garden borders. Provide the same culture as for *A. aflatunense.* The dried seed heads have some potential for indoor decoration. (See photo.)

Anemonopsis macrophylla   (false anemone)   12–36 in   Semishade   Zones 6–9
    FLOWERING SPAN: Late July to September
    NATURAL COLOR: Light purple to rose

DISTRIBUTION: Japan

The low-to-the-ground foliage mass appears as long-stalked, 10-in, multiply-compound, triangular leaves similar in form to the April-flowering *Actaea*. The nodding, waxy, 1½-in flowers arrive on loose, open branches similar to the Japanese anemone. This perennial from a genus of one species likes a deep, rich, moist, well-drained site and propagates easily by spring division or by seeding. Nothing appears to bother it.

Anthericum ramosum   18–24 in   Sun   Zones 5–9
   FLOWERING SPAN: Early July to August
   NATURAL COLOR: White
   DISTRIBUTION: Europe
      Very similar to *A. liliago* of June, the flowering of *A. ramosum* is smaller and daintier and develops on branched stems. Culture the same as for *A. liliago*.

Arnica montana   12–24 in   Sun   Zones 5–8
   FLOWERING SPAN: Mid-July to mid-August
   NATURAL COLOR: Orange-yellow
   DISTRIBUTION: Central Europe, southern Scandanavia
      Daisylike, 2–3-in flowers appear singly or paired on erect stems from a basal clump of broad, oval, hairy, 4–5-in leaves. Easily grown on any moist, well-drained, average-fertility soil in sun to semishade, it becomes wide-spreading and rank in soil that is overly rich. The deep rootstock of an established plant resists division or transplanting, and propagation is more successful from seeding or by separating very young plants. There are no diseases or insect pests of consequence.

Asclepias tuberosa   (butterfly weed, pleurisy root, Indian paintbrush)   24–36 in   Sun
   Zones 3–9
   FLOWERING SPAN: Early July to mid-August
   NATURAL COLOR: Bright orange
   DISTRIBUTION: New Hampshire to Florida, west to North Dakota and Arizona
      Strongly colorful, 2-in clusters of tiny, waxy, star-shaped florets stand erect on stout, branched stems and offer fragrant nectar to a host of flying insects, especially butterflies. The 4-in, pointed, rough-haired leaves are bright green, and the slender seed pods turn rich red in autumn. Provide a well-drained, acid, sandy soil in full sun and expect tolerance to some drought because of the deep taproots. Spring growth is very slow to appear, so mark planting locations earlier to avoid inadvertently digging out the dormant roots. Propagate by careful division or root cuttings since seed does not readily germinate. It has no pests or diseases. Rare yet known to exist is a totally yellow form. (See photo.)

Aster × frikartii   24–36 in   Sun   Zones 5–9
FLOWERING SPAN: Early July to October
NATURAL COLOR: Bluish lavender
ORIGIN: Horticultural hybrid of *A. amellus* × *A. thomsonii*
    Long in bloom, the 2½-in, daisylike flowers have bright yellow centers above oblong, deep green, 1–2-in, rough-textured leaves. Cultivate in full sun or light shading on any well-drained, average-fertility, moist soil and propagate by spring division only. With the exception of red spider mite infestations during hot, dry summers, insects are uncommon, but mildew can be a problem in hot, humid weather. The superior cultivar 'Mönch' has larger blossoming, while 'Wonder of Staffa' is similar in bloom but is less rounded in form and top-heavy, requiring some staking. (See photo.)

Aster linarifolius   (savoryleaf aster, bristle aster)   6–20 in   Sun   Zones 3–9
FLOWERING SPAN: Mid-July to September
NATURAL COLOR: Lavender-pink to violet
DISTRIBUTION: Maine to Florida, west to Texas, Missouri, and Wisconsin
    The 1½-in needlelike, dark green leaves are not only stiff but also roughened and surround erect, much-branched flowering stems showing durable ¾-in, daisylike florets with deep yellow centers. The plant grows compactly neat on any light, well-drained, dry soil and is readily reproduced by spring division. Diseases and insect pests are infrequent. The cultivar 'Albus' has white petals; 'Purpureus' has purple ones; and 'Roseus' pink ones.

Astilbe chinensis   12–24 in   Semishade   Zones 4–8
FLOWERING SPAN: Late July to September
NATURAL COLOR: Deep pink-purple
DISTRIBUTION: China, Japan
    The narrow, compound, sharply toothed foliage of this species, which some authorities believe may actually be a hybrid itself, is composed of 2–3-in, hairy leaflets and set close to the ground. Spikes of very tiny florets appear on erect, slender stems. Provide a reasonably cool, semishaded location with constant moisture on a well-drained, average-fertility soil enriched with compost or humus. Either spring or autumn division is the simplest propagation method, and there are no troublesome diseases or pests. The cultivar 'Finale' is 15 in tall and carries pale lavender-pink blooms, while 'Pumila', only 10 in high with raspberry-colored flowers, is very drought-tolerant. Both cultivars bloom slightly later than the parent. (See photo.)

Astilbe simplicifolia   6–12 in   Semishade   Zones 4–8
FLOWERING SPAN: Early July to August
NATURAL COLOR: White

DISTRIBUTION: Japan

Unusual because it has simple, not compound foliage, this astilbe's 3-in, spearhead-shaped, somewhat glossy leaves are either deeply lobed or cut into ragged segments. The loose, airy flower panicles appear on slender stalks. Cultivate the same as for *A. chinensis*. The cultivar 'Sprite' has dark green foliage and shell pink blossoming on 10-in stems.

Belamcanda chinensis (Pardanthus chinensis) (blackberry lily, leopard flower) 15–36 in Sun Zones 5–9

FLOWERING SPAN: Late July to September

NATURAL COLOR: Deep orange, spotted red

DISTRIBUTION: China, Japan

The 2-in, star-shaped blossoms individually last only a day, but the buds are plentiful and occur on large, slender, branched, arching stalks. The irislike, erect, lance-shaped foliage grows 12–18 in tall from basal clumps, and the ripened seed pods open to show glossy, black seeds resembling a blackberry. These pods, when dried, make an interesting indoor decoration. Provide a rich, moist, sandy soil in sun to light shading and divide the tuberous rootstock in spring or midautumn. Propagation by seed gives much slower results. Diseases are rare, but iris borer is occasionally troublesome to the fleshy roots. Provide a winter mulch in severe climate areas.

Bletilla striata (hyacinthina) 10–24 in Semishade Zones 6–10

FLOWERING SPAN: Early July to mid-August

NATURAL COLOR: Carmine pink to purple

DISTRIBUTION: China, Japan

While not assuredly hardy in the coldest part of its normal range, this perennial can be worth a trial for its unusual flowering. The broad, glossy, spike leaves stretch almost 1 ft tall and are noticeably ribbed. The slender flower stalk carries 6–10 durable, cattleya-orchidlike, 1-in blossoms. Install tubers in a constantly moist but well-drained, sandy soil enriched with peat moss, compost, or humus during early spring or midautumn. Divide crowded colonies right after flowering. In very cold areas mulch heavily. Pests and diseases are uncommon. Available but scarce is a white cultivar, 'Alba'.

Briza media (quaking grass) 18–24 in Sun Zones 5–9

FLOWERING SPAN: Early July to November

NATURAL COLOR: Purplish to gray

DISTRIBUTION: Eurasia, Connecticut to southeastern Ontario to Michigan

Ornamental grasses for garden use afford some easy-to-grow choices for accent and later indoor decoration. The ¼-in-wide leaves on this grass are not particularly noteworthy (they somewhat resemble bamboo), but the slender flower stalks are very appealing and make handsome bouquets when dried. The locket-shaped, ½-in, nodding fruits appear in great abundance on wiry, branched stems which move easily in breezes for a visual bonus. Plant in a well-drained, moist, average-fertility soil with full sun and propagate by division in early spring or autumn. This perennial accepts modest drought satisfactorily. Diseases and insect nuisances are uncommon.

Calluna vulgaris (heather, Scotch heather) 6–36 in Sun Zones 4–8
  FLOWERING SPAN: Mid-July to October
  NATURAL COLOR: Rosy pink
  DISTRIBUTION: Europe, Asia Minor

This one-species perennial combines outstanding adaptability to drought and seashore conditions with a lengthy blooming time. Although technically a low shrub, it is popularly considered a perennial and is frequently listed as such in plant catalogs. This evergreen ground cover has ⅛-in, scalelike leaves tightly clasping slender, semierect stems to create an almost square-foliaged appearance. The tall, thin, terminal spikes of bell-shaped, ⅛-in florets are highly attractive to bees and retain interest with faded coloring long beyond the blooming season. The dried flowering remains intact through winter in a tan or gray color, and some cultivars offer winter foliage hues as well. Cut flowers last indoors.

Best grown in a sandy, peaty, well-drained, acid soil low in fertility, it can be safely spring-pruned for neatness and compactness since the seasonal flowering comes from new stems. Covering lightly with evergreen boughs in winter prevents foliage discoloration on exposed, windy sites, but these plants are hardy without any protection. Spring division, late summer stem cuttings, and stem layering are all effective propagation methods. Water new plantings generously until established. A leaf fungus in hot, humid weather occasionally browns the tips, but insects are not common.

The list of cultivars is impressive, including: 'Alba', 24 in, white; 'Alba Minor', 12 in, white; 'Alba Plena', 12 in, white, double-flowered; 'Alportii', 24 in, crimson; 'Aurea' ('Aureifolia'), 12 in, purple, scant bloom, gold-tipped leaves; 'Camla' ('County Wicklow'), 18 in, shell pink, double; 'Coccinea', 18 in, deep red with gray-green foliage; 'Cuprea', 18 in, pale mauve with golden yellow new growth; 'Foxii', 10 in, lavender-pink'; 'Hammondii', 30 in, white, vigorous; 'Hammondii Aureifolia', 20 in, white with gold-tipped leaves; 'H. E. Beale', 24 in, bright rosy pink, very long flower spikes; 'Hirsuta' ('Tomentosa'), 18 in, pink with gray foliage; 'Kupholdii', 6 in, deep lavender; 'Peter Sparkes', 18 in, deep pink, double; 'Robert Chapman', 20 in, soft purple with leaves first gold, then orange, finally red; 'Searlei', 20 in, white, late-blooming; and 'Tib', 20 in, deep red-purple, double, early. New cultivar introductions are reasonably frequent. (See photos. Also pictured with *Yucca filamentosa*.)

Campanula lactiflora 30–48 in Sun Zones 6–9
FLOWERING SPAN: Mid-July to mid-August
NATURAL COLOR: Off-white, pale blue
DISTRIBUTION: Caucasus Mountains

The bell-shaped, open-faced, 1½-in florets come massed in sizeable, top-heavy clusters above 2–3-in, deep green, lancelike, sawtoothed, robust foliage. It thrives in full sun on a deep, fertile, constantly moist soil but also adapts well to light shading. Spring division of the thick, fleshy rootstock, along with spring stem cuttings, is recommended for propagation. It appears unbothered by diseases or pests. The cultivar 'Alba' has pure white blossoms: 'Caerulea' carries light blue ones; and 'Loddon Anna' shows pinkish white flowering.

Campanula sarmatica 12–24 in Sun Zones 4–8
FLOWERING SPAN: Early July to September
NATURAL COLOR: Grayish blue
DISTRIBUTION: Caucasus Mountains

Unusual but attractive for both its velvety, nodding, 1-in flowers and 3-in, leathery, wrinkled, hairy, gray-green foliage, the plant grows readily on any well-drained, rich, moist soil. Propagate by seed only. There are no apparent disease or insect problems.

Cassia marilandica (wild senna) 36–48 in Sun Zones 4–9
FLOWERING SPAN: Late July to September
NATURAL COLOR: Bright yellow
DISTRIBUTION: Pennsylvania to Florida, west to Kentucky, Iowa, and Texas

The plant has 6–10-in, pinnately compound leaves of light green with individual leaflets nearly 2 in long on sturdy, erect stems. Clusters of sweet pealike, 3-in florets with rich brown anthers come from the leaf axils and later develop into attractive, cylindrical, 4-in-long seed pods with autumn interest. Suitable for wild areas or the back of large borders, it adapts readily to almost any well-drained, moist soil in sun or light shade. Seeding or spring division propagates it easily, and it has no problems with pests or diseases. The species *C. hebecarpa,* found in the same growing range, is very similar but has more abundant flowers.

Centaurea macrocephala (yellow hardhead) 24–36 in Sun Zones 4–9
FLOWERING SPAN: Mid-July to September
NATURAL COLOR: Golden yellow
DISTRIBUTION: Armenia

The bold, 3-in, thistlelike blossoms are long-lasting and appear terminally above rough-haired, coarse-looking, sawtoothed basal leaves up to 4 in wide and close to 1 ft long. Best placed as background in borders, it enjoys full sun and any average-fertility, well-drained soil. Seed is the better propagation method, and there are no disease or insect nuisances of importance. (See photo.)

Centaurea ruthenica   36–60 in   Sun   Zones 5–9
FLOWERING SPAN: Early July to mid-August
NATURAL COLOR: Sulphur yellow
DISTRIBUTION: Romania to Caucasus to Siberia
    This species carries finely dissected, lancelike, rich green leaves and 2½-in, thistlelike, solitary blossoms. Cultivate the same as for *C. macrocephala.*

Chelone glabra   (turtlehead, snakehead, balmony)   24–36 in   Semishade   Zones 3–8
FLOWERING SPAN: Mid-July to September
NATURAL COLOR: Off-white to pinkish
DISTRIBUTION: Newfoundland to Georgia, west to Missouri and Minnesota
    The ¾–1-in, egg-shaped florets appearing in leafy, terminal stalks resemble their common namesakes to most observers. The paired leaves are lancelike, dark green, up to 6 in long, and widely spaced on the stems. The plant enjoys a rich, consistently moist, humusy soil, particularly along streams and swamps, yet it adapts readily to garden sites if kept well-watered and heavily mulched. Division is the practical method for propagation, and it appears to be free of diseases and pests.

Cimicifuga racemosa   (black cohosh, black snakeroot)   48–84 in   Semishade   Zones 3–9
FLOWERING SPAN: Early July to August
NATURAL COLOR: Creamy white
DISTRIBUTION: Massachusetts to Georgia, west to Tennessee and Missouri
    Dramatically bold in its foliage, the plant carries deep green, compound leaves up to 18 in. long which are thrice-divided, and the subdivided leaflets 3 times more. Erect, branched, wiry, very tall flowering spikes have strong-scented, bee-attracting florets with clawed petals emerging from noticeably round, ¼-in buds. The later seed capsules are suitable for drying and use indoors. It provides a handsome accent in shadowy woodlots and between border shrubs in semishade. Provide a constantly moist, well-drained, acid, humusy, deep soil and propagate by spring division only. It is unbothered by diseases or insects. The closely related species from West Virginia, *C. americana*, blooms a bit later, and its wandlike flower spikes are shorter. Both are very hardy and require little care. (See photo.)

Coreopsis rosea   12–24 in   Sun   Zones 3–8
FLOWERING SPAN: Early July to September
NATURAL COLOR: Rosy purple
DISTRIBUTION: Nova Scotia to Delaware
    While not overly showy in flower, the unusual coloring of this species has

some garden interest. Its 1-in, daisylike flowers appear on much-branched stems with very narrow, lancelike foliage 1–2 in long on the upper parts along with pinnately compound leaves at ground level. Differing from most of the other *Coreopsis* species by preferring constantly moist to wet locations, *C. rosea* grows readily on average-fertility soil in sun to light shading. Propagate by simple division in early spring or autumn. Nothing bothers it. A white cultivar, 'Alba', is also known along with an earlier, dwarfed form, 'Nana'.

Coreopsis verticillata (threadleaf coreopsis) 12–24 in Sun Zones 3–9
  FLOWERING SPAN: Early July to mid-August
  NATURAL COLOR: Brassy yellow
  DISTRIBUTION: Maryland to Florida, west to Arkansas
      The finely divided, compound leaves create a lacy, erect foliage mass (resembling dwarfed cosmos to some) which is topped by 1–2-in, jagged-tipped, thin-petaled, daisylike blossoms. The plant readily creeps by underground stems to form large but not invasive clumps which enjoy sun but will accept semishading remarkably well. It also has a good tolerance for dry soil although it grows better with more moisture in a well-drained, average-fertility site. Division either in spring or autumn is the simplest propagation method, and expect no problems from diseases or insects. There are several cultivars: 'Golden Showers', 18 in, bright gold; 'Grandiflora', with larger blossoms; 'Moonbeam', 24 in, pale yellow; and 'Zagreb', 12 in, dwarfed but not always reliably so. (See photos.)

Delphinium cardinale 24–48 in Sun Zones 8–10
  FLOWERING SPAN: Early July to August
  NATURAL COLOR: Orange-scarlet
  DISTRIBUTION: Southern California
      Blooming from seed in its first season, this tender perennial has an exciting color for garden use and can sometimes reach 72 in of flowering height in its native growing area. In garden locations, however, it usually stays smaller. It carries 2–6-in, finely divided foliage in basal clumps and produces spikes of 1½-in, single florets with yellow eyes. The leaves fade away after the flowering ends. Cultivate as for *D.* × *belladonna* of June and supply a light winter mulch in cold areas.

Deschampsia caespitosa (tufted hair grass) 24–60 in Sun Zones 5–9
  FLOWERING SPAN: Early July to late August
  NATURAL COLOR: Greenish white to purplish
  DISTRIBUTION: Greenland to Alaska, south to North Carolina and California, Eurasia
      Dense, evergreen clumps of ⅛-in-wide, flat or folded, slender leaves pro-

duce erect, airy flower panicles good for cutting and drying. This ornamental grass prefers a damp, average-fertility soil with full sun or light shade but will adapt nicely to somewhat drier conditions. Pests and diseases are not problematic. Propagate by spring division. The cultivar 'Bronzeschleier' ('Bronze Veil') carries bronze-yellow flowering; 'Goldgehänge' ('Gold Pendant') has golden yellow; 'Goldschleier' ('Gold Veil') bright yellow; and 'Tardiflora' blossoms somewhat later.

Dianthus superbus (lilac pink)   12–36 in   Sun   Zones 4–9
  FLOWERING SPAN: Early July to August
  NATURAL COLOR: Lilac, pale rose, pink
  DISTRIBUTION: Europe, eastern Asia, Japan
      The lacy, deeply fringed, very fragrant, 1½–2-in blossoms appear on tall, slender, branched stems above light green, glossy, 2-in, narrow, lancelike foliage clumps. The plant can quickly overbloom itself into extinction, however, and probably should be propagated by annual seeding to maintain its presence in a garden border. Provide a rich, moist, well-drained site with full sun. Pests and diseases affect it less than self-exhaustion. The 'Loveliness Strain' is neater-looking in appearance with red, purple, or pink flowering but has no more endurance than the parent.

Echinacea purpurea (Rudbeckia purpurea) (purple coneflower)   12–48 in   Sun Zones 3–9
  FLOWERING SPAN: Early July to mid-September
  NATURAL COLOR: Purplish crimson
  DISTRIBUTION: Ohio to Iowa, south to Louisiana and Georgia
      Easily tolerant of heat and drought, this wildflower carries abundant, 4-in, daisylike flowers with drooping, widely spaced petals and raised, mahogany-colored centers, which have great appeal for butterflies. Its coarse-looking, 8-in-long, lancelike foliage is hairy and belongs in the rear of borders. Any well-drained, sandy, moderately fertile soil in full sun suits it. Division of the root clumps in spring or root cuttings propagate it readily, but do not divide frequently since the plant resents too much disturbance when established. Japanese beetles and mildew are often the chief problems. The cultivars are superior: 'Bright Star', 30 in, rosy red with a maroon center; 'Robert Bloom', 30 in, carmine-purple with an orange center, long-flowering; 'The King', 36 in, coral red with a maroon center; 'White Lustre', 30 in, almost-white with a bronze center; and 'White Swan', 18 in, pure white with a maroon center. All are very hardy. (See photo.)

Echinops humilis (ritro) (small globe thistle)   24–36 in   Sun   Zones 3–8
  FLOWERING SPAN: Mid-July to mid-August
  NATURAL COLOR: Steel blue

DISTRIBUTION: Western Asia

The striking foliage of this perennial is matched by its novel, ball-shaped, terminal flower heads. Its deeply lobed, 9-in, lancelike, dark green leaves have very downy, whitened undersides and are tipped with many fragile spines. Branched, green flower stalks carry 2-in-wide globes of tightly packed, tubular, star-pointed florets that can be cut when fully colored and dried for indoor decoration. Any average-fertility, well-drained, somewhat dry site in full sun is workable. Propagate by spring division, root cuttings, or seeding. It may self-seed generously in some areas to become weedy. The cultivar 'Taplow Blue' has bright blue, 3-in flower heads, while 'Veitch's Blue' is deep blue and somewhat taller. (See photo.)

Echinops sphaerocephalus (great globe thistle) 60–84 in Sun Zones 3–8
FLOWERING SPAN: Mid-July to mid-August
NATURAL COLOR: Pale blue to whitish
DISTRIBUTION: Central and southern Europe, western Asia

The stems of this species are ribbed and greenish white while its 10–14-in leaves are light green, rough-surfaced, and pinnately lobed with spiny tips. The undersurfaces of the leaves are whitened or gray and woolly—less whitened than those of *E. humilis*—and are clasped around the stems at the lowest level. The ball-shaped blossoming is up to 2 in wide and silvered. Culture is identical for both species, and the dried seedheads are also desirable for indoor use.

Erigeron aurantiacus (double orange daisy, orange fleabane) 6–10 in Sun Zones 4–9
FLOWERING SPAN: Mid-July to mid-August
NATURAL COLOR: Bright orange
DISTRIBUTION: Turkestan

Somewhat twisted, oblong, velvety, 3–4-in leaves clasp the erect, thin stems below the solitary, 2-in, semidouble, daisylike flowering of this perennial. Performing better if given some noonday shade, it grows easily in any sandy, low-fertility location that is well-drained but reasonably moist. Seeding or division in spring or autumn propagates it, and only the "aster yellows" disease is troublesome.

Erigeron aureus 2–6 in Semishade Zones 4–8
FLOWERING SPAN: Mid-July to mid-August
NATURAL COLOR: Bright golden yellow
DISTRIBUTION: Cascade Mountains of western Canada and Washington

Useful as a rock garden accent in semishade, the plant has a basal group of downy, warped, trowel-shaped, 3-in leaves and daisylike, 1-in, double flowers. Culture is the same as for *E. aurantiacus* except that this species prefers acid, humusy soil.

Erigeron × *hybridus* 9–30 in Sun Zones 5–9
>FLOWERING SPAN: Late July to early October
>NATURAL COLOR: Pink to deep violet
>ORIGIN: Horticultural hybrid of many species
>   This showy and long-flowering hybrid resembles the autumn-blooming perennial aster with its sturdy, leafy stems and clusters of 1–2-in, yellow-eyed, daisylike flowers. The outer petals are whisker-thin, arranged in several overlapping rows, and grow best where summers are cool. Cultivate as for *E. aurantiacus* but propagate by division only since seed of this hybrid produces erratic results. A sizeable list of attractive cultivars is available: 'Amity', lilac-rose; 'Azure Fairy', lavender; 'Charity', light pink; 'Dunkelste Aller' ('Darkest of All'), violet-blue; 'Dignity', violet; 'Double Beauty', deep violet, double-flowered; 'Felicity', deep pink; 'Festivity', lilac-pink; 'Foerster's Liebling', bright pink, semidouble; 'Gaiety', deep pink; 'Rose Jewel' ('Pink Jewel'), pale pink to lavender pink; 'Prosperity', mauve blue, semidouble; 'Sincerity', lavender-blue; and 'Wuppertal', deep violet.

Eryngium alpinum 18–24 in Sun Zones 3–9
>FLOWERING SPAN: Mid-July to September
>NATURAL COLOR: Metallic blue, white
>DISTRIBUTION: Europe
>   Novel throughout in appearance, this hardy perennial normally carries 1½-in, terminal blooms on steel blue stems and has prickly, blue-green foliage. The flowers are dominated by conspicuously raised, central domes surrounded with jagged, flattened, widely spaced bracts. The much-divided, stiff, prickly, 4–6-in leaves are tinged with blue and often palmately cut. Any part of the plant can be cut and dried for decorative use indoors. Provide a somewhat dry, light, rich, sandy soil in full sun. Division of the fanglike roots shocks the plant, and although root cuttings are a possible propagation technique, seeding is really the best method—but use only newly ripened seed for the best germination. Leaf miners and beetles can disfigure the foliage along with crown rot and leaf spot diseases. (See photo.)

Eryngium amethystinum (sea holly) 12–18 in Sun Zones 3–9
>FLOWERING SPAN: Early July to September
>NATURAL COLOR: Deep blue
>DISTRIBUTION: Europe
>   Much-branched and bushy in appearance, the blossoms, leaf bracts, and upper stems are shaded from steel blue to amethyst. The oval, 1½-in flower heads are surrounded by ragged collars of spiny bracts above deeply cut, green foliage. Cultivate the same as for *E. alpinum.*

Eryngium yuccifolium (button snakeroot, rattlesnake master) 24–42 in Sun
Zones 3–9
FLOWERING SPAN: Mid-July to mid-August
NATURAL COLOR: Ivory white
DISTRIBUTION: Connecticut to Florida, west to Texas, Kansas, and Minnesota
 Native to bogs and marshes, this wildflower has branched flower stalks with rounded, 1-in blossom heads composed of many tubular florets tightly packed together. The narrow, rigid, spiny, gray-green leaves can be up to 24 in long and remain near ground level. Effective as a sunny border accent, the plant strangely adapts to either a dry or a very moist soil when used in gardens. It may need wintertime mulching in severe climate areas. The blossoming can be cut and dried for decorative purposes. Seeding is the most assured method for reproduction, and there are no pest or disease problems. (See photo.)

Eupatorium rugosum (ageratoides, fraseri) (white snakeroot) 24–48 in Sun
Zones 3–8
FLOWERING SPAN: Mid-July to mid-September
NATURAL COLOR: Bright white
DISTRIBUTION: Eastern North America
 Showy and long in bloom, this heavily branched plant has many flat clusters of ¼-in, buttonlike blossoms and 3–6-in, nettlelike foliage. Poisonous if any part of the plant is chewed or swallowed, it should not be planted where young, adventuresome children might investigate it too closely. Browsing cows that feed on this plant develop toxic milk. Best grown in a sunny, constantly moist location well-endowed with humus, it blooms satisfactorily, but less vigorously, in semishade. Remaining dormant long into spring, the plant can be propagated by spring division only if the vigorous portions of the plant are used. Collected seedlings or nursery stock are other methods of increase. Diseases are not common, but leaf miners can disfigure the foliage.

Euphorbia corollata (flowering spurge) 18–36 in Sun Zones 3–9
FLOWERING SPAN: Early July to mid-August
NATURAL COLOR: White
DISTRIBUTION: Ontario to Florida, west to Texas
 A tough, long-lived, dependable plant for garden use, it has true, minuscule flowers surrounded by showy white leaf bracts above narrow, blunt-tipped, 2-in, smooth leaves which turn rich red in autumn. Handsome in borders or woodlot edges as a baby's-breath substitute, it thrives on a light, sandy, well-drained soil held to the dry side. Seeding, summer stem cuttings, and division in spring or autumn readily propagate it. There seem to be no bothersome pests or diseases.

Filipendula camtschatica (Spiraea camtschatica)   48–96 in   Semishade   Zones 2–7
  FLOWERING SPAN: Early July to August
  NATURAL COLOR: Creamy white
  DISTRIBUTION: Manchuria, Kamchatka Peninsula of Siberia
        This airy, graceful perennial carries very large plumes of ¼-in, fragrant florets and is especially noticeable at dusk. Culture is the same as for the June-blooming *F. purpurea,* but this species is far hardier.

Galega officinalis   (goat's rue)   24–60 in   Sun   Zones 3–9
  FLOWERING SPAN: Early July to September
  NATURAL COLOR: Lilac, pinkish lilac
  DISTRIBUTION: Central Europe to Iran
        Not commonly grown in gardens but easily adaptable and long-flowering, this bushy plant has graceful, pinnately compound, lancelike leaflets and showy, sweet pea-shaped, 1-in florets in 4–6-in terminal clusters. It likes full sun best but will adapt to modest shading on any moist, well-drained, average-fertility soil. Division in spring or autumn, plus seeding, reproduces it satisfactorily. Aphids and cutworms bother the stems and leaves, and mildew can disfigure the plant during hot, humid weather. The cultivar 'Alba' has white blossoming.

Galtonia candicans (Hyacinthus candicans)   (summer hyacinth)   24–48 in   Sun
  Zones 5–9
  FLOWERING SPAN: Mid-July to mid-August
  NATURAL COLOR: Milky white
  DISTRIBUTION: South Africa
        Showy in flower as a border background, the stiff, erect flower spike of this bulb carries 20–30 slightly fragrant, nodding, 1½-in florets. The straplike, 2-in-wide, gray-green leaves form a floppy basal clump and can stretch to 42 in in length. Simple to grow in any constantly moist, well-drained, sandy, humusy soil with full sun, it requires heavy mulching in severe winter climates. Lifting in autumn and replanting in spring may prove the wiser culture in those areas. Late spring installation of new colonies as well as bulb offsets from established but overcrowded groupings propagates it readily. Pests and diseases are uncommon. (See photo.)

Gaultheria procumbens   (checkerberry, wintergreen, teaberry)   4–6 in   Semishade
  Zones 3–8
  FLOWERING SPAN: Early July to August
  NATURAL COLOR: White, pinkish white
  DISTRIBUTION: Newfoundland to Manitoba, south to Georgia and Alabama
        Widely distributed in acid woodlots and tolerant of a variety of soils and

exposures, this evergreen ground cover has dark green, glossy, 1–2-in, oval leaves shielding waxy, drooping, ½-in florets in small clusters. These blooms later produce ¼–½-in, edible, scarlet fruit with a somewhat minty flavor. Slow to expand, it prefers a sandy, peaty, moist, well-drained location free of excessive root competition from vigorous shrubs or other perennials. Propagate by division since seed and cuttings are difficult to manage successfully. Nothing seems to bother it. This plant was the original, natural source of oil of wintergreen. (See photo.)

Gentiana asclepiadea (willow gentian) 18–30 in Semishade Zones 5–9
FLOWERING SPAN: Mid-July to September
NATURAL COLOR: Deep blue
DISTRIBUTION: Central and southern Europe, Caucasus Mountains
The slender, arching stems carry light green, willowlike, 2–3-in leaves and are terminally set with 6–8 in of conspicuous, tubular, 1½-in blossoms. Provide a permanent site with acid, humusy, constantly moist, cool conditions since this perennial resents transplanting. Early spring division of young plants is workable but risky, and seeding into individual pots, while slow for results, is the preferred reproduction technique. No insect is troublesome, but rust disease occasionally disfigures the foliage. There is a scarce white form, 'Alba', which has green markings on the florets.

Gentiana lutea (yellow gentian) 24–60 in Semishade Zones 6–9
FLOWERING SPAN: Mid-July to mid-August
NATURAL COLOR: Rich yellow
DISTRIBUTION: Europe, Asia Minor
Stoutly erect, the showy flower stalks are encircled by widely spaced whorls of star-shaped, 1-in, tubular blossoms in groups of 20 or more. The spear-shaped, 6–12-in leaves carry 5–7 noticeable veins. Cultivate as for G. *asclepiadea,* but only container seeding works for propagation.

Gentiana septemfida (cordifolia) (crested gentian) 8–12 in Semishade Zones 3–9
FLOWERING SPAN: Mid-July to mid-August
NATURAL COLOR: Deep blue
DISTRIBUTION: Asia Minor
Here the bell-shaped, 2-in, lacy-edged blossoms have white throats and appear in small, headlike clusters on squarish, semierect stems with 1½-in, oval leaves. Provide a moist, gravelly, well-drained soil, either acid or slightly alkaline. Reproduction is best handled by seeding into pots, and avoid disturbing the roots at any time. Pests and diseases are uncommon. This species and G. *lagodechiana* from the Caucasus are often confused due to their close general appearance, but G. *lagodechiana* carries 1½-in, tubular flowering. (See photo.)

Gypsophila acutifolia   36–72 in   Sun   Zones 3–8
FLOWERING SPAN: Mid-July to September
NATURAL COLOR: White
DISTRIBUTION: Romania, southern Ukraine, Caucasus Mountains
      All gypsophila thrive in alkaline soils, but acid garden conditions can be amended by initial soil conditioning and by an annual application of ground limestone around the base of each plant. The tall, airy sprays of much-branched flower panicles have ¼-in florets and provide a long-lasting mistlike effect in borders. The flowers can be cut and dried easily for indoor decoration when in full bloom. The slender, brittle stems have narrow, 3-in, green, lancelike leaves very widely spaced. When young this species is similar in general appearance to the more readily available G. *paniculata* and its cultivars, but it is far taller at maturity. Provide a sunny location on an average-fertility, somewhat dry site, and plant for permanence since its deep taproots resent later disturbance. Reproduce by seeding or by summer stem cuttings. Troublesome diseases and insect pests are unknown.

Gypsophila paniculata   (baby's-breath)   24–36 in   Sun   Zones 3–8
FLOWERING SPAN: Mid-July to mid-August
NATURAL COLOR: White
DISTRIBUTION: Central and southern Europe, central Asia
      Normally as broad as it is tall, the plant carries 3-in, gray-green, lance-shaped leaves scattered below the mass of wiry, branched flower stems with their profusion of ¼-in, single florets. These can be cut and dried at full bloom for indoor decoration. Its culture is identical with that for the taller G. *acutifolia,* which it closely resembles. Only seeding reproduces it satisfactorily, and even that technique is not entirely reliable. The double-flowered cultivars are usually root-grafted at the nursery and cannot be considered for division at all. Summer stem cuttings are a variable but possible propagation alternative.
      Growers have supplanted the parent species with this list of desirable cultivars: 'Bristol Fairy', 36 in, white, double-flowered, impressive; 'Compacta Plena', 18 in, white, double, long-lived; 'Compacta Plena Rosea', 18 in, pink-toned, double; 'Flamingo', 36 in, mauve-pink, double, larger blossoms; 'Perfecta', 48 in, white, double, larger-blossoming form of 'Bristol Fairy'; 'Pink Fairy', 18 in, light pink, double, larger-flowered; 'Pink Star', 24 in, pink, double, large flowers; 'Schneeflocke' ('Snowflake'), 36 in, white, double, durable in hot areas; and 'Rosenschleier' ('Rosy Veil'), 15 in, pale pink, semidouble. (See photo.)

Helianthus decapetalus   (thinleaf sunflower)   24–60 in   Sun   Zones 5–9
FLOWERING SPAN: Late July to October
NATURAL COLOR: Bright yellow
DISTRIBUTION: Maine to Georgia, west to Wisconsin and Iowa

The loosely set, 10-petaled blossoms have darker yellow centers and appear terminally above 3–8-in, broad, coarse-textured, lancelike leaves with slightly hairy undersides. Adaptable to any light, moist soil in full sun, it prefers a neutral to alkaline condition. Regular division not only propagates the plant readily but actually improves its performance since it eagerly spreads itself to the point of overcrowding. Diseases are uncommon but aphids, beetles, and leaf miners are regular pests.

Helianthus × multiflorus   48–72 in   Sun   Zones 3–9
FLOWERING SPAN: Late July to October
NATURAL COLOR: Bright yellow
ORIGIN: Horticultural hybrid of *H. annuus × H. decapetalus*
    The 3–5-in, daisylike flowering can be single, double or semidouble, and the erect stems have lancelike, deep green leaves up to 10 in long. A vigorous spreader requiring frequent division and wide spacing between plants—itself or other perennials—it has the same cultural needs as *H. decapetalus.* The cultivars are superior: 'Flore Pleno', bright yellow, double; and 'Loddon Gold', golden yellow, double.

Heliopsis helianthoides (laevis)   36–60 in   Sun   Zones 4–9
FLOWERING SPAN: Mid-July to October
NATURAL COLOR: Golden yellow
DISTRIBUTION: New York to Michigan, south to Mississippi, Alabama, and Georgia
    Widely distributed, this short-lived wildflower has 3–5-in, mostly smooth, stalked, thin leaves on erect stems and carries its 1½–2½ in, long-stemmed, daisylike flowering in generously branched abundance. Resistant to drought, the plant grows well in any sunny, well-drained, average-fertility soil kept on the dry side. Spring division or summer stem cuttings readily propagate it. The general pest list includes aphids, leaf miners, and various beetles, but diseases are uncommon. All the cultivars are superior: 'Goldgrünherz' ('Gold Greenheart'), 36 in, double with an emerald green center as it opens; 'Goldgefleder' ('Golden Plume'), 48 in, semidouble, deep yellow; 'Light of Loddon', 36 in, bright yellow, semidouble; 'Patula', 36 in, orange-yellow, semidouble; and 'Sommesonne' ('Summer Sun'), 42 in, orange, single-flowered.

Hemerocallis citrina   (citron daylily)   24–48 in   Sun   Zones 3–10
FLOWERING SPAN: Early July to August
NATURAL COLOR: Lemon yellow
DISTRIBUTION: China
    Normally, daylilies blossom only during daylight hours, but in this species the flowering is surprisingly nocturnal, appearing in late afternoon and con-

tinuing until dawn. Its many leafless flower scapes bud prolifically and rise out of a basal mound of deep green, 1½-in-wide, straplike leaves between 30–45 in long. The trumpet-shaped, 4–6-in flowers are modestly fragrant. Parent of many hybrids, the plant enjoys any moist, humusy, well-drained, average-fertility location in sun or light shading. Division in either spring or midautumn is the simplest propagation technique, yet seeding is also productive, if slower. The entire genus is remarkably free of diseases and pests of any consequence and is also agreeably adaptive to heat and dryness.

Hemerocallis fulva (orange daylily, tawny daylily) 48–60 in Sun Zones 3–10
FLOWERING SPAN: Early July to August
NATURAL COLOR: Rusty orange
DISTRIBUTION: Europe, Asia, eastern United States

Often mistakenly called "tiger lily" by the uninitiated, this durable and exceptional colonizer is highly useful for stabilizing steep embankments with poor soil in full sun. Nothing defeats its urge to grow. The plant has 18–24-in, bright green, narrow, straplike foliage in a base mound and clusters of 6–12 unscented, 5-in blossoms on erect, stiff scapes. Cultivate as for *H. citrina,* but know that it is even less fussy about accepting less than ideal growing conditions. The commonly seen cultivar 'Europa' does not set seed but has fertile pollen. The double-flowered 'Kwanso' (from the Chinese word *Hsuan-ts'ao*) has 2-in-wide leaves, a long-lasting bloom, and also no seed pods. Obviously, both cultivars can be reproduced only by division. (See photos.)

Hemerocallis × *hybrida* 15–48 in Sun Zones 4–10
FLOWERING SPAN: Early July to mid-August
NATURAL COLOR: Solid and blended colorings of yellow, orange, red, pink, and mahogany from pale to vivid, along with many bicolors
ORIGIN: Horticultural hybrid mainly from European and North American sources using a wide variety of species and cultivars

The continuing interest in daylily breeding over the past decades has given us a wealth of new colorings and flower sizes that is both astounding and welcome. No other perennial has received such hybridization attention, with the result that dozens of new introductions are now expected annually. One of the grandest improvements surely is the production of tetraploid cultivars with richer, more intense colorings, heavier petals, more branching and increased budding of the scapes, plus noticeable vigor. Many even have ruffled petals or different colored margins. From a scientific point of view, tetraploid plants have twice the number of chromosomes as diploid plants (the earlier cultural breakthrough). This doubling provides the impetus for all the horticultural benefits just described. Whenever possible, select a tetraploid cultivar before any other type. These data now are normally emphasized in catalogs.

Make note, too, that *Hemerocallis* includes some very late-blooming forms, such as those with evergreen foliage for use in mild winter zones, and also tall plants with flowering 60 in or more high. These are not necessarily tetraploids, but their existence at least indicates the potential for increasingly varied forms that further development of daylilies could bring. Whether used as a border specimen or as a lush ground cover bedding, they are tough, reliable, and adaptable perennials with a long life span. If handled carefully, they can even be transplanted while in flower. Include some of them in every sunny garden, and cultivate as for *H. citrina.*

The following arbitrarily brief listing of named cultivars gives some clue to the range of colorings available today: 'Apricot Surprise', soft apricot, ruffled; 'Artist Etching', apricot-pink, ruffled; 'Bowl of Roses', rosy salmon; 'Carolyn Criswell', canary yellow; 'Chicago Apache', rich scarlet; 'Chicago Atlas', plum; 'Chicago Blue Eyes', lavender; 'Chicago Gold Coast', deep gold; 'Chicago Petticoats', shell pink; 'Eenie Weenie', light yellow, dwarfed; 'Evening Gown', melon-pink; 'Heavenly Grace', light pink; 'Heaven's Trophy', creamy pink, ruffled; 'Hyperion', lemon yellow, enjoyed for scent and durability for over 50 years; 'James Marsh', bright scarlet; 'Mission Moonlight', ivory; 'Mountain Anemone', plum; 'Orange Blaze', vivid red-orange; 'Persian Shrine', burgundy red; 'Petite Palace Rose', rosy pink; 'Pink Tangerine', pinkish tangerine, ruffled; 'Root Beer', deep cherry red; 'Silver Trumpet', lavender, ruffled; 'Stella de Oro', golden yellow, dwarfed, reblooms; 'Summer Wine', purplish red; 'Temple Bells', cantaloupe; 'Witchhazel', cinnamon-orange; and 'Yellow Lady Slipper', bright yellow. (See photos.)

Hibiscus moscheutos   (common rose mallow, mallow rose, swamp rose mallow)
60–96 in   Sun   Zones 5–9
FLOWERING SPAN: Late July to September
NATURAL COLOR: White, pink, rose, all with a red center
DISTRIBUTION: Massachusetts to Alabama, west to Michigan

The giant 6–8-in, saucer-shaped blossoms are the largest produced by any herbaceous perennial known today. They appear terminally clustered on tall, erect stems with 8-in, lancelike to broadly ovate leaves indented with 3–5 lobes which are densely covered with white hairs beneath. Native to marshy areas, the plant adapts well to gardens with rich, constantly moist, well-drained soil in sun to light shading. Spring division or seeding propagates it readily, but division alone is the recommended technique for cultivars. Aphids, white fly, stem rot, and leaf spot disease are frequent problems in some growing areas. The cultivars have supplanted the parent today: 'Ann Arundel', magenta-pink; 'Lady Baltimore', lavender-pink; and 'Southern Belle Series', mixed colorings of red, pink, or white, 10-in blossoming, dwarfed at 36 in tall. (See photos.)

Hosta crispula   (whiterim plantain lily)   18–30 in   Semishade   Zones 3–9
   FLOWERING SPAN: Mid-July to early August
   NATURAL COLOR: Lavender
   DISTRIBUTION: Japan

   Plantain lilies not only possess the remarkable duality of having attractive flowers and conspicuous foliage, but their reliable hardiness, tolerance to drought, and willing adaptability to deep shading (for a show of leaves and less blossom impact) extend their usefulness far beyond that of most other perennials. None enjoys constant sunlight, strong wind, or poor drainage, yet all attempt to cope with any growing conditions. Their popularity is richly deserved. The correct identification of the separate species and cultivars, however, still puzzles botanists and growers. At one time, too, this genus was called *Funkia,* and that name, though now invalid, is still used by some older growers and gardeners even today. All new hosta cultivars are now registered with the American Hosta Society and the University of Minnesota Landscape Arboretum.

   Foliage is the main asset of *Hosta,* and it appears in mounds at ground level in a variety of colorings from light to dark green, yellow-green to almost-yellow, and blue-green to grayish green with leaves lancelike, heart-shaped, or oval in form. Some are streaked, mottled, or margined in white to yellow as a bonus. When grown well, any hosta creates an exceptional summertime ground cover with secondary interest from its flowering. All of the types blend well with each other and offer splendid possibilities for texture and color in shaded areas.

   The blossoms are funnel-shaped, carry noticeable stamens, last but a day or two, and are generated from a quantity of usually tall, leafless scapes rising out of the center of the foliage clump. The majority have scentless or mildly fragrant blossoming, and the flower scapes last when cut for indoor use. All produce a later collection of sausage-shaped seedheads, but the seed is not always viable for propagation.

   Hostas thrive and spread widely in a consistently moist, humusy, well-drained soil of average fertility. Division is the usual propagation technique. Some of the large-leaved forms can create a dense, almost solid mass of ropelike roots that requires an ax to separate. True to form, the plant accepts this bizarre treatment without dismay. Midautumn is preferable to spring division, when newly emerging, furled foliage can be easily damaged in handling. Autumn separation of old leaves avoids this drawback. Diseases are uncommon, but slugs and snails can be ruinous to leaves in any season of growth.

   The species *H. crispula* has somewhat wavy, white-margined, lancelike, medium green, partially puckered leaves up to 8 in long and 4–6 in wide on stalks nearly 1 ft in length. Vigorous and wide-spreading, its showy foliage is superior to its loosely set, 2-in floret display. It sets viable seed annually. (See photos.)

Hosta fortunei   (Fortune's plantain lily)   18–48 in   Semishade   Zones 3–9
   FLOWERING SPAN: Early July to August
   NATURAL COLOR: Pale lilac to violet

DISTRIBUTION: Japan

Late to emerge from dormancy, the plant carries grayish green, 6–12-in leaves with spearhead or trowel outlines. Flowering appears on 36–48-in scapes with spikes of 1–1½-in florets. Both the parent and its cultivars make effective masses for ground cover. Cultivate as for *H. crispula*. The cultivar list presents some fascinating variations: 'Albo-picta', pale yellow with deep green margins in spring but all green later; 'Aurea', pale yellow with creamy borders on emerging, becoming pale green in summer; 'Gloriosa', oval green foliage margined narrowly in white; 'Francee', 15–18 in, persistently dark green, heart-shaped leaves rimmed with white; and 'Marginato-alba', broader-leaved with irregular but wide white edges, late to flower. (See photo.)

Hosta sieboldiana (glauca) (Siebold plantain lily) 18–24 in Semishade Zones 3–9
FLOWERING SPAN: Early July to August
NATURAL COLOR: Pale lilac to almost-white
DISTRIBUTION: Japan

Strikingly noticeable in foliage, this species has heart-shaped, large leaves 15 in long and 10 in wide of metallic blue-green with conspicuous, wrinkled ribbing. Sometimes it is referred to by gardeners as the "seersucker plant." Its low-set flower stalks have compactly arranged, 1½-in florets. Care as for *H. crispula*. The cultivar 'Elegans' develops even larger and more intensely colored leaves; its offshoot cultivar 'Color Glory' adapts to more sunlight and shows yellow-green foliage bordered in olive green; while 'Frances Williams' has cupped leaves with bold, golden edges. (See photo.)

Hosta tokudama 9–12 in Semishade Zones 3–9
FLOWERING SPAN: Early July to August
NATURAL COLOR: Milky white
DISTRIBUTION: Japan

The rounded, cupped, seersuckerlike, 9-in foliage is gray-blue and might be considered a smaller edition of *H. sieboldiana*. These leaves catch and hold debris easily, so choose a location with this negative effect in mind. Slow to expand, the plant has urn-shaped florets in low, dense spikes. Provide the same care as for *H. crispula*. The cultivar 'Akebono' has a noticeably yellow leaf center, while 'Aureo-nebulosa' is similar but less intensely yellow. 'Flavo-circinalis' carries a wide, irregular, yellow leaf margin.

Hosta undulata (wavyleaf plantain lily) 12–15 in Semishade Zones 3–9
FLOWERING SPAN: Mid-July to mid-August
NATURAL COLOR: Pale lavender
DISTRIBUTION: Japan, China

Commonly found in gardens, the plant develops 4–6-in, oval, sharp-pointed, broadly undulating leaves with a central splash of cream or white. The slender flower stalks have 2-in florets with purple anthers but set no seed. The cultivars include: 'Albo-marginata', green and gray-green leaf centers with irregular margins of cream, quick-growing, tolerant of more sunlight; 'Erromena', solid green foliage, useful for deep shade; 'Univittata', rounded foliage mass, green-leaved with white streaking; and 'Variegata', spiral-tipped leaves irregularly striped in white at the centers, wavy-margined, 10 in tall. Grow any of these the same as for *H. crispula*. (See photo.)

Hosta ventricosa (blue plantain lily) 18–30 in Semishade Zones 3–9
FLOWERING SPAN: Early July to late July
NATURAL COLOR: Deep to pale violet
DISTRIBUTION: Eastern Asia
  This species has 5–7-in-long, heart-shaped, deep green leaves half again as wide with tapering, pointed ends. Stiffly erect, slender flower stalks are loosely strung with 1½–2-in florets striped in blue which flare into bell shapes at the ends. The plant readily sets viable seed. Cultivate as for *H. crispula*. (See photo.)

Inula ensifolia (swordleaf inula) 18–24 in Sun Zones 3–9
FLOWERING SPAN: Mid-July to September
NATURAL COLOR: Bright yellow
DISTRIBUTION: Europe
  Long-lasting, daisylike, solitary, 1–2-in flowers appear above dull green, slender, pointed, 4-in leaves on this vigorous perennial. It grows well in any average-fertility, moist, well-drained soil and can be propagated either by spring division or by seeding. Its chief problem is mildew. The cultivar 'Golden Beauty' flowers earlier, has golden yellow blossoms, and is slightly taller.

Inula hookeri (Hooker inula) 18–24 in Sun Zones 4–9
FLOWERING SPAN: Late July to mid-September
NATURAL COLOR: Greenish yellow
DISTRIBUTION: Himalaya Mountains
  The blossoming of this inula is 3 in wide with long, very whiskery petals around a yellow center. Its foliage is oval, downy, soft green, and 3–5 in long. This plant is top-heavy when in flower and needs to be staked for support. Cultivate the same as for *I. ensifolia*.

Inula orientalis (glandulosa) (Caucasian inula) 18–24 in Sun Zones 3–9
FLOWERING SPAN: Early July to August
NATURAL COLOR: Golden yellow

DISTRIBUTION: Caucasus Mountains

The solitary, daisylike flowers are 2–3-in wide and show a noticeably raised central disc surrounded by rows of raggedy, narrow petals which are broader than those of *I. hookeri*. Its lancelike foliage is 4–6 in long, up to 4 in wide, and clasps the stems at the base of the plant. It needs the same care as *I. ensifolia*.

Iris ensata (kaempferi) (Japanese iris) 24–36 in Sun Zones 5–9
FLOWERING SPAN: Early July to August
NATURAL COLOR: Reddish purple
DISTRIBUTION: Japan, China, Korea

The last major iris to bloom, this rhizomatous, apogon (beardless) species has flat-opening flowers often 8 in across on unbranched stalks normally set with 3 buds per stem. The slender, erect, swordlike foliage is 18–24 in tall and carries prominent, identifying midribs. While the assumption is very common that this species demands a waterside, marshy location—which it does accept if well-drained in winter—the plant actually just prefers extra-generous moisture when blooming. It does, however, have an aversion to high heat, dryness, and the use of lime, bonemeal, or wood ashes anywhere near its roots. Provide a consistently damp, acid, humusy, cool, well-drained soil in sun to light shading. Easily divided for propagation, it tolerates spring separation best. There are no troublesome pests or diseases.

While the cultivar listing does not yet offer a truly pink flower, the selections available are still impressive: 'Attraction', gray-white with a purple overlay; 'Bright Inspiration', bright yellow; 'Crimson Goddess', coppery red; 'Geihan', sparkling white; 'Jeweled Kimono', bluish lavender, double; 'Juno', rosy purple; 'Pink Frost', rosy lavender, double; 'Pink Pearl', flesh pink with a darker center; 'Purple Splendor', rich purple, double; 'Pyramid', bluish violet with a white center, double; 'Rising Sun', glowing yellow; 'Rose Anna', wine red; 'Snowy Goddess', white with a flush of gold, double; and 'Snowy Hills', white, double. The majority of these cultivar names are translations from the Japanese, and catalogs may list either the original or the English identity—sometimes both—but with no assured regularity. (See photo.)

Lathyrus latifolius (perennial pea) 48–96 in Sun Zones 3–9
FLOWERING SPAN: Mid-July to September
NATURAL COLOR: Rosy magenta, white
DISTRIBUTION: Europe, United States

A scrambling, vinelike perennial undaunted by soil, exposure, or most climate conditions, this vigorous plant has nonfragrant clusters of 1½-in, sweet pealike florets at the ends of 8–12-in stalks emerging from the axils of the gray-green, lancelike, parallel-veined leaves appearing in pairs on conspicuously winged stems. As a voluminous disguiser of rock piles, fences, or trellises, it adapts to almost any growing condition but blossoms best in full sun. Seed is the recommended propagation method. Nothing bothers it. The cultivar 'Alba' has white flowering, and while pink, purple, or red colorings are sometimes offered by seed companies, seedlings often produce only a random mix of these intended hues. (See photos.)

Lavandula angustifolia (officinalis, vera, spica) (English lavender) 24–36 in Sun Zones 5–10
FLOWERING SPAN: Late July to September
NATURAL COLOR: Lavender-blue
DISTRIBUTION: Mediterranean Europe and North Africa

The sweet scent of the leaves and flowers of this woody herb is familiar to almost everyone since the plant has been cultivated for centuries and used frequently in aromatic sachets. Its needlelike, blunt-tipped, 1-in leaves are silvery green and tightly set along slender stems. Many tall, gray spikes of terminal, ½-in, fragrant florets dominate the billowy foliage mass, and these blossoms can readily be cut and dried for durable indoor decoration. A light, sandy, alkaline, somewhat dry soil in full sun encourages the best growth. Fertilize infrequently but mulch heavily for winter in cold areas. Prune away old wood each spring to produce more flowers. There are no bothersome pests or diseases. Propagate by spring cuttings only. The cultivar list includes: 'Alba', white; 'Atropurpurea', deep purple; 'Compacta', dwarfed; 'Dutch', dark blue; 'Hidcote', dark purple, tender, slow-growing; 'Munstead', lavender-blue; 'Rosea', rosy pink; 'Twickel Purple', purple with very long flower stalks; and 'Waltham', dark purple. (See photo.)

Liatris spicata (spike gayfeather) 24–60 in Sun Zones 3–10
FLOWERING SPAN: Mid-July to September
NATURAL COLOR: Rosy purple
DISTRIBUTION: Long Island, New York to Florida, west to Louisiana and Michigan

Spirals of ¼–½-in-wide, dark green, smooth leaves thread their way up the slender, unbranched stem of this plant, terminated with a densely crowded spike of ½-in, ragged-edged florets. Oddly, the blossoms open from the top down. Often found thriving near open streams and marshes in the wild, it can be garden-cultivated readily in any constantly moist, light, well-drained, average-fertility soil. It will not tolerate standing water ("wet feet") in winter, however. Plant in full sun or light shade and propagate by spring division or by seeding. It has no diseases or insect pests worth mentioning. The cultivar 'Kobold' is 18 in high, compact-growing, and rosy lavender; 'Silver Tips' grows 36 in tall with lavender blossoming. (See photo.)

Ligularia dentata (Senecio clivorum, Ligularia clivorum)   24–48 in   Semishade
   Zones 4–8
   FLOWERING SPAN: Late July to mid-September
   NATURAL COLOR: Deep yellow-orange
   DISTRIBUTION: China, Japan
      Conspicuous for foliage alone, the plant has rounded, 6–12-in, glossy leaves
   emerging first in deep bronze or purple but later becoming deep green.
   Flowering is from sturdy branched stalks with 2-in, daisylike, scented blossoms
   with brown centers. Provide a consistently moist, rich, well-drained soil and
   mulch well for winter in the colder areas of its range. Spring division, summer
   stem cuttings, or seeding reproduces it, and aphids appear to be the main affliction. The compact cultivar 'Desdemona' has dark purple undersides to the leaves;
   'Orange Queen' is green on both sides with larger, more orange-colored
   flowering; and 'Othello' is similar in appearance to 'Desdemona' but smaller.
   (See photo.)

Ligularia przewalskii (Senecio przewalskii)   48–60 in   Sun   Zones 4–9
   FLOWERING SPAN: Late July to mid-September
   NATURAL COLOR: Bright yellow
   DISTRIBUTION: Northern China
      The deeply cut, serrated, 8–12-in, arrow-pointed leaves form generous
   mounds at ground level prior to the emergence of the long-lasting, strikingly
   attractive, very tall flower spikes. The ragged-looking, loosely set, 1-in florets
   appear on deep purple stems and terminate the final foot of the spike. Thriving in
   any rich, constantly moist, well-drained location in sun, it is best propagated by
   division in either spring or midautumn. There are no important disease or insect
   nuisances. The superior cultivar 'The Rocket' blooms a bit later and has more
   triangular foliage. It has a special preference for avoiding late afternoon sunlight
   and wilts quickly on dry sites. This cultivar may be occasionally listed as a form of
   L. stenocephala in some catalogs. (See photo.)

Lilium (lily)   24–96 in   Sun   Zones 4–8
   FLOWERING SPAN: Early July to mid-September
   NATURAL COLOR: White, yellow, red, orange, pink, plus many bicolors
   DISTRIBUTION: Northern Hemisphere
      The midsummer-blooming hybrid lilies normally have larger blossoms,
   heavier bud clusters, and greater overall size. Their culture, however, is identical
   with that provided in the June entry on *Lilium*. (See photos.)

Classification of Hybrid Lilies

July-blooming Hybrid Lilies

DIVISION 4: American hybrids: From 48–96 in tall with 4–6-in, turban-shaped blossoms and elongated pedicels. Derived from native American species, these are tall-stemmed; stem-rooting.

EXAMPLES: 'Bellingham Hybrids', speckled orange and red shadings, vigorous, easy-to-grow; 'Buttercup', deep yellow, heavily spotted with brown, only partly recurved petals; and 'Shuksan', gold, spotted in crimson-maroon, strongly recurved petals.

DIVISION 5: Longiflorum hybrids: From 36–72 in tall with 6–8-in, trumpet-shaped, scented blossoms. Having the characteristics of *L. longiflorum* and *L. formosanum.*

EXAMPLES: 'Holland's Glory', pure white, 36–48 in, the hardiest cultivar; 'Mount Everest', waxy white with a gold flush inside, 60–72 in; and 'White Queen', white with a greenish throat, 36–48 in tall.

DIVISION 6: Aurelian or trumpet hybrids: From 48–60 in tall with 6–10-in, fragrant blossoms of varying shapes. Having the characteristics of the Asiatic hybrids. Except for the cultivars of *L. auratum* and *L. speciosum,* which bloom earlier, these bloom in mid-July and early August.

CHINESE TRUMPET OR FUNNEL-SHAPED-FLOWERING EXAMPLES: 'Black Dragon Strain', white with extensive dark maroon flush outside and gold-throated inside; 'Golden Splendor', deep gold, prefers light shade; 'Green Magic Strain', white with minty green throat as well as petal reverse; 'Limelight', chartreuse yellow; 'Moonlight Strain', greenish yellow; 'Pink Perfection Strain', purplish pink fading to deep pink, prefers semishade; 'Royal Gold', bright golden yellow; and 'Sentinal Strain', pure white.

BOWL-SHAPED-FLOWERING EXAMPLES: 'First Love', pink outside with gold inside and a pale green throat; 'Heart's Desire', blend of white, cream, and yellowish orange; and 'Thunderbolt', vivid greenish orange.

PENDANT-FLOWERING EXAMPLES: 'Golden Showers', buttery yellow with a brownish exterior, vigorous; and 'Reliance', golden yellow.

SUNBURST OR STAR-SHAPED-FLOWERING EXAMPLES: 'Bright Star', ivory white with an apricot center; 'Golden Sunburst Strain', deep gold; 'Pink Sunburst', purplish pink; 'Silver Sunburst Strain', white to cream with a gold throat; and 'White Henryi', white with a deep orange throat.

Lilium auratum (goldband lily) 60–84 in Sun Zones 4–8
  FLOWERING SPAN: Mid-July to mid-August
  NATURAL COLOR: White, striped yellow
  DISTRIBUTION: Japan
    Spectacularly large, 10–12-in, bowl-shaped blossoms heavy with a spicy scent appear in generous clusters on purple-green, erect stems with 6–8-in, narrow, lance-shaped leaves up to 2 in wide. Each petal is centrally striped in rich yellow with crimson freckling. Striking when set against an evergreen backdrop, the large bulb (which is still eaten as food in parts of rural Japan) is short-lived but usually produces an effective showing at least for several seasons. Disliking alkaline, overfertilized, poorly drained locations, this plant is highly susceptible to mosaic disease, which means immediate discard into the trash and no replanting of any lily in the same area for several years. Install this stem-rooting bulb in a moist, well-drained, humusy, average-fertility, acid soil and provide extra water during dry spells, especially when flowering. Offset bulbs or bulb scales are better for propagation than seed, which, although free of mosaic disease, germinates very slowly and erratically.
    The variety *platyphyllum* is larger in every respect. The cultivar list includes: 'Album', pure white; 'Pictum', white with gold banding terminating in crimson tips and dense, crimson spotting; 'Praecos', earlier-flowering; 'Rubro-vittatum', deep crimson banding and spotting; 'Rubrum', broader crimson stripes; and 'Variegata', gold-striped with yellow spotting. (See photo.)

Lilium bulbiferum (orange lily) 24–48 in Sun Zones 4–8
  FLOWERING SPAN: Early July to August
  NATURAL COLOR: Bright orange-red
  DISTRIBUTION: Eastern and central Europe
    Simple to grow in almost any well-drained soil, this stem-rooting bulb has erect, chalice-shaped, 3–4-in, sterile flowers with brown to orange spotting. It has the novel habit, however, of providing tiny, round, reproductive bulbils in the axils of its 3–4-in, slender, lancelike leaves just below the flowers. Any light, rich, porous soil in sun to light shade is satisfactory, but the bulb adapts to lesser growing conditions. Propagation by offsets or bulb scales produces quicker results than the bulbils. Nothing important bothers it. The 60-in variety *croceum* has light orange, 3-in blossoms.

Lilium lancifolium (tigrinum) (tiger lily) 24–60 in Sun Zones 3–8
  FLOWERING SPAN: Mid-July to late August
  NATURAL COLOR: Salmon-red
  DISTRIBUTION: Korea, Japan, western China
    Sharing honors with *L. candidum* of June for thousands of years in cultivation, this sturdy plant carries up to 20 unscented, black-spotted, 3–5-in blooms on

purple-colored stems which are overlaid with a cobweblike fuzz. Not suitable for alkaline soils, the bulb thrives in any average-fertility, well-drained, acid location with sun or light shading. The sterile blossoms produce no seed, but tiny, round bulbils are evident in the axils of the glossy, 6-in, linear leaves and when mature scatter broadly. Germination is high and readily contributes to dense colonization. While not susceptible to pests or diseases itself, it can harbor the damaging mosaic disease, which may be spread by aphids to nearby, vulnerable Asiatic types of lilies. The double-flowered but scarce cultivar, 'Flore-pleno', is strikingly effective for accent; 'Splendens' is rich red with more spotting, increased budding, and later bloom; and 'Superbum' is bright orange. Additional hybridization efforts to improve the color range are currently in progress. (See photo.)

Lilium pardalinum (leopard lily) 48–84 in Semishade Zones 6–9
FLOWERING SPAN: Early July to August
NATURAL COLOR: Light red-orange
DISTRIBUTION: Southwestern Oregon to southern California
    Easily grown and vigorously spreading, this lily has 3–4-in, drooping, turk's-cap blossoms with heavy sprinklings of red or maroon spots, mainly close to the orange centers. The linear, 5–7-in leaves are arranged in whorls up the stem. It prefers a light, humusy, constantly damp but well-drained soil with semishading but accepts more sun if kept very moist. Propagate by bulb offsets or scales, and do not be concerned about pests or diseases. The cultivar 'Giganteum', also commonly known as the "sunset lily" in some areas, has larger, bright yellow flowers spotted in brown and with red-tipped petals. (See photo.)

Lilium philadelphicum (wood lily, orange-cup lily) 12–36 in Sun Zones 4–8
FLOWERING SPAN: Early July to August
NATURAL COLOR: Orange to vivid orange-red
DISTRIBUTION: Maine to southern Ontario, south to Delaware, North Carolina, and Kentucky
    This up-facing wild lily has 3–4-in blossoms in clusters of 5 above narrow, linear leaves up to 4 in long arranged in whorls on the stem. The wide petals have very tapered ends and carry deep purple spotting. Not always adaptable to garden culture, it likes a light, rich, moist, well-drained soil in full sun or light shade. Seed is very slow to produce results, and propagation is better from bulb scales or offsets. Diseases and insects are not troublesome.

Lilium regale (myriophyllum) (regal lily, royal lily) 36–72 in Sun Zones 4–8
FLOWERING SPAN: Early July to early August
NATURAL COLOR: White

DISTRIBUTION: Western China

One of the most popular garden additions, this lily has an enticing fragrance. Its heavy clustering of 3–6-in, funnel-shaped blossoms perches atop sturdy, wiry stems with deep green, 3–5-in, narrow, linear leaves. The outside of the flower is flushed with rosy purple between dark purple veins, while the interior is white overlaid with canary yellow at the throat. Tolerant of alkaline as well as acid conditions, it grows easily with full sun or light shade on a light, rich, well-drained soil. Provide some shade at root level, easily managed with nearby perennials, such as *Astilbe,* which has fountainlike foliage. Reproduce by either bulb offsets or scales. There are no bothersome diseases or insect pests. The cultivar 'Album' is pure white. (See photo.)

Lilium superbum (canadense) (turk's-cap lily, American turk's-cap lily, swamp lily) 36–96 in Sun Zones 4–9

FLOWERING SPAN: Late July to September

NATURAL COLOR: Bright orange-scarlet

DISTRIBUTION: Southeastern New Hampshire to Georgia and Alabama

Native to meadows and marshes, this bulb becomes a sizeable plant with 15–20 turban-shaped, brown-spotted, 3–4-in flowers arranged pyramidally atop tall, sturdy stems set with whorls of 2–5-in, linear leaves. Disliking alkaline conditions, it grows best in a damp, acid, peaty soil with sun or light shade. Seed is sluggish to germinate, and propagation is speedier from bulb scales or offsets. While pests and diseases are not common, it can become susceptible to mosaic disease when grown near Asiatic lilies. Its appearance is very similar to *L. pardalinum* for flowering, but it differs by having a green "star" in the center of each blossom. (See photos.)

Limonium latifolium (Statice latifolia) (sea lavender, statice) 12–24 in Sun Zones 3–9

FLOWERING SPAN: Mid-July to September

NATURAL COLOR: Lilac blue

DISTRIBUTION: Romania, Bulgaria, southern Russia

Highly resistant to damage from salt spray and even to being covered occasionally at the shore by salt water, this semievergreen perennial has a loose cluster of ground-level, leathery, elliptical leaves up to 10 in long set in a sprawling fashion. Airy panicles of ⅛-in, trumpet-shaped florets, which can expand to 18 in in width, appear on wiry, much-branched stems. When cut and dried, these flower stalks make long-lasting indoor decorations. Provide a sandy, well-drained, average-fertility soil in full sun, and propagate only by seeding. It has no problems with diseases or pests. The cultivar 'Collier's Pink' shows rosy blossoming, while 'Violetta' carries violet florets. (See photo.)

Lobelia cardinalis (cardinal flower, Indian pink) 24–36 in Sun Zones 2–8
    FLOWERING SPAN: Late July to September
    NATURAL COLOR: Bright scarlet
    DISTRIBUTION: Southeastern Canada to Florida, west to east Texas and Minnesota
        Erect, slender, purple-red, unbranched stalks produce brilliantly showy, terminal blossoms composed of many 1–2-in, tubular florets, which end in 3-lobed sets of downturned petals. The narrow, 2–4-in leaves are tapered at both ends. This very hardy perennial grows best in a constantly moist, peaty, acid, rich soil with sun or even semishade. Although it self-seeds readily if its location is ideal, the plant can also be propagated by division or by springtime softwood cuttings. Insects are no bother, but both rust disease on the foliage and rhizoctonia crown rot can be serious afflictions at times. Butterflies and hummingbirds are readily attracted to the plant. Several cultivars exist: 'Alba', white and hard to find, better propagated by division since seed produces erratic results; 'Bees' Flame', intensely scarlet; 'Rosea', pink-toned, propagate only by division; and 'The Bishop', velvety scarlet with bronze-green foliage. (See photo.)

Lycoris squamigera (Amaryllis hallii) (autumn lycoris, resurrection lily) 12–30 in Sun
    Zones 5–10
    FLOWERING SPAN: Mid-July to early August
    NATURAL COLOR: Rosy lilac, pink
    DISTRIBUTION: Japan
        This bulb behaves like *Colchicum autumnale* (autumn crocus) of September by producing spring leaves which disappear before the actual blossom emerges from the vacant ground. The foliage is straplike, up to 12 in long, and about 1 in wide. A slender, leafless stalk produces the summertime bloom in a terminal cluster of 2–3-in, lilylike, fragrant florets banded in light yellow. Install in a moist, well-drained, average-fertility location with sun or light shading and reproduce by taking bulb offsets. There appear to be no disfiguring pests or diseases. Plant initially in late autumn.

Lysimachia clethroides (gooseneck loosestrife, gooseneck) 24–36 in Sun Zones 5–8
    FLOWERING SPAN: Mid-July to September
    NATURAL COLOR: White
    DISTRIBUTION: Japan, China
        Vigorously expansive underground stems quickly spread this durable perennial over a wide area if left unchecked. It is as rampant as mint but more difficult to restrain since any rooted fragment will continue to grow. Its erect stems have 3–6-in, lancelike leaves which usually turn golden by midautumn, depending upon the chemical composition of the soil. Nodding, densely packed, terminal spikes of star-shaped, ½-in unscented florets with recurving tips can be made to rebloom by promptly removing the spent blossoming. These flower stalks last

well when cut. Any well-drained, average-fertility, moderately moist soil in sun or light shade is suitable, but the plant tends to invasiveness on rich, constantly moist sites. Spring or midautumn division is the easiest propagation method, and there are no nusiances from diseases or insects. (See photo.)

Lythrum salicaria (purple loosestrife)   24–72 in   Sun   Zones 3–9
  FLOWERING SPAN: Mid-July to late August
  NATURAL COLOR: Reddish purple
  DISTRIBUTION: Europe, United States
      Widely occurring in marshy areas, the plant has graceful, leafy, branched spikes of slender, ¾-in, star-shaped florets with wavy petals above deep green, 4-in-long, willowlike foliage. It tends to rampantly overseed any area which is constantly moist and in full sun, and there are no hampering pests or diseases of consequence. The new cultivars, which are more restrained and seed infrequently, are preferred for garden use and should be divided in spring or autumn for reproduction. The list includes: 'Dropmore Purple', rich violet, 30 in; 'Feuerkerze' ('Firecandle'), 36 in, vivid rosy red; 'Morden Gleam', 48 in, carmine-pink; 'Morden's Pink', 36 in, rosy pink; 'Morden Rose', 36 in, rose; 'Robert', 24 in, purplish pink, more tolerant of wet conditions; and 'The Beacon', 24 in, deep carmine-red. (See photo.)

Lythrum virgatum (wand loosestrife)   24–36 in   Sun   Zones 3–9
  FLOWERING SPAN: Early July to August
  NATURAL COLOR: Rosy purple
  DISTRIBUTION: Europe, northern Asia, Massachusetts, and New Hampshire
      Very similar in appearance to *L. salicaria,* this plant is usually more compact and smaller overall. Culture for both is identical. The cultivar 'Rose Queen' is recommended for its clear pink flowering.

Macleaya cordata (Bocconia cordata) (plume poppy, tree celandine)   72–96 in   Sun   Zones 4–9
  FLOWERING SPAN: Mid-July to mid-August
  NATURAL COLOR: Pinkish white
  DISTRIBUTION: China, Japan
      Boldly tropical in leaf appearance, the foliage of this plant is composed of 8–12-in, thin, gray-green, somewhat heart-shaped leaves with numerous scalloped margins and noticeably silvered undersides. Its unbranched, grayish stems also carry sizeable, feathery, terminal masses of petalless florets which can be successfully cut and dried for indoor use. Vigorously invasive from creeping, underground stems which continue growing even from fragments if disturbed, the plant needs careful placement. Adaptable to either sun or light shade, it prefers a

constantly moist, rich soil and can easily be spring propagated by division or root cuttings. Diseases and insect pests are unknown. The species *M. microcarpa* from central China is very similar but shorter, between 72–84 in, and is less invasive. Its fine cultivar 'Coral Plume' shows a salmon overtone on the blossoming. (See photos.)

Malva moschata (musk mallow) 24–36 in Sun Zones 3–9
  FLOWERING SPAN: Early July to September
  NATURAL COLOR: Rosy pink
  DISTRIBUTION: Europe, North Africa, northeastern United States
      Generally similar to the June-blooming *M. alcea,* the deep green, 3-in leaves of *M. moschata* are more dissected in their fingered appearance, and the total silhouette is more compact. Its 2-in, satiny flowers appear in terminal clusters. Cultivate the same for both. The cultivar 'Alba' is pure white, and 'Rosea' is rosy mauve.

Mentha species (mint) 3–30 in Sun Zones 5–10
  FLOWERING SPAN: Early July to September
  NATURAL COLOR: Purple, pink, white
  DISTRIBUTION: North Temperate Zone
      The aromatic leaves of this well-known perennial herb have been used for centuries horticulturally in gardens and commercially as flavoring and in making perfume. Its squared stems have opposite leaves and terminate in small spikes of very tiny florets. Often invasive and weedy if left untended, the plant accepts any moist, average-fertility, well-drained soil in sun or semishade. Any form is propagated readily by spring division, summer stem cuttings, or separation of the stem runners. Rust disease is the main affliction. The commonly used species are: *M. citrata* (bergamot mint), *M. ×piperita* (peppermint), *M. ×piperita* var. *citrata* (orange mint), *M. suaveolens* (apple mint), *M. suaveolens* 'Variegata' (pineapple mint), and *M. spicata* (spearmint).

Phlox paniculata (decussata) (perennial phlox, summer phlox) 24–48 in Sun Zones 3–9
  FLOWERING SPAN: Mid-July to late September
  NATURAL COLOR: Purplish pink
  DISTRIBUTION: New York to Iowa, south to Arkansas and Georgia
      The poorly colored parent is rarely used in gardens now since the wide array of hybrid improvements easily supplants it. These cultivars have 1-in, sweetly scented, disc-shaped florets generously massed in wide, pyramidal heads atop erect, woody stems with thin, dull green, lancelike, 3–6-in leaves. They cut well for indoor use. Foliage mildew is prevalent where air drainage is sluggish and the

weather hot and humid. They thrive on any moist, average-fertility, well-drained soil improved beforehand with generous amounts of compost or humus in either full sun or light shade. Any plant reblooms with smaller, axillary flowering if the terminal blossoming is removed quickly after it fades. This is a desirable effort because seedlings from hybrid plants revert to the original parent coloring of near-magenta. Thinning out some of the new stem growth in spring not only produces larger flowers but also aids in forestalling mildew, rust disease, and red spider infestations. Spring or autumn division is the usual method for propagation.

The extensive cultivar list includes plants that bloom later, that have color-contrasted centers or "eyes," increased flower head size, plus a color palette of white, pink, salmon, red, pale blue, lavender, and plum. The English strain 'Symons-Jeune' has increased mildew-resistance and a set of bright-colored, fragrant selections. The following examples illustrate the wide range of options developed by a number of hybridizers: 'American Legion', 48 in, vivid rosy red; 'B. Compte', 30 in, deep plum red; 'Blue Ice', 40 in, pink fading to almost-white; 'Bonny Maid', 30 in, pale blue-violet; 'Bright Eyes', 24 in, pale pink with a crimson eye; 'Cecil Hanbury', 30 in, salmon-orange with a carmine eye; 'Charlotte', 30 in, light lavender with a white eye; 'Charmaine', 36 in, cherry red; 'Chintz', 36 in, pink with a red eye; 'Colorado', 36 in, salmon-orange; 'Dodo Hanbury Forbes', 36 in, clear pink, massive head; 'Dresden China', 36 in, shell pink; 'Eva Foerster', 18 in, salmon-rose with a white eye; 'Excelsior', 48 in, rich magenta; 'Fairest One', 18 in, pale pink with a cerise eye; 'Fairy's Petticoat', 42 in, pale pink with a darker pink eye, huge heads; 'Juliet', 24 in, pale pink; 'Lilac Time', 48 in, clear lilac-blue; 'Mother of Pearl', 36 in, white; 'Fujiyama' ('Mount Fuji'), 36 in, pure white with oversized heads; 'Orange Perfection', 30 in, salmon-orange; 'Pinafore Pink', 18 in, bright pink with a darker pink eye; 'Prince Charming', 48 in, glowing scarlet; 'Prince George', 36 in, intense scarlet; 'Prince of Orange', 36 in, orange-red; 'Progress', 30 in, light blue with a purple-blue eye; 'Rembrandt', 36 in, pure white; 'Royalty', 42 in, rich purple; 'Sir John Falstaff', 30 in, salmon-pink, enormous florets and huge heads; 'Snowdrift', 24 in, bluish white; 'Spitfire' ('Frau A. von Mauthner'), 30 in, salmon-orange; 'Starfire', 30 in, vivid cherry red; 'Vintage Wine', 36 in, claret red; 'White Admiral', 36 in, white with giant-sized heads; and 'World Peace', 42 in, white. (See photos.)

Physalis alkekengi (franchetii) (Chinese lantern)   12–24 in   Sun   Zones 2–8
FLOWERING SPAN: Early July to August
NATURAL COLOR: White
DISTRIBUTION: Southeastern Europe to Japan

Certainly not grown for its unimpressive flowering, this vigorously creeping perennial produces inflated, papery, orange-red capsules in late summer. The capsule is about 2 in long and encloses an edible but bland-tasting red fruit. When cut as the color of the capsule strengthens, the zig-zag stems can be dried for long-lasting indoor use. Any moist, rich soil in sun or light shade suits it, and spring division of the fleshy roots or seeding works equally well for propagation. Flea beetles are an important foliage pest, but diseases are uncommon. The 8-in-high cultivar, 'Pygmea', is less rampant and adapts to a wider range of growing conditions. (See photo.)

Physostegia virginiana (Virginia lions-heart, false dragonhead, obedience)
24–48 in Semishade Zones 3–9
FLOWERING SPAN: Early July to September
NATURAL COLOR: Purplish rose
DISTRIBUTION: New Brunswick to South Carolina, west to Missouri and Minnesota
    The strongly erect, squarish stems carry dark green, deeply toothed, willowlike, 3–5-in leaves and 8–10-in terminal spikes of 1-in tubular florets arranged in 4 matched rows up the stalk. The common name "obedience" is from the oddity of the individual florets: when bent to another position, they retain that orientation. Although tolerant of full sun if kept consistently very moist, the plant does better in light shade to semishade and expands vigorously if provided with ideal growing conditions. Plant in a constantly moist, humusy, average-fertility soil and divide every 3rd spring to maintain longevity. Occasionally rust disease bothers the leaves, but insects make no inroads. The cultivar list is sizeable: 'Alba', pure white; 'Bouquet Rose', 36 in, rose, late to bloom; 'Rosy Spire', 36 in, deep rose, late-flowering; 'Summer Glow', 42 in, pale pink; 'Summer Snow', 24 in, pure white and less expansive than 'Alba'; 'Vivid', 24 in, bright rose, late-blooming; and 'Variegata', 18 in, striking green-and-white foliage but only pale lavender flowering. (See photos.)

Potentilla nepalensis (coccinea, formosa) (Nepal cinquefoil) 15–18 in Sun Zones 5–9
FLOWERING SPAN: Mid-July to September
NATURAL COLOR: Deep rose
DISTRIBUTION: Himalaya Mountains
    With this species the palmately compound leaves have 5 2-in leaflets and are green on both sides, while the branched flower stalks carry 1-in, somewhat furry, cup-shaped blossoms. Provide a rich, well-drained, somewhat dry soil and do not overwater. Seeding or spring division propagates it equally well, and only occasional leaf spot disease is bothersome. The dwarfed cultivar 'Miss Wilmott' is cherry red with a darker center, while 'Roxana' is deep salmon-pink and grows 18 in tall.

Rudbeckia fulgida (orange coneflower) 24–36 in Sun Zones 3–9
FLOWERING SPAN: Late July to October
NATURAL COLOR: Deep orange-yellow

DISTRIBUTION: New Jersey to northern Florida, west to Illinois

The narrow, coarse-toothed, 3–6-in, lancelike leaves are generally hidden by masses of daisylike flowers on well-grown plants. Its constantly creeping or sprawling flower stalks readily enlarge into a bushy display of 3-in blossoms with downturned petals surrounding a black cone. Best grown in full sun, it accepts light shade and dryness well and prefers a heavy soil, provided it is well-drained at all times. Division in spring or autumn is the recommended propagation technique, and it seems to have no troublesome diseases or insect pests. The cultivar 'Goldsturm' ('Goldstorm') is about 24 in tall and covered generously with golden yellow, 3–4-in blossoming. (See photo.)

Rudbeckia laciniata (cutleaf coneflower) 30–84 in Sun Zones 3–9
FLOWERING SPAN: Mid-July to September
NATURAL COLOR: Golden yellow
DISTRIBUTION: Southeastern Canada to northern Florida, west to the Rocky Mountains

With this species the deeply incised, 3–6-in leaves are rich green and show ragged teeth along the margins. The daisylike flowers have a raised, greenish yellow center. Plant in a moist, average-fertility, well-drained soil and reproduce by simple division in spring or autumn. It has no pest or disease difficulties. The double-flowered cultivar 'Golden Glow' (also known as 'Hortensia') has 3-in blossoms, spreads rapidly, grows to 48–60 in high, and flowers later; however, it is very prone to aphid infestation. Superior to it is 'Goldquelle', with chrome yellow, double blossoms, a more refined expansion habit, fewer aphid problems, and later flowering.

Ruta graveolens (common rue) 24–36 in Sun Zones 4–9
FLOWERING SPAN: Mid-July to mid-August
NATURAL COLOR: Dull yellow
DISTRIBUTION: Southern Europe

Raised primarily for its attractive, blue-green foliage instead of its nondescript, ½-in flowers, this drought-tolerant, evergreen subshrub must have a sheltered location and heavy winter mulching in the coldest areas of its range. Its much-divided, round-lobed, pinnately compound leaves have ½-in leaflets that are pungently aromatic when bruised. Some people can develop a mild rash when exposed to the oils. The plant's bushiness can be utilized as a modest hedge, especially since annual spring pruning encourages further bushiness. Grow in any moist, average-fertility, well-drained location and propagate by spring division or by seeding. The larger-growing cultivars 'Blue Beauty', 'Blue Mound', and 'Jackman's Blue' are all very similar with intensely blue-green foliage and differ mainly in outline and growing height. When young, each looks much like the other. (See photo.)

Salvia farinacea (mealycup sage) 24–36 in Sun Zones 7–10
FLOWERING SPAN: Mid-July to mid-August
NATURAL COLOR: Deep violet-blue
DISTRIBUTION: Texas, eastern New Mexico

Perhaps better treated as an annual since the plant usually dies right after flowering, it is appealing for its generally felted appearance. The showy flowers are ½ in long and appear in congested terminal whorls on branched stems. Each floret is covered with dense, white hairs to present a "mealy" look. The 1½–3-in, lance-shaped, hairy leaves are gray-green with toothed margins. Well-drained, rich, reasonably moist soil is best and only seeding can propagate it. Occasionally, white fly can become a pest, but there are no diseases of importance. The cultivar 'Blue Bedder' is a superior selection.

Salvia pratensis (haematodes) (meadow clary, bloodvein sage) 12–36 in Sun Zones 4–9
FLOWERING SPAN: Early July to September
NATURAL COLOR: Bluish violet
DISTRIBUTION: Europe, Morocco

With this durable—but extremely variable—species the 6-in, heart-shaped, blue-green leaves have noticeable red veining and remain in a basal rosette below the much-branched flower stalks with their loosely arranged, ½-in, hooded florets set in whorls. Provide the same care as for *S. farinacea,* and while this plant is also short-lived, it self-seeds readily.

Sedum album (white stonecrop) 4–8 in Sun Zones 4–9
FLOWERING SPAN: Early July to August
NATURAL COLOR: White
DISTRIBUTION: Europe, North Africa, western Asia

Another of the fine ground cover plants in the genus, this mat-making species has sausage-shaped, ½-in reddish green leaves and airy clusters of erect, starry blossoming. Full sun produces the most flowering, yet the plant accepts modest shading as well. A light, sandy soil of average fertility encourages rapid growth, and simple division at any time in the growing season is the simplest reproduction method. Diseases and insect nuisances are uncommon. There are many cultivars with minor differences, but only 'Murale', showing deep purple leaves, has any special value worth noting. (See photo.)

Sedum hispanicum (glaucum) 3–6 in Sun Zones 4–9
FLOWERING SPAN: Early July to August
NATURAL COLOR: Pinkish white
DISTRIBUTION: Southern Europe, southwestern Asia

The tightly compressed, gray-green, ¼–½-in, cylindrical foliage of this creeper turns reddish as it ages and the leaf tips have small, raised dots. Its branched, flat-topped flower clusters carry starry, ½-in florets. The plant's culture is identical with that for *S. album,* and it may perform as a biennial in some northern growing areas.

Sedum kamtschaticum   6–12 in   Sun   Zones 4–9
 FLOWERING SPAN: Early July to August
 NATURAL COLOR: Golden yellow
 DISTRIBUTION: Japan, Korea, Kamchatka Peninsula of Siberia
   A clump-forming species with trailing stems, the plant has bright green, pulpy, mostly 1½-in, spoon-shaped leaves and sizeable clusters of ½-in, star-shaped florets. The later seed pods become deep red and offer an effective bonus. Tolerant of light shading, it needs the same culture as *S. album.* The cultivar 'Middendorfianum' carries dark green, needlelike foliage turning bronze in the autumn but is a reluctant bloomer, while 'Variegatum' has leaves narrowly bordered in cream. (See photo.)

Sedum reflexum   6–8 in   Sun   Zones 4–9
 FLOWERING SPAN: Early July to August
 NATURAL COLOR: Bright greenish yellow
 DISTRIBUTION: Europe
   The ½-in, starry flowers have pale chocolate markings, and the ½-in, pulpy leaves are crowded toward the growing tip. This foliage is occasionally used abroad in soups and salads. Cultivate the same as for *S. album* except that the plant enjoys a dry soil at all times. The cultivar 'Minus' is dwarfed. (See photo.)

Sedum spurium   4–8 in   Sun   Zones 3–9
 FLOWERING SPAN: Mid-July to early August
 NATURAL COLOR: Purplish pink
 DISTRIBUTION: Caucasus
   Eventually becoming a rampant creeper even in modest shade, the plant has 1-in, oval, wavy-edged leaves paired on trailing stems which root as they touch earth. Its star-shaped, ragged flowering comes in tight, 2-in clusters on reddened stalks and is heavier when in full sun. This hardy, durable ground cover needs the same culture as *S. album.* Its cultivars include: 'Coccineum' with erect, deep pink flowering and reddish stems; 'Dragon's Blood', ruby red blossoms and bronzed leaves; and 'Royal Pink', rich pink flowers. (See photos.)

Senecio cineraria (Cineraria maritima)   (silver groundsel, dusty miller)   18–24 in
Sun   Zones 4–8
FLOWERING SPAN: Mid-July to September
NATURAL COLOR: Yellow
DISTRIBUTION: Mediterranean Europe

Grown mainly for its stiff, woolly-white foliage, the insignificant, terminal flower clusters of ¼-in, daisylike blooms can be removed to create a compact outline. The lancelike, 2–6-in leaves are very deeply indented with rounded lobes and present a ferny appearance for a noticeable accent. Grown best in full sun, it tolerates light shading well and needs winter protection in the severe climate areas of its range. Provide a rich, well-drained, consistently moist location and propagate by spring division, summer stem cuttings, or seeding. Aphid infestations are the main nuisance. (See photo.)

Solidago × hybrida   (goldenrod)   12–60 in   Sun   Zones 3–9
FLOWERING SPAN: Late July to November
NATURAL COLOR: Medium yellow to deep yellow
ORIGIN: Horticultural hybrid of uncertain parentage but probably derived from *S. canadensis* (of eastern North America) × *S. virgaurea* (of Europe)

Incorrectly blamed for hay-fever allergies more properly assigned to ragweed (*Ambrosia* species), which is in flower at the same time, the sizeable, fluffy plumes of these colorful, long-lasting perennials are more appreciated in Europe than in the United States. Hybridization by European growers has produced a wealth of different sizes, colorings, and blooming times worth investigating. Rampant if overfertilized, the plant enjoys a well-drained, average-fertility, somewhat dry soil in full sun or light shading, and it can be transplanted even in full bloom. It is a durable cut flower. Simple division is the easiest propagation method, but seeding works, too. Rust disease on the dull green, willowlike foliage is disfiguring, but insect pests are uncommon. Some of the popular cultivars are: 'Crown of Rays', 18 in, mustard yellow; 'Gold Dwarf', 12 in, deep yellow; 'Goldenmosa', 36 in, golden yellow, early; 'Golden Shower', 42 in, bright yellow; 'Golden Thumb', 12 in, deep yellow; 'Golden Wings', 60 in, bright gold; 'Laurin', 15 in, bright yellow; 'Lemore', 30 in, lemon yellow; 'Leraft', 36 in, bright gold, late; 'Peter Pan', 24 in, canary yellow, late; and 'Queenie', 12 in, deep yellow. (See photos.)

× *Solidaster luteus*   18–30 in   Sun   Zones 4–9
FLOWERING SPAN: Mid-July to September
NATURAL COLOR: Canary yellow
ORIGIN: Horticultural hybrid from 1910 between an unknown *Solidago* species and *Aster ptarmicoides*

Heavy clusters of ½-in, daisylike blossoms appear on widely branched, mostly erect stems in an outline which can billow and sprawl to 48 in in width. The 4–6-in, lancelike leaves are similar to those of goldenrod, while the flowering is much like an aster's. Provide an average-fertility, moderately moist, well-drained location in full sun or light shade and reproduce by either spring or late autumn division only. Bothersome pests and diseases are infrequent. (See photo.)

Teucrium chamaedrys (wall germander) 12–24 in Sun Zones 5–9
FLOWERING SPAN: Mid-July to mid-August
NATURAL COLOR: Pale to deep purple
DISTRIBUTION: Europe, southwestern Asia
    Useful either as an airy ground cover or as a clipped edging at sunny borders, the plant has erect, woody stems and deep green, oval, hairy, ½-in leaves tightly arranged on the stalks. Its tubular, ¾-in florets appear in whorled clusters and are often spotted with white or rose. Generally evergreen in the mildest areas of its range, it usually requires a winter covering in severe climates. Any light, well-drained, average-fertility soil is suitable, and propagation is simplest by division in the spring. Diseases and insect pests are rarely troublesome. The cultivar 'Prostratum' is dwarfed and conspicuously flattened in appearance.

Thalictrum rochebrunianum 48–72 in Sun Zones 5–9
FLOWERING SPAN: Late July to September
NATURAL COLOR: Rosy lavender
DISTRIBUTION: Japan
    The dainty, fernlike, gray-green foliage is robustly presented on blue-green, hollow stems below airy panicles of ½-in, globular florets with conspicuous, yellow, protruding stamens. Considered the cold-hardiest species of the genus, its culture is identical with that of the May-blooming *T. aquilegifolium.* (See photo.)

Thalictrum speciosissimum (glaucum) 24–60 in Sun Zones 5–9
FLOWERING SPAN: Mid-July to September
NATURAL COLOR: Light yellow
DISTRIBUTION: Portugal, Spain, northwestern Africa
    The blue-green, compound leaves, scented blossoming, and flower color add up to special distinction with this species. Cultivate the same as for *T. aquilegifolium* of May.

Veronica longifolia (maritima) 24–48 in Sun Zones 4–9
FLOWERING SPAN: Mid-July to September
NATURAL COLOR: Lilac-blue

DISTRIBUTION: Central Europe, northern Asia, eastern North America

In this species the gray-green, lancelike, 3–4-in leaves appear on stiffly erect stems either in pairs or whorls of 3. The narrow, densely crowded flower spikes are generously produced and are good for cutting. Their tall size, however, often requires staking for support. Any moist, well-drained, average-fertility soil in sun to light shade is suitable. Reproduction is simplest by division, although seeding is also workable. Pests and diseases are uncommon. The variety *subsessilis* is 36 in tall, royal blue, stiffly erect, and densely flowered. Cultivars include: 'Alba', 24 in, ivory white; 'Blue Giant', 48 in, lavender-blue; 'Foerster's Blue', 18 in, deep blue; 'Romiley Purple', 18 in, dark purple; and 'Rosea', 24 in, deep pink. (See photos.)

Yucca filamentosa (Adam's-needle) 48–72 in Sun Zones 5–10
FLOWERING SPAN: Early July to mid-August
NATURAL COLOR: Creamy white
DISTRIBUTION: North Carolina to Florida and Mississippi

The sizeable foliage of this evergreen plant is conspicuous throughout the year. Its swordlike leaves are 1 in wide and from 12–36 in long with short, curly threads along the margins. They terminate in a recurved, spoonlike outline. The main stalk is stout and short, and the stiff, sharply pointed leaves are tightly arranged around it in radiating whorls to create a large, ground-level foliage mass. A solitary, very rigid, asparaguslike flower stalk emerges from the center of the clump. As it enlarges it develops many side branches and 1–2-in, drooping bell-like, 2-in florets. Provide a sun-drenched, sandy soil which is consistently well-drained and moderately dry. Propagate by division of young plants only because established specimens have deep, large-as-an-arm roots that resent disturbance. Older plants can, however, be dug up and the roots sliced into 4–6-in-long pieces for reproduction—at the loss, of course, of the former plant. Leaf blotch disease may occasionally disfigure the foliage, while caterpillars and beetles sometimes bother the blossoms. Some cultivars are: 'Bright Edge' with creamy leaf margins; 'Golden Sword' with leaves centrally striped in yellow or yellowish green, somewhat tender; and 'Variegata' with foliage striped in creamy yellow. All are very drought-tolerant. (See photos.)

Yucca flaccida 48–84 in Sun Zones 5–10
FLOWERING SPAN: Early July to mid-August
NATURAL COLOR: Off-white
DISTRIBUTION: North Carolina to Alabama

Often confused with its look-alike relative, *Y. filamentosa,* the thick foliage of *Y. flaccida* hangs downward and the leaf margin fibers are straight. Its flower stalk is usually more openly constructed, but the florets are the same size for both. Culture is identical. The cultivar 'Ivory Tower' has much showier blossoming.

August

WHITE

Anaphalis margaritacea
Anemone vitifolia
Artemisia lactiflora
Artemisia ludoviciana
Artemisia schmidtiana
Aster novae-angliae cvs.
Boltonia asteroides

Chrysanthemum parthenium
Chrysanthemum serotinum
Hosta plantaginea
Hosta sieboldii
Liatris pycnostachya cvs.
Lilium cvs.
Lilium speciosum

Liriope spicata
Lobelia siphilitica cvs.
Phalaris arundinacea
Polygonum affine
Sedum spectabile cvs.
Stokesia laevis cvs.
Veronicastrum virginicum

YELLOW

Artemisia absinthium
Artemisia stellerana
Chrysopsis mariana
Helenium autumnale

Kniphofia uvaria cvs.
Lilium henryi cvs.
Pityopsis falcata
Rudbeckia hirta

Santolina chamaecyparissus
Santolina virens

ORANGE

Helenium autumnale cvs.
Kniphofia uvaria cvs.

Lilium henryi
Rudbeckia hirta cvs.

RED

Aster novae-angliae cvs.
Helenium autumnale cvs.
Kniphofia uvaria

Lilium cvs.
Lilium speciosum cvs.
Sedum spectabile cvs.

Sedum × 'Ruby Glow'
Sedum telephium cvs.

PINK

Aster amellus cvs.
Aster novae-angliae
Boltonia asteroides
Chelone lyonii
Crocus kotschyanus

Dianthus biflorus
Kniphofia uvaria cvs.
Lilium cvs.
Lilium speciosum cvs.
Molinia caerulea

Polygonum affine
Polygonum cuspidatum var.
  compactum
Sedum sieboldii
Sedum spectabile

PURPLE/LAVENDER

Aconitum carmichaelii
Aster amellus
Aster novae-angliae
Aster spectabilis
Astilbe chinensis var.
  taquetii
Boltonia asteroides

Chelone obliqua
Crocus kotschyanus var.
  leucopharynx
Hosta decorata
Hosta lancifolia
Liatris pycnostachya
Liatris scariosa

Liriope muscari
Liriope spicata
Pennisetum alopecuroides
Sedum telephium
Thalictrum delvayi

_____ B L U E _____

Boltonia asteroides var.　　Eupatorium coelestinum　　Stokesia laevis cvs.
　latisquama　　　　　　Gentiana andrewsii　　　Veronicastrum virginicum
Ceratostigma plumbaginoides　Lobelia siphilitica
Clematis heracleifolia　　　Salvia azurea

_____ B I C O L O R _____

Helenium autumnale cvs.　　Lilium cvs.　　　　　　Pennisetum alopecuroides
Kniphofia uvaria cvs.　　　Lilium speciosum cvs.　　Rudbeckia hirta cvs.

(Photos for August are between pages 240 and 241.)

_____ T H E　P L A N T S _____

Aconitum carmichaelii (fischeri) (azure monkshood) 24–60 in Semishade Zones 3–8
　FLOWERING SPAN: Mid-August to October
　NATURAL COLOR: Rich purple-blue
　DISTRIBUTION: China
　　Erect, rigid, almost branchless stems carry dark green, glossy, 2–6-in, thick leaves cleft nearly to the base into three parts, which are further lobed and sawtooth-edged. The 1-in, hooded blossoms are taller than broad and appear terminally on stiff, unbranched stalks. Cultivate as for *A.* × *bicolor* of July. The taller variety *wilsonii* has lighter blue flowering and is top-heavy to require support staking.

Anaphalis margaritacea (pearly everlasting) 12–36 in Semishade Zones 3–9
　FLOWERING SPAN: Early August to October
　NATURAL COLOR: Pearly white
　DISTRIBUTION: Northeastern Asia, North America
　　Easily adaptable to a wide range of soils and exposures, the plant produces erect, unbranched stems with 2–4-in, lancelike, woolly, silvery gray foliage and terminal clusters of ¼–½-in blossoms mainly composed of whitened leaf bracts. Although tolerant of both full sun or deep shade as well as dry, poor soil, it performs best on a well-drained, moist, average-fertility soil in semishade. The flower stalks can be cut and easily dried for indoor decoration. Propagate by spring division, spring stem cuttings, or seeding. Nothing bothers it, yet the plant itself may tend to invasiveness if it finds all growing conditions highly favorable. The choice variety *yedoensis* has deep gray foliage and larger blossoms, which are also good for cutting and drying. It tends to be less invasive, too. (See photo.)

Anemone vitifolia (grapeleaf anemone) 24–36 in Semishade Zones 5–8

FLOWERING SPAN: Late August to October

NATURAL COLOR: White

DISTRIBUTION: Northern India, Burma, western China

The earliest of the autumn anemones to bloom, it produces a heavy basal clump of long-stalked, much-cut foliage resembling grape leaves with woolly white undersides. The erect, thin stems carry 2–3-in, saucer-shaped flowers showing raised, yellow-toned centers. A rich, moist, well-drained, humusy soil with morning light and afternoon shading is preferred. Spring division or seeding is the reproduction method. Diseases or pests are uncommon, but the plant needs winter protection in the coldest areas. Its 30-in cultivar 'Robustissima' has silvery pink blossoms on sturdier stems and is somewhat hardier. Some botanists believe this cultivar actually is a form of *A. tomentosa* from the Himalaya Mountains. (See photo.)

Artemisia absinthium (absinthe, common wormwood) 30–48 in Sun Zones 4–9

FLOWERING SPAN: Early August to October

NATURAL COLOR: Greenish yellow

DISTRIBUTION: Europe, northeastern United States, southeastern Canada

Few of the *Artemisia* species are raised for their flowering but for their attractive foliage, which on most types can be cut and dried successfully for durable indoor decoration. The 2–4-in, aromatic, pinnately cut, lance-shaped leaves of *A. absinthium* are silver-coated and useful, when dried, as a tea with medicinal powers. They also are used to flavor the liqueur absinthe. The plant's erect, somewhat woody stems are terminated with numerous but insignificant clusters of ⅛-in blossoming. Any dry, well-drained soil is suitable in sun or light shade, and propagation is by division, by seeding, or stem cuttings. The main affliction is rust disease on the foliage. The cultivar 'Lambrook Silver' has a more silvery appearance, is 36 in high, and rapid-growing, while the tender 'Powis Castle' reaches only 24 in with feathery foliage. (See photo.)

Artemisia lactiflora (white mugwort) 48–60 in Semishade Zones 4–9

FLOWERING SPAN: Mid-August to October

NATURAL COLOR: Creamy white

DISTRIBUTION: China

Here the 6–9-in, deeply incised, fragrant leaves are deep green above and slightly silvered beneath. Clusters of scented but minute blossoms appear in decorative plumes on erect, purplish stems. The plant prefers a rich, constantly moist, well-drained soil with half-shade. Spring division, summer stem cuttings, or seeding works equally for propagation. Insects are not bothersome, but rust disease can disfigure the leaves.

Artemisia ludoviciana (gnaphalodes) (western mugwort, white sage) 30–36 in Sun Zones 5–9

FLOWERING SPAN: Mid-August to October

NATURAL COLOR: White

DISTRIBUTION: Southern Colorado to southern California and western Texas

Showy for its silver-gray foliage more than for its large panicles of tiny flowers, the plant has 1½–4-in, aromatic, lancelike leaves sometimes lobed or with ragged edges. A well-grown plant makes a sizeable, feathery accent with good cutting qualities for drying as indoor decoration. Any light, well-drained, somewhat dry soil in sun or light shading is acceptable. Propagate by spring division, summer stem cuttings, or seeding. It can become invasive. Rust disease is a foliage problem, and in severe climates mulch heavily for winter. The cultivar 'Silver King' carries glistening foliage and stems, but the leaves are generally blunt-tipped. 'Silver Queen' is very similar but not as tall or broad. (See photo.)

Artemisia schmidtiana 12–24 in Sun Zones 4–9

FLOWERING SPAN: Mid-August to October

NATURAL COLOR: Creamy white

DISTRIBUTION: Japan

This parent plant seems to have disappeared from culture, supplanted by its cultivar 'Silver Mound' (sometimes listed as 'Silver Dome') with a domed, neat habit; silvery, much-cut, feathery, 2-in leaves; and hardly more than a foot of height. Overfeeding and too much shade cause the very slender mass of stems to flop over, exposing the center. Removing the disclike, tiny flowering when it appears maintains the plant's symmetry better. Reproduce by spring division or summer stem cuttings only. There are no insect pests or diseases. (See photo.)

Artemisia stellerana (beach wormwood, dusty miller, old woman) 18–30 in Sun Zones 4–9

FLOWERING SPAN: Early August to October

NATURAL COLOR: Soft yellow

DISTRIBUTION: Northeastern Asia, Quebec to Delaware

Prized for its strikingly white, woolly, 2–4-in, lancelike but much-cut foliage, this hardy species is nonaromatic, carries ¼-in, globe-shaped flowers in heavy, spiked clusterings, and thrives along seacoasts. For gardens provide a well-drained, sandy, somewhat dry location in full sun. Spring division or summer stem cuttings propagate it equally. Disease and insect pests are uncommon. (See photo.)

Aster amellus (Italian aster) 18–24 in   Sun   Zones 4–9
>   FLOWERING SPAN: Early August to mid-September
>   NATURAL COLOR: Violet-purple
>   DISTRIBUTION: Central and southeastern Europe, western Asia

Showy and in blossom for a lengthy period, the plant carries daisylike, 2-in, scented flowers with yellow centers in terminal clusters above gray-green, lancelike, rough-surfaced leaves up to 5 in long. Adaptable to modest drought, it prefers a moist, average-fertility, well-drained soil in sun or light shade. Mildew is an occasional foliage problem, but insects are not bothersome. Propagate by spring division, summer stem cuttings, or seeding. Its cultivars include: 'King George', deep violet; 'Perry's Variety', almost red; 'Rudolph Goethe', deep lavender; 'Sonia', clear pink; 'Triumph', violet-blue, early; and 'Violet Queen', rich violet.

Aster novae-angliae (New England aster) 36–72 in   Sun   Zones 3–8
>   FLOWERING SPAN: Late August to October
>   NATURAL COLOR: Deep violet-purple, lavender, pink
>   DISTRIBUTION: Vermont to Alabama, west to North Dakota, Wyoming, and New Mexico

Widely distributed naturally in fields and meadows, this aster has erect, woody stalks with distinguishing, stem-clasping, 3–5-in, lancelike, gray-green, hairy leaves. The 2-in, daisylike flowers occur in clusters of 40–50 florets with yellow centers. A moist-to-wet, average-fertility soil in sun or light shade is its preference, and when heavily mulched and kept cool, it should retain its lower leaves. (Lower leaf loss can be a problem with this species.) Spring division, summer stem cuttings, and seeding are the propagation techniques. Mildew in humid, hot weather can disfigure the leaves and blossoms, but insects appear to avoid it. The cultivar list includes: 'Alma Pötschke', bright rose-pink, long-lasting; 'Barr's Pink', rosy pink; 'Harrington's Pink', clear pink, semidouble, late-blooming; 'Incomparabilis', reddish purple; 'Mount Rainier', creamy white; 'September Ruby', rich red; and 'Treasure', deep lilac. (See photos.)

Aster spectabilis (seaside aster) 18–36 in   Sun   Zones 4–9
>   FLOWERING SPAN: Mid-August to October
>   NATURAL COLOR: Bright violet to purple
>   DISTRIBUTION: Coastlines of Massachusetts to South Carolina

Quickly spreading by slender, underground runners, this wildflower has 3–5-in, dark green, oval leaves and 1–1½-in, daisylike blossoms with yellow centers arranged in terminal clusters showing leafy bracts. In nature it enjoys a sandy, acid, reasonably moist location in sun or light shade, but the plant adapts to garden use and heavier soil. It is not troubled by pests or diseases. Division is the simplest propagation method.

Astilbe chinensis var. *taquettii*   24–42 in   Sun   Zones 4–8
FLOWERING SPAN: Early August to September
NATURAL COLOR: Magenta-purple
DISTRIBUTION: Eastern China

    Unusual for its late bloom and tall habit, this species of *Astilbe* is not commonly cultivated today, but its cultivar 'Superba' is much admired. It has 6–9-in panicles of magenta pink flowers on stiffly erect, somewhat reddened stems with red-tinted, compound leaves in a heavy, basal mass. 'Superba' accepts greater heat and drought than most other astilbes. Cultivate as for the June-blooming *A.* × *arendsii.* (See photo.)

Boltonia asteroides (glastifolia)   48–96 in   Sun   Zones 3–9
FLOWERING SPAN: Late August to October
NATURAL COLOR: White, violet, pink, purple
DISTRIBUTION: Eastern United States

    In overall appearance it resembles a perennial aster, but the ¾-in, yellow, central disc of the daisylike flower of *B. asteroides* is raised and rounded. The narrow, lancelike, somewhat thickened, 3–5-in, gray-green leaves on much-divided, stiffly erect stems rarely need support. Any average-fertility, moderately moist, well-drained site in sun or light shading is acceptable. Division is the better propagation method, yet seed germinates reasonably well. Nothing appears to bother it. The preferred cultivar, 'Snowbank', is 60 in high and carries pure white flowers with yellow centers. It blooms somewhat later, as does the weak-stemmed 'Pink Beauty', at 48 in. The variety *latisquama* from the central United States is violet-blue with ½-in florets set in denser clusters. Its cultivar 'Nana' is only 36 in high. (See photo.)

Ceratostigma plumbaginoides (Plumbago larpentiae)   (leadwort, plumbago)   6–10 in   Sun Zones 5–9
FLOWERING SPAN: Mid-August to October
NATURAL COLOR: Cobalt blue
DISTRIBUTION: Western China

    Vividly colorful in flower, this perennial is better grown in semishade in the warmer parts of its range. Long in bloom as a dense ground cover, it has trailing, wiry, glossy stems and bright green, 1–3-in, bristle-tipped leaves wider at the upper end. The ¾-in, rounded florets appear in tight clusters on reddish stalks and continue flowering even after the foliage takes on a bronze cast by late September. Provide a consistently moist, well-drained, humusy soil and propagate either by spring division or by summer stem cuttings. There are no special diseases or pests of importance. Mulch for winter in areas of severe cold. (See photo.)

Anaphalis margaritacea

Anemone vitifolia
'Robustissima'

Artemisia absinthium

Artemisia ludoviciana
'Silver Queen'

Artemisia schmidtiana
'Silver Mound'

Artemisia stellerana

Aster novae-angliae
cultivars

Aster novae-angliae
'Alma Pötschke'

Astilbe chinensis var. *taquetii* 'Superba'

Boltonia asteroides 'Snowbank' and 'Pink Beauty'

Ceratostigma plumbaginoides in plant wall

Chelone lyonii

Chrysanthemum parthenium
'Ultra Double White'

Chrysopsis mariana

Clematis heracleifolia

Eupatorium coelestinum

Helenium autumnale
'Butterpat'

Hosta lancifolia

Hosta lancifolia

Hosta plantaginea
'Honeybells'

Hosta plantaginea
'Royal Standard'

Hosta sieboldii
'Kabitan'

Kniphofia uvaria
'Bees' Lemon'

Liatris pycnostachya

Liatris pycnostachya
'White Spire'

Liatris scariosa

Lilium (Oriental Hybrids: Flat-faced)
'Imperial Gold Strain'

Lilium (Oriental Hybrids: Flat-faced)
'Imperial Crimson Strain'

Lilium henryi

Lilium speciosum
'Album'

Lilium speciosum
'Grand Commander'

Liriope muscari
'Variegata'

Pennisetum alopecuroides

Phalaris arundinacea var. *picta*

Polygonum cuspidatum var. *compactum*

Rudbeckia hirta

Rudbeckia hirta
'Double Gloriosa Daisy'

Salvia azurea

Santolina chamaecyparissus

Sedum × 'Ruby Glow'

Sedum × 'Ruby Glow'

Sedum sieboldii

Sedum spectabile

Sedum spectabile
'Autumn Joy'

Sedum spectabile
'Brilliant'

Sedum spectabile
'Star Dust'

Sedum telephium

Stokesia laevis

Veronicastrum virginicum

Chelone lyonii (pink turtlehead, snakehead) 24–36 in Semishade Zones 4–9
  FLOWERING SPAN: Early August to mid-September
  NATURAL COLOR: Rosy pink
  DISTRIBUTION: Mountains of North Carolina, South Carolina, and Tennessee
      Native to swampy places, *C. lyonii* requires a consistently moist, humusy soil
  in gardens and is intolerant of full sun at any time. The deep green, oval, 4–6-in,
  coarsely toothed, long-pointed, glossy leaves appear below terminal, short spikes
  of 1-in, tubular, hooded florets. Spring division, summer stem cuttings, and
  seeding reproduce it equally well, and there are no nuisances from diseases or
  insects. Keep heavily mulched for the best growth. (See photo.)

Chelone obliqua 18–24 in Semishade Zones 4–9
  FLOWERING SPAN: Early August to mid-September
  NATURAL COLOR: Rosy purple
  DISTRIBUTION: Maryland to Florida, west to Tennessee and Mississippi
      Less vigorous but more attractively colored than *C. lyonii*, this long-
  flowering species has 6–8-in, dark green, glossy leaves tapering back to a
  broadened stem stalk. Culture for both is identical.

Chrysanthemum parthenium (Matricaria capensis, M. eximia) (feverfew) 12–36 in Sun
  Zones 4–9
  FLOWERING SPAN: Early August to mid-September
  NATURAL COLOR: White
  DISTRIBUTION: Southeastern Europe, Caucasus Mountains, North America
      Because it is not reliably hardy in all areas of its range but does self-seed
  eagerly, this perennial should perhaps be treated in some gardens as an over-
  productive annual. The 1-in, ball-like flowers have a prominent, yellow center
  and appear on much-branched stalks above pungent, oval, 3-in, bisected foliage.
  Install in a well-drained, moist, sandy soil for the longest durability and mulch for
  winter in severely cold areas. Disease and pest nuisances are occasional problems,
  but none makes any serious inroads. Use summer stem cuttings to propagate most
  cultivars. The cultivar list includes: 'Aureum', with greenish yellow foliage and a
  short life; 'Golden Ball', bright gold flowering, dwarfed; 'Ultra Double White',
  very double blossoms plus generous self-seeding; and 'White Stars', just 6 in tall.
  (See photo.)

Chrysanthemum serotinum (uliginosum, Pyrethrum uliginosum) (giant daisy, high daisy)
  48–84 in Sun Zones 3–9
  FLOWERING SPAN: Mid-August to October
  NATURAL COLOR: White
  DISTRIBUTION: Central Europe

Impressive in the background of borders, this sturdy, upright plant is densely branched and carries 2½–3-in, yellow-centered blossoms in terminal clusters above narrow, coarsely toothed, 3–4-in, light green, lancelike leaves. It has a decided preference for very moist sites and enjoys a rich, heavy soil. Spring division, seeding, and root suckers all reproduce it readily, and there appear to be no problems with diseases or insect pests.

Chrysopsis mariana (Heterotheca mariana) (Maryland aster) 8–28 in Sun Zones 4–9
FLOWERING SPAN: Mid-August to mid-September
NATURAL COLOR: Bright yellow
DISTRIBUTION: Eastern New York to Ohio, south to eastern Texas and Florida
Useful for dry, sandy locations in full sun, especially at seashores, the plant has smooth, 2–3-in, broad, lancelike leaves up to 9 in long with lighter-colored midveins. The erect, silky-haired stems terminate with 1½–2-in, daisylike flowers in showy clusters. Pinch back new growth during spring and early summer to encourage bushiness and greater flowering later. Spring division or seeding is the recommended propagation method. There are no disease or insect nuisances of importance. (See photo.)

Clematis heracleifolia 36–48 in Sun Zones 3–9
FLOWERING SPAN: Mid-August to mid-September
NATURAL COLOR: Pale blue
DISTRIBUTION: Eastern China
The 3-parted, compound, 4–6-in, bright green leaves on this vigorous, shrubby perennial may appear coarse, but the hyacinthlike, 1-in, tubular, scented flowers in terminal clusters add useful color to late summer borders. Later, silvery, fluffy seedheads—typical for *Clematis* species—further enhance the plant. Provide a well-drained, slightly acid, humusy soil with reasonable moisture and propagate by spring division, summer stem cuttings, or seeding. Unfortunately, the large foliage mass is prone to disfigurement from blister beetles, tarnished plant bugs, red spider mites, and leaf spot disease. The earlier-flowering variety *davidiana,* with its rich blue coloring, is preferred over the parent, as are the cultivars 'Crepuscule', with sky blue blossoms but faint scent, and 'Wyevale Blue', with conspicuously larger flowers of medium blue and noteworthy fragrance. (See photo.)

Crocus kotschyanus (zonatus) 3–4 in Sun Zones 3–9
FLOWERING SPAN: Late August to mid-September
NATURAL COLOR: Pink to pale rose
DISTRIBUTION: Mountains of southern Turkey to Lebanon
Perhaps the earliest of the autumn-blooming crocuses, this bulb develops short, fine-textured leaves and blossoming distinguished by 2 yellow-orange spots on the inside of each petal base. The flower throat itself is yellow. Plant

initially in spring on any well-drained, average-fertility site in full sun and expect it to enlarge freely. There are no problems from pests or diseases. The bluish lavender variety *leucopharynx (karduchorum)* blooms later and shows a creamy white throat without the orange spotting.

Dianthus biflorus (cinnabarinus)   10–16 in   Sun   Zones 4–8
FLOWERING SPAN: Mid-August to mid-September
NATURAL COLOR: Magenta pink
DISTRIBUTION: Mountains of central and southern Greece
    A tuft of rigid, grasslike leaves produces squarish stems with linear leaves and terminal clusters of ½-in, toothed blossoms somewhat like sweet William. Provide a rich, moist, well-drained soil and propagate by spring division only. Diseases and insect pests are not common.

Eupatorium coelestinum (Conoclinium coelestinum)   (mistflower, blue boneset, hardy ageratum)   18–36 in   Sun   Zones 6–10
FLOWERING SPAN: Mid-August to mid-September
NATURAL COLOR: Bright violet-blue
DISTRIBUTION: New Jersy to Florida, west to Texas and Illinois, West Indies
    Upright, thin stems with widely spaced, elongated, triangular, 2-in, wrinkled leaves produce 3–4-in-wide heads of fuzzy, ½-in florets that resemble the annual ageratum, a related plant. Rapidly expanding on any light, humusy, moist, well-drained site in sun or light shading, the plant can be propagated equally by spring division, summer stem cuttings, or seeding. Insects are no bother, but rhizoctonia crown rot and botrytis disease are often serious problems. (See photo.)

Gentiana andrewsii   (bottle gentian, closed gentian)   18–24 in   Semishade   Zones 3–8
FLOWERING SPAN: Early August to mid-September
NATURAL COLOR: Purplish blue
DISTRIBUTION: Eastern North America
    Novel because the football-shaped, 1¼-in blossoms never open (they self-fertilize in complete privacy), this perennial wildflower carries 4-in, lancelike leaves on slender, erect stems. The terminal, stemless, clustered flowering is also tightly surrounded by leafy bracts. Growing any gentian well in garden spaces is an exacting process slightly different for each species. This one likes a deep, cool, humusy soil in semishade that is consistently moist, well-drained, and acid. Seeding, although slow for flowering results, is the most rewarding propagation technique. Often confused with its close look-alike, *G. clausa* (blind gentian), and differing by only minor details of blossoming, you may need to be a botanist to distinguish them correctly.

Helenium autumnale (sneezeweed) 24–60 in Sun Zones 3–9
FLOWERING SPAN: Early August to October
NATURAL COLOR: Bright yellow
DISTRIBUTION: Quebec to Florida, west to British Columbia and Arizona

Flowering freely for many weeks, the plant has clusters of 1½–2-in, terminal flowers with raised central discs above 4–6-in, smooth-surfaced, lancelike leaves on stout, erect stems. Provide a consistently moist, rich soil in full sun and propagate by spring division, summertime stem cuttings, or seeding. The main affliction is root aphids. Hybrid cultivars provide an extensive color range: 'Brilliant', 36 in, blendings of orange, brown, and yellow; 'Bruno', 36 in, deep red-brown; 'Butterpat', 30 in, clear, golden yellow; 'Chipperfield Orange', 48 in, gold; 'Coppelia', 36 in, deep coppery orange; 'Copper Spray', 42 in, coppery orange; 'Crimson Beauty', 24 in, mahogany brown; 'Goldene Jugend' ('Golden Youth'), 36 in, deep yellow; 'Gold Fox', 36 in, orange-brown; 'Mahogany', 36 in, bronze-red; 'Moerheim Beauty', 36 in, reddish brown; 'Riverton Beauty', 48 in, yellow and maroon; and 'Waldtraut', 24 in, coppery orange. (See photo.)

Hosta decorata 12–24 in Semishade Zones 3–9
FLOWERING SPAN: Early August to September
NATURAL COLOR: Deep violet
DISTRIBUTION: Origin unclear, probably Japan

Slow to spread, this perennial has dark green, blunt-tipped, spearhead-shaped leaves up to 6 in long with a ½-in, white margin down to the stem stalk. The 2-in florets on stiff scapes later become viable seed capsules. This species is very often listed in catalogs as 'Thomas Hogg'. Culture is the same as for the July species *H. crispula.* The cultivar 'Butter Rim' has yellowish leaf margins.

Hosta lancifolia (japonica) (narrow-leaved plantain lily) 15–24 in Semishade Zones 3–9
FLOWERING SPAN: Mid-August to mid-September
NATURAL COLOR: Deep violet
DISTRIBUTION: Japan

The 2–5-in, glossy, dark green, lancelike foliage is only 2–3 in wide and appears as a dense mound even under very dry growing conditions. Its scape produces 6–10 1½-in florets which fade to pale lilac with age. This is a very hardy and dependable *Hosta* species for difficult sites, yet it rarely sets seed. Care for it the same as for the July-blooming *H. crispula.* (See photos.)

Hosta plantaginea (subcordata) (fragrant plantain lily) 12–30 in Semishade Zones 3–9
FLOWERING SPAN: Mid-August to mid-September

NATURAL COLOR: Waxy white

DISTRIBUTION: China, Japan

Delightfully scented 3–5-in, tubular blossoms open during late afternoon and continue until dawn. The plant has noticeably veined, light green, waxy, 12–18-in, heart-shaped leaves ending in sharp points. Cultivate as for the July-blooming *H. crispula*. The variety *grandiflora* produces longer, wider-opening florets and is worth finding. Now a rare, double-flowered form named 'Aphrodite' is becoming available for the first time since the parent was discovered many decades ago, and it, too, will be a special garden asset. The cultivar 'Honeybells' has only a mild fragrance but produces many erect flower scapes up to 36 in tall above rich, green foliage. 'Royal Standard' is 30–36 in high with smaller but fragrant florets and tolerates almost full sunlight without scorching. It is, however, tender and suitable for Zones 6–9 at best. (See photos.)

Hosta sieboldii (albomarginata, lancifolia var. *albomarginata)* 9–12 in Semishade Zones 3–9

FLOWERING SPAN: Mid-August to mid-September

NATURAL COLOR: White

DISTRIBUTION: Japan

At first glance *H. sieboldii* could be mistaken for *H. lancifolia,* except that its 4–5-in, very narrow, deep green leaves are wavy-margined, dull-finished on top, and shiny beneath. The pendant, bell-shaped florets are prominently veined in deep purple. The cultivar 'Kabitan' has almost all-yellow to greenish yellow foliage with a green edging, while 'Subcrocea' carries entirely yellow leaves with wavier margins. All create neat edging for shaded borders. Grow as for *H. crispula* of July. (See photo.)

Kniphofia uvaria (alooides) (poker plant, torch flower, torch lily) 24–42 in Sun Zones 6–10

FLOWERING SPAN: Early August to mid-September

NATURAL COLOR: Red, becoming yellow with age

DISTRIBUTION: South Africa

Similar to the June-blossoming *K. tuckii* in general form, this species has gray-green, ¾-in-wide leaves often stretching to 36 in in length in a disheveled, ground-level mass. The terminal flower spikes carry many 1½–2-in, down-hanging, tubular florets tightly packed into noticeable displays attractive to hummingbirds. Provide a rich, deep, constantly moist soil which is very well drained at all times, and mulch heavily for winter in severe climate areas. In the colder zones it might be advisable to dig out the ropelike roots each autumn and store them since the plant is tender. Propagate either by spring division of this thick rootstock, which then takes a few years for reflowering, or by seeding, which will likely produce some mixed blossom colorings.

The parent has now been supplanted by a wide range of cultivars: 'Ada', 42 in, deep orange; 'Bees' Lemon', 36 in, lemon yellow; 'Bees' Sunset', 30 in, gold with light red shading; 'Earliest of All', 30 in, coral, early-blooming; 'Gold Mine', 36 in, rich yellow, late-flowering; 'H. C. Mills', 42 in, gold and red; 'Little Maid', 24 in, creamy white, late; 'Maid of Orleans', 42 in, creamy white, tinged pink; 'Modesta', 24 in, ivory with a pink overcast; 'Primrose Beauty', 30 in, pale yellow, early; 'Royal Standard', 42 in, bright red and yellow; 'Samuel's Sensation', 60 in, fiery red; and 'Vanilla', 24 in, pale yellow, early. (See photo.)

Liatris pycnostachya (Kansas gayfeather) 36–60 in Sun Zones 3–9
FLOWERING SPAN: Mid-August to mid-September
NATURAL COLOR: Rosy lavender
DISTRIBUTION: South Dakota to Indiana, south to Texas, Louisiana, and Florida
The wandlike spikes of this species have closely set, fuzzy blossoms and more densely arranged foliage up to 14 in long than the July-blossoming *L. spicata*; otherwise, it is very similar. Give it a moderately fertile location which is consistently moist. Although the plant accepts more shade to flower, its stems will become crooked instead of stiffly erect. Because seed is slow to germinate, propagate by spring division only. Mulch for winter in severely cold areas. The later-blooming cultivar "September Glory' shows deep purple flowers on stalks 48 in tall, while 'White Spire', also late, has white blossoming and is just 30 in high. Butterflies are attracted in quantity to all *Liatris* species. (See photos.)

Liatris scariosa (dense blazing star) 12–36 in Sun Zones 3–9
FLOWERING SPAN: Mid-August to mid-September
NATURAL COLOR: Deep lavender
DISTRIBUTION: Mountains of southern Pennsylvania to northern Georgia
The florets of *L. scariosa* open almost all at once for a noticeable show of color. Its stiff stems are usually covered with downy white hairs, and the 10-in-long lancelike leaves around the base of the plant are about 2 in wide. The 1-in florets have distinct stalks and are openly set on the stems. While tolerant to modest drought, the plant prefers a rich, moist, well-drained soil. Spring division or seeding is the recommended propagation method. Occasionally, leaf spot disease is troublesome, but insects are no threat. (See photo.)

Lilium (lily) 24–96 in Sun Zones 4–8
FLOWERING SPAN: Early August to October
NATURAL COLOR: White, pink, crimson
DISTRIBUTION: Northern Hemisphere
These last-to-flower hybrid lilies are normally bigger, sturdier and more colorful than their earlier-blooming relatives. Their culture is discussed in the June entry for *Lilium*. (See photos.)

Classification of Hybrid Lilies

August-blooming Hybrid Lilies

DIVISION 7: Oriental hybrids: From 24–96 tall with 6–12-in, highly fragrant blossoms derived from *L. auratum, L. speciosum, L. japonicum, L. rubellum,* plus any crosses made with *L. henryi.* These hybrids are usually stem-rooting bulbs.

BOWL-SHAPED-FLOWERING EXAMPLES: 'Cotton Candy', white with pink tips; 'Empress of India', deep pink outside, dark crimson inside; 'Midnight Star', white with dramatic dark red banding; and 'Ruby Jewels', deep crimson throughout.

FLAT-FACED-FLOWERING EXAMPLES: 'Arctic Treasures', icy white, needs semi-shade; 'Coralbee', salmon-pink; 'Dorothea', rich salmon-pink; 'Fanfare', garnet red with narrow white edges; 'Imperial Crimson Strain', mostly deep crimson with white margins and heavy spotting; 'Imperial Gold Strain', white with gold center banding plus heavy, dark red spotting; 'Imperial Silver Strain', white with moderate, dark brown spotting; and 'Pink Ribbons', light crimson with center banding of deep rose.

RECURVED-PETAL EXAMPLES: 'Allegra', pure white with slightly recurved petals; 'Allura', light pink fading to lilac-purple; 'El Toro', rich red; 'Everest', pure white with a slightly greenish throat; 'Journey's End', lavender-crimson; 'Red Jamboree', deep red with white margins; 'Red Ruby', dark red throughout; 'Sans Souci', medium pink with white edges and dark spotting; and 'Sprite', deep crimson with silvery edges.

TRUMPET-FLOWERING EXAMPLE: 'Parkman Strain', various tints and shades of crimson or white; few of this type have been hybridized at this time.

Lilium henryi   60–84 in   Semishade   Zones 4–8
FLOWERING SPAN: Early August to September
NATURAL COLOR: Salmon-orange
DISTRIBUTION: China

Not just lime-loving, this stem-rooting bulb detests acidity (do not incorporate peat moss into its soil) and locations in full sun. The 5-in foliage is lancelike at the base but changes to 1-in ovals near the blossoming. These thick, dark green, glossy leaves appear on thin, wiry stems which flop over easily and require early support staking in borders. This arching, drooping habit can be used to good effect, however, by draping plants over walls or fences. Its 4-in, turk's-cap, black-spotted blossoms are scentless and occur in clusters of 4 to 20. Division every few years is recommended in spring to keep the plant vigorous. Provide a moist, well-drained, alkaline, highly composted soil with semishading, and install new colonies in the spring. Insects are not bothersome, but mosaic disease is prevalent in many growing areas. The cultivar 'Citrinum' has pale yellow flowers. (See photo.)

Lilium speciosum (showy lily, Japanese lily) 48–60 in Sun Zones 4–8
FLOWERING SPAN: Mid-August to mid-September
NATURAL COLOR: White, pink, both with crimson spotting
DISTRIBUTION: Southern Japan

Reliable, hardy, and fragrant, this stem-rooting bulb produces many outward-facing, nodding, 4–6-in flowers on very elongated stalks above deep green, thick, lancelike leaves up to 7 in long. The waxy, fleshy petals are strongly recurved and wavy margined around prominent, extended stamens. Its slender stems tend to arch and need support staking when in flower for greater effectiveness. Disliking alkaline soil under any circumstances, the plant prefers a rich, deep, humusy, acid location with consistent moisture and excellent drainage. Bulb scales or offsets propagate it readily, and new installations should be made in spring. Insects and diseases present no special difficulties. The cultivar list includes: 'Album', pure white; 'Grand Commander', crimson with deep red spotting and white edges; 'Kraetzeri', white with a central greenish stripe and orange-brown stamens: 'Lucie Wilson', rosy pink edged in white with very deep red spots: 'Magnificum', rose with deep crimson spotting and 8-in blossoms; 'Roseum', rosy pink; 'Rubrum', carmine-pink with broad, white margins and 8-in flowers; 'Uchida', deep crimson with white edges; and 'White Champion', pure white, superior to 'Album'. (See photos.)

Liriope muscari (*muscari* var. *densiflora*, *graminifolia* var. *densiflora*) (big blue lilyturf) 12–18 in Semishade Zones 6–9
FLOWERING SPAN: Early August to mid-September
NATURAL COLOR: Dark violet
DISTRIBUTION: Japan, China

Successful as a ground cover or edging even in dry, shaded locations, this tufted, grasslike plant has ¾-in-wide, firm, glossy, deep green, arching leaves up to 24 in long. Its many spikes of thickly clustered ¼-in florets rise from the center of the foliage for showy color accent. While not reliable in the colder areas of its range, it performs well in a moderately rich, constantly moist, well-drained location in semishade to full shade (with reduced flowering). Shearing back winter-damaged leaves in early spring encourages new growth of bright green. Rapid when established, it can easily be spring-propagated by simple division of the thick tubers. Disease-resistant and pest-free, the plant may also produce late-season clusters of blue-black berries under ideal conditions.

The list of cultivars is generous: 'Grandiflora', light lavender; 'John Burch', lavender, crested or cockscomblike flower spikes; 'Majestic', violet, narrower foliage, distorted flower clusters; 'Monroe White' (var. *monroei*), pure white, slender leaves; 'Silvery Midget', violet, dwarfed, foliage edged in pale yellow; 'Silvery Sunproof', violet, sun-tolerant, leaves striped with white and pale yellow; and 'Variegata', dark violet, foliage creamy with green striping, fades with too much sun, tender. (See photo.)

Liriope spicata   (creeping lilyturf)   6–10 in   Semishade   Zones 6–10
FLOWERING SPAN: Early August to mid-September
NATURAL COLOR: Pale lilac to almost-white
DISTRIBUTION: China, Vietnam

With this species, the foliage is only ¼ in wide and carries tiny, translucent teeth along the margins. Dark green and glossy like *L. muscari,* these leaves rarely exceed 15 in and should be cut back in spring for the quick reappearance of fresh, new, brighter foliage. Expansive to the point of invasiveness when conditions are to its liking, the plant accepts more shading and greater soil moisture; otherwise, grow as for *L. muscari.* The short flower stalks are at foliage level and less conspicuous.

Lobelia siphilitica   (great lobelia, blue cardinal flower)   24–36 in   Sun   Zones 4–9
FLOWERING SPAN: Mid-August to late September
NATURAL COLOR: Bright blue
DISTRIBUTION: Maine to Mississippi, west to Texas and South Dakota

Toothed, lancelike, thin, 3–6-in leaves crowd stems which terminate in a 6–8-in spike of ribbed, tubular, 1-in florets with downturned, pointed lobes. Accepting more heat than *L. cardinalis* of July, the plant thrives in a boggy, neutral soil but can be garden-grown if kept wet at all times. In cold areas divide for propagation in the spring; in warmer zones in either spring or autumn. Seeding and offsets also reproduce it readily. Insects are no bother, but rust disease and rhizoctonia crown rot are serious problems. Its cultivars are known but hard to find: 'Alba', pure white and tender, and 'Nana', dwarfed at 18 in.

Molinia caerulea   (purple moor grass)   18–24 in   Sun   Zones 4–8
FLOWERING SPAN: Mid-August to November
NATURAL COLOR: Purplish pink
DISTRIBUTION: Southwestern and northern Asia

Medium to fine, ¼-in leaves taper to needlelike points and appear in dense clumps with this ornamental grass. Preferring a neutral to acid, consistently moist, average-fertility soil with good drainage, it expands slowly even in full sunlight. The clusters of slender flower stalks are topped with spikelets between 6–8 in long and are good for cutting and can be dried for later indoor decoration. Propagate by spring division only. Diseases and pests are rare. The cultivar 'Variegata' carries white, horizontal stripes on the foliage, is somewhat less hardy, and accepts semishading well.

Pennisetum alopecuroides   (Chinese pennisetum, fountain grass)   24–42 in   Sun   Zones 5–9
FLOWERING SPAN: Mid-August to November
NATURAL COLOR: Coppery tan to purplish tan

DISTRIBUTION: Eastern Asia

The ⅛-in-wide, light green leaves of this drought-tolerant grass can elongate to 30 in and form dense clumps. The slender flowering stalks have soft, caterpillarlike, bristly spikelet heads up to 3 in long, and the entire plant has a fountainlike appearance. Eventually the flower heads turn gray-toned and are excellent for cutting and drying. Provide an average-fertility, moderately moist, well-drained site in bright sun and divide only in spring for propagation. There are no pests or diseases. (See photo.)

Phalaris arundinacea (reed canary grass) 24–60 in Sun Zones 4–9
FLOWERING SPAN: Early August to late August
NATURAL COLOR: White to cream
DISTRIBUTION: Northern North America, Eurasia

Ornamentally useful along wet embankments of streams or ponds, the grasslike, ½-in-wide leaves are green and are eventually topped by stalks of erect plumes with many tiny florets. Eagerly spreading by underground stems, the plant needs to be confined in gardens or it will overwhelm the space. Spring division is the recommended propagation method, and it willingly grows on any average-fertility, moist soil in sun to light shading. The colorful-foliaged variety *picta* (ribbon grass) has leaves attractively striped in white, is somewhat less exuberant in expanding, and is shorter. Diseases and insect nuisances are uncommon. (See photo.)

Pityopsis falcata (Chrysopsis falcata) 4–16 in Sun Zones 4–9
FLOWERING SPAN: Early August to mid-September
NATURAL COLOR: Golden yellow
DISTRIBUTION: Coastal Massachusetts to coastal southern New Jersey

A hardy, trailing perennial suitable for acid, sandy soils exposed to seashore conditions, it can also be grown in gardens successfully in any sunny, average-fertility, light, well-drained, acidic location. Pinching back new growth during spring encourages greater flowering later. Its narrow, deep green leaves are 2–3 in long, somewhat hairy, and become incurved around the blossoming. The silver-haired flower stalks carry erect, solitary, ¾-in, daisylike blooms. Spring division or seeding propagate it readily, and there are no important pests or diseases.

Polygonum affine (Himalayan fleece flower) 12–15 in Sun Zones 3–9
FLOWERING SPAN: Mid-August to mid-October
NATURAL COLOR: Rosy pink to white
DISTRIBUTION: Himalaya Mountains

Potentially evergreen (or perhaps better labeled "ever-brown" during winter in cold areas), this mat-forming plant has 2–4-in, lancelike leaves which become reddened in autumn. The erect, stiff flower stalks have cylindrical, tightly packed, ⅛-in florets in 2–3-in heads, which are colored at the same time in rosy pink and whitish pink. Provide a constantly moist, average-fertility, well-drained site in sun or light shade. Diseases and pests are of little concern. Reproduce by spring division only.

Polygonum cuspidatum (Reynoutria japonica)   (Japanese knotweed, Mexican bamboo)
      36–96 in   Sun   Zones 3–9
      FLOWERING SPAN: Late August to October
      NATURAL COLOR: Greenish white to pinkish white
      DISTRIBUTION: Japan
      The weedy parent is not cultivated today, but the desirable variety *compactum,* which many nursery catalogs still incorrectly list as *P. reynoutria,* has much garden appeal. Able to endure a variety of soils and exposures, this nonrampant ground cover is well-suited to sun-drenched, semidry embankments because of its undemanding nature. The 1-in, heart-shaped leaves are marked with reddish veining and appear on red-toned stems. Heavy clusters of tiny florets cover the plant in late summer. Spring division is the easiest reproduction method. Nothing seems to bother it. (See photo.)

Rudbeckia hirta   (black-eyed Susan)   24–30 in   Sun   Zones 3–9
      FLOWERING SPAN: Early August to October
      NATURAL COLOR: Golden yellow
      DISTRIBUTION: Maine to Georgia, west to Alabama and Illinois
      Usually considered only a prolifically seeding annual or biennial, this short-lived perennial has 5-in, lancelike, coarsely toothed, roughened leaves; hairy stems; and 3–4-in, daisylike blossoms with dark brown centers. Best grown on dry, open sites of average fertility in full sun or light shade, its seeding vigor can overwhelm small spaces. Occasionally leaf miners bother the foliage, but the plant is normally pest- and disease-free. The earlier-flowering cultivar 'Gloriosa Daisy' has single, 5–7-in-wide, yellow blossoms shaded variously with orange and red-brown, while the double cultivar 'Double Gloriosa Daisy' shows only golden yellow flowering. Both of these are top-heavy when flowering and require support staking early. They are also generous about self-seeding in many directions. (See photos.)

Salvia azurea   (blue sage)   18–60 in   Sun   Zones 5–9
      FLOWERING SPAN: Late August to October
      NATURAL COLOR: Rich blue
      DISTRIBUTION: North Carolina to Florida, west to Texas, Nebraska, and Minnesota

This species has 2–3-in, narrow, linear, dark green leaves with prominent, lighter green veins. The terminal flower spikes are composed of loosely arranged, ¾-in, wide-lipped florets on slender, floppy stems needing staking. Provide a well-drained, average-fertility, modestly moist soil and propagate by simple division in spring. Seeding is also workable, but summer stem cuttings are often reluctant to set roots. White fly is the main difficulty, and plants grown in cold areas require winter protection. The more colorful variety *grandiflora,* sometimes listed as subspecies *pitcheri,* from the central United States carries larger, deeper blue blossoms. (See photo.)

Santolina chamaecyparissus (incana) (lavender cotton) 18–24 in Sun Zones 6–9
FLOWERING SPAN: Early August to mid-September
NATURAL COLOR: Yellow
DISTRIBUTION: Spain, North Africa
    Highly favored as a tightly clipped, low hedge or neat edging, the ¾-in globular flowers are rarely provided with any opportunity to show. If left untrimmed, the plant presents a mildly interesting blossom accent, yet it is the silvery gray, minutely divided, scalelike, aromatic foliage that is the real highlight. Unpruned, the plant tends to become open and bedraggled-looking unless propped-up with short stakes. Any well-drained, average-fertility, modestly moist soil in full sun suits its needs. The more reliable propagation technique is summer stem cuttings, which root easily in moistened sand. Severe winter climates do not allow this perennial to be more than an annual, and winter protection is recommended in all but the mildest zones of its range. Cut all plants back severely in spring to foster attractive new growth from the base. The cultivar 'Nana' is dwarfed, while 'Plumosus' develops lacy, very silvery foliage. (See photo.)

Santolina virens (viridis) 18–24 in Sun Zones 6–9
FLOWERING SPAN: Early August to mid-September
NATURAL COLOR: Medium yellow
DISTRIBUTION: Southern Europe
    The foliage of this *Santolina* species is deep green, but the plant's culture is identical to that listed for *S. chamaecyparissus. Santolina ericoides* is very similar in general appearance, but has cream-colored blossoming.

Sedum × 'Ruby Glow' (× 'Rosy Glow') 8–12 in Sun Zones 4–9
FLOWERING SPAN: Mid-August to October
NATURAL COLOR: Deep pink to ruby red
ORIGIN: Hybrid of uncertain parentage
    A sprawling, free-spreading ground cover with purplish gray, 1-in, rounded

leaves edged in deep red, this cultivar carries many flattened heads of ¼-in florets for a long blooming period. It likes full sun and an average-fertility, well-drained site which can become dry occasionally. Reproduction is easiest from spring division. The nearly identical cultivar 'Vera Jameson' is magenta-pink. Neither is troubled by insects or diseases of consequence. (See photos.)

Sedum sieboldii (October daphne) 6–9 in Sun Zones 5–9
  FLOWERING SPAN: Late August to October
  NATURAL COLOR: Bright pink
  DISTRIBUTION: Japan
    This outdoor trailing plant adapts surprisingly well to indoor pot culture. The thick, leathery, ¾-in, rounded bluish green leaves come in whorls of 3 with faint red margins. The numerous, ½-in florets occur in 2–3-in terminal clusters. Any well-drained, average-fertility soil in full sun to light shade is workable, and propagation is easily handled by spring division or summer stem cuttings. It is disease- and pest-free. The leaves of the colorful but less hardy cultivar 'Medio-variegatis' have a prominent yellow center. (See photo.)

Sedum spectabile (showy stonecrop) 12–24 in Sun Zones 4–9
  FLOWERING SPAN: Late August to October
  NATURAL COLOR: Pale pink
  DISTRIBUTION: China, Korea
    Drought-resistant and sturdy, this showy species carries thick, erect, succulent stems and heavy, oval, 2–3-in, pale green leaves set in whorls of 3 or 4. The 3–4-in, flat-topped clusters of tightly packed, ¼-in florets are attractive to butterflies and bees. While accepting almost any well-drained, average-fertility soil in sun or light shade, the plant appears to do its best in a clayey, moisture-retentive location. Spring division and summer stem cuttings are the usual reproduction techniques. Black aphids are an occasional problem, but diseases are not common.
    The cultivar list is extensive: 'Album', 15 in, creamy white; 'Atropurpureum', 18 in, rosy crimson; 'Brilliant', 18 in, raspberry red; 'Carmen', 12 in, rosy red, silvery green foliage; 'Meteor', 18 in, vivid pink; 'Star Dust', 18 in, ivory white to pale pink with blue-green leaves; and 'Variegatum', 15 in, pale pink, foliage mottled in cream. Many growers include the popular, 18-in 'Autumn Joy' in this classification, but some botanists believe this cultivar is botanically derived from the hybrid *S.* × *erythrostictum* instead. The matter is not yet resolved to anyone's satisfaction, and to increase the confusion, several authorities further suggest that 'Indian Chief' (see *S. telephium* below) is the same plant as 'Autumn Joy'. (See photos.)

Sedum telephium (liveforever)   12–18 in   Sun   Zones 4–9
FLOWERING SPAN: Mid-August to October
NATURAL COLOR: Reddish purple
DISTRIBUTION: Eastern Europe to Japan

An upright-growing perennial with few flower heads, this stonecrop has 2–3-in, spearhead-shaped, toothed leaves scattered up the succulent stems. The flower clusters are 3–4 in wide and composed of tightly set, ¼-in, starlike florets. Readily grown in any sandy, average-fertility soil in sun or light shade, it is better propagated either by seeding or by offsets removed in spring. The flower stalks can be cut and dried for use indoors. There seem to be no important diseases or insect nuisances. Occasionally some nurseries list the cultivars 'Autumn Joy' and 'Indian Chief' (see above for more data) under this species, but some botanists now think this is an unlikely association. The debate goes on. (See photo.)

Stokesia laevis (cyanea) (Stokes' aster)   12–24 in   Sun   Zones 5–9
FLOWERING SPAN: Early August to mid-September
NATURAL COLOR: Lavender-blue
DISTRIBUTION: South Carolina to Florida, west to Louisiana

While not reliable in the coldest parts of its range, the plant blooms in much of Florida during the winter months and all year in southern California. It resists heat and drought and remarkably accepts neglect no matter where it grows. The 3–4-in, ragged-petaled, asterlike flowering occurs on hairy, purplish stems above shiny, 6–8-in, lancelike leaves sparsely produced. Disliking standing water at the roots in any season, this perennial prefers a moist, well-drained, sandy soil with full sun or light shade. Divide in spring every few years to maintain vigor and also propagate by spring stem cuttings or by seeding. Pests and diseases are not usual. Shorter, improved-color cultivars now include: 'Alba', 12 in, white; 'Blue Danube', 15 in, bright blue, early, larger blossoming; 'Blue Moon', silvery blue, 12 in; 'Blue Star', 12 in, light blue; 'Praecox', 12 in, lavender; 'Rosea', rosy pink, 12 in; 'Silver Moon', icy blue with a rosy overcast, 12 in; and 'Superba', 10 in, lavender-blue (See photo.)

Thalictrum delvayi (dipterocarpum)   36–60 in   Semishade   Zones 5–9
FLOWERING SPAN: Mid-August to October
NATURAL COLOR: Deep lavender
DISTRIBUTION: Western China

This is the only *Thalictrum* species adaptable to high heat and humidity. The fernlike, pinnately compound foliage has rounded leaflets and appears on slender stems topped by airy panicles of ½–1-in florets with prominent, pale yellow stamens. Its graceful appearance is an asset for borders. Install on a moist, humusy, well-drained soil in semishade. If kept consistently very moist, the plant accommodates a greater amount of sun. Seeding is the recommended propagation method, and diseases or pests appear to shun it. The cultivar 'Album' is white, while the fully double 'Hewitt's Double', with its extended blooming period, cannot be reproduced successfully except by summer stem cuttings or root offsets.

Veronicastrum virginicum (Leptandra virginica, Veronica virginica) (Culver's root, Bowman's root)   48–84 in   Sun   Zones 3–9
    FLOWERING SPAN: Early August to late September
    NATURAL COLOR: Pale blue to white
    DISTRIBUTION: Massachusetts to Manitoba, south to Florida and Texas
    Noticeably sturdy, upright stems carry whorls of 5–9 lancelike, sharply toothed, 3–6-in, rich green leaves, and even at the listed growing height the plant rarely needs staking. Its veronicalike, 9-in flower spikes have densely set, ¼-in florets with prominent stamens and persist for a long time. Many smaller-sized side branches surround the central flowering. Provide a moist, slightly acid, average-fertility soil with good drainage in sun or light shade. Reproduce by spring division, summer stem cuttings, or by autumn-sown seed. The superior cultivar 'Album' is pure white with deeper green foliage. (See photo.)

September

WHITE

Anemone × hybrida cvs.
Aster novi-belgii cvs.
Aster 'Oregon-Pacific
  Strain'
Chrysanthemum × morifolium

Chrysanthemum nipponicum
Cimicifuga simplex
Colchicum autumnale cvs.
Colchicum speciosum cvs.
Cortaderia selloana

Crocus cancellatus
Crocus sativus cvs.
Crocus speciosus cvs.
Polygonum amplexicaule cvs.

YELLOW

Chrysanthemum × morifolium
Kirengeshoma palmata

ORANGE

Chrysanthemum × morifolium

RED

Aster novi-belgii cvs.
Chrysanthemum × morifolium
Polygonum amplexicaule cvs.

PINK

Anemone hupehensis cvs.
Anemone × hybrida cvs.
Aster novi-belgii cvs.
Aster 'Oregon-Pacific

Strain'
Chrysanthemum × morifolium
Chrysanthemum × rubellum
Colchicum autumnale

Colchicum speciosum cvs.
Cortaderia selloana
Crocus sativus

PURPLE/LAVENDER

Anemone hupehensis
Aster laevis
Aster novi-belgii
Aster 'Oregon-Pacific
  Strain'

Chrysanthemum × morifolium
Colchicum autumnale
Colchicum speciosum
Crocus cancellatus
Crocus longiflorus

Crocus pulchellus
Crocus sativus cvs.
Crocus speciosus

BLUE

Aster novi-belgii cvs.
Aster 'Oregon-Pacific
  Strain'
Crocus speciosus cvs.

BICOLOR

Calamagrostis × acutifolia
Chrysanthemum × morifolium

Colchicum speciosum cvs.
Crocus speciosus cvs.

Miscanthus sinensis

(Photos for September are between pages 264 and 265.)

================ T H E   P L A N T S _____

Anemone hupehensis (Japanese anemone) 18–24 in Semishade Zones 6–9
FLOWERING SPAN: Early September to mid-October
NATURAL COLOR: Rosy purple
DISTRIBUTION: Central China
   Dark green, unequally 3-lobed, toothed leaves form a husky basal clump of attractive foliage in this species. Rising out of it are many slender, erect flowering stems with much side branching and 2–3-in, saucer-shaped blossoms with noticeable yellow centers. Best grown in a sheltered location with full morning sun but only dappled afternoon light, it prefers a rich, deep, moist, humusy site. To avoid soft, disease-prone growth, fertilize with a light hand. Spring division, root cuttings, and seeding work equally for propagation. Diseases include smut, rust, mildew, and root decay, while various beetles damage the leaves and blossoms. In general it needs light mulching for winter in the coldest areas of its range. The 24-in variety *japonica* flowers later with rosy carmine blossoming. Its cultivar 'Superba' shows more vigor.

Anemone × hybrida 36–60 in Sun Zones 5–8
FLOWERING SPAN: Early September to late October
NATURAL COLOR: White, pink, purplish pink
ORIGIN: Horticultural hybrid of *A. hupehensis* var. *japonica* × *A. vitifolia*
   This very hardy plant has sturdy stems and abundant, attractive flowers up to 3 in wide either in single, semidouble, or double form, all with prominent yellow centers. Just about all of the late-blooming anemones offered for sale today are of this origin, yet catalog listings erroneously carry them as cultivars of *A. hupehensis* var. *japonica,* which is not wholly the situation. Grow as for *A. hupehensis* with the knowledge that far fewer diseases and insect pests bother them. The cultivar list includes: 'Alba' ('Honorine Jobert'), single, white; 'Alice', semidouble, rosy pink; 'Bressingham Glow', semidouble, rosy red; 'Krimhilde', semidouble, salmon; 'Lady Gilmour', semidouble, pink; 'Luise Uhink', single, white; 'Margarete', semidouble, deep pink; 'Marie Manchard', semidouble, white; 'Prinz Heinrich' ('Prince Henry'), double, deep rose; 'Profusion', single, deep rose; 'Queen Charlotte', semidouble, pink; 'September Charm', single, clear pink; 'September Sprite', single, rosy pink; and 'White Giant', single, larger blossoms, white. (See photo.)

Aster laevis (smooth aster) 24–36 in Sun Zones 3–8
FLOWERING SPAN: Early September to mid-October
NATURAL COLOR: Pale violet to blue
DISTRIBUTION: Southern Yukon to northeastern Oregon and New Mexico, east to Maine

Showy in flowering, the plant has erect stems with thick, lancelike, 1½-in-wide leaves which may have a whitish cast in some areas. Its flower clusters are terminal and carry many daisylike florets with gold centers. Groups of small, stem-clasping leaves usually occur below the blossoming. Any well-drained, average-fertility, modestly moist soil is suitable, and it endures drought satisfactorily. Spring division and seeding are the 2 reproduction techniques usually followed. Diseases and insect pests are infrequent.

Aster novi-belgii (New York aster) 24–48 in Sun Zones 4–8

FLOWERING SPAN: Early September to mid-October
NATURAL COLOR: Violet to purple, occasionally white or pink
DISTRIBUTION: Coastal Newfoundland to coastal Georgia

Similar in garden effectiveness to *A. novae-angliae* of August, this species differs by being shorter and having hairless stems and smooth, 2–5-in, lancelike leaves with evident teeth. Leafy bracts beneath the clusters of 2-in florets extend either outward or downward. Culture for both species is identical, including summer pinching-back of the expanding stems to foster greater compactness. An impressive list of cultivars is available. The following are considered tall at between 30 and 48 inches: 'Ada Ballard', mauve-blue; 'Autumn Glory', claret red; 'Bonningdale White', clear white, semidouble; 'Clarity', white; 'Crimson Brocade', bright red, double; 'Ernest Ballard', rosy crimson; 'Eventide', purple, semidouble; 'Glorious', carmine-pink; 'Marie Ballard', pale blue, double; 'Patricia Ballard', pink, double; 'Winston S. Churchill', ruby red. These cultivars (which may belong to *A.* × *dumosus*) are dwarfed at 9–18 in and have a mounded appearance: 'Alert', deep crimson; 'Alice Haslem', rosy pink, double; 'Audrey', pale blue; 'Jean', lilac-blue; 'Jenny', cerise-red; 'Little Red Boy', rosy red; 'Niobe', white; 'Peter Harrison', rosy pink; and 'Snowsprite', white. All have yellow eyes. (See photo.)

Aster 'Oregon-Pacific Strain' 10–15 in Sun Zones 4–8

FLOWERING SPAN: Early September to mid-October
NATURAL COLOR: White, pink, violet, blue
ORIGIN: Horticultural hybrid of *A. subspicatus* × *A. novi-belgii*

Hybridization created a compact group of plants literally covered with flowers, and 2-in flowers at that. Provide a rich, moist, well-drained site in full sun or light shading and propagate either by spring division, summer stem cuttings, or seed. Insects avoid the plant, but mildew, rust disease, and wilt disease (which turns the plant bright yellow) are important problems. The cultivars include: 'Bonny Blue', purplish blue; 'Canterbury Carpet', gentian blue; 'Pacific Amaranth', rosy purple; 'Persian Rose', rosy pink; 'Pink Bouquet', pink; 'Romany', plum purple; 'Snowball', white; 'Snow Flurry', bright white; 'Twilight', deep violet-blue; and 'White Fairy', clear white. (See photo.)

Calamagrostis × acutifolia (feather reed grass) 60–72 in Sun Zones 4–9
FLOWERING SPAN: Early September to November
NATURAL COLOR: Deep tan, fading to gray
ORIGIN: Horticultural hybrid of *C. arundinacea × C. epigeios*

One of the easiest ornamental grasses to raise, this species requires only full sun and a well-drained, average-fertility soil. The tall stems are stiffly erect when flowering, and the multitude of sizeable, feathery plumes are good for cutting and use indoors. Propagate by simple division in the spring. Diseases and insect pests are unknown. The cultivar 'Karl Foerster' is about 12 in shorter when in bloom and much showier. (See photo.)

Chrysanthemum × morifolium (hortorum) (garden chrysanthemum, florist's chrysanthemum) 9–48 in Sun Zones 4–9
FLOWERING SPAN: Early September to November
NATURAL COLOR: All but blue in every shade, tint, and hue
ORIGIN: Probably China with a high number of recent hybridization crossings from many sources

It would be difficult to find a more adaptable perennial than the chrysanthemum: it transplants readily in full bloom; is easily reproduced by several simple methods; grows well in a variety of soils; and offers a wide array of colorings, flower shapes, heights, and blooming times. Cut flowers keep amazingly well. Both the foliage and the blooms have a pungent odor regarded by almost everyone as the sign of autumn's arrival.

All types are represented by thick, aromatic, cleft foliage up to 3 in long along with semiwoody stems ending in clusters of various-sized florets. Shallow-rooted, they require a rich, well-drained, somewhat neutral, very moist soil with frequent—but light—applications of balanced fertilizer during the growing season. While described as winter-hardy, many types are not truly reliable left in the garden, even if mulched heavily, and are better dug and placed to winter-over safely in cold frames. Spring division of the old clump means discarding all woody parts in favor of fleshy, new growth. Pinching back the elongating stems (unnecessary for "cushion" chrysanthemums) until mid-July in short season areas promotes compactness and flowering potential while providing a source of additional plants. These pinched off cuttings, stripped of most of the bottom foliage, root easily when first dipped in a hormone mixture and then set into boxes of moistened builder's sand mixed with peat moss. Most of the cuttings bloom the first season. Disbudding for larger, terminal flowering is rarely done with garden plants. That is a commercial concern of florists' suppliers.

Every type appreciates consistent moisture and a loose mulch in summer. Tall sorts benefit also from early staking and loose tying with soft twine or plastic strips which allow the plant's natural configuration to stay evident. Shorter plants can be inconspicuously supported by inserting some twiggy, defoliated branch parts pruned earlier from trees and shrubs. This economical staking requires no tying.

Unfortunately, chrysanthemums are prone to many afflictions, such as aphids, root nematodes, red spider mites, blister beetles, leaf miners, thrips, mildew, leaf spot, black spot, rust, and botrytis disease. Of course, not all of these problems are annual nor are they evident in all growing areas or on all types of plants. Given reasonable care and room to grow, chrysanthemums are consistently rewarding.

The "cushion" types generally grow from 9–15 in tall and spread up to 30 in wide. They naturally branch readily and early, needing no pinching back for bushiness. Some come into flower intermittently during the summer, but even with these the autumn displays will still completely obscure the foliage. The various kinds of taller, upright chrysanthemums have proved confusing for their correct categorization, however, and the National Chrysanthemum Society of the United States has now cataloged the outdoor, major flower types as follows:

Pompon: Blossoms 1½–2 in wide in clusters formed of stiff, short petals creating a ball shape or else a yellow-centered, daisylike blossom with one row of loosely arranged petals; both are usually 24 in tall.

Button: Blossoms are less than 1 in across, clustered, and formed mainly of tightly packed petals; height is 24 in.

Decorative: Double blossoms 2–4 in wide without any noticeable, yellow center or "eye"; generally between 18–36 in tall.

Single: Daisylike, 2–3-in-wide blossoms with a conspicuous yellow center that is either flattened or only slightly raised; 12–18 in high.

The 6 other hardy types are: spoon, quill, anemone, spider, cascade, and exhibition. These are more difficult to grow well outdoors since they bloom very late and are easily distressed by frost unless carefully sheltered. They are perhaps better suited to greenhouse culture, except in very mild areas. Eventually, hybridization will produce garden-hardy sorts.

Since there are hundreds of cultivars available commercially throughout the United States, any listing here of recommended types would quickly be outdated or unsuited to all growing areas. Their basic low cost and ease of being dug and moved at any time make experimentation a simple, eye-appealing pleasure for anyone, whether browsing specialists' catalogs or seeking out garden center offerings. Every reliably hardy type makes a long-blooming addition to the garden border as well as to terrace tubs and planter boxes. Chrysanthemums are still one of the most cooperative perennials known. (See photos.)

Chrysanthemum nipponicum (Nippon daisy) 12–24 in Sun Zones 5–9

FLOWERING SPAN: Mid-September to November

NATURAL COLOR: White

DISTRIBUTION: Coastal Japan

Similar in bloom to the summertime shasta daisy (*Chrysanthemum × superbum*) the Nippon daisy has dark green foliage which is thick, blunt-tipped but lancelike, 3–4 in long, and toothed only at the farthest end. Unusual in that it carries woody stems which often persist unscathed through winter in mild areas, the entire plant normally dies to the ground in severely cold regions, even if sheltered. The 2–3-in blossoms are daisylike with a greenish yellow center, and each flower is solitary on a slender stem. Thriving at seashore locations, it adapts to garden use elsewhere with a humusy, moist, well-drained, average-fertility site. Spring division and summer stem cuttings are the usual reproduction methods, and there are no important pests or diseases. (See photo.)

Chrysanthemum × rubellum (zawadskii var. *latilobum)* 12–18 in Sun Zones 4–9
FLOWERING SPAN: Mid-September to November
NATURAL COLOR: Pink
DISTRIBUTION: Japan, Korea, northern China, Manchuria
Remarkably hardy and durable, this easily grown plant has purple-toned rhizomes and spreads quickly to form neat mounds in any moist, well-drained, average-fertility soil with full sun to light shade. The single, daisylike, 2½–3½-in flowers stand above somewhat hairy, 1½-in, wedge-shaped, cleft leaves. Propagate by spring division or summer stem cuttings. Diseases and insect nuisances are few and far between. The highly popular cultivar 'Clara Curtis' is slightly taller with rosy pink blossoms.

Cimicifuga simplex (foetida var. *intermedia)* (Kamchatka bugbane) 24–48 in Semishade Zones 3–9
FLOWERING SPAN: Mid-September to mid-October
NATURAL COLOR: Pure white
DISTRIBUTION: Siberia, Manchuria, Japan
Except for its lower height, this species is very similar in all aspects to the July-blooming *C. racemosa,* and its culture is identical. The cultivars 'Armleuchter', 'Elstead Variety', and 'White Pearl' offer taller flower stalks and varying degrees of gracefulness in appearance, but there is no special note of real distinction among them. (See photo.)

Colchicum autumnale (meadow saffron, autumn crocus, wonder bulb) 4–8 in Sun Zones 3–6
FLOWERING SPAN: Early September to October
NATURAL COLOR: Purple to white
DISTRIBUTION: Europe, North Africa
The planting of these large corms should occur as soon as they appear by early autumn in the local garden center or as they arrive by mail since they flower very early even out of the earth. Capable of producing its elongated blossoming just sitting openly on a windowsill because the bud was long preformed, this

novel plant should be installed in a consistently moist, well-drained, average-fertility location with full sun or light shading. The 6-petaled blossom opens to 2–3 in wide and appears in ongoing clusters without foliage at the time of bloom. The 3–8 straplike, 6–8-in leaves up to 2 in wide appear just in spring—to many gardeners' great surprise—but persist only until early July. Do not remove any foliage before it fades, or the corm will diminish in vigor and possibly fail to flower that season. Division of overcrowded colonies during late July or early August is the best propagation method. Pests and diseases are uncommon. Its cultivars include: 'Album', off-white; 'Album Plenum', double, off-white; 'Majus', purple-pink, the hardiest and most prolific for flowering; 'Minus', lilac, later-blooming; and 'Roseum', rosy pink. (See photo.)

Colchicum speciosum   8–12 in   Sun   Zones 3–6
   FLOWERING SPAN: Mid-September to mid-October
   NATURAL COLOR: Pale lilac to rosy lavender
   DISTRIBUTION: Asia Minor, eastern Mediterranean
   The largest and showiest of all the *Colchicum* species, these clustered, 6–8-in, tulip-shaped blossoms have white throats and open broadly. The long-lasting, sizeable spring foliage can be 12–15 in long and must be left in place until it totally fades, which may be late July. Although the blossoming has much appeal in the front of borders, the spring foliage can be quite distracting there. Evaluate this factor when first planting the corms in autumn. Cultivate the same as for *C. autumnale* but consider planting in grassy, wild areas which are infrequently mowed because of the overscaled spring-to-summer leaves.
   The cultivar list is extensive: 'Album', pure white; 'Atrorubens', purple-crimson; 'Autumn Queen', rosy violet; 'Conquest', deep violet, late; 'Disraeli', deep mauve; 'Huxley', deep rosy lilac, hard to find; 'Lilac Wonder', mauve-pink with a white base, very late to flower; 'Premier', pale rosy lilac; 'Princess Astrid', light violet; 'The Giant', dark lilac with a white base, late; 'Violet Queen', deep purple; and 'Waterlily', lilac-mauve, double-flowered, top-heavy blossoming, late-blooming.

Cortaderia selloana (argentea)   (pampas grass)   96–132 in   Sun   Zones 8–10
   FLOWERING SPAN: Early September to late November
   NATURAL COLOR: Silvery white to pale pink
   DISTRIBUTION: Brazil, Argentina, Chile
   As a lawn or waterside specimen in mild growing areas, this grass is unrivaled for its graceful, 12–24-in plumes and overall size. The masses of stems create huge clumps that defy later division, so place this perennial carefully. When plants are young, they can be separated in the spring for propagation, but that possibility quickly fades since the plants are quite vigorous. The luxuriant foliage has sharp edges and appears on sturdy, rigidly erect stems. The glistening

plumes retain their appeal, when cut, for many years indoors. Grow only in full sun on any moist, average-fertility soil. Pests and diseases are rare. The cultivar 'Monstrosa' has larger, creamier flower panicles, while 'Pumila' grows only 60 in tall with dense plumes of creamy white flowering. Several forms with variegated foliage are known but remain uncommon in cultivation. (See photo.)

Crocus cancellatus   3–4 in   Sun   Zones 5–8
   FLOWERING SPAN: Early September to October
   NATURAL COLOR: Deep lilac, white
   DISTRIBUTION: Greece, Asia Minor
      Novel in that the foliage appears right after the flowers fade, the bulb carries slender, grasslike leaves and large, globular blossoms with conspicuous veining or stripes in purple. The stigma is scarlet while the anthers are pale yellow. Any well-drained, modestly moist, average-fertility soil in full sun is suitable, yet richer soil encourages more rapid colonization. The corms prefer to be undisturbed, but if the flowering diminishes from overcrowding, then dig and separate soon after the foliage disappears. Install initial plantings in the summer. Diseases and insect nuisances are uncommon.

Crocus longiflorus   4–5 in   Sun   Zones 5–8
   FLOWERING SPAN: Late September to late October
   NATURAL COLOR: Bright lilac
   DISTRIBUTION: Southern Italy, Sicily, Malta
      Nicely scented, this species has long, sharp-pointed petals with an inner orange throat. Its culture is identical to that for *C. cancellatus*.

Crocus pulchellus   3–4 in   Sun   Zones 5–8
   FLOWERING SPAN: Mid-September to mid-October
   NATURAL COLOR: Pale lavender to bright lilac
   DISTRIBUTION: Turkey, Greece
      Simple to grow but slow to colonize, the flower shows a deep yellow inner throat, an orange-yellow stigma, and white anthers. Grow as for *C. cancellatus*. This species readily hybridizes with *C. speciosus* (see below).

Crocus sativus   (saffron crocus)   4–5 in   Sun   Zones 5–8
   FLOWERING SPAN: Late September to late October
   NATURAL COLOR: Pale pink to purplish mauve
   DISTRIBUTION: Now it is known only in cultivation
      Grown in Greece, Sicily, and England since ancient times, the plant is the source of saffron, used in coloring and flavoring food, but is no longer seen in its

Anemone × hybrida
'Alba'

Aster novi-belgii
cultivar

Aster
'Oregon-Pacific Strain'

Calamagrostis × acutifolia

Chrysanthemum × *morifolium* (Cushion Type) cultivar

Chrysanthemum × *morifolium* (Pompon Type) cultivar

Chrysanthemum × *morifolium* (Decorative Type) cultivar

Chrysanthemum × *morifolium* (Single Type) cultivar

Chrysanthemum × *morifolium* (Spoon Type) cultivar

Chrysanthemum × *morifolium* (Quill Type) cultivar

Chrysanthemum nipponicum

Cimicifuga simplex 'White Pearl'

Cortaderia selloana 'Pumila'

Colchicum autumnale 'Majus'

Kirengeshoma palmata

Miscanthus sinensis

Miscanthus sinensis
'Variegatus'

Miscanthus sinensis
'Zebrinus'

wild state. The orange, feathery stigma of the flower, when dried, provides the commercial reason for its cultivation because it is a valuable and scarce commodity. For garden interest, provide the corm with a very warm, sun-bright location and cultivate as for *C. cancellatus*. Abundant grasslike foliage appears with the large, globular blossoms, which open into wide-spreading stars. This flowering is unusual by staying open at all times, even at night and in poor weather. The cultivar 'Cashmirianus' is white with a vividly scarlet stigma.

Crocus speciosus   3–4 in   Sun   Zones 4–8
FLOWERING SPAN: Early September to October
NATURAL COLOR: Bluish lilac
DISTRIBUTION: Southeastern Europe to Iran

One of the easiest autumn crocus species to grow satisfactorily, *C. speciosus* is noticeably attractive with its funnel-shaped, 2½-in, fragrant blossoms striped in dark lilac to blue. The stigma becomes deep orange-red. Most flowers appear either before or just with the emerging leaves. It needs a rich, light, well-drained, modestly moist soil and is actually helped by forking its bed lightly when the corms are dormant since this distributes the many tiny cormlets. Self-seeding also promotes colonization. Several cultivars are known: 'Aitchisonii', pale lavender, large-flowered; 'Albus', creamy white; 'Artabir', pale lavender-blue; 'Cassiope', bluish lavender with a cream base; 'Oxonian', closest yet to blue but not nearly as vigorous as the parent; and 'Pollux', pale violet-blue.

Kirengeshoma palmata   (waxbells)   36–48 in   Semishade   Zones 5–9
FLOWERING SPAN: Early September to October
NATURAL COLOR: Pale yellow
DISTRIBUTION: Mountains of Japan

Here is a divertingly different, shrubby perennial with clear green, maplelike, 3–5-in leaves on arching, purple-toned stems. The waxy, 1½-in shuttlecock-shaped blossoms appear either terminally or in leaf-axil sprays. Provide a deep, acid, constantly moist soil with no more than dappled light. Propagate by careful division in the spring. Pests and diseases are unknown. (See photo.)

Miscanthus sinensis   (Japanese silver grass)   72–96 in   Sun   Zones 5–9
FLOWERING SPAN: Late September to late November
NATURAL COLOR: Brownish tan fading to buff gold
DISTRIBUTION: China, Japan

Expansive but not invasive, this clump-forming, robust, tall grass accepts either moist or dry locations equally and tolerates moderate shade as well. Useful as a seasonal screen when planted several deep, its sturdy, stiffly erect stems carry narrow, flat leaves up to 36 in long. Terminal, recurved flower plumes endure attractively through the winter and make good indoor decoration when cut and dried by late autumn. Propagate either by spring division or seeding. The cultivars include: 'Gracillimus', 60 in, with noticeably channeled foliage only ¼ in wide; 'Purpurescens', 48 in, with reddish leaves but reduced hardiness; 'Variegatus', 72 in, with leaves striped in white or cream; and 'Zebrinus', 72 in, showing either yellow or white banding on the foliage. (See photos.)

Polygonum amplexicaule (mountain fleece)   24–48 in   Sun   Zones 6–9
    FLOWERING SPAN: Early September to November
    NATURAL COLOR: Rosy red, white
    DISTRIBUTION: Himalaya Mountains

    Creating a wide-spreading mat of attractive foliage when it becomes well established, this perennial has 4–6-in, wavy-margined, heart-shaped leaves and slender, nodding flower stalks ending in spikes of ¼-in, tightly arranged florets up to 6 in long. Grow in a moist, well-drained, average-fertility soil either in full sun or light shading. Reproduce by spring division only. Insects are unknown, but leaf spot disease can be an occasional problem. The cultivar 'Album' has pinkish white blossoming, 'Atrosanguineum' is ruby red, and 'Firetail' develops larger, scarlet blooms.

Hardy Ferns

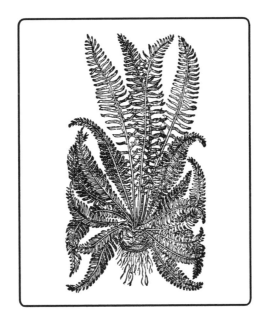

Hardy Ferns

Foliage is the main asset of ferns. Whether evergreen or deciduous, ferns are admired for their textural contrast, variety of sizes, and ability to endure in many light and soil conditions. Hardy ferns are reliable—but flowerless—perennials belonging to a major division of the plant kingdom called Pteridophyta, a Latinized Greek word translating to "feathery plant." Botanically, ferns are an evolutionary step below the seed-producing plants because they have no true flowering or fruiting. Their chief method for natural reproduction is by means of spores (a Greek word meaning "seed") often arranged in clustered, tiny heaps on the backsides of their leaf forms, called fronds. The dominant frond type is compound, and the primary leafy divisions from the main stalk are labeled pinnae. Some pinnae are directly set on the stalk, while others extend beyond it by means of petioles.

There are two major kinds of fern growth habits related to how the stems grow: creeping or clustered. Rootstocks with below-ground, creeping rhizomes form sizeable masses in time since they continually develop new foliage throughout the growing season. Any of these can become invasive. Ferns with raised crowns or clumps of clustered stems produce only central foliage concentrations, maintain the original number of springtime stems, and are more restrained in their expansion. The creeping sorts generally can be transplanted in either spring or autumn, while the clustered forms usually prefer only dormant lifting and separation. There are some ferns so sturdy they can even be mowed without future harm or dug up in thick sods like grass for transplanting. Most emerging fronds are colloquially called "fiddleheads" because of their tightly rolled, crozierlike shape. Several species can be collected, prepared, and eaten as a gourmet delicacy during spring.

In general ferns do their best where moisture is evenly available at all times and the soil rich in humus to allow easy penetration of the fine roots. A slightly acid to neutral, loose, sandy site, balanced in content between clay and humus, provides the basic soil mix for good growth of most ferns. Many enjoy semishaded conditions, but there are also some which do best in more sunlight. Because ferns resent having mud splashed on their foliage, they benefit greatly from a thick but loose-structured mulch at all times. In natural distributions they are often found growing satisfactorily with mosses in leaf litter and twiggy debris. New plantings in gardens can be helped along by an initial top-dressing of either moist peat moss, pine bark, compost, shredded plant parts, or any other vegetative mulching material not likely to generate a lot of heat as it decays. Ferns are no more difficult to establish than any other perennial once their basic growing needs are understood.

(Photos for Hardy Ferns are between pages 272 and 273.)

THE FERNS

Adiantum pedatum (American maidenhair, maidenhair fern, five-fingered fern)
8–20 in   Semishade   Zones 3–7
FOLIAGE COLOR: Light to medium green
DISTRIBUTION: Southeastern Canada to Georgia, west to Louisiana and Minnesota,
Pacific Northwest, eastern Asia

The many emerging, wiry stems are somewhat reddish but soon mature to
shiny black-brown with flat-spreading, delicate fronds arranged parallel to the
ground. Its leaf outline is 12–18 in wide and almost circular from fingerlike divisions of 4–12 narrow pinnae. When mature the fronds cut well and stay durable
for indoor use. Spores form on the undersides at the outer edges of the pinnae.
Grow in a loose, rich, slightly acid, constantly moist but well-drained soil in
reasonable light but never hot sun. The plant slowly expands from a creeping
rhizome and is normally propagated by rootstock cuttings. The spores are also
workable, however, if slow to develop. Snails and slugs are the primary
problems. (See photo.)

Asplenium platyneuron (ebeneum) (ebony spleenwort) 6–15 in   Sun   Zones 3–7
FOLIAGE COLOR: Deep green
DISTRIBUTION: Maine to Georgia, west to Colorado, South Africa

This fern displays 2 kinds of evergreen foliage: the tightly compressed
pinnae, 2–6 in long, of prostrate, sterile fronds plus stiffly erect, fertile fronds
stretching to 15 in and tapering at both ends. These 1–3-in-wide fertile fronds
have noticeable gaps between alternate pinnae and appear on purple-brown,
glossy petioles. A gravelly, alkaline soil enriched with humus or compost is to its
liking. Although it must be moist and reasonable cool, the plant also tolerates
modest dryness and light shade well. Propagate by spores located along the
midrib. There are no special diseases or pests.

Asplenium trichomanes (maidenhair spleenwort) 2–8 in   Semishade   Zones 3–7
FOLIAGE COLOR: Dark green
DISTRIBUTION: Europe, Asia, Nova Scotia to Georgia, west to Arizona and Alaska

Like *A. platyneuron,* this fern also has evergreen, sterile, prostrate fronds and
upright, fertile ones. These shorter, fertile fronds show lustrous, dark brown
stems and roundish pinnae which are notched at the upper edges. Spores are also
located along the midribs. Keep protected from too much wind and provide a
cool, moist, well-drained site high in humus and definitely alkaline. Some

growers place the plant between limestone rocks for best growth. Rootstock division in spring or spores are the recommended reproduction techniques. Tolerant of occasional dryness, this fern is mostly bothered by the eating habits of slugs and snails.

Athyrium filix-femina (Asplenium filix-femina) (lady fern) 18–36 in Sun Zones 3–7
FOLIAGE COLOR: Pale green to medium green
DISTRIBUTION: Temperate Northern Hemisphere
    The lance-shaped fronds are often 15 in wide with pinnae which are twice-divided and have fine teeth along the edges. Mature fronds often show a reddish or brownish cast on the upper surfaces. The tightly clustered pinnae near the tip end carry the curved spore cases. Slow to expand, this fern requires constant wetness since it is found naturally in swamps and at streamsides. A neutral, average-fertility, reliably moist soil out of high wind gives satisfactory results in gardens with full sun or light shading. Either spores or division of the thick, horizontal rootstock in spring readily duplicates it. No particular pest or disease is a bother. (See photo.)

Athyrium goeringianum (Japanese fern) 6–18 in Semishade Zones 3–7
FOLIAGE COLOR: Medium green
DISTRIBUTION: Japan, Taiwan
    Few raise the parent plant when the superior coloring of the variety *pictum* (painted fern) is available. This variety shows wine red or purplish petioles supporting pinnae of grayish green with noticeably silvery central striping. These 8-in-wide fronds are gracefully arched and present a special accent for a semishaded garden space. Slow to expand, it enjoys a neutral to slightly acid, moist, well-drained, average-fertility soil. Provide extra water in dry spells since the creeping rootstock continues with new growth until autumn. Its spores are set in a herring-bone pattern on the reverse of the pinnae, and they self-seed readily and easily to be the main reproduction technique. Careful spring division is another way to create more plants. Bothersome diseases and pests are not frequent. (See photo.)

Botrychium virginianum (rattlesnake fern) 6–30 in Shade Zones 3–7
FOLIAGE COLOR: Yellow-green changing to rich green
DISTRIBUTION: Most of southern Canada and the entire United States, Asia, Europe
    One of the earliest ferns to provide foliage in spring, the succulent stems are very brittle and carry triangular fronds with lacy looking pinnae. Its sterile, 24–30-in fronds may produce a fertile stalk which has rows of circular capsules resembling the rattles of a rattlesnake. Production of this fertile part is undependable from year to year. A moist, rich, loose, humusy, neutral soil in medium to deep shade helps it thrive, but rabbits, slugs, cutworms, and rodents

all enjoy feeding on the juicy stems. It has no fiddleheads and its fronds are fully formed beneath the ground in late winter and early spring. Because it carries long, fleshy roots, division is very risky; spore reproduction is the preferred propagation method. Diseases are rare.

Camptosorus rhizophyllus (walking fern) 4–9 in Semishade Zones 3–7

FOLIAGE COLOR: Medium green

DISTRIBUTION: Southeastern Canada to Georgia, west to Oklahoma and Minnesota

Novel for its reproduction method, this fern has simple, evergreen, wedge-shaped, or lancelike leaves with very elongated, tapering points which can vegetatively produce new offshoots where these tips touch the earth and root. Its spore cases are haphazardly arranged on the undersides of the foliage. While it tolerates moderate dryness satisfactorily, the fern likes a moist, humusy, alkaline soil, preferably in the damp crevice of a limestone rock. Propagate it either by spores or by careful separation of the leaf-tip offspring. Slugs can be devastating during hot, steamy weather, but diseases are uncommon.

Cheilanthes lanosa (tomentosa) (hairy lip fern, woolly lip fern) 6–20 in Semishade Zones 4–8

FOLIAGE COLOR: Medium yellow-green

DISTRIBUTION: Virginia to Georgia, west to Arizona and Mexico

The narrow, twice-divided fronds have purple-brown to blackish petioles covered densely with rust-colored, fine hairs above the very short main stems. Spores line the outside edge of each fertile pinna, which is also hairy. Drought can cause the entire plant to collapse, but sufficient rainfall brings its quick recovery. Providing extra water in dry spells forestalls this event. It prefers an acid, average-fertility soil, somewhat dry, and apppears to be immune to diseases and insect pests. Reproduce it only from spores.

Cystopteris bulbifera (berry bladder fern, bulblet bladder fern) 18–30 in Shade Zones 3–7

FOLIAGE COLOR: Yellow-green

DISTRIBUTION: Southeastern Canada to Georgia, west to Arizona

A graceful, tapering, twice-divided frond, 3–5 in wide, appears from a pink-green stem and carries 2 neat rows of spore cases along each pinna. At the junction of the pinna and the petiole, however, a pea-shaped bulblet forms. When this matures and drops, a new fern should develop. A cool, humusy, moist, alkaline soil is generally suitable, yet superior growth usually comes from having the slender rhizome packed tightly into a limestone rock crevice. Spring rootstock division or frond bulblets reproduce it equally. There are no disease or insect nuisances.

Adiantum pedatum

Athyrium filix-femina

Athyrium goeringianum var. *pictum*

Dennstaedtia punctilobula

Dryopteris cristata var. clintoniana

Dryopteris marginalis

Gymnocarpium dryopteris

Matteuccia pensylvanica

Onoclea sensibilis

Osmunda cinnamomea

Osmunda claytoniana

Osmunda regalis

Polypodium virginianum

Polystichum acrostichoides

Pteridium aquilinum

Thelypteris noveboracensis

Thelypteris palustris

Cystopteris fragilis (Filix fragilis) (brittle fern, fragile fern) 4–12 in Shade
Zones 3–8
FOLIAGE COLOR: Medium green
DISTRIBUTION: Temperate Northern Hemisphere

The twice-pinnate foliage on this species is widely spaced along the slender, somewhat brittle stems which are brown at the base but green above. The round-lobed pinnae carry only a few scattered spore cases prominently attached to the veins. Foliage emerges very early in spring, and the fern has a preference for a humusy, moist, alkaline location. Prolonged drought withers the foliage, but adequate rain quickly renews it. Supply additional water in dry times to avoid this condition. Spring division is the recommended propagation method. Diseases are no threat, but slugs and snails have a special liking for these semidrooping fronds.

Dennstaedtia punctilobula (Dicksonia punctilobula) (hay-scented fern, boulder fern)
18–30 in Sun Zones 3–8
FOLIAGE COLOR: Yellow-green
DISTRIBUTION: Eastern North America

Vigorous to the point of invasive, this feathery, thin-leaved fern is useful for covering slopes because it tolerates a wide variety of site exposures ranging from full sun to heavy shade plus almost any soil condition. Ruggedly hardy and dependable, it carries 10–12-in-wide, lancelike fronds on brown stems, and its pinnae, when bruised, have glands which secrete the odor of cut hay. Cup-shaped spore cases appear in a regular pattern on the underside of each pinna. Provide a humusy, average-fertility, acid soil, either wet or dry—or even both in turn. It is not fussy. Spring division of the clumped, above-ground rootstock is the simplest propagation technique. Diseases are unknown, but snails and thrips are often bothersome. (See photo.)

Diplazium acrostichoides (Asplenium acrostichoides, Athryrium thelypteroides) 20–36 in Sun
Zones 5–7
FOLIAGE COLOR: Yellow-green changing to deep green, then to russet-green
DISTRIBUTION: North Carolina to Georgia and Missouri, eastern Asia

Yellow stems produce 7-in-wide, lancelike fronds with noticeably deep notches between the simple, often toothed pinnae. Silvery spore cases are located on the veining of the fertile fronds and become blue-gray when mature. A rich, moist, acid soil in sun or light shade is suitable, and spring division is the preferred reproduction method. Insect pests and diseases are unusual.

Diplazium pycnocarpon (Asplenium angustifolium, Athyrium pycnocarpon) 20–40 in Shade
Zones 3–7
FOLIAGE COLOR: Bright green changing to dark green, finally to russet

DISTRIBUTION: Southeastern Canada to Georgia, west to Louisiana and Missouri

The triangular, 6-in-wide frond carries simple, lancelike pinnae which are openly spaced along the stalk above brown main stems. Often found naturally in association with *Dryopteris goldiana,* this fern is very slow to expand but does produce ongoing fronds until autumn. The spore cases make a herringbone pattern along the midvein of each fertile pinna. Either spring division of the above-ground rootstock or spores readily propagate it. It likes a cool, moist, rich, alkaline location in deep to moderate shading. Diseases and insect nuisances are unknown.

Dryopteris cristata (Aspidium cristatum) (crested wood fern, crested fern) 12–30 in Shade Zones 3–7

FOLIAGE COLOR: Dark green

DISTRIBUTION: Europe, northern Asia, southeastern Canada to Virginia, west to Arkansas

The sterile fronds are short, reasonably evergreen, and leathery, while the 4–6-in-wide fertile fronds are taller, erect, and carry blunt-ended pinnae turned horizontally in a stepladderlike fashion, which is characteristic of this group. The covered spores are round dots in generous display. Very wet—even mucky—locations are its habitat in cool, neutral to alkaline soil, yet it accepts garden conditions satisfactorily if kept consistently very moist. Spring division or spores work equally for propagation, and it appears untroubled by problems from diseases or insects. The variety *clintoniana* has broader fronds. (See photo.)

Dryopteris goldiana (Aspidium goldianum) (Goldie's wood fern) 30–48 in Shade Zones 3–7

FOLIAGE COLOR: Yellow-green to deep green

DISTRIBUTION: Northeastern North America

Having both the tallest and the widest fronds—up to 18 in across—of this genus, *D. goldiana* makes a dramatic addition to the woodlot garden. The foliage is oval in outline and appears from ground stems which have pale brown scales very shaggily arranged near the base. Its spore cases are precisely set in generous quantities along the veins of the pinnae. Provide a cool, moist, deep, humusy soil of neutral or slightly acid condition. Either spring division or spores reproduce it well, and there seem to be no bothersome insect pests or diseases.

Dryopteris marginalis (Aspidium marginale) (marginal shield fern, shield fern, leather wood fern) 15–30 in Shade Zones 3–7

FOLIAGE COLOR: Dark bluish green

DISTRIBUTION: Eastern North America

In preparation for its new season of spring growth, this slow-creeping fern forms a raised crown of inward-bending, dormant fronds that become a uniform circle of foliage in spring. The 5–8-in-wide, erect, broadly oval, leathery leaves carry large, round, blue-black spore cases arranged along the edges of the pinnae. These leaves are durable when cut for indoor decoration. A moist, deep, stony, leaf-composted soil from acid to slightly alkaline is suitable, and the plant tolerates anything from deep shade to intermittent sunlight if kept consistently very moist. Spores or spring division creates additional plants readily, and it seems to have no difficulties with pests or diseases. (See photo.)

Gymnocarpium dryopteris (Dryopteris disjuncta, Polypodium dryopteris) (oak fern)
4–11 in Semishade Zones 3–7
FOLIAGE COLOR: Yellow-green
DISTRIBUTION: Northern North America, Europe, Asia
These doubly pinnate fronds have broad-based, triangular shapes with an attractively graceful appearance. Creeping widely by black-colored rootstocks, it produces only sparse foliage in the acid, moist, cool woodlots of its natural environment. Rootstock cuttings, spring division, or spores reproduce it equally, and it is unencumbered by disease or insect nuisances. (See photo.)

Lygodium palmatum (Hartford fern, climbing fern) 24–60 in Semishade Zones 4–7
FOLIAGE COLOR: Light green
DISTRIBUTION: Massachusetts to Florida, west to Tennessee and Michigan
While not easy to grow well, this fern, with its novel, vinelike appearance, is worth a trial. The 1–3-in-wide, palmately shaped fronds appear paired and widely spaced along the stringy, dark brown, trailing or climbing stems. A light, moist, acid soil helps it thrive in gardens, but it is natural to swampy thickets. Reproduction is best handled only by spores. Both snails and strong winds seriously hamper its growth, but diseases are not known.

Matteuccia pensylvanica (Pteretis nodulosa) (ostrich fern) 36–84 in Semishade
Zones 3–7
FOLIAGE COLOR: Deep green
DISTRIBUTION: North America
The leathery, erect, plumelike, sterile fronds are graceful and very durable except in periods of drought, when they shrivel or scorch. They appear from sizeable raised domes which poke several inches above the earth. The shorter fertile fronds come from the center of the clump during late summer and are stiff but feathery looking and about 2 in wide. They turn deep brown at maturity, and when cut for indoor decoration are very durable. If kept consistently moist this fern accepts full sunlight, but it usually is more satisfied in a damp, humusy, average-fertility, cool site with semishade. Division in early spring is more

productive than spores for propagation, and nothing but drought seems to bother it. The shorter variety *struthiopteris* from Europe and Asia has shorter and less erect fronds which top out at 60 in of height. (See photo.)

Onoclea sensibilis (sensitive fern) 12–48 in Sun Zones 3–7
    FOLIAGE COLOR: Yellow-green, gray-green, or brownish green
    DISTRIBUTION: Eastern Europe, western Asia, southern Canada to Texas and Florida
    This one-species fern genus is acutely sensitive to late spring and early autumn frosts, which quickly damage the foliage. Otherwise, the fern is a relatively easy one to grow, but it can become invasive from the pencil-thick, creeping, ground-level rootstock. The triangular-shaped, deeply lobed, simple foliage can be up to 10 in long and is separately produced from the fertile portions. These persistent, 12–15-in, erect, slender, fertile parts produce heavy clusters of round, green spore cases which later become dark brown and are collectible for indoor use. Colloquially they are known as "bead sticks." A wet, marshy, acid-to-alkaline soil in strong sunlight is best, yet the plant cooperatively endures more shading and just consistent moisture. Propagate either by spring division or by spores. Diseases and insects appear to shun it. (See photo.)

Osmunda cinnamomea (cinnamon fern, fiddleheads) 24–60 in Semishade
Zones 4–7
    FOLIAGE COLOR: Pale green to deep green
    DISTRIBUTION: Asia, South America, West Indies, North America
    Widely distributed and adaptable to more sunlight if kept consistently moist, this is an almost-foolproof fern with a sluggish growth habit. It is not only garden-attractive but a nutrition-loaded, gourmet delicacy as well. The undeveloped spring fronds or "fiddleheads" are collected and boiled or eaten raw in salads in many parts of the world. The erect, fertile fronds, which are entirely separate from the outward-facing, fountainlike, sterile ones, produce thick, terminal collections of rounded spore cases that are first bright green, then golden brown, and finally deep brown. The plant enjoys a wet or consistently moist location of average fertility and an acid disposition. Duplicate it either by spring division or by spores. Pests and diseases are unknown. (See photo.)

Osmunda claytoniana (interrupted fern) 36–48 in Semishade Zones 4–7
    FOLIAGE COLOR: Yellow-green to dark green
    DISTRIBUTION: Asia, North America
    Not always as easy to grow as its cousin, *O. cinnamomea,* but just as edible, *O. claytoniana* prefers less acid soil and tolerates drier conditions satsifactorily, although the plants are generally shorter. Both the sterile and the fertile fronds are similar in size and general appearance, except that the fertile stalks are

interrupted by a noticeable clustering of spore cases about halfway up the stem. Reproduction can be handled either by spores or spring division. It is unbothered by any disease or insect nuisance. (See photo.)

Osmunda regalis (royal fern, flowering fern)   36–72 in   Semishade   Zones 3–7
  FOLIAGE COLOR: Light reddish green changing to deep green
  DISTRIBUTION: Europe, Africa

  A cluster of golden, spherical spore capsules crown the top of an otherwise sterile frond and give this fern the odd appearance of displaying true flowering. The foliage resembles that of a honeylocust (*Gleditsia*) with its bipinnate, openly spaced, thick pinnae. Very slow to expand, the plant maintains its accent individuality for a long time in one location. Only a very wet, highly acid soil makes it thrive, and it grows successfully even if flooded around the base. Short of digging up an entire plant, sowing spores is the most practical reproduction technique and is easily handled in springtime. There are no problems from diseases or insects. (See photo.)

Pellaea atropurpurea (purple cliff brake)   6–12 in   Semishade   Zones 5–7
  FOLIAGE COLOR: Pale green changing to gray-green, then to blue-green
  DISTRIBUTION: North America

  Semievergreen, this fern has purple-brown, hairy stems and oddly divided, leathery, stalked pinnae with a greater number of divisions on the lower segments than on the upper. Spores line the outer edges of the pinnae, which curve inward to protect them. Although tolerant of more sun than listed, it prefers some shading during the heat of the day and grows perhaps best on dry, limestone rocks. Sowing spores is the usual reproduction technique. Insects and diseases are uncommon.

Polypodium virginianum (rock polypody, American wall fern)   4–10 in   Semishade   Zones 2–7
  FOLIAGE COLOR: Yellow-green to medium green
  DISTRIBUTION: Eastern North America

  Sometimes locally identified as the "rock's cap" fern because a well-established specimen can completely swathe a small boulder in a mat of foliage, this plant has 2–3-in-wide, evergreen, leathery fronds and many tip-end spore cases. In the northerly part of its range it does best in cool, somewhat dry exposures with open shade, but if placed in semisunny areas it prefers more moisture. Accepting both acidic and alkaline soils well, the plant tolerates modest drought satisfactorily. Propagate either by spring division or rootstock cuttings, which readily develop. Nothing seems to bother it. The European species, *P. vulgare,* is very similar but has edible, sweet-tasting rootstocks. (See photo.)

Polystichum acrostichoides (Asplenium acrostichoides, Dryopteris acrostichoides) (Christmas fern, dagger fern, canker brake) 12–24 in Shade Zones 4–7
FOLIAGE COLOR: Light green changing to very deep green
DISTRIBUTION: Eastern North America

Attractive and durable when cut for indoor decoration, this evergreen fern has a neat, slow-to-expand outline composed of narrowly tapering fronds up to 5 in wide. Its spore cases are densely clustered at the tips of the fertile fronds. When emerging, the new growth is covered with white scales which later mature to brown and persist until the following season. Tolerant of more sunlight if kept consistently moist, the fern grows well in any rich, humusy, damp, well-drained soil. Division is the recommended propagation method, and there seem to be no diseases or insect nuisances. The plant has many natural variations from its widespread distribution, and some have been provided with localized names to identify the particular source when sold at nurseries or through catalogs. (See photo.)

Polystichum braunii (shield fern, Braun's holly fern) 18–24 in Shade Zones 3–7
FOLIAGE COLOR: Deep green
DISTRIBUTION: Europe

The 8-in-wide, gracefully arching, glossy fronds of this fern are, unfortunately, not fully evergreen, but its summertime attractiveness is a worthwhile garden asset. Long, brown scales appear on the short stems, and the lancelike fronds taper sharply on both ends. It prefers a cool, consistently moist, rich, well-drained soil with a neutral to slightly alkaline condition. Both spores and spring division are the usual reproduction techniques. It is not bothered by any insect or disease. The variety *purshii* (Pursh's holly fern) has thicker foliage.

Pteridium aquilinum (brake, pasture brake, braken) 36–48 in Semishade Zones 3–7
FOLIAGE COLOR: Dark green
DISTRIBUTION: Western North America, Michigan, Ontario, eastern Quebec

Apt to become weedy in a short time, this vigorous fern has leathery, thrice-divided, triangular fronds which can expand to 36 in wide. The emerging spring growth should not be eaten since the plant is now known to be carcinogenic. Growing equally well on either dry or moist sites which are very acid, it prefers a sandy, humusy location with room to expand. Easily transplanted or divided in spring, the plant has no problems with either diseases or insect pests. (See photo.)

Thelypteris hexagonoptera (Dryopteris hexagonoptera, Phegopteris hexagonoptera) (broad beech fern, beech fern) 10–15 in Shade Zones 3–7
FOLIAGE COLOR: Medium green

DISTRIBUTION: Eastern North America

Highly variable in form, the fronds are broadly triangular and up to 15 in wide with leafy ridges along the stalks connecting the lacelike divisions of the pinnae. Fragrant when bruised, the fronds usually make dense mats in the rich, moist, humusy, acid soil it prefers. The spore cases are tiny and round. Propagation can come from spring division, spores, and rootstock cuttings. Nothing troublesome bothers it.

Thelypteris noveboracensis (Dryopteris noveboracensis) (New York fern) 12–24 in
Zones 3–7
FOLIAGE COLOR: Pale green
DISTRIBUTION: Eastern North America

Rapid-growing to the point of quickly overcrowding itself, this fern has 7-in-wide, pale green fronds tapered at both ends. Spore cases are located along the edges of the pinnae. Consistently producing new foliage well into the summer, this fern can be divided readily or grown from spores. An acid, humusy soil, either moist or reasonably dry, is satisfactory, and the plant appears to be insect- and disease-free. (See photo.)

Thelypteris palustris (Dryopteris thelypteris) (marsh fern) 10–30 in Semishade
Zones 3–7
FOLIAGE COLOR: Bright green changing to gray green
DISTRIBUTION: Temperate North America

At home in bogs, marshes, and other wet places, this fern creeps widely from a cordlike rootstalk. The 6-in-wide fertile fronds have spore cases along the edges of the pinnae, which fold over to cover and protect them. Tolerant of either full sun or dense shade if kept wet at all seasons, it needs a rich, acid soil. Spring division or spores reproduce it readily, and only drought is its nemesis. (See photo.)

Thelypteris phegopteris (Dryopteris phegopteris) (long beech fern, narrow beech fern)
6–10 in Semishade Zones 3–7
FOLIAGE COLOR: Light green to yellow-green
DISTRIBUTION: Temperate Northern Hemisphere

One of the easiest ferns to grow well, this plant has a noticeable tendency to become quickly invasive. The 8-in-wide, triangular fronds, which are usually hairy throughout, appear on yellow-brown stalks carrying brown scales. Unique in outline, the frond's lowest set of pinnae is longer than the others and also points downward. Provide a constantly moist, acid, rich soil annually mulched with leafy compost. Propagate either by spring division or rootstock cuttings or by spores. No problematic nuisances come from insects or diseases.

Woodsia ilvensis (rusty woodsia, fragrant woodsia) 3–10 in Sun Zones 2–7
FOLIAGE COLOR: Light gray green changing to yellow-brown on the undersides
DISTRIBUTION: Cold, northern areas of Europe, Asia, North America

The 1½-in-wide, thick fronds are tapered at both ends, and although they brown and curl completely in prolonged drought, they recover quickly after adequate rain. This fern prefers a neutral to slightly acid, loose soil with moderate moisture, and because it is usually native-growing among boulders, it is highly suitable for sunny garden rockeries. Division is the simplest propagation technique, and there are no difficulties from any diseases or insect pests.

Woodsia obtusa (blunt-lobed woodsia, common woodsia) 6–15 in Shade
Zones 3–8
FOLIAGE COLOR: Gray green
DISTRIBUTION: Central United States to Florida

Yellow-green stems produce 4-in-wide fronds remaining reasonably evergreen where the climate is mild. Tiny white hairs cover both sides of the pinnae, and the ends of the pinnae are unusual by being blunt-tipped. It enjoys a well-drained, rocky, neutral, moist soil and can be reproduced satisfactorily by spring division or spores. Nothing much bothers it.

Woodwardia areolata (angustifolia) (netvein chain fern) 10–15 in Sun Zones 3–8
FOLIAGE COLOR: Dark green
DISTRIBUTION: Maine to Florida, west to Louisiana

These fronds are 3–4 in wide and glossy and have some resemblance in the sterile parts to the outline of *Onoclea sensibilis.* In this species, however, the leaves are narrower and have more space between divisions. Quickly spreading over wide stretches, it grows best in an acid, swampy soil yet will accept a well-drained, moist garden location without much trouble. Spring division or spores propagate it equally, and it appears to be unbothered by diseases or insects.

Woodwardia virginica (Blechnum virginica) (Virginia chain fern) 18–22 in Semishade
Zones 4–9
FOLIAGE COLOR: Dark green to yellow-green, depending on light conditions
DISTRIBUTION: Nova Scotia to Florida, west to Louisiana, Bermuda

Growing so rapidly when established that it may overwhelm any garden space, this fern has 5–9-in-wide fronds supported by green-brown stems which become black as they meet the ground. Its spores are interestingly arranged on the back of the pinnae both parallel to the midrib and also in an ascending herringbone pattern up the segments. Native to swampy, acid soils it can grow easily—if perhaps too vigorously—on a moist, average-fertility location in moderate shade in a garden. Division in spring is the simplest method for increasing the plants. Nothing bothers it.

Useful Lists

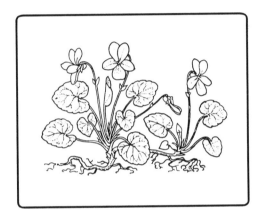

Perennials Blooming 6 Weeks or More

	Sun	Semi-shade	Shade
MARCH			
Erica carnea	x		
Helleborus niger		x	
Helleborus orientalis		x	
APRIL			
Brunnera macrophylla		x	
Dicentra cucullaria		x	
Dicentra eximia		x	
Hepatica acutiloba			x
Hepatica americana			x
Omphalodes verna		x	
Pachysandra procumbens		x	
Polemonium reptans		x	
Primula denticulata		x	
Pulmonaria saccharata		x	
Trillium sessile			x
Vinca minor 'Bowlesii'	x		
Viola cornuta	x		
Viola odorata		x	
Viola palmata		x	
Viola sororia		x	
Viola tricolor	x		
MAY			
Anemone canadensis		x	
Anemone sylvestris		x	
Anemonella thalictroides		x	
Aquilegia caerulea	x		
Aquilegia chrysantha	x		
Aquilegia × hybrida	x		
Arenaria verna		x	
Armeria maritima	x		
Armeria plantaginea	x		
Campanula elatines	x		
Campanula poscharskyana	x		
Cerastium arvense	x		

	Sun	Semi-shade	Shade
Corydalis lutea		x	
Delphinium nudicaule	x		
Dianthus × allwoodii	x		
Dicentra formosa		x	
Dicentra spectabilis		x	
Dodecatheon meadia		x	
Doronicum cordatum	x		
Doronicum pardalianches	x		
Epimedium × youngianum		x	
Erigeron glaucus	x		
Geranium endressii	x		
Geranium sanguineum	x		
Geum × borisii	x		
Geum quellyon	x		
Geum rivale		x	
Geum triflorum		x	
Hutchinsia alpina		x	
Hypoxis hirsuta	x		
Lamium maculatum		x	
Linum perenne	x		
Myosotis scorpioides	x		
Myosotis sylvatica		x	
Patrinia triloba	x		
Phlox divaricata		x	
Phlox stolonifera		x	
Polemonium caeruleum		x	
Potentilla anserina	x		
Potentilla argentea	x		
Potentilla tridentata	x		
Ranunculus aconitifolius		x	
Ranunculus acris	x		
Ranunculus montanus	x		
Ranunculus repens	x		
Saxifraga virginiensis	x		
Silene caroliniana	x		
Silene quadrifida	x		

	Sun	Semi-shade	Shade
Symphytum grandiflorum	x		
Symphytum officinale	x		
Thalictrum aquilegifolium	x		
Thermopsis montana	x		
Tradescantia × andersoniana	x		
Trollius europaeus		x	
Veronica officinalis			x
Veronica pectinata	x		
Viola canadensis		x	
Viola hastata		x	
Viola pedata	x		
Xerophyllum asphodeloides		x	
JUNE			
Achillea filipendulina	x		
Achillea ptarmica	x		
Achillea tomentosa	x		
Allium karataviense	x		
Anemone virginiana		x	
Anthemis tinctoria	x		
Anthericum liliago	x		
Aquilegia skinneri	x		
Astilbe × arendsii		x	
Campanula carpatica	x		
Campanula glomerata	x		
Campanula latifolia	x		
Campanula persicifolia	x		
Campanula portenschlagiana	x		
Campanula rotundifolia	x		
Catananche caerulea	x		
Centaurea dealbata	x		
Centaurea montana	x		
Centranthus ruber	x		
Cephalaria gigantea	x		
Chrysanthemum coccineum	x		
Chrysanthemum × superbum	x		
Chrysogonum virginianum		x	
Clematis integrifolia	x		
Clematis recta	x		
Coreopsis auriculata	x		

	Sun	Semi-shade	Shade
Coreopsis grandiflora	x		
Coreopsis lanceolata	x		
Coronilla varia	x		
Delphinium elatum	x		
Dianthus alpinus		x	
Dianthus barbatus	x		
Dianthus × latifolius	x		
Digitalis grandiflora		x	
Eremurus himalaicus	x		
Eremurus robustus	x		
Erigeron speciosus	x		
Filipendula purpurea		x	
Filipendula ulmaria		x	
Filipendula vulgaris	x		
Hesperis matronalis	x		
Heuchera × brizoides	x		
Heuchera sanguinea	x		
Heuchera villosa	x		
Hieracium villosum	x		
Kniphofia tuckii	x		
Leontopodium alpinum	x		
Leontopodium leontopodiodes	x		
Lewisia cotyledon		x	
Lewisia rediviva	x		
Lewisia tweedyi	x		
Lotus corniculatus	x		
Lupinus polyphyllus	x		
Lupinus × 'Russell Hybrids'	x		
Lychnis chalcedonica	x		
Lychnis flos-cuculi	x		
Lychnis flos-jovis	x		
Lysimachia nummularia		x	
Malva alcea	x		
Monarda didyma	x		
Nepeta × faassenii	x		
Oenothera fruticosa	x		
Oenothera missouriensis	x		
Oenothera tetragona	x		
Penstemon × gloxinoides	x		
Phlox maculata	x		
Platycodon grandiflorus	x		
Polygonum bistorta	x		

	Sun	Semi-shade	Shade
Potentilla argyrophylla	x		
Potentilla atrosanguinea	x		
Salvia × superba	x		
Saponaria ocymoides	x		
Saxifraga aizoides		x	
Saxifraga cotyledon		x	
Saxifraga paniculata		x	
Scabiosa caucasica	x		
Scabiosa columbaria	x		
Scabiosa graminifolia	x		
Sedum aizoon	x		
Sedum pulchellum		x	
Sedum rosea	x		
Sedum telephioides	x		
Sempervivum cultivars	x		
Sidalcea candida	x		
Sidalcea malviflora	x		
Silene schafta	x		
Silene virginica		x	
Stachys byzantina	x		
Stachys grandiflora	x		
Thymus × citriodorus	x		
Verbascum chaixii	x		
Verbascum × hybridum	x		
Veronica incana	x		
Veronica spicata	x		

JULY

	Sun	Semi-shade	Shade
Achillea millefolium	x		
Aconitum × bicolor		x	
Aconitum lycoctonum		x	
Aconitum napellus		x	
Alcea rosea	x		
Asclepias tuberosa	x		
Aster × frikartii	x		
Aster linarifolius	x		
Bletilla striata		x	
Briza media	x		
Calluna vulgaris	x		
Campanula sarmatica	x		
Centaurea macrocephala	x		
Centaurea ruthenica	x		
Chelone glabra		x	
Coreopsis rosea	x		
Coreopsis verticillata	x		

	Sun	Semi-shade	Shade
Deschampsia caespitosa	x		
Echinacea purpurea	x		
Erigeron × hybridus	x		
Eryngium alpinum	x		
Eryngium amethystinum	x		
Eupatorium rugosum	x		
Euphorbia corollata	x		
Galega officinalis	x		
Gentiana asclepiadea		x	
Gypsophila acutifolia	x		
Helianthus decapetalus	x		
Helianthus helianthoides	x		
Helianthus × multiflorus	x		
Hemerocallis × hybrida	x		
Inula ensifolia	x		
Inula hookeri	x		
Lathyrus latifolius	x		
Liatris spicata	x		
Ligularia dentata		x	
Ligularia przewalskii	x		
Lilium lancifolium	x		
Limonium latifolium	x		
Lysimachia clethroides	x		
Lythrum salicaria	x		
Malva moschata	x		
Phlox paniculata	x		
Physostegia virginiana		x	
Potentilla nepalensis	x		
Rudbeckia fulgida	x		
Rudbeckia laciniata	x		
Salvia pratensis	x		
Senecio cineraria	x		
Solidago × hybrida	x		
× Solidaster luteus	x		
Thalictrum speciosissimum	x		
Veronica longifolia	x		
Yucca filamentosa	x		
Yucca flaccida	x		

AUGUST

	Sun	Semi-shade	Shade
Aconitum carmichaelii		x	
Anaphalis margaritacea		x	
Artemisia absinthium	x		

	Sun	Semi-shade	Shade
Artemisia lactiflora	x		
Artemisia ludoviciana	x		
Artemisia schmidtiana	x		
Artemisia stellerana	x		
Aster amellus	x		
Aster spectabilis	x		
Astilbe chinensis var. taquetii	x		
Boltonia asteroides	x		
Ceratostigma plumbaginoides	x		
Chelone lyonii		x	
Chelone obliqua		x	
Chrysanthemum parthenium	x		
Chrysanthemum serotinum	x		
Gentiana andrewsii		x	
Helenium autumnale	x		
Kniphofia uvaria	x		
Liriope muscari		x	
Liriope spicata		x	
Lobelia siphilitica	x		
Molinia caerulea	x		
Pennisetum alopecuroides	x		
Pityopsis falcata	x		
Polygonum affine	x		
Rudbeckia hirta	x		

	Sun	Semi-shade	Shade
Salvia azurea	x		
Santolina chamaecyparissus	x		
Santolina virens	x		
Sedum × 'Ruby Glow'	x		
Sedum telephium	x		
Stokesia laevis	x		
Thalictrum delvayi		x	
Veronicastrum virginicum	x		

SEPTEMBER

	Sun	Semi-shade	Shade
Anemone hupehensis		x	
Anemone × hybrida	x		
Aster laevis	x		
Aster novi-belgii	x		
Aster 'Oregon-Pacific Strain'	x		
Calamagrostis × acutifolia	x		
Chrysanthemum × morifolium	x		
Chrysanthemum nipponicum	x		
Cortaderia selloana	x		
Miscanthus sinensis	x		
Polygonum amplexicaule	x		

Perennials Having Attractive Foliage Throughout the Growing Season

	Sun	Semi-shade	Shade
APRIL			
Alchemilla alpina	x		
Bergenia cordifolia		x	
Bergenia crassifolia		x	
Caulophyllum thalictroides			x
Euphorbia epithymoides	x		
Euphorbia myrsinites	x		
Pachysandra terminalis		x	
Pulmonaria angustifolia		x	
Pulmonaria montana		x	
Pulmonaria officinalis		x	
Pulmonaria saccharata		x	
Vinca minor	x		
MAY			
Amsonia tabernaemontana		x	
Asarum europaeum		x	
Astrantia major	x		
Baptisia australis	x		
Baptisia leucantha		x	
Clintonia borealis			x
Cornus canadensis			x
Corydalis lutea		x	
Dryas octopetala	x		
Epimedium species		x	
Galax urceolata		x	
Galium odoratum		x	
Geranium sanguineum	x		
Iberis sempervirens	x		
Lamium maculatum		x	
Paeonia lactiflora	x		
Podophyllum hexandrum		x	

	Sun	Semi-shade	Shade
Podophyllum peltatum		x	
Polygonatum biflorum		x	
Polygonatum commutatum		x	
Polygonatum multiflorum		x	
Potentilla tridentata	x		
Saxifraga virginiensis	x		
Sedum species	x		
Tiarella cordifolia		x	
Tiarella wherryi		x	
Veronica gentianoides	x		
Waldsteinia fragaroides		x	
JUNE			
Achillea filipendulina	x		
Achillea tomentosa	x		
Antennaria dioica	x		
Astilbe × *arendsii*		x	
Centaurea gymnocarpa	x		
Cerastium biebersteinii	x		
Coreopsis auriculata	x		
Dianthus species	x		
Dictamnus albus	x		
Filipendula ulmaria 'Aureo-variegata'		x	
Heuchera sanguinea	x		
Heuchera villosa	x		
Leontopodium alpinum	x		
Leontopodium leontopodiodes	x		
Lewisia cotyledon		x	
Lewisia tweedyi	x		
Lychnis coronaria	x		
Meconopsis cambrica		x	
Nepeta × *faassenii*	x		
Opuntia humifusa	x		

	Sun	Semi-shade	Shade
Potentilla argyrophylla	x		
Saxifraga aizoides		x	
Saxifraga cotyledon		x	
Saxifraga paniculata		x	
Scabiosa graminifolia	x		
Sedum species	x		
Sempervivum cultivars	x		
Shortia galacifolia			x
Shortia uniflora			x
Stachys byzantina	x		
Thymus × citriodorus	x		
Verbascum chaixii	x		
Veronica incana	x		
JULY			
Aconitum species		x	
Briza media	x		
Calluna vulgaris	x		
Cassia marilandica	x		
Coreopsis verticillata	x		
Deschampsia caespitosa	x		
Echinops humilis	x		
Echinops sphaerocephalus	x		
Eryngium alpinum	x		
Eryngium amethystinum	x		
Euphorbia corollata	x		
Hosta species		x	
Iris ensata	x		
Lathyrus latifolus	x		
Ligularia dentata		x	
Ligularia przewalskii	x		
Limonium latifolium	x		
Lysimachia clethroides	x		
Macleaya cordata	x		
Ruta graveolens	x		
Salvia pratensis	x		
Sedum species	x		
Teucrium chamaedrys	x		
Thalictrum speciosissimum	x		
Yucca filamentosa	x		
Yucca flaccida	x		

	Sun	Semi-shade	Shade
AUGUST			
Anaphalis margaritacea		x	
Artemisia species	x		
Boltonia asteroides	x		
Ceratostigma plumbaginoides	x		
Hosta species		x	
Liriope muscari		x	
Liriope spicata		x	
Molinia caerulea	x		
Pennisetum alopecuroides	x		
Phalaris arundinacea var. picta	x		
Santolina chamaecyparissus	x		
Santolina virens	x		
Sedum species	x		
SEPTEMBER			
Calamagrostis × acutifolia	x		
Cortaderia selloana	x		
Kirengeshoma palmata		x	
Miscanthus sinensis	x		
FERNS			
Adiantum pedatum		x	
Asplenium platyneuron	x		
Asplenium trichomanes		x	
Athyrium filix-femina	x		
Athyrium goeringianum		x	
Botrychium virginianum			x
Camptosorus rhizophyllus		x	
Cystopteris bulbifera			x
Dennstaedtia punctilobula	x		
Diplazium acrostichoides	x		
Diplazium pycnocarpon			x
Dryopteris cristata			x
Dryopteris goldiana			x

	Sun	Semi-shade	Shade		Sun	Semi-shade	Shade
Dryopteris marginalis			x	Polystichum braunii			x
Gymnocarpium dryopteris		x		Pteridium aquilinum		x	
Onoclea sensibilis	x			Thelypteris hexagonoptera			x
Osmunda cinnamomea		x		Thelypteris noveboracensis		x	
Osmunda claytoniana		x		Thelypteris phegopteris		x	
Osmunda regalis		x		Woodsia obtusa			x
Pellaea atropurpurea		x		Woodwardia areolata	x		
Polypodium virginianum		x		Woodwardia virginica		x	
Polystichum acrostichoides			x				

Perennials Having Persistent Winter Foliage

	Sun	Semi-shade	Shade		Sun	Semi-shade	Shade
MARCH				MAY			
Erica carnea	x			Aethionema coridifolium	x		
Helleborus niger		x		Aethionema grandiflorum	x		
Helleborus orientalis		x		Aethionema × warleyense	x		
				Asarum europaeum		x	
APRIL				Cornus canadensis			x
Arabis procurrens	x			Dianthus deltoides	x		
Aurinia saxatilis	x			Dianthus gratianopolitanus	x		
Bergenia cordifolia		x		Dryas octopetala	x		
Bergenia crassifolia		x		Epimedium species		x	
Claytonia caroliniana		x		Galax urceolata		x	
Hepatica acutiloba			x	Iberis saxatilis	x		
Hepatica americana			x	Iberis sempervirens	x		
Iris verna		x		Phlox stolonifera		x	
Muscari species	x			Potentilla tridentata	x		
Pachysandra procumbens		x		Veronica chamaedrys	x		
Pachysandra terminalis		x		Veronica officinalis			x
Phlox subulata	x			Veronica pectinata	x		
Primula auricula		x		Waldsteinia fragaroides		x	
Primula × polyantha		x					
Primula veris		x					
Primula vulgaris		x					
Vinca minor	x						

	Sun	Semi-shade	Shade
JUNE			
Campanula			
portenschlagiana	x		
Cerastium			
tomentosum	x		
Chrysogonum			
virginianum		x	
Coreopsis auriculata	x		
Genista sagittalis	x		
Helianthemum			
nummularium	x		
Heuchera sanguinea	x		
Lewisia cotyledon		x	
Lewisia rediviva	x		
Oenothera fruticosa	x		
Saponaria ocymoides	x		
Saxifraga species		x	
Sempervivum			
cultivars	x		
Shortia galacifolia			x
Shortia uniflora			x
Thymus × *citriodorus*	x		
JULY			
Calluna vulgaris	x		
Deschampsia			
caespitosa	x		
Gaultheria			
procumbens		x	
Lavandula angustifolia	x		

	Sun	Semi-shade	Shade
Ruta graveolens	x		
Sedum album	x		
Sedum spurium	x		
Teucrium chamaedrys	x		
Yucca filamentosa	x		
Yucca flaccida	x		
AUGUST			
Liriope muscari		x	
Liriope spicata		x	
Polygonum affine	x		
Santolina			
chamaecyparissus	x		
Santolina virens	x		
FERNS			
Asplenium			
platyneuron	x		
Asplenium			
trichomanes		x	
Camptosorus			
rhizophyllus		x	
Dryopteris cristata			x
Lygodium palmatum		x	
Pellaea atropurpurea		x	
Polypodium			
virginianum		x	
Polystichum			
acrostichoides			x
Woodsia obtusa			x

Perennials Showing Ornamental Fruit or Dried Flower and Seed Head Possibilities

	Sun	Semi-shade	Shade
APRIL			
Actaea pachypoda fruit			x
Actaea rubra fruit			x
Anemone caroliniana seed head	x		
Anemone patens seed head	x		
Anemone pulsatilla seed head	x		
Caulophyllum thalictroides fruit		x	
Trillium undulatum fruit		x	
Tulipa tarda seed head	x		
MAY			
Alchemilla mollis flower	x		
Anemone alpina seed head	x		
Arisaema triphyllum fruit		x	
Clintonia borealis fruit			x
Cornus canadensis fruit			x
Dryas octopetala seed head	x		
Geum triflorum seed head		x	
Jeffersonia diphylla fruit		x	
Podophyllum hexandrum fruit		x	

	Sun	Semi-shade	Shade
Podophyllum peltatum fruit		x	
Smilacina racemosa fruit		x	
JUNE			
Achillea filipendulina flower	x		
Allium christophii seed head	x		
Anemone virginiana seed head		x	
Astilbe × arendsii flower		x	
Catananche caerulea flower	x		
Dictamnus albus seed head	x		
Dipsacus sativus seed head	x		
Opuntia humifusa fruit	x		
JULY			
Belamcanda chinensis fruit	x		
Briza media flower	x		
Cimicifuga racemosa seed head		x	
Deschampsia caespitosa flower	x		
Echinops humilis flower	x		
Echniops sphaerocephalus flower	x		

	Sun	Semi-shade	Shade
Eryngium species flower	x		
Gaultheria procumbens fruit		x	
Lavandula angustifolia flower	x		
Limonium latifolium flower	x		
Macleaya cordata flower	x		
Physalis alkekengi seed head	x		
AUGUST			
Anaphalis margaritacea flower		x	
Molinia caerulea flower	x		

	Sun	Semi-shade	Shade
Pennisetum alopecuroides flower	x		
SEPTEMBER			
Calamagrostis × acutifolia flower	x		
Cortaderia selloana flower	x		
Miscanthus sinensis flower	x		
FERNS			
Matteuccia pensylvanica seed head			x
Onoclea sensibilis seed head	x		

Perennials Exhibiting Satisfactory Drought Tolerance

	Sun	Semi-shade	Shade
MARCH			
Crocus tomasinianus	x		
Eranthis cilicica	x		
Eranthis hyemalis	x		
Erica carnea	x		
APRIL			
Anemone caroliniana	x		
Anemone patens	x		
Anemone pulsatilla	x		
Arabis alpina	x		
Arabis caucasica	x		
Aubrieta deltoidea	x		
Aurinia saxatilis	x		
Euphorbia epithymoides	x		

	Sun	Semi-shade	Shade
Euphorbia myrsinites	x		
Ornithogalum nutans	x		
Phlox × procumbens	x		
Phlox subulata	x		
Primula sieboldii		x	
Tulipa aucheriana	x		
Tulipa clusiana	x		
Tulipa eichleri	x		
Tulipa greigii	x		
Tulipa kaufmanniana	x		
Tulipa kolpakowskiana	x		
Tulipa linifolia	x		
Tulipa tarda	x		
Tulipa turkestanica	x		
Tulipa whittalii	x		

	Sun	Semi-shade	Shade		Sun	Semi-shade	Shade
Viola palmata		x		*Centaurea montana*	x		
Viola pubescens		x		*Cersastium biebersteinii*	x		
				Coronilla varia	x		
MAY				*Delphinium × belladonna*	x		
Aethionema coridifolium	x			*Delphinium elatum*	x		
Aethionema grandiflorum	x			*Delphinium grandiflorum*	x		
Aethionema × warleyense	x			*Dianthus × latifolius*	x		
Anemone alpina	x			*Dictamnus albus*	x		
Camassia cusickii	x			*Erigeron speciosus*	x		
Campanula poscharskyana		x		*Gaillardia × grandiflora*	x		
Cerastium arvense	x			*Genista sagittalis*	x		
Corydalis lutea		x		*Gypsophila repens*	x		
Cypripedium acaule		x		*Helianthemum nummularium*	x		
Dianthus deltoides	x			*Hemerocallis middendorffii*		x	
Erigeron glaucus	x			*Hieracium villosum*	x		
Iberis saxatilis	x			*Kniphofia tuckii*	x		
Lamium maculatum		x		*Lewisia* species	x		
Lithospermum canescens	x			*Lotus corniculatus*	x		
Lychnis viscaria	x			*Lychnis chalcedonica*	x		
Ornithogalum umbellatum	x			*Lychnis coronaria*	x		
Phlox pilosa	x			*Malva alcea*	x		
Polygonatum biflorum	x			*Oenothera missouriensis*	x		
Potentilla argentea	x			*Oenothera tetragona*	x		
Potentilla tridentata	x			*Opuntia humifusa*	x		
Saxifraga virginiensis	x			*Potentilla argyrophylla*	x		
Sedum acre	x			*Potentilla atrosanguinea*	x		
Silene caroliniana	x			*Salvia × superba*	x		
Viola pedata	x			*Saponaria ocymoides*	x		
Waldsteinia fragaroides		x		*Sedum aizoon*	x		
				Sedum rosea	x		
JUNE				*Sedum sexangulare*	x		
Achillea ageratifolia	x			*Sedum telephioides*	x		
Achillea clavennae	x			*Sempervivum* cultivars	x		
Achillea filipendulina	x			*Thymus × citriodorus*	x		
Achillea tomentosa	x						
Allium cyaneum	x						
Allium ostrowskianum	x			JULY			
Antennaria dioica	x			*Achillea millefolium*	x		
Anthemis tinctoria	x			*Asclepias tuberosa*	x		
Catananche caerulea	x						
Centaurea dealbata	x						
Centaurea gymnocarpa	x						

	Sun	Semi-shade	Shade
Aster linarifolius	x		
Briza media	x		
Calluna vulgaris	x		
Cassia marilandica	x		
Coreopsis verticillata	x		
Echinacea purpurea	x		
Echinops humilis	x		
Echinops sphaerocephalus	x		
Eryngium alpinum	x		
Eryngium amethystinum	x		
Eryngium yuccifolium	x		
Euphorbia corollata	x		
Gypsophila acutifilia	x		
Gypsophila paniculata	x		
Hemerocallis species	x		
Hosta species		x	
Lathyrus latifolius	x		
Lavandula angustifolia	x		
Limonium latifolium	x		
Malva moschata	x		
Potentilla nepalensis	x		
Rudbeckia fulgida	x		
Sedum species	x		
Solidago × hybrida	x		
Yucca filamentosa	x		
Yucca flaccida	x		
AUGUST			
Anaphalis margaritacea		x	

	Sun	Semi-shade	Shade
Artemisia species	x		
Aster spectabilis	x		
Chrysanthemum parthenium	x		
Chrysopsis mariana	x		
Hosta species		x	
Pennisetum alopecuroides	x		
Pityopsis falcata	x		
Polygonum cuspidatum	x		
Rudbeckia hirta	x		
Salvia azurea	x		
Santolina chamaecyparissus	x		
Santolina virens	x		
Sedum species	x		
SEPTEMBER			
Aster laevis	x		
Chrysanthemum nipponicum	x		
Miscanthus sinensis	x		
FERNS			
Dennstaedtia punctilobula	x		
Osmunda claytoniana		x	
Pellaea atropurpurea		x	
Pteridium aquilinum		x	
Thelypteris noveboracensis		x	

Perennials Enjoying Constantly Moist Conditions

	Sun	Semi-shade	Shade		Sun	Semi-shade	Shade
APRIL				*Podophyllum*			
Anemone nemorosa		x		*hexandrum*		x	
Anemone quinquefolia		x		*Podophyllum peltatum*		x	
Anemone				*Polemonium*			
ranunculoides		x		*caeruleum*		x	
Caltha palustris		x		*Polygonatum*			
Claytonia caroliniana		x		*commutatum*			x
Claytonia virginica		x		*Primula* species		x	
Leucojum aestivum	x			*Trollius asiaticus*	x		
Polemonium reptans		x		*Trollius europaeus*		x	
Primula species		x		*Trollius japonicus*		x	
Trillium species		x					
Vinca minor	x			**JUNE**			
Viola blanda		x		*Aquilegia longissima*	x		
				Aruncus dioicus		x	
MAY				*Chrysanthemum* ×			
Anemone canadensis		x		*superbum*	x		
Baptisia leucantha		x		*Cypripedium reginae*		x	
Camassia quamash	x			*Dodecatheon jeffreyi*		x	
Clintonia borealis			x	*Filipendula* species		x	
Cornus canadensis			x	*Lilium canadense*		x	
Cypripedium candidum		x		*Lysimachia vulgaris*	x		
Dicentra spectabilis		x		*Phlox carolina*	x		
Dodecatheon				*Phlox maculata*	x		
pulchellum		x		*Platycodon*			
Doronicum cordatum		x		*grandiflorus*	x		
Doronicum				*Polemonium boreale*		x	
pardalianches	x			*Primula* species		x	
Doronicum				*Scabiosa caucasica*	x		
plantagineum	x			*Scabiosa graminifolia*	x		
Geum rivale		x		*Shortia uniflora*			x
Geum triflorum		x		*Trollius ledebourii*		x	
Hutchinsia alpina		x		*Valeriana officinalis*	x		
Iris pseudacorus	x						
Mazus reptans		x		**JULY**			
Myosotis scorpioides	x			*Astilbe chinensis*		x	
Patrinia triloba	x			*Bletilla striata*		x	
Phlox divaricata		x		*Campanula lactiflora*	x		
Phlox stolonifera		x		*Chelone glabra*		x	
				Cimicifuga racemosa		x	

	Sun	Semi-shade	Shade		Sun	Semi-shade	Shade
Coreopsis rosea	x			Liatris pycnostachya	x		
Deschampsia caespitosa	x			Liriope muscari		x	
				Liriope spicata		x	
Filipendula camtschatica		x		Lobelia siphilitica	x		
Gentiana asclepiadea		x		Molinia caerulea	x		
Gentiana lutea		x		Phalaris arundinacea	x		
Hibiscus moscheutos	x						
Hosta species		x		SEPTEMBER			
Iris ensata	x			Cimicifuga simplex		x	
Liatris spicata	x			Cortaderia selloana	x		
Ligularia dentata		x					
Ligularia przewalskii	x			FERNS			
Lilium pardalinum		x		Adiantum pedatum		x	
Lilium superbum	x			Athyrium filix-femina	x		
Lobelia cardinalis	x			Dennstaedtia punctilobula	x		
Lythrum salicaria	x			Dryopteris cristata			x
Lythrum virgatum	x			Lygodium palmatum		x	
Macleaya cordata	x			Onoclea sensibilis	x		
				Osmunda cinnamomea		x	
AUGUST				Osmunda regalis		x	
Chelone lyonii		x		Polystichum braunii			x
Chelone obliqua		x		Thelypteris palustris		x	
Chrysanthemum serotinum	x			Thelypteris phegopteris		x	
Gentiana andrewsii		x		Woodwardia areolata	x		
Hosta species		x		Woodwardia virginica		x	
Kniphofia uvaria	x						

Perennials Preferring Semishade

	Dry	Moist	Wet
MARCH			
Galanthus species		x	
Helleborus species		x	
APRIL			
Anemone apennina		x	
Anemone blanda		x	
Anemone nemorosa		x	
Anemone quinquefolia		x	
Anemone ranunculoides		x	
Aquilegia canadensis		x	
Bergenia species		x	
Brunnera macrophylla		x	
Caltha palustris			x
Claytonia species		x	
Dicentra species		x	
Erythronium species		x	
Iris verna		x	
Leucojum species		x	
Mertensia virginica		x	
Omphalodes verna		x	
Pachysandra species		x	
Polemonium reptans		x	
Primula species		x	
Pulmonaria species		x	
Sanguinaria canadensis		x	
Trillium undulatum		x	
Viola blanda		x	
Viola odorata		x	
Viola palmata		x	
Viola pubescens	x		
Viola sororia		x	
Viola tricolor		x	
MAY			
Anemone species		x	
Aquilegia × *hybrida*		x	
Arisaema triphyllum		x	
Baptisia leucantha		x	

	Dry	Moist	Wet
Campanula poscharskyana		x	
Convallaria majalis		x	
Corydalis lutea		x	
Cypripedium acaule		x	
Cypripedium calceolus var. *pubescens*		x	
Cypripedium candidum			x
Dicentra species		x	
Dodecatheon species		x	
Doronicum cordatum		x	
Endymion species		x	
Epimedium species		x	
Galium odorata		x	
Geranium maculatum		x	
Geum rivale			x
Geum triflorum		x	
Hedyotis purpurea	x		
Hutchinsia alpina		x	
Iris cristata		x	
Iris gracilipes		x	
Jeffersonia species		x	
Lamium maculatum		x	
Mazus reptans		x	
Myosotis sylvatica		x	
Phlox divaricata		x	
Phlox stolonifera		x	
Podophyllum species		x	
Polemonium caeruleum		x	
Polygonatum biflorum		x	
Polygonatum commutatum		x	
Primula species		x	
Smilacina racemosa		x	
Tiarella species		x	
Trollius europaeus		x	
Trollius japonicus		x	
Viola canadensis		x	
Viola hastata		x	
Viola lutea		x	

	Dry	Moist	Wet
Viola sagittata		x	
Waldsteinia fragaroides		x	
Xerophyllum asphodeloides		x	

JUNE

	Dry	Moist	Wet
Anemone virginiana		x	
Aruncus dioicus		x	
Astilbe × arendsii		x	
Chrysogonum virginianum		x	
Cyripedium reginae		x	
Dianthus alpinus		x	
Digitalis species		x	
Dodecatheon jeffreyi		x	
Filipendula species		x	
Lewisia cotyledon		x	
Lilium canadense		x	
Lilium hansonii		x	
Lilium martagon		x	
Lysimachia nummularia		x	
Lysimachia punctata		x	
Meconopsis cambrica		x	
Polemonium boreale		x	
Primula species		x	
Saxifraga species		x	
Sedum pulchellum		x	
Silene virginica		x	
Trollius ledebourii		x	

JULY

	Dry	Moist	Wet
Aconitum species		x	
Anemonopsis macrophylla		x	
Astilbe chinensis		x	
Bletilla striata		x	

	Dry	Moist	Wet
Chelone glabra		x	
Cimicifuga racemosa		x	
Erigeron aureus		x	
Filipendula camtschatica		x	
Gaultheria procumbens		x	
Gentiana species		x	
Hosta species		x	
Ligularia dentata		x	
Lilium pardalinum		x	

AUGUST

	Dry	Moist	Wet
Anaphalis margaritacea	x		
Anemone vitifolia		x	
Chelone species		x	
Gentiana andrewsii		x	
Hosta species		x	
Lilium henryi		x	
Liriope species		x	
Thalictrum delvayi		x	

SEPTEMBER

	Dry	Moist	Wet
Anemone hupehensis		x	
Cimicifuga simplex		x	
Kirengeshoma palmata		x	

FERNS

	Dry	Moist	Wet
Adiantum pedatum		x	
Lygodium palmatum		x	
Osmunda cinnamomea		x	
Osmunda regalis		x	
Thelypteris palustris		x	
Thelypteris phegopteris		x	
Woodwardia virginica		x	

Perennials Accepting Deep Shade

	Dry	Moist	Wet
APRIL			
Actaea pachypoda		x	
Actaea rubra		x	
Caulophyllum thalictroides		x	
Hepatica acutiloba		x	
Hepatica americana		x	
Pachysandra procumbens		x	
Pachysandra terminalis		x	
Trillium nivale		x	
Trillium sessile		x	
MAY			
Asarum europaeum		x	
Clintonia borealis		x	
Clintonia umbellata		x	
Cornus canadensis		x	
Polygonatum biflorum		x	
Polygonatum commutatum		x	
Polygonatum multiflorum		x	
Polygonatum odoratum		x	
Uvularia grandiflora		x	
Uvularia perfoliata		x	
Uvularia sessilifolia		x	
Veronica officinalis		x	

	Dry	Moist	Wet
APRIL			
Shortia galacifolia		x	
Shortia uniflora		x	
JULY			
Hosta species		x	
AUGUST			
Hosta species		x	
FERNS			
Botrychium virginianum		x	
Cystopteris bulbifera		x	
Cystopteris fragilis		x	
Diplazium pycnocarpon		x	
Dryopteris cristata			x
Dryopteris goldiana		x	
Dryopteris marginalis		x	
Polystichum acrostichoides		x	
Polystichum braunii		x	
Thelypteris hexagonoptera		x	
Woodsia obtusa		x	

Bibliography

Aden, Paul. 1988. *The Hosta Book*. Portland, OR: Timber Press.

Bloom, Alan. 1971. *Perennials for Your Garden*. Nottingham, Nottinghamshire, UK: Floraprint.

———. 1980. *Alpines for Your Garden*. Nottingham, Nottinghamshire, UK: Floraprint.

Brown, Emily. 1986. *Landscaping with Perennials*. Portland, OR: Timber Press.

Clausen, Ruth R., and Nicolas H. Ekstrom. 1989. *Perennials for American Gardens*. New York: Random House.

Cox, Jeff, and Marilyn Cox. 1985. *The Perennial Garden*. Emmaus, PA: Rodale Press.

Crockett, James Underwood. 1971. *The Time-Life Encyclopedia of Gardening: Bulbs*. New York: Time-Life Books.

———. 1971. *The Time-Life Encyclopedia of Gardening: Lawns and Ground Covers*. New York: Time-Life Books.

———. 1972. *The Time-Life Encyclopedia of Gardening: Perennials*. New York: Time-Life Books.

Everett, Thomas H. 1980. *The New York Botanical Garden Illustrated Encyclopedia of Horticulture*. 10 vols. New York and London: Garland.

Foster, F. Gordon. 1971. *Ferns to Know and Grow*. New York: Hawthorn Books.

Hay, Roy, and Patrick M. Synge. 1969. *The Color Dictionary of Flowers and Plants for Home and Garden*. New York: Crown.

Hebb, Robert S. 1975. *Low Maintenance Perennials*. Jamaica Plain, MA: The Arnold Arboretum of Harvard University.

Know Your Garden Series: Bulbs and Perennials. 1984. Portland, OR: Timber Press.

Liberty Hyde Bailey Hortorium. 1976. *Hortus Third: A Concise Dictionary of Plants Cultivated in the United States and Canada*. 3rd ed. New York: Macmillan; London: Collier Macmillan.

McGourty, Frederick. 1989. *The Perennial Gardener*. Boston: Houghton Mifflin.

Ottesen, Carole. 1989. *Ornamental Grasses*. New York: McGraw-Hill.

Petrova, Ing. Eva. 1975. *Flowering Bulbs*. London and New York: Hamlyn.

Pizzetti, Ippolito, and Henry Crocker. 1968. *Flowers, A Guide for Your Garden*. New York: Harry N. Abrams.

Reader's Digest. 1984. *Reader's Digest Guide to Creative Gardening*. London and New York: Reader's Digest Association Limited.

Rickett, Harold William. 1966–1973. *Wildflowers of the United States.* 6 vols. New York: McGraw-Hill.

Sabuco, John J. 1987. *The Best of the Hardiest.* 2nd ed. Flossmoor, IL: Good Earth Publishing.

Taylor's Guide to Ground Covers, Vines & Grasses. 1987. Boston: Houghton Mifflin.

The American Horticultural Society. 1982. *Illustrated Encylopedia of Gardening: Perennials.* Mount Vernon, VA: The American Horticultural Society.

_____ . 1989. *Encyclopedia of Garden Plants.* New York: Macmillan.

Thomas, Graham Stuart. 1990. *Perennial Garden Plants or the Modern Florilegium.* 3rd ed. Portland, OR: Sagapress/Timber Press.

Time-Life Books. 1988. *The Time-Life Gardener's Guide: Perennials.* Alexandria, VA: Time-Life Books.

_____ . 1989. *The Time-Life Gardener's Guide: Bulbs.* Alexandria, VA: Time-Life Books.

_____ . 1989. *The Time-Life Gardener's Guide: Lawns and Ground Covers.* Alexandria, VA: Time-Life Books.

_____ . 1989. *The Time-Life Gardener's Guide: Wildflowers.* Alexandria, VA: Time-Life Books.

Index

Metric Conversion Graph

CENTIMETERS / INCHES

About the Author

Joseph Hudak is a nationally recognized landscape architect who has served more than 3000 individual and corporate clients in the course of his 40-year practice. A graduate of The Pennsylvania State University, he was affiliated for 25 years with the nation's oldest landscape architectural firm, Olmsted Associates of Brookline, Massachusetts, now a national historic site. Mr. Hudak was the plant materials instructor for 20 years in the Department of Landscape Architecture at Harvard University's Graduate School of Design and also taught for five years at the Radcliffe Seminars Program. He has been an officer of the American Society of Landscape Architects at both the local chapter and national levels and in 1992 was elevated to Fellow.

Today Mr. Hudak is an avid gardener, photographer, and practicing landscape architect. He enjoys lecturing here and abroad and occasionally contributes to the pages of *Horticulture*, *American Horticulturist*, and *Organic Gardening*. His essays also appear in *Taylor's Guide to Garden Design* (1988) and the *Handbook of Specialty Elements in Architecture* (1982).

He is the author of the popular *Shrubs in the Landscape* (1984); *Trees for Every Purpose* (1980), which received the Helen S. Hull Literary Award in 1981 from the National Council of State Garden Clubs; and the original *Gardening with Perennials Month by Month*. This American classic on perennials, first published in 1976 and reprinted in 1985, was taken as a selection of the Garden Book Club and is largely responsible for the current popularity of perennials. Mr. Hudak lives and gardens in Westwood, Massachusetts.